CONDUCT
AND
CONSCIENCE

THE SOCIALIZATION OF INTERNALIZED
CONTROL OVER BEHAVIOR

CONDUCT AND CONSCIENCE

THE SOCIALIZATION
OF INTERNALIZED CONTROL
OVER BEHAVIOR

JUSTIN ARONFREED

UNIVERSITY OF PENNSYLVANIA

1968

ACADEMIC PRESS   New York   London

ACADEMIC PRESS, INC.
111 Fifth Avenue, New York, New York 10003

United Kingdom Edition published by
ACADEMIC PRESS, INC. (LONDON) LTD.
Berkeley Square House, London W.1

LIBRARY OF CONGRESS CATALOG CARD NUMBER: 68-26638

PRINTED IN THE UNITED STATES OF AMERICA

PREFACE

This monograph began as a manuscript that was commissioned, with far more modest intentions, by the Social Science Research Council. A much shorter version was first presented at a conference which was sponsored by the committee that the Council had established for the purpose of advancing research and theory in the area of socialization. The members of that committee were: John Clausen (Chairman), Orville G. Brim, Alex Inkeles, Ronald Lippitt, Eleanor E. Maccoby, and M. Brewster Smith. I am indebted to these people for their having provided the original social stimulus for the germination of the monograph, and to many other participants at the original conference for their generous reactions to its initial form. Martin L. Hoffman was the organizer of the conference, and was also a patient source of encouragement while the manuscript was growing toward its final shape. I owe a special debt of gratitude to M. Brewster Smith for his intelligent and sympathetic reading of an intermediate version of the manuscript.

In the beginning, the manuscript confined itself to the description of a few experiments which were addressed to an account of the mechanisms of translation between the child's social experience and its internalized control of behavior. There were also some brief excursions into the theoretical implications of the experiments. As time went on, the manuscript underwent two metamorphoses which began to seem preordained. The first transformation grew out of my perception that it was difficult to conceptualize the mechanisms of internalization without a more general treatment of socialization. The second and final transformation was an escalation of the phenomena of socialization into a theoretical conception of the learning process. As the monograph now stands, the first two chapters present a synopsis of the major problems which are to be engaged in any attempt to understand the origins of conduct and conscience. The third chapter redefines these problems in the context of a concept of internalization. The fourth chapter is the theoretical core of the monograph. It sets forth an initial conception of the mechanisms of learning which underlie socialization. The remaining eight chapters, while they contain a certain amount of additional theoretical material, are primarily descriptive and experimental analyses of specific internalized products of socialization, from the perspective of the fourth chapter.

It gives me a great deal of pleasure to acknowledge the contribution that has been made to my thinking about the nature of socialization by many interesting conversations with a number of near and distant colleagues. I must also offer my apologies to some of these people if it was not always apparent to them that our conversations were being digested into this monograph. Since my fondness for such conversations exceeds the capacity of my memory, I cannot thank as many people as I would like. But I can single out the following individuals: Albert Bandura, Urie Bronfenbrenner, Francis W. Irwin, Lawrence Kohlberg, Eleanor E. Maccoby, Daniel R. Miller, Walter Mischel, Harris Savin, Robert R. Sears, Richard L. Solomon, the late Richard H. Walters, John W. M. Whiting, and David R. Williams.

The National Institutes of Health provided support for most of the empirical work that appears here. The National Science Foundation provided a senior postdoctoral award for a year's retreat as a Fellow of the Center for Advanced Study in the Behavioral Sciences. In the hospitable intellectual climate of the Center, I was able to confront the requirements of a theory of socialization at close range.

I am very grateful to Isabelle Friedman for her superb assistance in the preparation of the manuscript.

Finally, I acknowledge an irredeemable debt to my wife and children, from whom I have taken much instruction concerning the problems of socialization.

Philadelphia, Pennsylvania   JUSTIN ARONFREED
June, 1968

CONTENTS

CONDUCT
AND
CONSCIENCE

THE SOCIALIZATION OF INTERNALIZED
CONTROL OVER BEHAVIOR

CHAPTER ONE

CONSCIENCE
AND
MORAL JUDGEMENT

Conscience is the term that has been used traditionally to refer to the cognitive and affective processes which constitute an internalized moral governor over an individual's conduct. In the classical Greek conceptions of morality (Plato, *The Republic;* Aristotle, *Nichomachean Ethics*), there was nothing that would really correspond to what we today might call conscience. The Greeks thought of moral judgement as an essentially rational phenomenon. And they did not perceive it in the powerful affective components which we are now inclined to regard as indispensable to internalized control over social conduct. Some later writers also have emphasized the place of intellect in moral judgement—particularly Bentham, J. S. Mill, and the modern British ethical intuitionists (for example, G. E. Moore, in *Principia Ethica,* 1903). But the more striking historical trend has been toward increasing emphasis on the affective, inarticulate, and impelling features of conscience. As early as the writings of Augustine, we begin to find the concept of an internal agency of control and sanction that commends, warns, and chastises in terms which refer to strong affective states. Many other moral philosophers have been careful to distinguish between the functions of cognition and affect in the control of conduct. Philosophers who have taken very different approaches to a conception of moral judgement—Aquinas, Locke, Hume, Kant, and Kierkegaard—have in common their distinction between the understanding and the will, or between thought and the motivation to act. Interest in the affective components of moral judgement is also apparent among more contemporary ethical theorists (Ayer, 1935; Perry, 1926; Stevenson, 1944), who have given much attention to the affective core that morality has in common with other kinds of value systems.

The emergence of the behavioral and social sciences provided a naturalistic view of conscience which gave even more attention to its affective and motivational properties. The use of "natural philosophy" also fostered an expanded conception of the dimensions of value which were to be included within conscience. Moral philosophy generally had taken the view that morality was concerned only with fundamental human relationships. Values were considered to be moral when they were addressed to desires and constraints which had direct implications for the welfare of others. Moral

---

[1] A distinction is sometimes made between *moral* and *ethical* thought, when ethics is used to refer to the theoretical foundations of a moral point of view. The distinction is not required here.

2

values were described with a language that conveyed attachment and obligation to other human beings. They were analyzed with respect to concepts of freedom, responsibility, authority, and the distribution and possession of material goods. An analysis of moral value yielded a set of principles of conduct which could be tested against their beneficial or harmful consequences for the participants in a social relationship and for society as a whole. Moral cognition had much to do, then, with the evaluation of the goodness or rightness of actions by reference to their impact on others.

From the point of view of traditional moral philosophy, contemporary naturalistic conceptions of conscience often subsume a much broader array of value systems than might properly be called moral. In some of these value systems, the consequences of an act for others are relatively insignificant as determinants of the act's evaluation. It is quite common today to find that the term conscience is used in a sense that embraces dimensions of value which pertain to cleanliness, to sexual habits, to proficiency and persistence in achievement, and to a great many other highly individualized and personal segments of human behavior.

At least four distinct sources of influence can be discerned in tracing the broadening of the concept of conscience. One source can be found in the cultural relativism which social anthropologists introduced into the interpretation of their field studies. Following the early work of Boas and of Malinowski, there has been a continuous tradition of attention to cross-cultural variations among societies in the substance of their dominant values. More recently, there has been much interest in the predictability of different value systems from child-rearing practices and from the forms of primary social institutions. A second source of influence can be traced to social-psychological theories of development which emphasized the child's ability to adopt the roles and normative structures of its socializing agents. This source was first clearly visible in the developmental theories of Baldwin (1906), McDougall (1908), and Mead (1934). Its more persistent form is in concepts which treat conscience as the internalized representation of either the normative standards or the role-relationships to which the child has been exposed as a result of interactions with its socializing agents (Newcomb, 1950; Parsons and Bales *et al.,* 1955). These conceptions would describe moral standards of conduct in much the same way that they would describe the standards which are appropriate to sex role, to achievement, or to social conformity in general.

The psychoanalytic concept of the superego was a third source of the dilution of the moral connotations of conscience. From his observation of the behavior of adults, Freud (1927, 1936, Chapter 8) drew the inference that children acquired many forms of control over their behavior which did not require conscious volition, even though they had become independent of external reward or punishment. He took the view that the superego embraced a variety of internalized controls, some of which operated in a mechanical manner without the mediation of articulate standards of judgement. These irrational forms of behavioral control often were described as though they were more involuntary than they were evaluative. They were attributed to the limited verbal and cognitive capacities of the young child, and also to the repression of early experiences which had been associated with intense anxiety. Even in those areas of conduct where a person's actions were thought to be governed by explicit standards which were available to consciousness and verbalization, it was presumed that such standards took into account more than simply the person's intentions and the consequences of his actions for others. The directness of expression of a drive, the choice of object of the drive, and other aspects of motivated behavior, were all linked to the operation of conscience. And the mechanism that Freud suggested for the formation of the superego was an identification with a parental figure that went far beyond an adoption of the parent's moral viewpoint.

A final source of an expanded conception of conscience lies in behavioristic theories of social learning. The earliest forms of such theories were based primarily on studies of animals (Holt, 1931; Miller and Dollard, 1941; Thorndike, 1911). These theories tried to explain how the behavior of one organism could be patterned after the behavior of another through external rewards and punishments. They were not addressed to the problem of how social behavior became independent of direct external reinforcement. More recent extensions of these theories have attempted to account for internalized control of behavior by setting forth learning mechanisms which are not entirely dependent on external reinforcement of the child's observable actions (Aronfreed, 1964; Mowrer, 1960b, Chapter 3; Sears, Maccoby, and Levin, 1957, Chapter 10; Whiting and Child, 1953, Chapter 11). The mechanisms generally attempt to specify how the adoption of the evaluative responses of socializing agents might become intrinsically reinforcing to a child. However, the cognitive dimensions of evaluative responses are not examined in any detail. The emphasis is rather on their generalized function in the mediation of affective states and overt behavior. Accordingly, from the point of view of social learning theories, conscience is composed of value systems which mediate conduct in many areas of social behavior. Dimensions of value which are specifically moral are not given any particular functional significance.

There are numerous illustrations of how the term conscience is now used in ways which would seem to extend its application well beyond the traditional perimeter of moral judgement. It is used, for example, to refer to value orientations which support self-denial of pleasure, effort in the face of adversity, and other self-directive patterns of behavior, many of which are well captured in concepts such as "Protestant ethic" (Weber, 1930) or "inner-direction" (Riesman, Denney, and Glazer, 1950). Surveys which aim to uncover the child-rearing antecedents of conscience examine not only the socialization of such behavioral domains as aggression—which would easily lend itself to moral evaluation—but also the socialization of the child's dependence on the mother, of its toilet habits, and of its manipulative and exploratory dispositions. It is interesting to note that some recent general treatments of value (Hare, 1952; Pepper, 1958) have reacted against an overemphasis on the common psychological foundations of different kinds of value, and have tried to demonstrate the utility of distinguishing between moral and nonmoral systems of value. Of course, there are unavoidable semantic problems of definition in the question of what constitutes moral judgement. Nevertheless, it may prove useful to recognize that moral judgement is only one sector of the multiple value systems which are now commonly regarded as the substance of conscience.

Even the broadest definition of the standards of value to be included within conscience must be constrained by certain criterial boundaries. It seems clear that many kinds of standards—for example, those which are applicable to taste or to physical skill—do not belong under the rubric of conscience, even though they may be derived from social experience. If we wanted to describe conscience fairly liberally, we might say that it subsumes those evaluative standards which apply to what we ordinarily call *conduct*. But conduct itself designates a vast set of behavioral dispositions which have been molded by the child's intercourse with a social environment. We will see that much of conduct can be internally governed without the evaluative support of conscience. And even within the great body of evaluative cognition which children do acquire during the socialization of their conduct, the intensity of affectivity will vary as a function of the nature of the social experience through which specific values have been transmitted. The behavior of parents and of other agents of the social transmission of values will establish different intensities of value for the child in different areas of conduct. The usual connotations of conscience might therefore be conveyed more accurately if we were to narrow its definition even further by a criterion of affective intensity. We might restrict the province of conscience to those areas of conduct where social experience has attached substantial affective value to the child's cognitive representation and evaluation of its own behavior.

❧ CHAPTER TWO ❧

THE RELATIONSHIP
BETWEEN
CONDUCT AND CONSCIENCE

Conscience is not a prerequisite of internalized control over conduct. There are large areas of conduct for which internal monitors are established on the basis of the child's status as a conditionable animal, rather than on the basis of its status as a highly cognitive and verbal animal. Common observation compels us to see that internalized control of behavior does not require evaluative cognition. The prohibitions to which many household pets are trained often will continue to be evident in their behavior when they are temporarily free of external human control. Most parents discover that even preverbal children are capable of some acquired control over their own actions in the absence of external surveillance. An eighteen-month-old child may have only the beginnings of verbal comprehension; yet its behavioral restraints on touching dangerous objects or running into the street may show some independence of direct supervision, if it has had earlier experience with the punitive consequences of such actions.

The first signs of the internalization of anxiety and of anxiety-reducing maneuvers, in reaction to committed transgressions, also usually appear at a quite early age, when the child would not yet be expected to function under the control of self-evaluative resources. Likewise, very young children frequently will show their pleasure overtly when they have performed an act for which they have been rewarded previously, even when it seems highly unlikely that socializing agents could originally have communicated a cognitive standard for evaluating the act in question. It appears that even much older children often show internalized dispositions to confess their transgressions, or to make reparation for the consequences of their actions, without showing any evidence of the intercession of evaluative standards (Aronfreed, 1961). Adults also have many internalized forms of conduct which can be elicited with a mechanical immediacy that could hardly require evaluative decision-making processes. These forms of conduct sometimes seem not even to be under voluntary control.

The findings of a number of recent experiments confirm the observation that internalized control of social behavior can be acquired without the engagement of evaluative cognition. For example, when children are punished for their choices of attractive toys during experimental paradigms of socialization, without being given any explanation or further criterion for the occurrence of punishment, they continue to show the behavioral suppression that has been induced by the punishment training, during a subsequent test of internalization, when they are apparently free of any surveillance or risk of disclosure of their actions (Aronfreed and Reber, 1965; Aronfreed, 1966). The effectiveness of the internalized behavioral suppression that is produced under these conditions of learning is very closely determined by the immediacy with which punishment has followed the originally punished choices. The results of similar punishment-training experiments, which have been conducted in R. L. Solomon's laboratory (Mowrer, 1960b, pp. 399–404; Solomon, Turner, and Lessac, 1968), indicate that dogs also will sometimes suppress punished behavior, and display affective reactions to their failures of suppression, after the agent of punishment is no longer present.

Other experimental paradigms of socialization, which have been designed to examine the origin of self-criticism as an internalized reaction to transgression (Aronfreed, 1964), have demonstrated the conditions of aversive learning under which a child will reproduce a verbal component of the punishment of a socializing agent, and apply the component to its own punished behavior, when neither the verbal label nor the behavior has had any previous evaluative significance for the child. There also have been recent experimental findings which indicate that the child's suppression or performance of behavior that is ordinarily under some social constraint may be sharply affected by the mere observation of the punitive consequences of similar behavior on the part of another child or an adult, even though the child itself has not been exposed to the same consequences (Bandura, 1965a; Walters and Parke, 1964a). The techniques which are used in this latter type of experiment make no direct attempt to change the child's evaluative standards in the direction of the reported behavioral effects. Bandura, Ross, and Ross (1963c) reported, in fact, that some children expressed disapproval of the aggressive behavior which they had observed, but nevertheless engaged in similar behavior if they had seen it produce rewarding consequences for the other person.

Although it is generally assumed that values are the most significant source of control over social conduct (see, for example, Thibaut and Kelley, 1959), the available evidence usually points to great discrepancies between children's verbal expression of evaluative standards and their actual behavior in a real social context. Just as internalized control of conduct does not presuppose conscience, it is conversely true that conscience does not insure internalized control of conduct. Knowledge of the standards of conduct to which a child subscribes will often not permit an accurate prediction of its behavior under conditions where the child is not exposed to the surveillance or reactions of external agents of control. Of course, we are in a much better position to predict the child's behavior if we know something about its standards than if we know nothing at all. But the evidence on this problem, though it is somewhat difficult to interpret, indicates that an adequate theory of internalization must account for non-reflexive relationships between conduct and conscience.

Hartshorne and May (1928) found only a small degree of correlation between the child's knowledge of common social standards and its internalized control of behavior in situations which were designed to test for honesty. Other investigators (Brogden, 1940; Terman *et al.,* 1925) also have observed large discrepancies between the child's verbalized knowledge of standards of conduct and its actual resistance to the opportunity to cheat when it was ostensibly not under surveillance. It is even more interesting to note that there does not appear to be any greater uniformity when one looks at the relationship between the child's control of its own conduct and its verbal description of the evaluative processes which it would use in applying standards to specific situations. It is well known that children in western society commonly show what may be called an increasingly internalized orientation of conscience, as they advance in age, when they are asked to give verbal expression to their evaluation of the determinants and consequences of conduct (Boehm, 1962; Kohlberg, 1963a; Lerner, 1937; MacRae, 1954; Piaget, 1948). But this shift in the orientation of conscience frequently is found not to be accompanied by corresponding changes in the predictability of conduct. There is no indication, for example, of age-related increments in the general effectiveness of children's control over their own behavior in situations which are designed to test their honesty (Hartshorne and May, 1928; Sears, Rau, and Alpert, 1965, Chapter 6).

In one study in which both conduct and conscience were assessed for the same children, Grinder (1964) found that an increasingly internalized orientation of conscience with advancing age was not paralleled by increases of internalized behavioral conformity to the rules of an achievement game. Medinnus (1966) also has reported an absence of consistent relationships between behavioral and cognitive indices of internalization for the same children. The initial appearance of altruistic and sympathetic behavior among young children shows some correlation with age. But even these forms of conduct do not show consistent changes of extent or frequency among children who are beyond the age of five or six years (Handlon and Gross, 1959; Murphy, 1937; Turner, 1948; Ugurel-Semin, 1952; Wright, 1942).

We might infer from the findings of the studies which are cited above that a certain level of internalized control over conduct is established during the earlier years of socialization, and that it remains relatively constant across changes in its cognitive foundations. But the findings of other studies, which attempt to map the child's conscience in even greater detail, suggest that conduct and conscience are not really divorced from one another to such an extent. Piaget (1948) observed that scrupulous conformity to the rules of a game of marbles was more characteristic of older children, who subscribed to the rules as cooperative social contracts, than it was of younger children, who perceived the rules as absolute constraints which were externally imposed by authority. Kohlberg (1964, 1969) has reported a number of correlations which also appear to confirm the expectation that the child's social behavior could hardly be insensitive to the cognitive control of evaluative standards. For example, the probability of a child's cheating in a test of honesty is inversely related to the degree of internalized orientation toward principled morality that characterizes the child's verbal decisions in hypothetical conflict situations. Hoffman (1963, 1968) has found that children differ in their internalized dispositions to react to their own transgressions, as measured by a story-completion device, in ways which are related to the classification of their verbal expressions of conscience as having a dominant orientation which is externalized, conventional, or humanistic.

The inconsistencies among the findings of different studies may be attributable, at least in part, to the fact that the affective components of conscience exercise a highly variable motivational control over conduct. Their motivational linkages may be differentially activated by complex variations in the child's cognition of the information that is carried in specific social stimulus situations. There should certainly be some kind of predictable relationship between a child's expressions of conscience and its overt conduct. But it is extremely difficult to build into situational assessments of actual behavior the same variety and structural complexity which can be presented hypothetically to elicit the child's verbal expression and application of values. An understanding of how values control conduct may therefore derive considerably more from a close theoretical and experimental analysis of their affective and cognitive mediational properties than it will from attempts to simply correlate the behavioral and cognitive products of naturalistic social experience.

As a concrete illustration of the difficulty of predicting conduct from conscience, consider the following actions of a seven-year-old child: Her younger brother is perched precariously on the ottoman, and has just given her a mild affront. She draws back and positions herself to push him off the ottoman, unaware that she is under observation. She hesitates, removes a sharp-edged toy from the area of floor on which he will obviously fall, and is then about to carry through her original intention, when she becomes aware of my presence and sheepishly withdraws. A few minutes later, while we are talking about another matter, she spontaneously offers the view that it would have been wrong to push her brother. She further observes that she "ought not to make him fall," because he might have been hurt and because she is supposed to take care of him. Apparently, she is quite capable of pushing her brother off the ottoman, in the absence of any higher authority. Yet her verbalization clearly reveals the rudiments of conscience. She criticizes her intended act both in terms of its harmful consequences and in terms of her obligation toward someone to whom she has a special socially defined attachment. She does not lack conscience, then, nor does she lack one of its appropriate connections to action, as we can infer from her removal of the sharp-edged toy. It would seem, however, that she is dependent on external mediation of its other possible connections to action. To put the case in another way, we might say that the anxiety which is generated by her cognitive resources for the evaluation of her incipient transgression is not yet sufficient to motivate her suppression of the transgression. But the necessary intensity of anxiety can be elicited by external social cues which provide information about the probability of punishment.

The fact that conduct often does not follow from the evaluative structure of conscience emphasizes the importance of the affective correlates of cognitive processes. When an act comes under the evaluation of conscience, it is placed on some specific cognitive dimensions or standards. This cognitive placement does not in itself define the assignment of value. Valuational phenomena have irreducible affective components. And the control of behavior through evaluative cognition must be closely monitored by the nature and intensity of the affective correlates of cognitive representation, as well as by the informational substance of the cognition itself. One aspect of conscience that helps us to identify its presence, and to distinguish it from other evaluative systems, such as those which might govern etiquette or behavior that is appropriate to a professional role, is our own experience of its affective intensity and our observation of the same intensity when it is apparent in the behavior of others. The antecedents of conscience tend to be highly concentrated in the child's early relationships with a few socializing agents, to whom it has very strong affective attachments. Other kinds of value systems may tend to be acquired more gradually in the context of multiple social relationships which are weaker in affective attachment and distributed in time well beyond childhood.

It seems very likely that the powerful affective components of conscience are reflected in the sense of essential unanalyzable rightness or impelling obligation that we sometimes perceive in its operation. Variability in the changes of affective state which are attached to evaluative cognition undoubtedly hold much of the key to the apparent complexities of the relationship between conduct and conscience. Recognition of these affective properties of conscience allows us to see that conscience may govern conduct in ways which are lawful but not necessarily rational.

CHAPTER THREE

THE CONCEPT
OF
INTERNALIZATION

The power and durability of the effects of early learning on the child's later social behavior are the central problems in an account of socialization. It is obvious that the external contingencies of the child's immediate social environment exercise a profound control over its behavior throughout the course of socialization. The more remarkable consequence of social experience, however, is that it gives the child's acquired behavioral dispositions a stability which shows an increasing independence of external control. The young child's social behavior is initially highly dependent on the affective value of external events which are transmitted through the presence and activity of its socializing agents. But its behavior gradually comes to be governed extensively by internal monitors. These internal monitors assume many of the functions of the external controls which were originally required to establish the behavior.

Terms such as internalization or interiorization sometimes have been used to refer to a process in which an internal cognitive model is formed for the representation of behavior that was originally overt or public (Piaget, 1951; Vygotsky, 1962). The concept of internalization is also often used to refer to the child's adoption of social norms or roles as its own, and to the resulting evaluative control of its behavior by some of the most complex functions of cognitive and verbal processes (Kohlberg, 1969; Piaget, 1948). These concepts actually pertain to special and rather formidable cases of a much wider variety of cognitive and affective mechanisms which can translate the child's social experience into its capacity for internalized control over behavior. Concepts of internalization which are constructed on a base of representational and evaluative capacities rest very heavily on the extraordinary ability of human beings to acquire cognitive structures with which they can process information about their behavior and their environment. Such structures will sometimes function as powerful determinants of social behavior. But the representational and evaluative functions of cognitive structures are only a part of the broader conceptual resources which we require for an understanding of the total spectrum of ways in which socialization may produce internalized control over the child's behavior.

The mechanisms for internalized control of behavior carry the motivational and informational functions of many of the externally structured determinants of the child's earlier experience. They are superimposed upon, and sometimes displace, the functional properties of concrete exter-

16

nal events. And they take a number of forms, many of which are relatively simple transformations of the affective and cognitive input that the child has received from its social environment. The cognitive models which are available to the child for the representation and storage of sequentially structured patterns of behavior are an extensive and powerful type of transformation of social experience. But great repertoires of the child's social behavior also come under internalized control through the simpler transformations which are produced by conditioning and direct instrumental training, as well as through various kinds of cognitive acquisitions which are less imposing than a representational model. Likewise, evaluative cognition is only a part of the monitoring system which socialization can produce for internalized affective control of behavior. The place of values in the mediation of affective control of the child's behavior can be assessed more accurately if we first take into account that large areas of social behavior can be brought under internalized control without the engagement of evaluative cognition.

THE PERSISTENCE OF LEARNED BEHAVIOR

If we temporarily put aside conscience and focus our attention on conduct, we can make a useful initial approach to the concept of internalization. We might consider an act to be internalized to the extent that its maintenance has become independent of external outcomes—that is, to the extent that its reinforcing consequences are internally mediated, without the support of external events such as reward or punishment. Accordingly, we would use the concept of internalization to refer to the intrinsically reinforcing status of the act, without regard to the specific mechanisms of the reinforcement. This broad use of the concept would make it applicable to every area of social conduct. And yet internalization would certainly not be synonymous with socialization, since much of a child's socially acquired behavior remains heavily dependent on its immediate external consequences.

The range of this kind of concept of internalization can be demonstrated by pointing out its relevance to the persistence which animals sometimes show in their maintenance of certain forms of learned behavior. The work of Solomon and his colleagues (Solomon, Kamin, and Wynne, 1953; Solomon and Wynne, 1954), on the avoidance learning of dogs under intense punishment, is a particularly interesting illustration of the strong resistance to extinction that an animal's behavior may have in the absence of its original reinforcing external outcomes. After a small number of pairings of a warning signal with electric shock of very high magnitude, a dog will quickly hurdle a barrier into an adjacent shock-free compartment at the occurrence of the signal alone. The dog may continue to make this response for hundreds of trials, even though the shock has been removed from the situation and the dog's response is therefore no longer instrumental to the avoidance of shock. Since the response continues to occur for a long period of time, when the original aversive contingencies of the learning situation have been withdrawn, it may be said to show some degree of internalization. There are many other experiments which confirm the observation that animals may show great stability of both active avoidance and behavioral suppression when the aversive outcomes of alternative behavior have been suspended (Boroczi, Storms, and Broen, 1964; Church, 1963; D'Amato, Fazzaro, and Etkin, 1967; Solomon and Brush, 1956; Whiting and Mowrer, 1943). The persistence of their behavior is especially notable when it has been acquired originally under the control of intense aversive stimulation. The findings of such experiments are analogous to the common observation that the behavioral products of human socialization under aversive control are sometimes highly resistant to changes in external contingencies. Children often maintain their acquired behavioral suppressions under circumstances where the suppressions are no longer appropriate and may even have aversive consequences.

Closer examination of some of the paradigms which have been used to demonstrate the persistence of the behavior of animals under aversive control often reveals that the behavior may actually be quite limited in its independence of external consequences. Even though the animal is no longer exposed to onset and termination of the aversive stimulation that was used to motivate learning, conditions frequently are arranged so that its behavior will continue to produce the termination of external cues which originally had the function of warning signals. To the extent that such cues have acquired secondary aversive value through their previous association with the onset of shock, their termination may reduce conditioned anxiety and thus constitute a reinforcing event. There is a considerable amount of evidence that the termination of conditioned aversive stimuli does have reinforcing properties (Bolles, Stokes, and Younger, 1966; E. S. Brush, 1957; Church, Brush, and Solomon, 1956; Kamin, 1957; Mowrer and Lamoreaux, 1942; Solomon and Wynne, 1953). Moreover, the stability of the animal's behavior may also be reinforced by its control over stimuli which have been associated with absence or termination of shock. For example, in the studies which were reported by Solomon and his co-workers, the dogs may have produced environmental stimulus changes which acted as safety signals whenever they leaped the barrier. These stimuli may have acquired reinforcement value as conditioned inhibitors of anxiety, through their previous contiguity with the absence or termination of shock (Dinsmoor and Clayton, 1966; Kinsman and Bixenstine, 1968; Murray and Strandberg, 1965; Rescorla and LoLordo, 1965; Weisman et al., 1966).

There are other types of experimental paradigms in which the learned behavior of animals has been maintained with an apparently greater independence of external consequences. In many instances where punishment produces suppression of a highly motivated reward-oriented act, the suppression may show strong resistance to extinction after the punishment contingency has been eliminated, even though suppression has no other reinforcing external consequences (Boroczi et al., 1964; Church, 1963; Solomon, 1964). Sidman (1953, 1955) has shown that rats who are trained to make a response at regular intervals, in order to avoid shock in the absence of any external signal, will continue to do so for a long period of time after they are no longer subjected to the shock.

Perhaps the most striking demonstrations of the persistence of aversive control over behavior appear in those studies in which escape- or avoidance-trained acts are themselves subsequently exposed to the suppressive effects of punishment. Although punishment of an animal's avoidance behavior sometimes has been shown to facilitate the extinction of the behavior (F. R. Brush, 1957; Seligman and Campbell, 1965), particularly when the punishment is intense or prolonged (Kintz and Bruning, 1967), there are a variety of conditions under which the behavior may be extremely resistant to extinction when it is being repeatedly punished. A number of experiments have demonstrated the remarkable persistence of escape- or avoidance-trained behavior after shock has become the consequence of its performance rather than of its nonperformance (Brown, Martin, and Morrow, 1964; Gwinn, 1949; Melvin and Smith, 1967; Migler, 1963; Sidman and Boren, 1957; Solomon et al., 1953). Sandler and Davidson (1967) have found that monkeys will continue their punished avoidance behavior even when they have available a nonpunished active behavioral alternative for the avoidance of shock.

The conditions under which these effects are obtained suggest that they may be attributable to the generalized anxiety which is elicited by punishment of the animal's previously learned escape or avoidance behavior, and to the resulting increment of motivation for the behavior that has become attached to external situational cues. This inference appears to be supported by the fact that the behavior remains persistent even when the aversive stimulation which has been used in its acquisition is different in quality from the punishment which is used during the attempt to extinguish the behavior (Melvin and Martin, 1967).

The extensive modifications of behavior which animals can acquire under the control of positive reinforcement do not seem to have the same kind of persistence that is sometimes seen in the behavioral changes which are acquired under aversive control. It has been noted for many years that the training paradigms of the animal laboratory produce persistence of behavior under aversive control more readily than they produce persistence under positive control (Brown, 1953; Miller, 1951). Behavior that has been learned because it is instrumental to getting food may have some stability when the food is no longer available (Wolfe, 1936). The stability can be bolstered by the use of training schedules in which the original positive reinforcement occurs as a highly intermittent and sometimes unpredictable outcome of the appropriate behavior (Ferster and Skinner, 1957; Lawrence and Festinger, 1962; Morse, 1966; Uhl and Young, 1967). Stability also may be enhanced by the occurrence of other external stimulus outcomes which have acquired some secondary positive reinforcement value through their previous association with the food (Kimble, 1961; Skinner, 1938). And when secondary reinforcing stimuli are used independently to maintain behavior, they may produce somewhat more stability if they occur only as infrequent outcomes of the behavior, particularly if they have had an intermittent association with the primary reinforcement that was used in the original training (Fox and King, 1961; Knott and Clayton, 1966; Zimmerman, 1957). Nevertheless, the persistence of the behavioral effects of learning through positive reinforcement is generally quite limited in its duration when the original reinforcement has been completely terminated (Myers, 1958; Wike, 1966).

The observed contrast between the relative stabilities of positive and aversive control over the learned behavior of animals may have some instructive implications for the strength and autonomy of those components of human social learning which are respectively derived from positive and aversive experience. It is quite possible that aversive affective states of substantial magnitude can be conditioned more easily than can corresponding positive affective states—not only to external stimuli, but also to the stimuli which are inherent in behavior and to cognitive representations. For human beings as well as for animals, aversive affectivity may have a relatively sharp onset and termination, in comparison to what may be the slower gradients of excitation and inhibition of positive affectivity, particularly when positive affectivity is closely tied to basic biological functions such as feeding. However, there are other reasons to suppose that this extrapolation from animals to humans is a limited one. The socialization of the child takes place through stimulus channels and cognitive processes which are inherently socially oriented. The effects of this social transmission may not be entirely predictable from the effects of the nonsocial medium that is generally used to study learning in animals.

Positive control over the maintenance of human behavior may have the advantage of support by reinforcing events which are socially transmitted and have a much richer variety than the positive reinforcers that are commonly shown to be effective for many other mammals. The value of some reinforcing social stimuli may have a large innate or maturational component, so that its establishment during early childhood and its subsequent persistence do not require the stimuli to be continually associated with the reduction of strong motivational states. It seems clear that much of the behavior of the higher animals can be controlled by stimulus events whose reinforcement or incentive value is neither acquired nor sustained by an association with the reduction of physiological deficits (Berlyne, 1960; Harlow, 1953; Hebb, 1958; Seward, 1963). The observations of Harlow and his collaborators (Harlow and Harlow, 1965; Harlow and Zimmerman, 1959), on the behavior of monkeys who have been deprived of social stimulation during their early experience, indicate that the formation of social attachments among primates gives a strong and durable positive value to a variety of social stimuli, and that the retention of this value is not dependent on an association of the stimuli with the reduction of what are conventionally regarded as primary drives.

Other recent analyses of social attachment suggest that there may be unlearned species-specific dispositions which prime certain social stimuli to acquire increments of positive value, quite independently of their relationship to the reduction of physiological needs, and possibly as a function of the young organism's sheer frequency of contact with the stimuli during critical periods of development (Foss, 1963; Scott and Fuller, 1965; Walters and Parke, 1965). Lövaas *et al.* (1966b) have used hungry autistic children to demonstrate that even social stimuli whose positive value has been established through an association with food may independently maintain behavior over an impressive duration of time. It appears, then, that at least some classes of social stimuli are capable of acquiring a very durable kind of positive control over the child's behavior. Since the affective value of these stimuli is not constrained by their temporal relationship to physiological states of deficit or to consummatory responses (in contrast to what is typically the case in the animal laboratory), the presence of the stimuli can immediately elicit high magnitudes of positive affectivity which are readily conditionable to other stimuli.

Even when allowance is made for the great qualitative range of the social stimuli which may retain durable reinforcement value for human beings, it often seems that people are singularly persistent in the maintenance of behavior patterns which are not supported by observable external reinforcement. We must be careful, however, not to overestimate the difference between animals and humans in their capacities to sustain behavior in the absence of reinforcing external outcomes. It has already been pointed out that training schedules on which an animal's learned behavior receives only intermittent positive reinforcement may make the behavior more tenacious when reinforcement is entirely withdrawn. Such schedules closely resemble the infrequent occurrences of social reinforcement which people commonly experience for their cumulative or sequential patterns of social behavior. Children also show more resistance to extinction of behavior that has been established on the basis of partial positive reinforcement (Bijou and Baer, 1966; Brackbill, 1958; Cowan and Walters, 1963). And their behavior under the control of intermittent reinforcement may have some of the same long-term stability that is sometimes seen in the behavior of animals (Long *et al.,* 1958).

The conditions under which children are socialized necessarily provide highly intermittent reinforcement of learned behavior. One would therefore expect that young children would quickly acquire dispositions to maintain certain forms of behavior for considerable periods of time without reinforcing consequences. These dispositions would be strengthened by the occasional reinstatement of reinforcement that would accompany the child's continuing exposure to a social environment. The great variability in delay of reward that is characteristic of the socialization process may also augment the persistence of a child's previously rewarded behavior under the subsequent temporary absence of reward. Recent studies of the learned behavior of rats have shown that partial delay-of-reward enhances resistance to extinction, particularly when intermittent delays are concentrated in time (Capaldi, 1967; Donin, Surridge, and Amsel, 1967).

Intermittent or inconsistent aversive contingencies also may increase the persistence of behavior that has been acquired under the control of positive reinforcement. For example, the punishment of an animal's previously or intermittently rewarded behavior will, under certain conditions, increase the subsequent resistance to extinction of the behavior when all outcomes are withdrawn (Lawrence and Festinger, 1962; Logan and Wagner, 1965; Martin, 1963; Martin and Ross, 1964). Behavior that continues to be rewarded may also be made resistant to a high frequency of punishment that has been introduced gradually on an intermittent schedule (Banks, 1966, 1967; Sandler, 1964). Much of the social behavior that children learn on the basis of reward also will be subjected to intermittent and generally mild forms of punishment which may enhance the persistence of the behavior. Lack of consistency among the outcomes of a specific form of behavior are an inevitable consequence of differences in disposition among the child's caretakers and peers, of differences over time in the reactions of a specific agent of socialization, and of variation in the situational appropriateness of the behavior.

There are a number of other respects in which socialized human behavior may not be so free as it sometimes appears to be of the external support that is usually required to maintain the learned behavior of animals. The social environment contains many sources of acquired positive and aversive control over the child's behavior, other than explicit rewards or punishments. The apparently intrinsically mediated value of some forms of conduct actually may be continually reinstated by external consequences which are both infrequent and not easily observable. Much of a child's behavior can be controlled by subtle interpersonal cues which transmit its positive or aversive outcomes. The child may not even be fully aware of how it uses such cues as indicators of social approval or disapproval.

Many extended or serial patterns of social behavior probably are maintained by the intermittent control that components of the behavior have over the occurrence of positive or aversive social stimuli. For example, some kinds of minimal social cues may retain their positive reinforcement value for the child because they serve as intervening signals of a highly valued and well-established rewarding outcome that will follow a long sequence of behavior. Experiments in the animal laboratory have demonstrated that extended sequences of behavior can be maintained by secondary reinforcers which are contingent on distinct components of the behavior, provided that primary reinforcement occurs at the termination of the sequence (deLorge, 1967; Kelleher, 1966; Kelleher and Gollub, 1962; Zimmerman, 1963). Under the appropriate conditions, the behavior may be maintained under an extremely long delay in the occurrence of the primary reinforcement (Ferster and Hammer, 1965). Premack (1965) has argued that such behavior sequences are also sustained because of the very high probability of occurrence and the value of terminal components which are in effect unconditioned responses to the final reinforcing event.

The observation that conduct which appears to be internalized may actually be controlled by a wide range of social stimulus consequences raises the interesting question of how the acquired value of the social stimuli could be maintained if it were still dependent to some extent on an association with more "primary" positive or aversive events. In the case of positive social reinforcers, the durability of their acquired value for the child may be increased by their intermittent occurrence in the socialization process, and also by their inconsistent relationship to other events through which their value was originally established (Myers and Myers, 1963; Myers and Myers, 1966). However, a more important source of the persistent value of some positive social stimuli may lie in its establishment under conditions where the child's behavior is not dominated by the requirement of reducing the intensity of a strong motivational state. Hall (1967) has found that children persist in their positive valuations of a visual form long after the form is no longer associated with the reward of a penny, even though the form originally is paired consistently with the penny in order to establish its value.

Wyckoff (1959) has pointed out that positive secondary reinforcers may quickly lose their acquired value in the animal laboratory because they so rapidly cease to be signals of the control which a specific act can exercise over the contingent occurrence of a more highly valued reinforcing event. There is evidence to support the view that the acquired reinforcement value of stimuli which have been associated with reward can be predicted from their previous informational value as signals of the occurrence of the reward (Egger and Miller, 1962). But the conditions under which children are socialized are much less likely to make the acquired reinforcement value of social stimuli dependent on their function as signals of other more highly valued outcomes of a particular act. The acquired reinforcers of the socialization process may often be social stimuli which have had their value originally established by their presence as elements in a larger stimulus compound. And children may have unlearned predispositions to orient and attend to some of these social stimuli, and to continue to respond to them with positive affectivity, quite independently of any informational value that the stimuli may have acquired through their relationship to other events.

Socialization provides a much greater variety of stimulus contingencies and behavioral options than do the relatively restrictive paradigms of the animal laboratory. For example, the positive value of many social stimuli may be acquired and maintained through their associations with a complex of events of more established value, rather than through their narrow function as signals of the occurrence of a single type of reward. Children may also introduce a great deal of variation into the behavior which they use to control the rewarding resources of a social environment, with the result that the effectiveness of a specific act may be a less crucial determinant of whether a positive social stimulus will maintain its acquired reinforcement value. The findings of some experiments with both animals and children suggest that acquired positive reinforcers may be more effective when they are used independently to establish new behavior than when they are used to maintain old behavior (Egger and Miller, 1962; Fort, 1965; Zimmerman, 1959).

Perhaps the most significant determinant of the durability of acquired social reinforcers is their frequent establishment under contingencies which are not controlled by the overt behavior of the child. There is mounting evidence, from experiments with animals, that initially neutral stimuli can acquire the value of secondary reinforcers simply through their association with other stimuli which function as events of unconditioned or established value. This phenomenon does not appear to require that the neutral stimulus act as a discriminative cue for a specific response (Ferster and Skinner, 1957; Kelleher and Gollub, 1962). Nor does it require even that the animal's behavior produce the contingency between the primary and secondary stimuli (Knott and Clayton, 1966; Stein, 1958). Zimmerman and Hanford (1966) have reported an interesting study in which the learned behavior of pigeons was maintained, for very long periods, by an intermittent secondary reinforcer. The conditioned positive value of the reinforcer was established and sustained by independent pairing with presentations of food which were not contingent on the pigeon's behavior. A substantial part of the positive value that social reinforcers acquire for a child may also be established by their intermittent relationship to other kinds of pleasurable events which are not selectively contingent on the child's specific overt acts. To the extent that these acquired reinforcers are not established on the basis of their value as signals of the child's instrumental control over other reinforcing events, they would tend to retain more easily their subsequent value as independent reinforcing outcomes of the child's overt behavior. Of course, any loss of their acquired value would also be replenished, from time to time, by their further association with other stimuli whose positive value had not been attenuated.

The acquired aversive properties of social stimuli provide another powerful source of external support for maintenance of the child's social behavior. We already have noted that the onset and termination of stimuli which have been associated with shock may retain an independent value for the motivation and reinforcement of learned behavior in animals. And we also have noted that stimuli which have been associated with termination or absence of shock may likewise acquire independent reinforcement value. Human socialization produces an extensive set of conditioned aversive stimuli which can act as warning signals or generalized suppressors of the child's behavior. The value of these social stimuli is acquired originally through their association with the child's direct experience of punishment and of other forms of aversive stimulation which have an unlearned or already established value. Common observation reveals that warning signals are frequently transmitted in the behavior of the child's socializing agents, and that the conditioned aversive value of such signals can be a potent source of control over the child's behavior, even though the contingent support of punishment may be very infrequent. Conversely, the termination of warning signals, or the occurrence of social stimuli which have been associated with punishment-avoidance, may independently function as reinforcing safety signals for the child's behavioral alternatives to a punishable transgression (Aronfreed, 1964, 1966).

Experiments in the animal laboratory show that the conditioned aversive value of a stimulus tends to generalize widely to other similar stimuli, which can also then be effective in activating or suppressing behavior (Desiderato, 1964; Hearst, 1962; Hoffman and Fleshler, 1961; Miller, 1959). There is some evidence that a stimulus will independently retain its acquired aversive control over behavior for longer periods of time if it has been originally paired only intermittently with primary aversive stimulation (Wagner, Siegel, and Fein, 1967). In general, it appears that conditioned aversive value is less dependent than is conditioned positive value on the informational function of a stimulus in signalling the occurrence of an event of more primary or established value (an instructive comparison can be made, for example, between the findings of Egger and Miller, 1962, and those of Seligman, 1966). The contrast suggests the possibility that there may be differences between anticipatory positive and aversive states in the timing and pattern of their control by informational signals. These differences may in turn account for the fact that conditioned aversive stimuli maintain independent value more easily than do conditioned positive stimuli, when they are removed from the conditions under which their value was acquired.

The persistence of the conditioned aversive value of a stimulus can also be increased by infrequent reinstatements of a temporal association between the stimulus and primary aversive stimulation that is not contingent on overt behavior. A well-established avoidance response can be maintained, for a very long time, by an occasional unavoidable and unpredictable shock that is entirely unrelated to an animal's choice of behavior—apparently as a result of the aversive motivational value that becomes attached to external situational cues (Kelleher, Riddle, and Cook, 1963; Sidman, Herrnstein, and Conrad, 1957). Long-term suppression of a highly motivated act can be induced by punishing the act with conditioned aversive stimulus outcomes whose value is maintained by infrequent pairing with shock, under conditions where the shock itself is never used as an outcome of the punished behavior (Hake and Azrin, 1965). Hoffman,

Fleshler, and Jensen (1963) have reported that a tone which was paired with unavoidable "free" shock would later independently suppress a pigeon's ongoing behavior even after a two and one-half year interval during which it was not used.

These findings in the animal laboratory are directly relevant to an understanding of how the socialization process produces durable and pervasive forms of external aversive stimulus control over the child's behavior. It is obvious that socialization will give aversive value to a matrix of social and nonsocial stimuli which have an intermittent temporal relationship either to explicit punishment of the child's behavior or to other kinds of aversive experience which are not necessarily contingent on the child's actions. The acquired activating, reinforcing, and suppressive effects of the occurrence or termination of these secondary aversive stimuli would spread, through generalization and cognitive representation, to an even broader range of situational cues.

Many conditioned social stimuli may show an indefinite retention of their value for aversive control of the child's behavior, because they are occasionally paired with the more highly aversive experience of punishment. In other instances, the onset of a situational social cue may have a persistent suppressive effect on a child's potential transgressions, or its termination may have a durable reinforcing effect on behavioral alternatives to transgression, because the cue retains an association with a broad base of aversive experience, rather than because it has been associated specifically with punishment. For example, cues which convey the fatigue or irritability of socializing agents, or which indicate the dangerous nonsocial consequences of an act, may suppress the child's behavior because of their previous association with its direct experience of other aversive events which were only incidentally or not at all under its own control. Moreover, since a great variety of such external cues are available to the child, it need not rely too heavily on any one cue. As a result, a specific cue would be slow to lose its acquired value as an informational signal of aversive contingencies.

It is also important to recognize that social behavior can be maintained by reinforcing external consequences which were not operative when the behavior was originally established. For example, a child may learn to suppress an act because suppression has been instrumental in avoiding or otherwise controlling the punitive consequences of the act. If the suppression is later elicited in the absence of any objective risk of punishment, it may be regarded as having acquired an internalized motivation. But the suppression may then facilitate the child's performance of more socially desirable alternatives to the punished act, which subsequently receive approval or other forms of positive social reinforcement. Social reinforcement can also support the maintenance of conduct that has been acquired originally without the direct training which is imposed by the positive or aversive consequences of the child's overt behavior. Very substantial repertoires of behavior are acquired through the disposition of children to observe and imitate their social models (Aronfreed, 1969; Bandura and Walters, 1963a). The value of such imitative behavior for the child often will be enhanced by the direct positive reinforcement to which the behavior is subsequently exposed.

A child's conduct may be externally maintained in still another way when it is governed by the child's empathic or vicarious response to its observable consequences for others, rather than by its directly positive or aversive consequences for the child. Of course, the effectiveness of this kind of external support of conduct already implies a certain degree of internalization in another and more extended sense of the concept, which we will shortly examine more closely—the sense in which some cognitive representation must necessarily have been imposed on the immediate concrete properties of social stimulus events.

Some of the forms of human behavior which are most commonly cited as evidence of long-term internalized control—for example, the suppression of certain types of aggression, or constraints on the manner and place of eliminative functions—may derive much of their persistence from their initial acquisition under conditions of a relatively high magnitude of aversive experience, at a time when children still have only a limited capacity for cognitive representation of the contingencies among external events and of the relationship between such events and their own behavior. If the child has not been able to give a cognitive representation to the original contingencies of socialization, then its behavioral dispositions are unlikely to make it aware of how the contingencies may have changed. It is clear that the behavior which animals learn under aversive control is often inflexible when it does not drift sufficiently toward a retest of the original contingencies of learning. For example, the persistence of behavior that has been learned in order to avoid shock sometimes prevents an animal from discovering that the behavior is no longer required (Church, 1963; Solomon and Brush, 1956).

Two of the most effective techniques for eliminating the avoidance behavior of animals are those which first prevent the behavior in the presence of the conditioned warning stimuli (Black, 1958; Carlson and Black,

1959; Solomon *et al.,* 1953; Weinberger, 1965), or which counter-condition the effects of positive stimuli to the cues of the avoidance situation (Hall, 1955; Nelson, 1966). Both of these techniques would increase the animal's exposure to conditioned aversive stimuli to the point where the value of the stimuli would undergo some extinction as a result of their dissociation from the occurrence of shock. There is experimental evidence that acquired aversive control over human behavior is also more resistant to extinction when conditions are arranged to prevent the subject's awareness and cognitive representation of changes in the contingencies which were present during learning (Logan, 1951; Spence and Platt, 1967). Conversely, extinction of avoidance behavior may be facilitated in human subjects by the withdrawal of salient external cues which were previously coterminous with the occurrence of punishment (Banks, 1965).

When we attempt to estimate the extent to which various areas of human conduct are independent of the control of external reinforcement, we must also take into account the resistance of the conduct to the motivation for alternative forms of behavior. In the paradigms which are used to study the persistence of learned behavior in animals, it is typically the case that the behavior must compete with other behavioral alternatives which may be in the service of very strong motivation. Under these conditions, the learned behavior will naturally be less durable if its motivation is weakened, or if the original contingencies which established its value are withdrawn from the situation. Where there is a choice, for example, between the suppression and the performance of behavior that will lead to reduction of a strong hunger drive, the suppressive effects of electric shock may extinguish fairly quickly when suppression is no longer instrumental to shock-avoidance (Estes, 1944; Miller, 1959).

The internalized control that people exercise over their conduct may be much less likely to be placed in competition with behavioral dispositions which have a motivation that is strong enough to jeopardize the control. However, when strongly competitive dispositions are induced by temporary changes in normative social constraints, long-standing behavioral suppressions can sometimes be released fairly easily (Brown, 1954; Festinger, Pepitone, and Newcomb, 1952; Kelley *et al.,* 1965; Singer, Brush, and Lublin, 1965). It appears that people can readily be induced to administer electric shock to others, for example, even though they have previously clearly stated their opposition to doing so (Brock and Buss, 1964; Glass, 1964). And under conditions of unusual stress or social pressure, people will sometimes relinquish patterns of conduct which appeared to have been very firmly internalized (Bettelheim, 1943; Lifton, 1961; Milgram, 1963; Schein, 1957).

We may conclude that there is some continuity between animals and humans in the conditions which determine the stability of their acquired behavior. But we cannot infer from the continuity that animals and humans have comparable resources for internalization. On the contrary, it appears that people do have a much greater capacity than animals for internalized control over their behavior, and that they sometimes are able to maintain the control for substantial periods of time without external support. It may be that human conduct more easily maintains its acquired intrinsic value because its reinforcing consequences often have the advantage of being carried in the cognitive representations for which human beings are so uniquely equipped.

A number of recent experiments have demonstrated the variety of conditions of learning which can be used to induce some degree of internalized control over the conduct of children (Aronfreed, 1964, 1966; Aronfreed and Paskal, 1966; Aronfreed and Reber, 1965; Bandura, 1965a; Bandura and Kupers, 1964; Grusec, 1966; Mischel and Grusec, 1966; Mischel and Liebert, 1966; Parke and Walters, 1967; Walters and Parke, 1964a; Walters, Parke, and Cane, 1965). These conditions include the observation of the behavior of other people, and of the consequences of their behavior, as well as the application of reward and punishment to the child's own behavior. Although the studies which are cited generally do not attempt to assess the persistence of internalization over any substantial period of time, they do reveal some of the ways in which it is possible to obtain predictable control over conduct in situations which appear to be entirely private, or in which it is at least clear that the child's behavioral choices will not produce differential social reward or punishment.

The concept of internalization that has been advanced here does not assume that conduct can become divorced from the stimulus control of the external environment. Even the most highly internalized forms of control over conduct must remain dependent on external situational cues, if they are to be elicited under appropriate conditions. When the absence of support from external events is used to define the internalized status of an act, the criterion of internalization refers only to whether the act has become independent of its outcomes for the actor. There is a sense, of course, in which every act necessarily introduces some change into the total complex of the individual's stimulation from the external environment. But the concept of internalization is anchored more specifically to those external consequences of an act which are conveyed through a social medium and which have some affective value for the actor. The external cues which elicit and control conduct bear upon a criterion of internalization only to the extent that they either signal or represent potential social consequences for the actor—as they might, for example, in the case of cues which convey surveillance or the power of socializing agents to reward and punish.

External situational cues continue to govern internalized conduct not only through the control which they exercise over the selection of appropriate behavior, but also through their specification of the conditions under which particular forms of conduct will maintain their acquired intrinsic values. It is quite common, for example, to find that young children internalize their control of behavior more concretely than their socializing agents might have intended. They may learn to suppress an act that has been previously punished, and to do so effectively even in the absence of external surveillance by their parents. But they may then show no evidence of suppression when their environmental cues are slightly different from those under which they were originally trained. This kind of slippage in behavioral control may reflect restrictions on the conditions of learning rather than a failure of internalization. The suppression may be still highly internalized in the presence of the original external cues, but its intrinsic reinforcement value has been too narrowly tied to these cues.

The power of external stimulus control over internalized conduct can also be seen in the appropriate discriminations which children learn to make. There are very few acts which are always treated in the same way by socializing agents, without regard to the situational context in which they occur. Thus, for example, certain kinds of aggressive behavior may be punished when they are directed toward some social objects, but may be tolerated or even reinforced when they are directed to other objects. Accordingly, when the child must subsequently control its aggressive behavior in the absence of its primary agents of socialization, the intrinsic value of suppression will be governed in part by specific situational cues.

It may be noted, finally, that the control of the social environment over the maintenance of the child's internalized conduct is ordinarily not limited to the precise stimulus situations in which the child previously has experienced positive or aversive outcomes of its behavior. External stimulus control over the child's behavior is broadened and refined by the effects of generalization, discrimination, and a number of other phenomena which are indigenous to conditioning and learning (Honig, 1966; Prokasy, 1965). And an even greater range and complexity of external control over the child's behavior are attained when the cues and contingencies of specific situations are subordinated to the representational power of cognition and language.

The maintenance of either a specific act or a sequential pattern of behavior, under the control of appropriate environmental cues, requires some form of mediational bridging if outcomes of significant value are suspended or delayed for substantial periods of time. Investigators in the animal laboratory sometimes have devised ingenious arrangements for making learned behavior more persistent through the use of stimuli which have a conditional value as signals of the later occurrence of a delayed reward or punishment (for example, the experiments which are reported by Bixenstine, 1956, and by Ferster and Hammer, 1965). But the cognitive capacities of children attain a greater power than those of animals, and become a more effective means of bridging the long intervals of time which may pass between their behavior and the occurrence of social rewards or punishments. Children are capable of highly articulate representations of the eventual outcomes of their behavior, even when the behavior may not be directly observable to others. And they can also give an accurate cognitive representation to the contingency between intermittent signals of conditional value and the final outcome of a sustained sequence of behavior.

INTERNAL AND EXTERNAL ORIENTATION

The criterion of internalization that we have examined thus far is essentially the criterion of resistance to extinction. It applies to the persistence of behavior in the absence of reinforcing external outcomes, or to the independent maintenance of behavior by outcomes whose value was originally dependent on their conditional relationship to events of more established value. Such a criterion defines the internalized status of the maintenance of an act only by reference to its external consequences for the actor. And because surveillance is such an immediate representation of the potential consequences of behavior in a social environment, the criterion usually is extended to require that conduct remain stable in the absence of surveillance. In most empirical tests for internalized control of conduct in children, the absence of surveillance is actually taken in itself as a pragmatic criterion of internalization, since it is often used in situations where it is reasonable to assume that the child does not expect its actions to be known to others (Aronfreed, 1968).

The actual external consequences of an act for the actor, and the potential consequences which are represented in surveillance, are indispensable reference points for a criterion of internalization. When conduct is maintained in the absence of such external support, its reinforcing consequences must somehow be carried in its intrinsic correlates. However, neither surveillance nor the actual consequences of a person's conduct are sufficient criteria to make the full range of significant distinctions which we might wish to make in developing the concept of internalization. Much of the internalized control of conduct is mediated through the cognitive operations of conscience, which people can use to represent and evaluate their behavior in a variety of ways. The representational and evaluative functions of conscience vary in the concreteness or abstraction of their reference to the external outcomes of conduct, and also in the directness with which they translate such outcomes into their value for the individual. A complete analysis of the concept of internalization can therefore be made only by taking into account the cognitive determinants of conduct as well as its dependence on external consequences.

When we allow for the cognitive processes which may be superimposed on concrete external stimulus events, the concept of internalization can be greatly extended to make some important distinctions among a number of different kinds of evaluative control over conduct. These different forms of evaluative control may be thought of as lying along a continuum of *internal versus external orientation.* The applicability of such a continuum is apparent in the many ways in which conscience may represent the consequences of conduct. For example, an individual's perception of social observation and potential consequences of his actions is not always coordinate to the actual conditions of surveillance. From a child's point of view, its actions may result in maintenance of parental affection, or in avoidance of punishment, despite the absence of any objective indicators of these contingencies. Adults also may behave in accordance with their perception of surveillance by temporal or spiritual agents who are not physically present. Whiting (1959) cites examples of entire societies whose internalization of conduct remains highly dependent on the nonveridical perception of surveillance by both real and imaginary agents of social control. Even when a person may perceive that his conduct is private in its immediate context, his actions may be influenced by his expectation that they will later come to the attention of other people, or by his cognitive representation of how other people have responded to his actions in the past.

The examples of the operation of conscience which are cited above illustrate a cognitive focus on the direct social consequences of an act for the actor. Conscience may also operate, however, through other forms of evaluative cognition which are less externally oriented, but which can nevertheless exert a powerful influence on behavior. There are many criteria of value which can exercise control over conduct even though they do not represent its direct consequences for the individual. People may evaluate their actions with respect to the standards or practices of those whom they hold in esteem or authority, without necessarily being oriented toward the consequences which their actions will have for themselves. They may also evaluate the consequences of their actions in accordance with their standards for the maintenance of satisfactory affiliative or contractual relationships within a social system. Or they may apply broader principles which are oriented to the intrinsic goodness or rightness of the effects of their actions upon the welfare of others. These different evaluative schemata vary in their cognitive substance and in the extent of their formal abstraction from concrete external referents. They would occupy different positions on a continuum of internal versus external orientation, and they would have different implications for the resistance of conduct to change under the pressure of external social influence. Yet all of these schemata are capable of controlling conduct without any concrete reference to external consequences of reward or punishment.

Even within the large repertoires of conduct which are continually supported by the individual's direct experience of their external consequences, cognition makes very strong representational and evaluative impositions on the functional properties of external events. When the maintenance of a behavioral disposition is dependent on explicit rewards and punishments, or on less explicit but equally powerful outcomes such as social approval and disapproval, there are still cognitive interventions to take into account in determining how the value of the behavior is controlled by its outcomes. The value of the outcome of an act is often mediated by the evaluative function of cognitive processes which are engaged by the outcomes. For example, social reward and punishment may control conduct in part because they serve as cues to elicit an individual's evaluation of the consequences of his actions for others. The effects of the reward and punishment are then mediated by the value that is carried in the cognitive structures which they activate, as well as by whatever value may be inherent in the concrete stimulus properties of the external events through which they are transmitted.

The very direction of the value of external outcomes of behavior may be determined by a child's cognitive representation of the contingencies in its social environment. Recent experiments on the social control of children's performance in various tasks have shown, for example, that the absence of any reaction to a child's behavioral choices can assume aversive or positive value merely by the effects of contrast to the alternative occurrence of verbal reward or punishment (Crandall, Good, and Crandall, 1964; Offenbach, 1966). The effect of a socially transmitted reinforcer on a child's behavior can also be augmented by explicit instructions which verbalize the informational status of the reinforcer as a signal of a correct choice (Cairns, 1967).

Some of the most persuasive evidence of cognitive control over the value of reward and punishment can be found in studies of the variability in their effects on behavior. Rotter (1966) has shown that the effects of external reinforcement on behavior in various task settings are systematically influenced by the individual's expectations about how closely the occurrence of rewarding events will be determined by his own performance. Even more striking evidence, although it is somewhat more indirect, appears in the strong preference that both children and adults have for rewards and punishments which are under the close control of their own behavior, and also in their preference for informational signals which enable them to predict the outcomes of their behavior (Belanger and Sattler, 1967; Lanzetta and Driscoll, 1966; Lefcourt, 1966; Metzner, 1963). Information about the occurrence or timing of outcomes apparently is valued even though it permits no modification of their nature or schedule. Active control over outcomes will compensate for delay in reward, and will often be preferred even when it produces an immediate aversive outcome. These preferences are a very general and pervasive phenomenon; they also have been demonstrated repeatedly in the behavior of animals (Bower, McLean, and Meacham, 1966; Gibbon, 1967; Lockard, 1963; Sidman and Boren, 1957).

The effects of behavioral and informational contingencies on the value of external outcomes carry an even broader implication for the social control of conduct. These effects emphasize the fact that the value of the outcomes which we identify as social reward and punishment are not entirely and immediately contained in their concrete stimulus properties. Their value is subordinated to the individual's affective and motivational dispositions, as well as to his capacity for cognitive representation. Thus, for example, affective and cognitive dispositions may introduce variability into the locus of control over conduct that is maintained by a person's empathic or vicarious reactions to its consequences. Many common forms of social behavior are maintained on the basis of their actual or anticipated consequences for others. They may be intermittently reinforced because they produce visible evidence of pleasure or relief of distress for another person. These forms of behavior often are emitted, however, under conditions where others are necessarily cognizant of the individual who is the source of a beneficent action. The consequences of the action for others may therefore elicit that individual's perception of the implicit approval or affection in which others will hold him. Even when a person may be responding empathically or vicariously to the consequences of his actions for others, without any cognitive representation of their direct consequences for himself, the locus of control over the reinforcement of his conduct may still vary in its dependence on observable external events. The reinforcement may lie in the person's empathic affective response to directly observable cues which indicate the effects of his action upon another person. But the reinforcement may also be mediated by cognitive processes through which the person represents and evaluates the beneficial consequences of his action for the other person, quite independently of the immediate visibility of the consequences.

The concept of a continuum of internal versus external orientation is also very useful in any attempt to understand the variable results of the different types of paradigms which have been used to assess behavioral or cognitive conformity to social influence and constraint. There have been a great many demonstrations of the conformity of adults to the judgements, demands, or actions of others, in situations where they are exposed in varying degrees to the direct social pressure of both observation and implicit or explicit approval or disapproval (Allen and Crutchfield, 1963; Asch, 1956; Endler, 1966; Jacobs and Campbell, 1961; Milgram, 1964). The social conformity that can be induced in such paradigms is also readily demonstrable in the behavior and evaluative judgements of children (Abelson and Lesser, 1959; Harper *et al.,* 1965; Hetherington, 1965; Jakubczak and Walters, 1959). Additional evidence of children's dispositions to conform under these conditions can be found in numerous experiments which are reported as demonstrations of learning through observation of a social model. We will look more closely at these experiments in our later analysis of observational learning and imitation.

Among the many experiments which demonstrate a controlled induction of conformity, there are a few whose results have the interesting feature of an apparent persistence of the effect for some period of time after the original exposure to social pressure. However, the observations of persistence generally are made under conditions in which the subjects might well perceive that there is external knowledge or surveillance of their behavior. Stone (1967) recently has shown that verbal reinforcement of a person's judgements of the movement of a visual stimulus will quickly eliminate the perceptual norms which had been established earlier by the person's exposure to the judgements of others.

In a second type of paradigm, direct observations of potential social transgressions are made in a relatively public situation, where the subject's perceived risk of nonconformity may be substantial, even though he is not under immediate surveillance (Kimbrell and Blake, 1958; Lefkowitz, Blake, and Mouton, 1955). Finally, there have been a number of assessments of children's suppression of prohibited behavior in situations which appear to be quite private (Burton, Maccoby, and Allinsmith, 1961; Grinder, 1962; Hartshorne and May, 1928; Sears, Rau, and Alpert, 1965, Chapter 6). The extent and persistence of the conformity that one observes in these different types of paradigms seem to be determined in part by the amount of social pressure that is being used to elicit choices or judgements which are already under some degree of internalized control. This inference is supported by the findings of other experiments, in which controlled variation of the public-private dimension has produced the more or less obvious expected differences in conformity (Argyle, 1957; Gerard, 1964; Kelman, 1965). At the same time, it is rather surprising to find that situational constraints which represent very different points on a public-private dimension often appear not to be very different in the sheer amount of conformity which they induce (see, for example, Berg and Bass, 1961). The roughly comparable effects of the different types of paradigms suggest that people may tend to fall back on more internalized resources for the control of their behavior when external monitors are suspended or made uncertain.

There is a variety of evidence that points to the rough equivalence of the effectiveness of internal and external monitors in the control of social behavior. For example, experiments with both adults and children indicate that private conformity may be induced merely by the influence of information about the choices of others (Deutsch and Gerard, 1955; Iscoe and Williams, 1963). This finding suggests that there may be a certain amount of reinforcement value in a person's prediction or matching of the actions and judgements of other people in his social environment, even when his own choices are unknown to others. Secondly, it appears that objective risk and gain may not weigh very heavily on external social control over conduct, perhaps because variability in the real probabilities of reward and punishment undergoes some shrinkage when it is translated into the individual's perception of the probabilities. Rettig and Rawson (1963) found that people's estimates of the situations in which others might perform "unethical" acts were much more influenced by the potential intensity of punishment than they were by the potential probability.

The most direct evidence of the relationship between internal and external monitors of conduct may lie in the findings of experiments which suggest a compensatory balance between the individual's internalized evaluative control over his behavior and the magnitude or salience of its rewarding or punitive external consequences. Rettig (1966) observed that students who performed a task as isolated individuals were more honest than those who performed as members of groups in which there were no apparent constraints on cheating. In contrast, when students in a group setting were exposed to a high level of communication about the potential punitive consequences of cheating, they tended to be as honest as the students who performed in isolation. In many recent experiments on cognitive change under the influence of various magnitudes of social pressure for behavioral conformity, there is also evidence that the individual's own evaluative resources are more extensively called into play when external control of the behavior is relatively weak (Aronson and Carlsmith, 1963; Festinger and Carlsmith, 1959; Freedman, 1965; Raven and Fishbein, 1961) or when an already established motivation is a more significant determinant of conduct (Mills, 1958). The findings of these experiments very probably reflect their subjects' past histories of learning to engage the sliding scales of their own values, in order to accommodate their internalized control of conduct, when the role of external monitors has been diminished or blurred.

There also may be acquired differences of disposition among individuals in their orientation toward the locus of control over their conduct. For example, children who are more susceptible to the influence of the judgements of others are also more likely to violate social prohibitions when they are not under direct external constraints (Lesser and Abelson, 1959). But they are less likely to be able to postpone immediate rewards for delayed and more valuable rewards (Mischel, 1961b). Rettig and Sinha (1966) found that college students who were most oriented to risk of external censure for transgression were also most likely to be deceitful in a situation where their deceit appeared to be undetectable to others.

The reactions which people have to their committed social transgressions also reveal interesting differences when they are separated along a continuum of internal versus external orientation, even after they are sufficiently internalized to have become independent of direct surveillance (Aronfreed, 1961). Self-criticism might be regarded as the most internally oriented type of reaction to transgression, since its occurrence can be virtually independent of any particular context of external support. Reactions such as confession and apology have a much greater dependence on an external supportive context than does self-criticism, since they can function only in the presence of social agents. Moreover, these reactions often bring about a resolution of transgression through their external social consequences in the form of either punishment or forgiveness. Reparative reactions would seem to have a roughly intermediate position between self-criticism and reactions such as confession or apology. Although reparation does not necessarily require an external social presence, many reparative actions do in fact bring the transgressor into direct contact with the person to whom reparation is made. Some forms of reparation cannot be carried out without exposing an otherwise private transgression to others. And even when they are completely private, reparative reactions are always directed toward an external target.

There are also some common internalized reactions to transgression which are entirely oriented toward an external resolution of the transgression—for example, the avoidance of anticipated discovery and punishment, the punitive interpretation of fortuitous events, or even the use of direct attempts to elicit punishment. The context of social support that is sometimes required for the elicitation of certain reactions to transgression reveals still more subtle differences of internal versus external orientation. Confession and corrective modifications of behavior may be self-initiated. But they may also be externally initiated by various kinds of influence from the observed behavior or verbalized values of other people (even when the transgression itself may be unknown to others). Some internalized reactions to transgression may be displayed publicly in order to win external approval or forgiveness. Still another kind of external orientation is apparent when the assistance of other people is used in order to carry out a corrective action.

A very interesting kind of evidence of variation on a continuum of internal versus external orientation appears in the expressions of conscience which are verbalized by both children and adults, when they are asked to state their rationales for the evaluation of different forms of conduct in hypothetical situations. Although differences of orientation clearly exist in the evaluative cognition of adults (Adorno *et al.*, 1950; McCord and Clemes, 1964; McCord and McCord, 1960), the differences have been investigated more extensively among children. The most widely known differences in the orientation of conscience among children are those which are reported by Piaget (1948), who makes essentially one basic distinction between absolute and relative morality. But more elaborate distinctions are made in the reports of surveys which have been carried out by Kohlberg (1963a, 1964, 1969) and by others (Hoffman 1968; Hoffman and Saltzstein, 1967). Among the findings which emerge from the work of Piaget and of Kohlberg are some striking differences of orientation among children who differ in age or in other indices of developmental status. These developmental differences will be examined in some detail in Chapter Ten, where they will be used to analyze the role of social experience as the generator of changes in the structure of conscience. Here we need only describe the predominant differences, without regard to their developmental order, in order to illustrate their relevance to a continuum of internal versus external orientation.

When asked for their reasons for asserting that certain actions are more correct or desirable than others, children sometimes point to the direct consequences of the actions for the actor. In other cases, they may justify the actions on the grounds of conformity to the rules which are imposed by authority. Or they may rely on more abstract principles of social interaction, such as those which take account of the welfare of others. When they are asked to assign appropriate punishments, they may judge transgressions either in terms of their visibly harmful consequences or in terms of the intentions of the transgressor. They may advocate external retribution in the resolution of transgressions, or they may suggest that the transgressor take the initiative through restitution. When they are asked about situations in which conventional rules might be changed, they may insist that the constraints of authority are inviolate, or they may agree that the rules could be modified. They also vary in their disposition to perceive that transgression will lead to punitive consequences in a more or less inevitable and impersonal way. All of these variations represent clear differences of cognitive position on a continuum of internal versus external orientation.

CHAPTER FOUR

MECHANISMS
OF
SOCIALIZATION

As an introduction to the mechanisms of socialization, it will be useful if we first briefly formalize a few terms and concepts. The general theoretical context of this formalization is one in which changes of affective state are assumed to be fundamental to the learning processes which form the basis of socialization. The child's acquired behavioral dispositions are initially highly dependent on its experience of external events which may be either contingent or noncontingent on its own behavior. The most important medium for the transmission of these events is the behavior of the child's socializing agents. Exposure to a social environment produces socialized control over the child's behavior because of the nature and magnitude of the changes of affectivity which are elicited in the child by specific environmental events.

The mechanisms of socialization also produce a shift in the locus of control over the affectivity that has become associated with the child's behavior. Internalization takes place to the extent that changes of affectivity are transferred from the mediation of external monitors to the mediation of monitors which are more intrinsically correlated to the child's performance or representation of an act. The shift or transfer takes place essentially through a process of conditioning. It is not necessary to assume, however, that a firmly internalized form of behavior always remains under affective control. Some forms of behavior may be automatized out of the sequence of changes of affective state through which they were originally established (Hebb, 1949; Solomon and Wynne, 1954).

It is important to distinguish between two types of internal monitors which are available to the child for the mediation of conditioned affectivity and the control of its own behavior. The first type of monitor consists of the behavioral cues which are directly inherent in the child's overt performance of an act—for example, the proprioceptive or visual cues which are intrinsically produced for the child by its own behavior. The second type of monitor consists of the more complex information in *cognitive* processes, which give the child the capacity to represent and evaluate both its own behavior and the external situational context in which the behavior occurs. The cues which are directly inherent in the child's behavior are crucial to the establishment of the earliest forms of internalized transmission of affectivity. And they continue to have an extensive monitoring function throughout the course of socialization. Cognitive processes have much broader and more powerful mediational functions. But their control of affective states emerges more slowly with advancing development. Although the cognitive processes of the young child are closely tied to its overt behavior—a phenomenon that is especially clear in the extensive observations which have been made by Piaget (1952)—cognition becomes increasingly independent of its original behavioral correlates as it gradually acquires more representational and anticipatory functions.

Affective states may be divided into two basic classes: *positive* (pleasurable) and *aversive* (unpleasant or painful) states. Each of these two classes includes a number of variations in the specific quality of affective experience. The qualitative variations are governed by the cognitive framework in which the arousal of affectivity occurs. Schachter and his collaborators (Schachter, 1964; Schachter and Singer, 1962) have reported experiments which are suggestive illustrations of the control of the specific quality of a person's affective arousal by information from the social environment. The basic distinction between positive and aversive states is sufficient, however, for a preliminary outline of the mechanisms of internalization. The stimuli in the child's social environment may be described in terms of either their positive or aversive properties, when it can be inferred that they have the capacity to induce corresponding affective states in the child. Other stimuli may be characterized by properties which reduce or inhibit the arousal of one of the two basic affective states.

The affective value of many significant classes of social stimuli is, of course, acquired rather than innate. But the value of some classes of social stimuli may be more or less predetermined by an interaction between the child's unlearned predispositions and its exposure to specific forms of experience which are ordinarily present at early and critical junctures of its development. Studies of the early development of social attachment in the human infant clearly suggest that certain types of change in social stimulation—for example, stimulus changes which are associated with the presence or absence of the mother or caretaker—very quickly acquire positive or aversive value (Ambrose, 1961; Casler, 1961; Gewirtz, 1965; Schaffer and Emerson, 1964; Spitz and Wolf, 1946). The uniformity of the behavioral manifestation and timing of this phenomenon can hardly be attributed merely to conditioning, since the contingencies which are required for conditioning would be expected to vary more among infants in accordance with their treatment. An excellent summary of the evidence on the effects of early experience in fixing the value of social stimuli for the human infant can be found in a forthcoming review by Maccoby (1969). It should also be noted that many of the forms of stimulation which a child receives from a social environment may have a value that is inherent in their novelty, in their complexity, or in other properties which appear to be derived from the developmental ethology of the child's affective and cognitive dispositions, rather than from any previous association with the child's attachment to a nurturant caretaker (Cantor, 1963; Hunt, 1965; Kessen and Mandler, 1961; Munsinger and Kessen, 1964).

Experiments on the early social attachments of animals also have demonstrated that the value of social stimuli becomes relatively fixed by specific experience within a fairly narrow range of developmental time (Cairns, 1966; Harlow and Zimmerman, 1959; Hess, 1959; Mason, 1961; Scott, 1963). The strong unlearned bias in the maintenance of the value of these stimuli is indicated in the resistance of social attachment to conditions which would ordinarily be expected to produce extinction or suppression (Cairns and Johnson, 1965; Harlow and Harlow, 1965; Hess, 1959). A fully established social attachment across two different species can sometimes be strong enough to supplant agonistic or flight reactions which would otherwise occur under natural conditions (Denenberg, Hudgens, and Zarrow, 1964; Kuo, 1960).

The behavioral dispositions which the young of many species of animals show toward their social environment also confirms an inference that is compelled by the common observation of children in their naturalistic settings: that it is not possible to account for social behavior without drawing a fundamental distinction between positive and aversive affective control (see, for example, the analysis of approach and withdrawal behavior that is suggested by Schnierla, 1959). The requirement of a dichotomy of positive and aversive states is also apparent in general theories of motivation (Miller, 1963; Young, 1961). And it is strongly supported by the evidence of neurophysiological approaches to problems of motivation and reinforcement (Deutsch and Howarth, 1963; Glickman and Schiff, 1967; Grossman and Grossman, 1966; Olds, 1955).

The induction of changes of affective state governs the child's acquisition and maintenance of social behavior through a number of different kinds of contingencies. *Outcomes* constitute one pervasive class of these contingencies. An outcome is a stimulus event that is selectively contingent on the occurrence of a specific form of overt behavior. Many of the external socially transmitted outcomes of a child's behavior—for example, direct rewards or punishments—induce affective change in the child. They also assume a very important role in producing internalized control of behavior, because they attach changes of affectivity directly to the behavioral and cognitive monitors which are intrinsically correlated to the child's acts.

Outcomes may have the status of *reinforcers*. Reinforcers strengthen or maintain the behavior on which they are contingent. Their effects are reflected, for example, in the increased probability that the same behavior will appear again, when situational cues are similar to those under which the reinforcement occurred. The reinforcing properties of outcomes are a function of their induction of positive affect or of their inhibition or reduction of aversive affect. Other outcomes have the status of *suppressors*. Suppressors decrease the probability of occurrence of the behavior on which they are contingent. The suppressive properties of outcomes are a function of their induction of aversive affect or of their inhibition or reduction of positive affect.

Internalized control of behavior can also be established through another broad class of contingencies in the social environment. This second class of contingencies can change the child's behavioral dispositions through the affective value of external stimulus events which are not necessarily the outcomes of the child's overt behavior. It is the child's observation of others, rather than the consequences of its own emitted behavior, that initiates this kind of learning. The observable behavior of socializing agents directly transmits stimulation which has a significant affective impact on the child. It also occurs in close proximity with a great many other stimulus events of affective value. Moreover, the child has the capacity for cognitive representation of much of the behavior that it observes. As a result of the contingencies between its observation of the behavior of others and its changes of affectivity, the child's cognitive representation of the behavior (and the behavior itself) will often acquire a self-contained or inherent affective value. The child may then reproduce the behavior, under the control of appropriate external cues, when the acquired value of the behavior corresponds to a reinforcing change of affective state. Thus, just as in the case of outcome contingencies, the observation of the behavior of others can produce a direct attachment of affective value to the cognitive and intrinsic stimulus correlates of the child's own behavior, with the effect that the behavior becomes independent to some extent of its external consequences. This kind of observational learning is the basis of the child's imitation of social models, and also of other forms of behavioral change which can be initiated without the control of outcomes.

An understanding of the mechanisms of socialization requires a more general understanding of the affective and cognitive mechanisms of learning. This outline of the mechanisms, and its subsequent expansion, rest on both extensions and modifications of traditional concepts of the learning process. The conception of the transmission of affectivity to internalized control is heavily influenced by Pavlovian conditioning concepts of excitation and inhibition (Pavlov, 1927), and especially by recent Russian work which demonstrates the applicability of conditioning paradigms to an impressive range of the phenomena of learning in children (Bronshtein *et al.,* 1958; Elkonin, 1957; Ivanov-Smolenski, 1959; Kasatkin, 1957). The conception of the control of affectivity over overt behavior is influenced to some extent by recent theoretical developments concerning the relationship between Pavlovian conditioning and behavior-contingent training (Konorski, 1964; Mowrer, 1960a; Rescorla and Solomon, 1967; Spence, 1956). These developments also can be applied to certain problems which are inherent in an account of observational learning. However, the model of the learning process that will be used here gives a fundamental place to the representational and evaluative functions of cognitive processes.

Cognition will be considered primarily with respect to its role in the mediation of the child's affectivity and in the consequent control of its behavior. Although cognitive change itself is a major ingredient of socialization, its mechanisms will not be analyzed in any detail. This treatment is dictated in part by the fact that concepts of learning which are drawn from the study of socialization appear to be most seminal when they are used to account for the modification of behavior. We do not yet seem to have a comparably powerful body of concepts which can be applied to the learning of values or to other phenomena of cognitive change.

It should also be observed that the mechanisms of socialization are not exclusively applicable to the child. But since early experience has such a profound and lasting influence on human social behavior, it seems appropriate to phrase most of the outline of the mechanisms in terms of learning during childhood.

BEHAVIOR-CONTINGENT LEARNING

A very great part of socialization takes place through the reinforcing and suppressive effects of outcomes of the child's overt behavior. These outcomes occur in the onset, termination, or modulation of various socially transmitted stimuli which have a positive or aversive value for the child. The requirements of this form of learning are that the child must emit some overt behavior, and that a contingency be established between the behavior and its outcome. It is frequently the case that the outcome can be effective only if it follows the behavior within a relatively short span of time. The time over which an outcome may follow an act and still be effective can be greatly expanded, however, if it can be bridged by the child's cognitive representation of the act. Behavior becomes internalized when its elicitation, under the control of appropriate cues, shows some independence of its external outcomes. When an act and its outcomes have been paired on a sufficient number of occasions, the affective change that is induced in the child by the outcomes may become directly attached (conditioned) to the intrinsic behavioral cues or cognitive representations which are associated with the act. Components of this affectivity may then be evoked by the intrinsic correlates of the act even in the subsequent absence of any external consequences.

The kind of learning that is being described here is commonly known as instrumental or operant training. The application of some of its principles to both positive and aversive control of behavior is described extensively in general treatments of the phenomena of learning (Ferster and Skinner, 1957; Honig, 1966; Logan and Wagner, 1965; Skinner, 1938). These principles have been employed very widely in experimental studies of the control of both social and nonsocial outcomes over the learning or performance of infants and children in a variety of settings and tasks. Summaries of this work may be found in a number of recent reviews (Bijou and Baer, 1966; Krasner and Ullman, 1965; Lipsitt, 1963; Papoušek, 1967; Stevenson, 1965), which are notable for their very heavy emphasis on positive control of behavior. It is a matter of some interest that the emphasis appears to be reversed in those investigations which have focussed on the problem of internalization. There is a remarkable scarcity of work on the internalized consequences of the direct training that can be imposed on the child's behavior by social reward or other kinds of positive social reinforcement. In contrast, a great many studies have given detailed attention to direct training as a source of internalized aversive control over the child's behavior, in both the naturalistic context of parental discipline and the experimental context of punishment learning in the laboratory (Aronfreed, 1968; Walters and Parke, 1967).

A number of investigations of behavior-contingent learning in children have demonstrated that the child's motivational dispositions determine the effectiveness of positive social reinforcement. This is a finding that bears directly on the question of how the stimulus features of a social environment acquire and maintain their affective value for the child. Deprivation of food and water is used quite commonly to control the motivational states of animals, and thus to bring their behavior under the control of appropriate reinforcers (Kimble, 1961). The effects of both rewards and punishments on the maintenance of learned behavior in animals also can be sharply modified by either gradual or abrupt changes in the magnitude or the value of the outcomes to which an animal has become adapted over short periods of time (Crespi, 1942; Gleitman and Steinman, 1964; Hake, Azrin, and Oxford, 1967; Sandler, 1964; Spear, 1967). In much the same way, deprivation or satiation can produce a transitory situational enhancement or reduction of the value which specific forms of social stimulation may have for the child. The original finding by Gewirtz and Baer (1958a, 1958b) of an enhanced effectiveness of positive verbal reinforcers in shaping the performance of young chidren in a simple task, after the children had been exposed to brief periods of social isolation, has since been amply confirmed and extended (Stevenson, 1965; Walters and Parke, 1964b). Conversely, a concentrated exposure to verbal social reinforcement may temporarily reduce its value for the child (Gewirtz and Baer, 1958b; Landau and Gewirtz, 1967). However, the fact that the attentional and affective value of social stimuli also may be controlled by more permanent dispositions of the child, which arise out of the total history of its social experience (Maccoby, 1969; Stevenson, 1965; Zigler and Williams, 1963), is undoubtedly of even greater importance to an understanding of the socialization process. The implications of such dispositions for the internalization of control over the child's behavior will be discussed more fully in a later chapter, where we will examine the effects of variations in child-rearing practices.

Some behavior-contingent learning takes place when socializing agents use their rewarding and punitive resources with the intention of modifying the child's behavior. Concrete rewards and punishments, praise and blame, and various other explicit indicators of approval or disapproval, are the most obvious and direct channels of behavior-contingent socialization.

Much of the child's social behavior is also shaped, however, by positive and aversive outcomes which are less consciously and intentionally determined. These outcomes may take the form of social stimulus changes which are quite small in their observable magnitude. The reactions of socializing agents to the child's behavior frequently are conveyed by subtle changes in the flow of their own behavior, through such media as physical contact, facial expression, posture, gesture, or pattern of speech. The social consequences of the child's behavior may shape its conduct even when they do not take the form of outcomes which the child experiences directly. Behavior-contingent learning may occur on the basis of the child's acquired capacity for empathic or vicarious experience, since the consequences of a child's actions for others may also function as positive or aversive outcomes if they induce corresponding changes of affectivity in the child.

Many of the social stimulus outcomes which shape a child's behavior may not be in the focus of awareness of either the child or the socializing agent. Nevertheless, they may be very effective in controlling the child's behavior, because of the affective value which they have acquired as a result of the child's past experience and of its unlearned predispositions. It seems quite clear that the Pavlovian conditioning of human subjects can occur in the absence of awareness of the contingency between conditioned and unconditioned stimuli (Kimble, 1962; Razran, 1949), and that this phenomenon may extend to the conditioning of affective value (see, for example, the report by Lacey and Smith, 1954, of the conditioning and generalization of "unconscious anxiety"). The affectivity that is induced in the child by the outcomes of its overt behavior could therefore be expected to become attached quite readily, without the requirement of awareness of the behavior-outcome contingency, to the intrinsic perceptual and cognitive monitors which are most closely associated with the behavior.

Some question has been raised recently about the conditions and extent of the learned modifications of overt behavior which are possible when people are unaware of behavior-outcome contingencies (Spielberger and DeNike, 1966). The findings of the earliest studies of social reinforcement of verbal behavior appeared to be in general agreement in suggesting that the phenomenon of learning without awareness could be produced under laboratory conditions (Cohen et al., 1954; Greenspoon, 1955; Taffel, 1955; Verplanck, 1956). More recent and sophisticated experimental designs appear to leave very little doubt that the phenomenon exists (Hefferline, Keenan, and Harford, 1962; Oakes, 1967). Bem (1965) has reported an especially interesting experiment in which subjects were unaware of the acquired control of external cues over their reactions to their own false confessions. Nevertheless, there is other evidence which indicates that behavior-contingent training is very much facilitated by a person's awareness of outcome contingencies (DeNike, 1964; Dulany, 1962), and that outcome control in the absence of awareness is more effective for behavior which is well established than it is for behavior which must be discovered in a learning situation (Eriksen, 1960; Turner and Solomon, 1962).

Another phenomenon that may be closely related to behavior modification without awareness of outcomes is the control that outcomes can apparently sometimes exercise over responses which ordinarily are expected to be more sensitive to the contingencies of Pavlovian conditioning (Kimmel, 1967). A number of studies have shown that the galvanic skin response, the heart rate, and other peripheral autonomic components which are commonly taken as indices of change in affective state, can be brought under the control of outcomes for human subjects (Greene, 1966; Kimmel, 1965; Kimmel and Baxter, 1964; Shearn, 1962). There recently have been some rather powerful demonstrations of the same type in the animal laboratory (Miller and Carmona, 1967; Miller and DiCara, 1967; Trowill, 1967). Recognition of this phenomenon raises the interesting possibility that the role of behavior-contingent learning in the socialization process is more extensive than we might first have supposed. It is conceivable, for example, that outcomes of the overt behavioral correlates of changes in the child's affectivity exercise some control over the conditioned activation and inhibition of the affectivity by social cues and cognitive representations.

Outcomes which the child perceives as explicit rewards and punishments are only a very partial inventory, then, of the outcomes which can be socially transmitted to cumulate the power of behavior-contingent learning. Reward and punishment might more appropriately be used to designate outcomes which are directly and intentionally addressed to the child with the purpose of controlling its subsequent behavior. Outcomes which the child perceives as having these properties may very possibly differ from other kinds of outcomes in their effects on its behavior. However, although the effectiveness of outcomes does not require the child to perceive the act-outcome contingency as an intentional form of social control, reward and punishment are the conventional generic terms which are used most frequently in reference to larger classes of reinforcing or suppressive consequences of an act. It will sometimes be a convenience to follow that usage here.

When changes of affective state become conditioned to the intrinsic correlates of an act, they spread beyond the cues which are immediately present during the overt performance of the act. Because of the variable duration of the outcomes of an act, and as a result of a certain amount of generalization, affectivity also becomes attached to intrinsic behavioral cues which just precede or follow the act in time. The anticipatory or intentional motor components of an act will therefore begin to acquire some affective control over the final commitment of the act. For example, the anxiety that is conditioned by punishment to the incipient motoric precursors of an act may be reduced simply by suppression of the act.

The temporal and behavioral span of the child's internalized monitors expands by orders of magnitude when cognitive representation is brought into play. Positive and aversive outcomes of the child's behavior must be kept closely tied to the behavior in order to be effective during the earlier phases of socialization. But the changes of affectivity which are induced by the outcomes also become increasingly attached to the cognitive representations which are correlated to the child's behavior, as the child's cognitive development progresses and the medium of socialization becomes more verbal. And just as in the case of cues which are inherent in the performance of an act, the cognitive representations which acquire affective value include not only those which are immediately contiguous with an act, but also those which precede or follow the act in time. As a result, the child's cognitive representation of its intentions, and its anticipation of the consequences of an act, may carry affective values which can regulate its behavior without being dependent on the actual performance of the act, even though the affective values may have been originally transmitted through the external outcomes of the child's overt behavior.

The child's ability to represent and evaluate an act also increases the duration of time over which outcomes of the act can be effective. Socializing agents may transmit the outcome of an act long after its occurrence. If they simultaneously elicit the child's cognitive representation of the act—for example, if they are able to induce the child's application of a standard of judgement to the act—then the affective value of the outcome may become directly attached to the cognitive representation (rather than only to the act itself). The child's representational and evaluative capacities can then assume a functional role in the mediation of the affective control of its subsequent behavior, when they later intervene before an overt occurrence of the same act. However, although the child's cognitive capacities become increasingly independent of its momentary overt actions, their maintenance of control over the child's behavior always remains dependent on their transmission of affective value to the motivation or reinforcement for the behavior. The affective value that is carried by cognitive representations can exercise control over the child's incipient and ongoing behavior only to the extent that the representations remain functionally responsive to the behavior.

In the case of behavior-contingent learning under the control of positive outcomes, internalization occurs when the pleasurable affective consequences of the outcomes become directly attached to the intrinsic correlates of an act. The act then acquires self-reinforcing properties—that is, its reinforcing affective consequences come to be elicited by the intrinsic behavioral cues or cognitive representations which are associated with its performance. For reasons which already have been noted, these changes of affectivity will tend to become attached to the intrinsic precursors of a previously rewarded act as well as to its actual performance. However, a gradient of reinforcement would be expected to produce some differential affective value between the intrinsic correlates of the incipient and the committed act, since it is originally the committed act that would ordinarily have been closer to its positive social outcomes for the child. The internalized choice of a previously rewarded act may also be facilitated by the frustration value that has become directly associated with nonrewarded alternative forms of behavior. Of course, the specific quality of the affect that becomes attached to the intrinsic correlates of an act will be determined by the cognitive context in which the child originally experiences the external consequences of the act.

A parallel but somewhat more detailed analysis is required to account for the internalized consequences of behavior-contingent learning under aversive outcomes. A great variety of distressful, noxious, or irritant stimuli can be socially transmitted as aversive outcomes of a child's behavior. For our purposes here, punishment may be used as the representative case. And the concept of anxiety may be used to designate the generalized aversive state that is induced in the child by various forms of punishment. Although the experience of this affective state may assume any one of a number of qualitatively distinct forms, in accordance with its cognitive context (see the analysis of fear, guilt, and shame in Chapter Nine), the concept of anxiety emphasizes its general motivational properties and its initial relationship to punishment. The basis of the internalized behavioral control that can be produced by punishment is the conditioning of anxiety to the intrinsic behavioral or cognitive correlates of the child's performance of a punished act. Punishment will also result in the attachment of conditioned anxiety to the behavioral and cognitive precursors of the act. The subsequent arousal of anxiety by intentions or other forerunners of the punished act, or by intrinsic correlates of the actual performance of the act, is the motivational source of its internalized behavioral suppression. In contrast, the anxiety that comes to be elicited by the intrinsic correlates of the completion of a previously punished act is the motivational source of various reactions to transgressions which the child perceives as having been already committed. The mechanisms through which punishment and anxiety bring about internalized control are essentially the same for both behavioral suppression and reactions to committed transgressions. Behavioral suppression provides the simpler paradigm, however, for the exposition of the mechanisms at this point.

When anxiety becomes directly attached to the intrinsic correlates of a punished act, certain components of the anxiety itself may interfere to some extent with the performance of the act, particularly if the anxiety is of high intensity. But the more important function of anxiety is to provide the motivation, and indirectly the reinforcement, for nonpunished behavioral alternatives to the punished act. These nonpunished alternatives may include other active forms of behavior as well as passive suppression of the punished act. The child's suppression of an ongoing transgression will sometimes avoid, terminate, or reduce the punitive outcome of the transgression. Likewise, the child's arrest of an incipient transgression often will avoid the impending punishment that is signalled in the behavioral cues of socializing agents. The external outcomes of suppression therefore have the effect of inhibiting or attenuating the anxiety that has been induced in the child by its past experience and current anticipation of punishment. And the inhibition or reduction of anxiety that is induced by these outcomes tends to become directly conditioned to the intrinsic perceptual and cognitive correlates of the nonpunished behavior on which the outcomes are contingent. Nonpunished alternatives to punished behavior also acquire intrinsic anxiety-reducing value because they often disrupt an incipient punished act and thus attenuate whatever anxiety may already have become attached to the intrinsic correlates of the act.

In summary, then, the aversive control of punished behavior becomes internalized when anxiety has been attached directly to the intrinsic correlates of a punished act, and when anxiety-reduction has been attached directly to the intrinsic correlates of nonpunished alternatives to the punished act. When these requirements have been met, suppression of the punished act and alternative forms of behavior become self-reinforcing—that is, their intrinsic correlates carry the affective consequences which are inherent in the reduction of anxiety.

There appears to be an interesting difference between the two behavior-contingent models of internalization which have been described, respectively, for the cases of positive and aversive control. The acquired motivational properties of both external events and intrinsic correlates of behavior are given a much more conspicuous place in the aversive case than they are in the positive case. This difference is probably not an accurate reflection of the realities of the socialization process. The activating properties of anxiety have been emphasized for many years in theories of learning and motivation (Malmo, 1957; Miller, 1948; Mowrer, 1939). And the acquired motivational value of both external and internal stimuli has been given a central position in more general treatments of aversive control of behavior (Mowrer, 1960a; Solomon and Brush, 1956). Theoretical conceptions and empirical studies of the role of positive reinforcement in learning also have given attention to acquired incentive values (Logan, 1960; Spence, 1956; Williams, 1965; Zamble, 1967). But the weight and power of the evidence for acquired positive incentive values are not so great as they are in the aversive case (there is substantial consistency on this point between the review by Miller in 1951 and the comparisons which are drawn many years later by Rescorla and Solomon in 1967). The difference in the status of the evidence for the two kinds of phenomena may possibly be related to differences between positive and aversive affective states in the temporal pattern of their excitation and inhibition—for example, it may be that changes of aversive affectivity are more rapid than changes of positive affectivity under the usual conditions of learning in the animal laboratory.

Acquired positive incentive values have been demonstrated in experiments with children (Lipsitt and Castaneda, 1958; Longstreth, 1962). Their establishment appears to be controlled by the same contingencies which establish the value of a secondary reinforcer for children (Sidowski, Kass, and Wilson, 1965). Acquired positive incentives would certainly be expected to make a significant contribution to socialization. They would be established by their association with the kinds of social stimulation which have a high magnitude of value for the child, and which can induce affectivity without the delay that would be imposed by the filter of a consummatory response system. Their significance for the mechanisms of internalization lies in the possibility that the child's intrinsic behavioral cues and cognitive representations might acquire positive incentive values which would provide a motivational base for the autonomy of its behavior.

Although positive and aversive outcomes can be separated conceptually, in the analysis of their respective effects on the child's behavior, they have a highly interdependent relationship in actual socialization episodes. Many learning situations may be characterized, for example, by jointly or intermittently rewarding and punitive outcomes of the same act (Dollard and Miller, 1950; Martin, 1963; Miller, 1959; Mowrer and Ullman, 1945). The integration over time of the changes of affective state which are induced by joint positive and aversive outcomes of the same act, particularly under conditions of differential delay between the two outcomes, is a phenomenon that deserves more attention in experimental studies of children's learning. For example, it is obvious that most of those forms of the child's behavior which are punished by socializing agents will usually have some reinforcing consequences of inherent or acquired value before the point in time at which punishment occurs. The effectiveness of punishment in producing suppression of an act must therefore often be superimposed on the effects of an earlier and more immediate positive reinforcement of the act. Renner (1966b) has reported two interesting experiments with rats which suggest that the aversive component of a simultaneous reward-punishment acts more effectively over delay time than does the positive component—another finding that may be related to differences between positive and aversive affectivities in the temporal pattern of their excitation and inhibition. Renner (1966a) also has reported that early experience with delay of reward facilitates the later learning of adult rats in situations where they must integrate the behavioral effects of delays in both reward and punishment.

An important kind of reciprocal relationship between the child's positive and aversive experience exists in some of the behavioral media of punishment which are available to socializing agents. Parents may transmit the aversive consequences of a child's behavior through withdrawal of affection or other kinds of decrements in pleasurable social stimulation. Alternatives to the punished behavior can then be reinforced by reinstatement of the positive social stimulation. The reduction of anxiety and the induction of a positive affective state can thus control the child's learning simultaneously, through the medium of a single social outcome.

Another kind of reciprocity between positive and aversive control, which undoubtedly pervades the socialization process, is the result of the affective consequences of disruption of an established contingency between the child's behavior and its positive reinforcing outcomes. The child will often initiate behavior that meets with interference by external social constraints.

Or it will find that its social environment has withdrawn or delayed the anticipated pleasurable or rewarding consequences of its behavior. These frustrating outcomes of the child's behavior may inhibit positive affectivity or induce aversive affectivity. And they may have effects on the child's behavior which are much like the effects of punishment and anxiety. They may produce internalized suppression, for example, when their affective value becomes attached directly to the intrinsic correlates of the child's frustrated acts.

The aversive consequences of the blocking of goal-directed behavior are a phenomenon that is crucial to the well-known theory concerning the relationship between frustration and aggression (Dollard, Doob, Miller, Mowrer, and Sears, 1939). More recent versions of the theory (Berkowitz, 1962) continue to emphasize blocking of motivated behavior as a source of frustration. Mandler and Watson (1966) have reported an experiment with adults which appears to confirm the common observation that interruption of well-established sequences of behavior may also elicit anxiety. And Endsley (1966) has shown that blocking may increase the amplitude of children's goal-oriented behavior. Much more of the empirical work on the motivational increments which are attributable to frustration has focussed, however, on behavior that is under the influence of delayed, withdrawn, or intermittent reward. The suspension or delay of established rewards will often enhance the speed, vigor, or resistance to extinction of the behavior on which the rewards have been contingent. Such effects have been demonstrated repeatedly in the learned behavior of animals (Amsel, 1962; Lawrence and Festinger, 1962). A number of studies have shown that withdrawal or delay of expected reward will enhance the incentive value of the reward for children, and will also enhance the value of stimuli which are associated with the reward (Knott, Nunnally, and Duchnowski, 1967; Mischel and Masters, 1966; Olds, 1953).

It seems quite clear that the incentive or motivational effects of withdrawal and delay of reward are only a temporary prelude to suppressive effects which imply the presence of an aversive state of affectivity. The inhibitory properties which stimuli can acquire for hungry animals, when they are used as signals of the absence or withdrawal of food, have been known for many years in the Pavlovian conditioning laboratory (Konorski, 1948, pp. 135–136; Pavlov, 1928, pp. 381–383). Konorski (1948, Chapter 12) was able to show that a dog would suppress its own leg flexion (against external forcing) if this movement had been associated with the withdrawal of food—an interesting prototype of internalization.

There are simliar implications in the finding by Amsel and Ward (1965) of resistance to discrimination in rats for whom the discriminative stimuli have been associated with frustration.

The most impressive evidence of the aversive properties of interruption and delay of reward can be found in their potency for suppression of behavior. Ferster has devised a number of paradigms which demonstrate that "time out" from an established schedule of reward can be used as a contingency to suppress the behavior of animals (Ferster, 1957, 1958; Ferster and Appel, 1961). Other investigators of animal behavior also have used suspension of a reward schedule or delay of reward to produce suppression or to motivate active escape behavior (Holder *et al.,* 1957; Kaufman and Baron, 1966; McMillan, 1967). Withdrawal of a reward schedule has been shown to be a highly effective suppressor of the behavior of children (Baer, 1960, 1961; Brackbill, 1958; Longstreth, 1960) and of the behavior of adults (Holz, Azrin, and Ayllon, 1963; Zimmerman and Baydan, 1963). It would be difficult to overestimate the extension that this phenomenon implies for the power that we must attribute to schedules of positive reinforcement in the control of the child's social behavior. The selective occurrence of reward contingencies makes it possible not only to reinforce one form of behavior, but also to frustrate and extinguish another. The controlled application of such selective contingencies has proven to be an extremely effective technique for the modification of children's social behavior (Bijou, 1965; Brown and Elliot, 1965; Etzel and Gewirtz, 1967; Zimmerman and Zimmerman, 1962).

The frequently reciprocal relationship of the positive and aversive components of behavior-contingent learning makes it difficult to assess their respective contributions to the internalization of conduct. Common observation makes it apparent that positive social reinforcement of the child's behavior is a very extensive channel of socialization. But the power of positive reinforcement may be considerably more limited in the acquisition and maintenance of those forms of social behavior which most require internalized control, because they are in competition with other forms of highly motivated behavior whose reinforcing consequences are relatively independent of experience or already well established. Restrictions on the effectiveness of positive reinforcement become immediately visible when we consider that opportunities for its occurrence are dependent on the child's performance of the acts which are to be reinforced. Many of the most socially desirable forms of conduct are very distant from the initially dominant patterns of behavior which they must displace. Socialization often imposes on the child extensive modification or even total suppression of behavioral dispositions which are powerfully motivated. These initial behavioral dispositions may have a strong unlearned component, or they may have been acquired during earlier phases of socialization to which they were more appropriate.

The difficulties which socializing agents frequently encounter in establishing the child's selective internalized controls over dependent and aggressive behavior are particularly common indicators of the distance between the earlier dominant patterns of the child's behavior and the desired end products of socialization. Since the distance is often quite great, the new behavior to be acquired may not occur spontaneously with any substantial frequency. It cannot therefore derive much reinforcement from its positive outcomes until there is a sharp alteration of relative probabilities within the child's behavioral repertoire. Such an alteration sometimes can be effected on the basis of the child's ability to learn from observation of the behavior of others. In many instances, however, the required behavioral modifications may not be salient in the behavior of others, or the child's observational learning may not compete successfully with the established value of the behavior to be modified.

These limitations on the efficacy of positive social reinforcement clearly reveal the reasons for giving a central place to punishment learning, and to other avenues of aversive control over socialization, in any attempt to account for the great range and durability of the internalized control over behavior which children are capable of acquiring. The aversive effects of punishment are a potent motivational source for the repeated modifications which are made in the child's predominant behavioral dispositions during the course of socialization. Punishment makes it possible for earlier behavior patterns to be suppressed to the point where new behavioral alternatives can be emitted with a higher frequency and exposed to the effects of positive reinforcement. Of course, punishment also contributes to internalization by providing the affective context for the very powerful reinforcement contingencies which are inherent in the reduction of anxiety.

The respective contributions of positive and aversive outcomes in shaping the child's social behavior are in part a function of the kind of behavior that is being shaped. Many forms of conduct which appear to acquire some internalized value through the effects of positive social reinforcement may have the advantage of being derivatives of a class of behavior that is organized around a very general and strong motivational disposition. The effect of positive social reinforcement on these forms of conduct is essentially that of superimposing another component of value on selected members of a group of behavioral alternatives, all of which have in common their already established reinforcing consequences—as when, for example, a mother reacts affectionately only to certain kinds of dependent behavior from her child, or rewards it only for constructive forms of aggression. Positive reinforcement alone would probably not be sufficient, however, to produce modifications of behavior which are completely discrepant with the child's initial motivational dispositions—for example, in situations where the child must learn that no dependent or aggressive act is permissible. Moreover, many of the largest behavioral changes which are required of the child, in the direction of independence or control of aggression, may not have a high probability of positive reinforcement even after they have begun to appear. They will often be perceived by socializing agents as the minimal normative requirements of conduct rather than as changes which have a distinctly rewardable value. These constraints on the applicability of positive reinforcement make it necessary to assume that many internalized forms of conduct could never be acquired without contingencies which introduce punishment and aversive control over the child's behavior.

The power and extent of aversive behavior-contingent learning appear to have been badly underestimated in some conceptions of the control of conduct (see, for example, Skinner, 1953, Chapter 12.) There was for many years a notable absence of attention to the effectiveness of punishment in producing aversive control over socialization and its internalized derivatives. This lack of attention to punishment may have reflected widely held assumptions about its "traumatic" emotional impact on the child; it may also have been influenced by certain social and educational philosophies which implied that punishment was undesirable and not required where the informed socializing agent could elicit the child's natural inclinations toward social growth through affection and permissiveness. Some early observations of punishment learning in animals did suggest that the behavioral effects of punishment were sometimes neither very marked nor durable (Estes, 1944; Skinner, 1938; Thorndike, 1932). Other studies indicated that punishment could disrupt the organization or adaptiveness of behavior (Liddell, 1944; Maier, 1949; Masserman, 1943). However, these studies characteristically examined the efficacy of punishment in eliminating behavior that was instrumental to the reduction of a very strong motivational state, in situations where alternative forms of relevant behavior were not available to the animal. In some of the studies, the animals were placed in essentially insoluble learning situations. The paradigms which were used in these studies did not, therefore, represent the conditions under which much of human socialization typically takes place. And it soon became apparent that punishment learning could be effective when paradigms were designed to be more similar to socialization in taking account of other constraints on the animal's behavior (Bixenstein, 1956; Masserman, 1946; Mowrer and Viek, 1948; Whiting and Mowrer, 1943).

In more recent years, a variety of highly effective paradigms of punishment learning have been devised for use with both children and animals (Aronfreed, 1966; Church, 1963; Parke and Walters, 1967; Solomon, 1964). These paradigms have demonstrated quite clearly the adaptiveness and stability of both the external and internalized control over behavior which can be induced by punishment. Punishment has been used to produce sharp and stable suppression of highly motivated behavior in animals (Boe and Church, 1967; Boroczi, Storms, and Broen, 1964; Hake and Azrin, 1965). Some investigators have reported comparable effects when they have used either deprivation of candy or electric shock to suppress the behavior of children (Blum and Kennedy, 1967; Lövaas, Schaeffer, and Simmons, 1965; Weingold and Webster, 1964). A large number of experiments have shown that verbal and other forms of punishment facilitate the discrimination learning of children (Brackbill and O'Hara, 1958; Spence, 1966; Spence and Segner, 1967; Stevenson, Weir, and Zigler, 1959), when reward and punishment are given for alternative behavioral choices (as compared to a reward versus no reward paradigm). The findings of other experiments on the discrimination learning of children have indicated that punishment alone is often more effective than reward alone (Meyer and Offenbach, 1962; Meyer and Seidman, 1961; Nelson, Reid, and Travers, 1965; Penney, 1967; Penney and Lupton, 1961).

There undoubtedly are certain conditions under which punishment may be ineffective or undesirable in the socialization of children. We will examine some of these conditions more fully in a later detailed analysis of the determinants of behavioral suppression. But limitations on the use of punishment should not prevent us from recognizing the massive contribution that it makes to the internalized control of conduct.

The analysis of behavior-contingent socialization cannot be completed without looking more closely at what appears to be a generalized reinforcement value that becomes associated with prediction and control of both positive and aversive outcomes. We have already noted that both humans and animals have strong preferences for outcomes whose occurrence or timing they control, and that they also appear to place a value upon information which predicts the outcomes. These components of the value of the outcomes of a behavioral choice have been demonstrated in many different experimental settings. They may possibly reflect the acquired value that has become attached to the control and confirmation of the anticipatory affective states which occur in the interval between behavior and its outcomes (although there may well also be an unlearned bias in the value of this kind of control over affectivity).

The acquired value of behavioral control and prediction of outcomes is a phenomenon that requires more attention in a conception of the mechanisms of internalization. It suggests that many forms of social behavior may be sustained not only by the value that inheres in the concrete stimulus properties of their outcomes, but also by the more intrinsic value that has become attached to their exercise of control over the outcomes. For example, people may often behave in such a way as to confirm their immediate control over social rewards and punishments which would otherwise have an uncertain probability of occurrence or delay.

Theoretical speculations about the development of motivational dispositions have given some attention to the reinforcement value of the child's control over the events in its environment (the analysis of competence by White, 1959, is a well-known example). Mischel and Grusec (1967) have found that children will choose an immediate and certain punishment in preference to a delayed and uncertain punishment, under conditions where the delayed punishment is larger and has a substantial probability of occurrence. The same study and many other investigations which Mischel (1966) has conducted indicate that children will often choose a delayed larger reward in preference to an immediate smaller reward, when their past experience or current expectations support their disposition to predict and control events in their social environment. Metzner (1963) gave children the opportunity to make choices of a larger delayed reward over a smaller immediate reward, and found that they were more likely to do so when their performance would be instrumental to attainment of the reward than they were when they would be required simply to await the occurrence of the reward. The author (Aronfreed, 1963) has shown that children will acquire a disposition to initiate reparation for their own transgressions if they first have been exposed to punishment training during which they are given the opportunity to evaluate their own actions and to control the magnitude of their punishment.

The importance of the locus of control over outcomes is also apparent in the findings of a number of experiments which have been conducted with adults. Some of these experiments (Lefcourt, 1966; Watson and Baumal, 1967) indicate that both the current and anticipated direction of control over outcomes will affect learning and performance, and that the effects are determined in part by the amount of control over outcomes that has characterized the individual's past experience in similar situations. Other experiments have shown that people are more likely to make choices which may produce an immediate electric shock (Badia *et al.,* 1966; D'Amato and Gumenik, 1960), or to elect an immediate and certain shock (Belanger and Sattler, 1967), when the alternative outcome is a delayed shock of uncertain occurrence and timing. This type of effect is most marked when the probability of the uncertain delayed shock is perceived to be substantial. Even when the timing of a shock is known, human subjects experience the interval of anticipation as being highly aversive. Breznitz (1967) found that college students preferred short intervals to longer intervals, when they were given a choice as to how long they would wait before receiving a shock that would be certain to occur at the chosen point in time. He also found that evidence of anxiety in heart-rate changes, during the last minute of the interval which preceded shock, was proportionate to the total length of the interval from the point of the signal which marked its onset.

People will also choose positive or aversive outcomes which are preceded by signals in preference to unsignalled outcomes, even though they have no control over the occurrence of the outcomes (Lanzetta and Driscoll, 1966). And their behavior may be more responsive to punishment when the magnitude of the actual punishment is consistent with the magnitude of the threatened punishment (French, Morrison, and Levinger, 1960). Kanfer and Goldfoot (1966) found that the most effective techniques for increasing the tolerance of pain by human subjects were those which permitted the subjects to exercise active control over distracting stimuli or over external markers of the duration of painful stimulation. Assessments of human behavior in stressful naturalistic situations also suggest that people are more resistant to stress when they perceive that they can exercise some control over external events (Janis, 1962; Withey, 1962).

There is an abundance of evidence of the value of behavioral control over outcomes, and of the value of informational signals of outcomes, in the findings of experiments with animals. For example, experience with inescapable shock has a debilitating effect on the subsequent active escape or avoidance learning of animals (Brookshire, Littman, and Stewart, 1961; Overmier and Seligman, 1967). This effect can be very durable, even in the absence of further exposure to shock, but it also can be prevented by immunizing the animal with an initial exposure to escapable shock training (Seligman and Maier, 1967). An immediate shock is apparently a less aversive outcome for animals than is a delayed shock (Renner, 1966b), and a shock of constant delay is less aversive than a variably delayed shock (Sidman, 1954), when the intervals of delay are not so long as to surpass the animal's ability to bridge the behavior-outcome contingency. The frequency of choice of immediate shock is quite striking when the choice terminates a warning signal that would otherwise remain until the postponed shock occurred (Gibbon, 1967; Sidman and Boren, 1957). In contrast, animals will show a marked preference for warning signals, when they are confronted with the alternative of exposure to the shock in the absence of any signal (Knapp, Kause, and Perkins, 1959; Lockard, 1963; Perkins *et al.,* 1966; Sidman, 1957). They will also avoid a difficult discrimination situation in which their control of outcomes is uncertain (Tighe and Leaton, 1966). And in a number of other aspects of their learned behavior, they display a bias toward the control of outcomes and of informational signals, even though the exercise of control may have no effect on the occurrence of reward or may in fact have aversive consequences (Bower, McLean, and Meacham, 1966; Hearst, 1967; Prokasy, 1956; Wyckoff, 1952).

There is some reason to think that informational signals have a greater value in the aversive control of behavior than they do in positive control of behavior, and that their value is less dependent in the aversive case on the precise temporal relationship which they originally had to the contingent events which established the value. For example, Egger and Miller (1962) found that informationally redundant stimuli did not acquire positive secondary reinforcement value. But Seligman (1966) found that redundant stimuli did acquire some secondary aversive value for the suppression of behavior. The difference once again suggests differences between anticipatory positive and aversive affective states in the temporal course of their excitation and inhibition. Similar implications may be present in the finding by Mischel and Grusec (1967) that children preferred smaller immediate punishments to larger delayed punishments, when the probability of occurrence of the larger outcome was substantial. In the case of rewards, however, the children generally preferred the larger delayed outcome to the smaller immediate outcome. Kelley and Ring (1961) exposed college students to "suspicious" and "trusting" training schedules, during which either negative evaluations of errors or positive evaluations of correct choices were respectively emphasized by the agent of training. Students whose performance was monitored by negative evaluation voluntarily brought their choices to the attention of the agent more often than did students whose performance was monitored by positive evaluation.

This outline of behavior-contingent mechanisms of socialization may be closed by re-emphasizing two important points which were made earlier in the analysis of the concept of internalization. The first point is that the internalization of conduct does not make it independent of the informational cues which are provided in the child's environment. Social and nonsocial situational cues continue to govern the child's choices among alternative acts even after the choices may have acquired an intrinsically reinforcing status. The internalized status of an act is a function of the mediation of affectivity by its intrinsic correlates, and not a function of its independence of external stimulus control. Discrete forms of conduct acquire and maintain their internalized value in association with specific situational cues. Even the most highly generalized forms of conduct reflect the variety and breadth of the stimulus control under which they were originally socialized. Their intrinsic value is never entirely free of the control of external cues.

The second point is that conduct, when it comes under internalized control, does not necessarily become insensitive to any further confirmation or modification by the child's experience of external social reality. The intrinsic value that is acquired by many forms of conduct often may continue to be replenished by the affective value of the external outcomes which they produce in their subsequent history. Because so much of the child's socialized behavior is maintained in an interpersonal context, the intrinsic and external determinants of its maintenance will tend to have a mutually supportive relationship.

There still remains, of course, the problem of understanding why some forms of conduct seem to become so highly internalized that they no longer require external support. These forms of conduct have what might be called extraordinary resistance to extinction. They may even be resistant to change after they have begun to have aversive consequences for the individual who retains them. As was noted earlier, their apparent autonomy may be attributable in part to their acquisition under reinforcing or suppressive contingencies of a very high affective intensity, and in part to the absence of a verbal context for their original learning. The motivation for these forms of conduct may be so strong, particularly when they are under aversive control, that it prevents the occurrence of behavioral alternatives which are less highly motivated, with the result that external social outcomes are never or only infrequently retested. However, many of the most autonomous forms of conduct are sustained not by the consequences of the child's training as a conditionable animal, but rather by the kind of learning that is made possible by the child's remarkable cognitive capacities. The persistence of these forms of conduct, in the absence of external reinforcement, seems to require a very durable mechanism for the intrinsic mediation of their affectivity. That mechanism may well lie within the extensive representational and evaluative power of human language and thought.

COGNITIVE AND VERBAL CONTROL

The outline of behavior-contingent mechanisms of socialization makes it apparent that much of a child's control over its conduct is mediated by representational and evaluative cognition which intervenes between concrete stimulus events and specific forms of behavior. We have already noted a number of ways in which verbal and other cognitive representations contribute to internalization—for example, by making it possible for the child to use intentions and anticipations to govern its actions, so that it is not entirely dependent on the immediate external outcomes of its overt behavior. The generalized mediational properties of representational and evaluative cognition also gradually give the child's social behavior its internal organization and breadth of applicability across many different concrete situations—in short, they give conduct its appearance of character. We will give some attention later to the transformation of the child's representational capacities into evaluative cognition, when we consider the role of experience in the development of social cognition (Chapter Ten). But we need now to look more closely at some of the functions of representational cognition itself.

One of the points of agreement among contemporary versions of a general behavior theory is on the requirement that direct stimulus control of behavior must often be subordinated to representational cognition (Beritov, 1964; Berlyne, 1965; Miller, Galanter, and Pribram, 1960; Osgood, 1957; Razran, 1961). A second and less visible point of agreement among these theories is on the requirement of a hierarchical relationship among different types of representational cognitive functions. These pivotal requirements of a behavior theory must be amplified to even larger proportions in a model of the socialization process, where one of the basic problems is an account of the internalized representational control of affectivity.

The most direct approach to a hierarchical ordering of cognitive functions in the control of learning has been in the work of Russian investigators who have been interested in the developmental transitions of verbal control over the motor behavior of children (Elkin, 1957; Ivanov-Smolenski, 1956; Luria, 1961). This work includes some effective demonstrations of the interlock between representational cognition and the phenomena of Pavlovian conditioning and behavior-contingent training. Western investigators also have demonstrated a developmental shift in verbal control of the motor behavior of children (Birch, 1966; White, 1965).

Lövaas (1961b, 1964) has shown that the effects of reinforcement on children's verbal behavior generalize to some extent to corresponding classes of nonverbal aggressive and feeding behavior. In the findings which emerge from some of this work, distinctions can be roughly discerned among at least three levels in the development of verbal representational control over behavior. In the developmental order of their appearance, the three levels might be described as follows: first, a level at which behavior is directly bound to the immediate control of concrete stimulus events; second, a level at which behavior can be controlled by verbal mediators which are more or less direct representations of concrete stimuli; and finally, a level at which behavior can be controlled by more symbolic and abstract verbal representation. Similar functional levels appear with some regularity in the analysis of the development of concept formation and thought processes in children (Bruner, Olver, and Greenfield et al., 1966; Inhelder and Piaget, 1958; Kessen and Kuhlman, 1962).

Economy of learning is one of the most important consequences of the development of cognitive and verbal control over behavior. Socialization confronts children with the task of the discriminative learning of a great many specific forms of behavior. The child must make fine distinctions among complex situational cues and among various acts which belong to the same general class of behavior. It would not master many of these complex discriminations if it were forced to rely only on concrete external and behavioral cues. But the cognitive resources which the child acquires, particularly when socialization takes place in a verbal medium, provide it with conceptual categories which can be broadly and yet selectively imposed on specific acts and situations, so that its behavior attains some freedom from immediate concrete stimulus events.

Representational concepts make it possible for the child to categorize and evaluate different acts along abstract dimensions which take multiple situational cues into account, and thus to find some integrative structural organization among specific forms of behavior whose concrete properties may be highly variable. The child's acquisition of concepts enables it to place actions which are overtly very different into the same class—for example, in terms of their common intentions or consequences for others. The mediational power of cognitive representation therefore allows the child's conduct to be governed with a certain amount of consistency that could not be produced if its actions were closely bound to immediate situational and behavioral cues. For example, the verbalization of enriched cognitive structures for the evaluation of the form and amplitude of aggressive behavior, when it is used in association with verbal punishment and deprivation of candy, has been found to facilitate children's acquisition of self-critical dispositions during the course of experimental paradigms of socialization (Aronfreed, Cutick, and Fagen, 1963).

The facilitation of children's discrimination learning by the use of verbal labels or instruction has been demonstrated in a wide variety of task settings (Jeffrey, 1953; McConnell, 1964; Reese, 1963; Spiker, 1963; Weir and Stevenson, 1959). When the learning situation entails transposition or reversal problems, the effects of verbal mediation are usually striking. The learning sets which Harlow (1959a) and others have demonstrated with monkeys, in the context of transposition or oddity problems, may be a prototype of cognitive representation in animals. Learning sets in the absence of externally provided verbal mediators can also be demonstrated in children (Kaufman and Peterson, 1958). But the use of explicit verbal mediation would be expected to introduce a sharp magnification of the efficiency of learning that requires transposition or reversal of cues. And the findings of experiments which have tested this expectation often indicate that verbal labelling produces what amounts to a qualitative transformation in the learning and performance of children (Kendler and Kendler, 1962; Kendler, 1963; Kuenne, 1946; Reese, 1966). Another kind of interesting example of the facilitative effect of verbal mediation appears in the recent report of an experiment by Kendler, Kendler, and Carrick (1966), in which verbal labels were found to enhance the probability that children would integrate two segments of behavior toward an inferential solution to a problem. Transposition, reversal, and the integration of sequential behavior would be important components of the child's ability to maintain consistent internalized control of its behavior across diversity in situational cues.

Another important consequence of the child's cognitive status is its ability to represent contingencies between acts and outcomes, and also to represent contingencies between external informational signals and other events of significant affective value. Such representations are probably the key to the difference between animals and children in their capacities for internalized control of behavior. Cognitive representation makes it possible for the affectivity that is induced by external contingencies to come under internalized control with great speed, and with maximally functional consistency across small variations in behavior and in external situational cues. As a result, affective control of the learning and maintenance of the child's behavior attains a large measure of freedom from the more concrete and variable stimulus topography that is available in the external environment and in the cues which are directly produced by the behavior itself.

It is quite clear that the introduction of verbal instruction or labelling into Pavlovian paradigms will produce dramatic increments of speed and discrimination in conditioning and extinction processes for human subjects (Chatterjee and Eriksen, 1962; Grings, 1965; Hill, 1967; Razran, 1961). The effects on conditioned heart rate, galvanic skin response, and other peripheral indicators of autonomic arousal, are especially powerful when verbal instruction is designed to enhance the subject's awareness of the contingency between conditioned and unconditioned stimuli. Mandel and Bridger (1967) have reported that verbal instruction concerning the dissociation between conditioned discriminative stimuli and shock facilitates extinction of the conditioned galvanic skin response, but only when conditioning has been obtained under relatively long interstimulus intervals (during which the subject has time to form a cognitive representation of the relevant contingency).

The representation and awareness of contingencies also have been shown to facilitate the rate and even the very occurrence of behavior-contingent learning. Both positive and aversive control of behavior can be made more effective for adults by verbal instruction concerning act-outcome contingencies, or by the subject's spontaneous awareness of contingencies or attempts to formulate them (Eriksen, 1960; Spielberger, Southard, and Hodges, 1966; Turner and Solomon, 1962). Parton and DeNike (1966) have observed that the effects of positive social reinforcement on the performance gains of children in a learning task are also most clearly visible in subjects who report cognitive strategies with respect to the reinforcement contingency. The experiments which are reported by Turner and Solomon (1962) are especially interesting, because they indicate that instruction about outcomes has a strongly facilitative effect on human avoidance training in which the instrumental act is a short-latency, involuntary response that would not ordinarily permit time for cognitive interventions such as the representation of the avoidance contingency. The extent to which cognitive control of the effects of outcomes may subordinate the control of actual behavioral contingencies is suggested in a cleverly designed experiment that is reported by Kaufman, Baron, and Kopp (1966). These investigators demonstrated that a subject's behavior, during three hours of operant training, could be dominated by initial instructions about contingent schedules of reinforcement, regardless of whether the instructions were accurate or inaccurate.

It may be that the most crucial function of cognitive representation in the socialization process is the mediation of the temporal gap between the child's behavior and its rewarding or punitive consequences. Laboratory investigations use delay of rewards and punishments as a window through which to look at underlying processes, such as gradients of reinforcement value, and also as a counterpoint to the much wider and more effective employment of immediate reward and punishment. But the delay of outcomes is indigenous to socialization. The child is a highly mobile creature who is often well removed in space and time from the socializing agents who control many of the outcomes of its behavior. Moreover, it must acquire, and maintain with some reliability, many different kinds of sequential patterns of behavior which traverse long segments of time before they produce a highly valued outcome. Accordingly, one of the major problems in an account of socialization is the problem of how the child is able to bridge the delays of outcome which are imposed by a social environment that is not immediately sensitive to many features of its behavior.

Investigators of animal behavior have been able to show that delayed outcomes, in the form of either reward or punishment, are less effective than immediate outcomes for the control of learning and performance under a variety of conditions (Kamin, 1959; Kimble 1961, pp. 140–160; Logan, 1960; Mowrer, 1960a, Chapter 10; Skinner, 1938). Many relatively short intervals of delay are yet long enough that animals seem unable to integrate the effects of the outcomes into their behavior, particularly when the outcomes have an aversive component (Mowrer and Ullman, 1945; Renner, 1964; Sidman, 1954). Delays of reward and punishment, without the provision of verbal mediation, have been shown to reduce the effectiveness of behavior-contingent learning in children (Penney and Lupton, 1961; Terrell, 1964; Walters, 1964). There is also considerable evidence that the establishment of the acquired excitatory value of conditioned stimuli, under the control of Pavlovian contingencies, is facilitated by short intervals of delay between the conditioned and unconditioned stimuli (Brush, Brush, and Solomon, 1955; Kimble, 1961, pp. 182–184; Prokasy, 1965)—a phenomenon that implies a sharp limitation on the extent to which the affectivity that is induced by delayed outcomes of the child's behavior can be conditioned to the concrete intrinsic behavioral correlates of its overt acts.

It has been suggested that the effectiveness of delayed outcomes might be increased if periods of delay were bridged by the cues from orienting responses toward stimuli which were associated with the outcomes (Renner, 1964; Spence, 1956). Wright and Smothergill (1967) have found that the discrimination learning of children under delayed reward is greatly facilitated when discriminative stimuli and response markers remain visible and salient during the delay. Brackbill's experiments indicate that delay of reward may actually facilitate the retention of discrimination learning in children, possibly as a result of the effect of delay in focussing the child's attention on the stimuli which are associated with the correct response and the anticipated reward (Brackbill, 1964; Brackbill and Kappy, 1962).

Skinner (1938, pp. 52–55, 102–108) made what appears to have been by far the most heuristic suggestion about the bridging of delay intervals (in the absence of cognitive mediation), when he observed that sequential components of behavior might become chained to one another through the acquired reinforcement value that became attached to their proprioceptive cues—apparently on the assumption that a gradient of reinforcement value from the final rewarding outcome would move backward in time across the components. This prototype of a model for the establishment of the internalized affective value of sequential behavior seems to have been confirmed by the later observations of Skinner (1948) and others (Ferster, 1953; Herrnstein, 1966), which revealed that animals would sometimes perform "superstitious" behavior—behavior that was irrelevant to the control of rewards—in the interval between a criterial form of behavior and the occurrence of the reward. Other investigators have shown that the control of both positive and aversive delayed outcomes over the behavior of animals may be bridged, in some cases for sizeable intervals of time, by external markers which have a value that is conditional on their role as informational signals of the final outcome of the behavior (Bixenstine, 1956; Fantino, 1966; Ferster and Hammer, 1965; Kelleher, 1966). Strickland and Grote (1967) found that symbols which were partial components of the final signal of a potential rewarding outcome could be used to induce human subjects to persist in losing sequences of gambling behavior. The persistence of the subjects was greatest when the symbols occurred early rather than late in the sequence.

The child's ability to give a cognitive representation to the contingencies between its behavior and delayed outcomes should produce a radical increment in the delay tolerances which are generally found in the behavior of animals. The verbal medium of socialization would provide the child with cognitive equipment that would greatly expand the length of delay time over which its behavior could be sensitive to outcomes. For example, socializing agents often use verbal labelling and evaluative standards of judgement to represent an act to the child, in direct conjunction with reward or punishment, well after the act already has been committed. The internalized affectivity that is induced by reward or punishment may then come to control the child's subsequent choices of the same act, because it can be elicited by the child's cognitive or verbal representation of the act, even though it was not attached originally to the concrete behavioral cues which would be inherently correlated to an overt performance of the act. Fagan and Witryol (1966) recently have reported findings which indicate that the detrimental effects of delay of reward on children's learning can be overcome by instructing the child to maintain a cognitive orientation toward the locus of reward during the interval of delay.

Cognitive representation also contributes to internalized control of conduct by bridging the discrepancy between the child's initial behavioral dispositions and later behavior that is closer to the expectations of socializing agents. Certain forms of socially desirable conduct will initially occur relatively infrequently in the child's behavior, even though they may have a high potential for acquiring intrinsic value through either behavior-contingent or observational learning. However, these forms of conduct may have earlier forerunners which, although they may be less consistently and strongly reinforced, nevertheless can serve as a base from which the child's behavior will move toward more socially reinforceable channels. For example, parents may strongly reinforce those actions of the young child which they perceive as explicit evidence of fairness or generosity, but may only weakly reinforce the tentative rudiments of such actions. The maintenance of the rudiments, until they can gravitate toward the still infrequent and more highly evolved forms of conduct, may be facilitated by some generalization of the greater value that is gradually becoming attached to the latter forms as a result of their heavier reinforcement. This generalization of value would more effectively maintain the rudimentary base of the terminal conduct if it were mediated by verbal labels or concepts which the child could impose across the entire class of relevant acts.

Finally, it may be noted, by way of introduction to the next section of this chapter, that cognitive representation is the foundation of observational and imitative learning. It provides the child with the means of acquiring and storing templates of the forms and consequences of the behavior of others. Cognitive representation also supplies the child with evaluative structures which may be applied both to its own behavior and the attributes of social models. Such structures may be germane to the phenomena which are sometimes collectively gathered under the concept of identification. Identification might be conceived of as a type of evaluative cognition that supports the child's perception of a broad similarity between itself and an external model.

OBSERVATIONAL LEARNING AND IMITATION

Children acquire many of their stable patterns of social behavior on the basis of their observation of the behavior of others. The behavior of the child's parents, and of its other agents of socialization, produces various kinds of stimulus change which have a significant affective value for the child. The close conjunction between the child's observation of the behavior and the induced changes of affectivity will often result in the direct attachment (conditioning) of affective value to the child's cognitive representation of the behavior. The child may then reproduce the behavior, under the control of external cues, if the value of its cognitive representation corresponds to a reinforcing change of affective state (the induction of positive affect or the reduction of aversive affect). The behavior has acquired a certain amount of intrinsic value through the affectivity that is carried by its cognitive correlates. A performance of the behavior will therefore be reinforced to some extent because it enhances or articulates its own cognitive representation.

All forms of observational social learning require that the child give some attention to the behavior of another person. They also require that the child use its cognitive capacities for the coding and storage of information from its social environment. For the development of a conception of the observational learning process, however, we will need to take careful note of certain differences among the forms which it may take. In particular, we must distinguish among forms of observational learning which differ in the detail and fidelity of the child's representation of the observed behavior. *Imitation* is the form of observational learning in which the child uses a representational model of the specific features or sequential structure of another person's behavior. Imitation may serve as a convenient initial reference point for a more general analysis of observational learning and its mechanisms of internalization.

A substantial amount of the observed behavior of its socializing agents is immediately addressed to the child and has a directly experienced affective value for it. The affective value may be inherent in the potentially replicable components of the behavior of a model—as, for example, when a parent uses certain characteristic forms of behavior to convey affection to the child or to relieve its distress. In other instances, the reproducible features of the model's behavior may initially have little inherent affective value for the child, but may occur in intimate contiguity with other features of the model's behavior which do have such value—for example, on those frequent occasions when a parent's task-oriented performance or display of social skills happens to be interwoven in time with the expression of affection or nurturance toward the child. Under either of these two types of contingency, the affective context of the child's observation may become directly associated with its cognitive representation of the observed behavior. And the behavior itself may acquire an intrinsic reproducible value that is no longer dependent on its original function as an external social medium for the induction of changes in affectivity.

The inherent affective value of the observed behavior of another person may also acquire a generalized and broader kind of control over the child's observational learning. It appears that children will often reproduce the expressive or stylistic behavior of others even when they are not the recipients or objects of the behavior. For example, some of the behavior that is used by others to express affectivity may elicit empathic changes of affective state in the child. In some cases, the behavior may have specific components or a sequential organization which the child has never observed previously. But the behavior may nevertheless have an affective value for the child because it is perceived as an instance of a broader class of behavior that already has acquired a generalized value. Children have a wealth of social experience, for example, with the consequences of both nurturant and aggressive behavior. They may accordingly become disposed to respond with some affectivity to even the relatively inconsequential expressive behavior of another person, if they perceive that behavior to be associated with a generalized nurturant or aggressive role.

A second and at least equally common set of contingencies for observational learning occurs when the observed behavior of others induces affectivity in the child as a result of its external outcomes, rather than because of any affective value that is inherent in the behavior itself. The prototype for these contingencies can be found in the child's countless opportunities for observation of the ways in which the behavior of others produces positive or aversive environmental consequences, including consequences of reward or punishment. The affective value of the outcomes can be directly attached to the child's cognitive representation of the observed behavior when the representation is sufficiently close in time to the child's observation or knowledge of the outcome. And the child's own performance of the behavior may therefore acquire some intrinsic value without first having been exposed to the control of the outcomes.

The affective control of learning by the observed outcomes of another person's behavior requires that the outcomes elicit some amount of affec-

tivity in the child, either because of their unconditioned properties or because of the value which they have acquired as a result of the child's past
experience. The outcomes of another person's behavior may be directly experienced by the child—for example, a mother's behavior may produce
pleasurable external consequences for both herself and the child. However,
the more frequent opportunities for observational learning are those where
the child only observes the outcomes and does not experience them directly. In this very common paradigm of socialization, the affective value
that controls the learning process will often reside entirely in the child's
observation of the outcomes of another person's behavior, or in its observation of the contingency between behavior and outcomes, rather than in
its observation of any social cues which provide direct information about
the affective experience of another person. For example, a child in a competitive situation might experience some distress rather than pleasure on
observing another child's success in producing rewards from the environment. But its distress would not necessarily prevent the value of the rewards
from becoming attached to its cognitive representation of the instrumentality of the other child's behavior. The same point can be illustrated in the
paradigms of observational learning which often have been used with animals. One monkey's cognitive representation of the behavior of another
monkey may acquire an affective value that is determined only by the environmental effects of the second monkey's actions (for example, the appearance of food), and not by social cues which transmit the experience of the
second monkey. The first monkey might learn just as well through observation if the point of a stick were used to make the environmental manipula-
tions which produce valued outcomes (provided that it pays attention).

Our analysis of the ways in which observational learning may be controlled by the outcomes of another person's behavior enables us to see that
empathic or vicarious experience is not a prerequisite of the affective value
of the outcomes for the child. We will argue later that the concept of empathic or vicarious experience is not very useful when it is invoked to account for every instance in which the child's behavior is influenced merely
by its observation of the consequences of another person's behavior. Empathic and vicarious are terms which might be reserved, with more precision and utility, for the child's affective response to its perception or cognitive representation of another person's experience. For the moment, it is
sufficient to point out that a child may often learn through observation of
the outcomes of another person's behavior, without being at all responsive
to social cues which indicate the experienced value of the outcomes for that

person. Of course, empathic or vicarious experience of the consequences of another person's behavior does sometimes carry the affective value that becomes attached to the child's cognitive representation of the behavior—for example, when changes of affectivity are induced in the child by social cues which indicate how the consequences of the behavior affect others (either the person whose behavior is observed or others who experience its effects).

We can now make an important distinction between the two major types of contingencies for observational learning which have been described: those in which affective value is directly transmitted in the observed behavior and those in which affective value is transmitted by outcomes of the behavior.

When the affective value of observed behavior is inherent in the behavior, then the child's affectivity will be governed quite closely by intrinsic stimulus features of the behavior itself, rather than by the instrumentality of the behavior in producing outcomes. This kind of control of the child's affectivity is especially characteristic of the behavior which socializing agents use to express or monitor their own affective states. Expressive behavior is highly affect-laden. There would ordinarily be sharp gradients of affective value associated with the onset and termination of its specific components. If there is potential reinforcement value in the changes of affectivity which are induced in the child by the behavior that it observes, the child will attend and give cognitive representation to the behavior with a high fidelity to its observable features of form or sequence. And the child may then reproduce the behavior itself with the same fidelity.

The concept of imitation has maximum utility when it is restricted to the kind of observational learning which produces a high degree of fidelity in the child's replication of another person's behavior. The original observed behavior and its cognitive representation by the child are, respectively, external and internal *models* for the subsequent replicative behavior of the child. The properties of the representation are those of a *cognitive template,* in the sense that the structure and topography of the behavior are stored for reproduction. The template need not be thought of as a simple copy or image of the original external model. Nor does it necessarily always produce a slavish behavioral reproduction of the external model. The template may be characterized more accurately as a construction on an external model. It may take the form of a simple copy in some instances. But it may also incorporate rules or operators which make it possible for the child to generate new behavioral derivatives of the model.

In contrast to the direct transmission of affective value by the behavior that the child observes, the transmission of affective value by the outcomes of observed behavior does not lend itself so readily to the child's representation of the precise form of the behavior. The control of affectivity by observed outcomes does provide, however, a basis for the child's representation of both discrete act-outcome contingencies and the sequence of components in a pattern of behavior. When the affective value of observed behavior is governed by its outcomes, it will often be the case that the outcomes are not controlled by specific structural or topographic features of the behavior. It is in fact very frequently the case that a great number of possible variations of behavior will produce essentially the same outcome. Since the value of such behavior is determined by its instrumental effects, and not by the gradients of affectivity which are associated with its intrinsic components, its cognitive representation by the child will tend to be quite gross and undifferentiated. The cognitive representation will have only minimal properties as a model for the subsequent behavior of the child. It will be only a very general representation of the direction of choices for engagement of the environment, with respect to relevant cues and instrumental effects. For example, a child may observe the rewarded behavioral choices of another person, and may then engage in the same general class of behavior. But its behavior may show very little of the specific structural or sequential features of the behavior which it has observed.

There are some forms of observational learning which may produce imitative fidelity to the form or sequence of observed behavior even though they are primarily under the affective control of the anticipated outcomes of the behavior to be reproduced. This kind of learning is the result of the child's observation of the control of valued outcomes by certain structural requirements in the behavior of another person. Under these conditions, the affective value of the outcomes may become attached to a high level of fidelity in the child's cognitive representation and behavioral reproduction of the original external model. The fidelity may be greatly facilitated by verbal instruction which gives the child a representation of the contingency between the criterial features of the behavior and the occurrence of the outcomes. For example, a girl may learn very intricate dance patterns partially on the basis of her observation of the differential social rewards which accrue to other girls who have mastered the patterns with varying degrees of fidelity to a model.

Since any form of observational learning requires that affective value be attached to the child's cognitive representation of the observed behavior, the child's own performance of the behavior will have some intrinsic value immediately upon its first occurrence. The mechanism of reinforcement here requires that the performance and the representation be closely enough correlated so that the performance can be controlled by the affective value of the representation, even though the child has not overtly performed the behavior during the period of observation. Or to put the requirement in another form, the child's behavior must be controlled by affective value that has been first conditioned to the intrinsic correlates of the behavior. Many experiments on the behavior of animals have demonstrated that external stimuli can acquire value for control over behavior in this way. A stimulus can be exposed to Pavlovian conditioning procedures which are designed to give it motivating or reinforcing properties, in the absence of the overt behavior that will subsequently be used to test its acquired value, and it can then be shown to exercise positive control over the behavior (Estes, 1948; Knott and Clayton, 1966; Sheffield, 1965; Stein, 1958; Williams, 1965). Parallel demonstrations have been made for aversive control over behavior (Rescorla and LoLordo, 1965; Solomon and Turner, 1962).

Of course, the intrinsic value that observational learning gives to some forms of behavior will be further supported by direct external reinforcement of the behavior, and to some extent by reinstatement of the original conditions of observation. Some of the behavioral products of the child's observational learning will extinguish if they are not reinforced or confirmed by the child's subsequent experience. Certain kinds of imitative behavior may gradually become automated and move out of the control of cognitive representation, provided that they continue to have reinforcing outcomes on at least an intermittent basis. Their affective control may be taken over by the self-produced cues which are directly inherent in their very performance. And they may then become stereotyped even though their reinforcing outcomes are not contingent on their precise form.

The requirements of any general conception of observational learning can be better appreciated if we look more closely at some of the constraints which are imposed by the relevant phenomena. We might begin by noting that the contingencies which embed the observed behavior of another person in an affective context will account only for the value that the behavior acquires for the child. They will not explain the child's capacity to reproduce an overt performance of the behavior. When learning occurs as a result of behavior-contingent outcomes, modifications of the child's behavior can be understood in terms of its initial repertoire. The child first emits behavior, and then the probability and form of various acts are changed as a result of their reinforcing or suppressive consequences. In the case of observational learning, however, it does not appear to be necessary for the child first to produce behavior which is similar to that of another person, and then to have the behavior reinforced and gradually modified by external outcomes. This freedom from the control of external outcomes is particularly characteristic of imitative learning.

It is very common to see children reproduce a detailed sequence of the relatively idiosyncratic behavior of a model, after having observed the behavior on only a few occasions, under conditions where it is obvious that the reproduction could not previously have had the benefit of external social reinforcement. The child's imitation may not even require whatever cues might have been provided by the sheer presence of the model, and it may be repeated privately many times without the support of social reinforcement. Even when it happens that the model's behavior was originally a reinforcing outcome of other acts which were initiated by the child (as is often the case), the child's subsequent imitation of the model cannot usually be attributed to behavior-contingent training, since the acts which were originally reinforced would ordinarily bear no resemblance to the behavior through which the model transmitted their reinforcement. The foundation of imitative learning appears to lie, then, in the conditions under which the child observes the model, rather than in the modification of the child's emitted behavior by external outcomes.

The effects of observational learning on the child's overt behavior may sometimes be attributable to a relatively undifferentiated similarity between the stimulus properties of another person's behavior and the inherent stimulus properties of behavior that the child would be disposed to emit spontaneously and independently of the opportunity for observation. Under these conditions, the affective value of the reproduced external stimulation would merely add a component of intrinsic reinforcement to behavior that is already predetermined by the child's unlearned or established dispositions. Mowrer (1950, Chapter 24, 1960b, Chapter 3) has suggested that the vocalization of infants may become intrinsically reinforcing through essentially the conditioning of positive affective value to self-produced stimulation that initially only grossly resembles the stimulation from an external social source. And it is quite possible that the same kind of mechanism contributes to some of the examples of infant behavior which Piaget (1951) describes as evidence of the second through the fourth stages in his conception of the development of imitative dispositions.

The movement of conditioned affective value across a gross similarity between social and self-produced stimulation would not account, however, for the kind of imitative behavior in which children so commonly reveal their capacity to program the most varied sequences and complex structure of the behavior of models. Children characteristically reproduce extensive samples of the motoric and verbal behavior patterns of their models. Their imitation often represents a very high-fidelity replication of the exact topography of a model's behavior. Moreover, it is sometimes quite striking to see the apparent suddenness with which an accurate imitative program will emerge in the child's overt behavior, after only very limited exposure to a model, and with every indication that the imitation is an innovative departure from any behavior pattern that is likely to occur spontaneously. The efficiency of observational learning in general has been noted even in those conceptions of learning which emphasize behavior-contingent training (Skinner, 1953, pp. 116–122). Bandura (1962) has argued persuasively that the behavioral dispositions of children will often make observational learning more effective than behavior-contingent training. And both laboratory and field investigators of primate behavior have pointed to the speed and stability of observational learning (Hall, 1963; Harlow, 1959b).

It is not possible, of course, for the child to be able to quickly and accurately reproduce a sequence of observed behavior whose components are entirely foreign to the elements which are already available in its repertoire. Comparisons of the relative speed of acquisition of corresponding cognitive and motor representations make it clear that motor representation is much slower in approaching fidelity to a model (Maccoby and Bee, 1965; Miller, Galanter, and Pribram, 1960, Chapter 6). Even when the performance of components of an imitative program may be facilitated by some response generalization from the child's already established behavioral resources, there is still the problem of accounting for the child's ability to reproduce the order of components in fairly complex sequences. Generalization from established behavioral elements would also not account for the high topographical precision with which some forms of imitation reproduce the behavior of a model.

Actually, the impression of speed and efficiency of behavioral change that one often has, when observing a child's imitation of a model, may be created in part by lack of familiarity with the past history of the child's exposure to similar models and of its opportunities to practice the imitative program. It is likely that any detailed analysis of the topography of a child's initial imitative reproductions would reveal only a low replicative fidelity to the precise structure and sequence of the model's behavior. But the child's imitation would tend to increase in fidelity, even under conditions of restricted practice. It is not uncommon, for example, to see behavior patterns which are already established in the child's repertoire begin to gravitate with imitative exactness toward the corresponding behavior of a model. Under the assumption that imitative performance is controlled, at least during the learning process, by the affectivity that has become intrinsically associated with the child's representation of a model, we would expect the reinforcement value of the imitation to be proportionate to the fidelity with which it represented the model. Since the affective value of the performance is in turn controlled by a cognitive template of the original external model, it would also be necessary to assume that the value of different degrees of fidelity of imitation is a function of a gradient of affectivity along the representational dimensions of the template. The intrinsic reinforcement value of the imitation would be monitored, then, by the match between the template and the flow of imitative behavior. And the control of magnitude of reinforcement by the fidelity of the match would account for the value of the high topographical precision of some forms of imitative behavior.

Although the child's observational learning may sometimes require opportunities for overt practice, particularly if it is to produce any high-fidelity imitative correspondence to the behavior of a model, common observation makes it obvious that children are capable of remarkably rapid and accurate modifications of behavior on the basis of brief observation of the behavior of others. The apparent speed with which observational learning can affect the child's overt behavior, and the fact that it often seems not to require the opportunity for externally reinforced practice, have suggested to some theorists that the child engages in covert rehearsal during or after the period of observation (Logan *et al.*, 1955, pp. 149–151; Maccoby, 1959; Sears, Maccoby, and Levin, 1957, Chapter 10).

If covert rehearsal is taken to designate a process that is at the level of cognitive representation, then it could have considerable utility in accounting for certain features of observational learning—for example, the assembly and structure of the behavioral elements of an imitative program. Bandura, Grusec, and Menlove (1966) have shown that children's reproduction of the components of a model's behavior, under the explicit requirements of a recall task, is facilitated by instructing them to verbally describe the behavior to themselves during their observation of the model. But covert rehearsal would not in itself appear to explain the precision that children are capable of showing in their overt imitative performance of behavior patterns which include relatively unfamiliar elements. Of course, children do often rehearse the behavior of a model with overt practice that is either private or miniaturized to the point where it is not easily observable. Berger (1966) has described some of the conditions under which adults also will engage intentionally in overt rehearsal of the observed motor patterns of a model. If a rehearsal were entirely representational, however, without the engagement of behavioral motor components, then it is difficult to see how the rehearsal could produce the fidelity of overt performance that a child may show in the imitation of relatively novel and complex behavior. Given that the behavior to be reproduced has any significant amount of novel structure or topography, some overt practice would be required before an imitative performance could attain the precision that is more easily available at the level of representational rehearsal.

Whatever the role of covert rehearsal may be in observational learning, it is clear that the child must have the capacity to store the program of behavior which is to be rehearsed. It is the complexity of the programs which can be reproduced in the case of imitation, and the fidelity that is sometimes possible under conditions of limited observation, which require us to assume that the child can form fairly rapidly a cognitive template of the model's behavior. There is a substantial amount of evidence which indicates that the child's capacity to store and reproduce the behavior of others is a function of more general changes in its cognitive capacities. Some of the normative tasks which were designed many years ago for use with young children, with the purpose of establishing criteria for the assessment of intelligence at different ages, regularly showed developmental increments in the ability to observe and copy motor or verbal patterns of varying complexity (Bühler, 1935; Gesell et al., 1940; Shirley, 1933; Terman and Merrill, 1937). The findings of studies which have been designed specifically to assess mimicry and role-playing also have shown increments of ability with age or intelligence (Berges and Lezine, 1963; Bowers and London, 1965; Kwint, 1934).

Piaget's (1951) more informal but extensive observations of the development of imitation in infants and very young children led him to the conclusion that children reproduced the observed behavior of others through a developmental progression of mechanisms, ranging from sensory-motor processes to representational thought. It is interesting to note that experiments which have been conducted by Leontiev (described by Pick, 1963), and by other Russian investigators (Chistovich, Klass, and Alekin, 1961), indicate that discrimination along auditory stimulus dimensions is facilitated by requiring the subject to use vocal reproductions of sounds as discriminative responses. The finding suggests the inference that cognitive templates of an external social model may also be strengthened and refined by corresponding imitative performances, even though they may have a different order of complexity than a psychophysical dimension.

The concept of a cognitive template for imitative learning also recommends itself because it allows for the fact that, from the point of view of the child's concrete perception, the model's behavior and the child's reproduction are usually very different in their stimulus properties. For example, children must rely on the visual modality for much of their observation of the nonverbal behavior of potential models. Their reproduction of the behavior might provide a rich variety of self-produced stimulation, particularly in the form of proprioceptive cues of movement. But it could hardly provide anything like the array of visual stimuli which were present during the observation of the model. It is for this reason that a conception of imitation which emphasizes the attachment of affectivity to proprioceptive cues or to sensory-motor linkages does not give a satisfactory account of imitation (for example, Mowrer, 1960b, pp. 112–116). The limitation of such a conception is apparent quite early in the history of the child's imitative dispositions. Piaget (1951) observes that older infants begin, during what he describes as the fifth stage of imitation, to reproduce behavior which their direct perception cannot possibly apprehend to be the same as that originally produced by an external model (for example, sticking out the tongue). However, if the affective value of imitation were a function of fidelity to a cognitive template, rather than of fidelity to the direct perceptual input from the original behavior of the model, then the value would not be attenuated by the discrepancy between the immediate stimulus properties of the model and those of the child's reproduction. The representational power of a cognitive template would thus make the child's control of imitation independent of the match between the direct perceptual feedback from its own behavior and the concrete form of the cues which were originally presented externally in the behavior of the model.

Because observational learning so often seems to occur under conditions where external reinforcing events cannot be identified, many theorists have taken the view that it can be understood in terms of contiguity mechanisms (Allport, 1924, pp. 240–241; Holt, 1931, pp. 112–119; Humphrey, 1921; Maccoby, 1959; Piaget, 1951, Part I; Sheffield, 1961). Generally speaking, these mechanisms are described in such a way as to make it clear that they do not require the child's replication of another person's behavior to be controlled by its affective value (although an apparent exception can be found in the analysis by Maccoby). It is of some interest that earlier theorists, who emphasized the child's unlearned disposition toward imitation (Baldwin, 1895; McDougall, 1908, pp. 102–106), suggested the existence of circular reflexes which had properties not unlike those of the contiguity mechanisms which have been proposed for imitative learning.

It is possible that early experience does often structure a close temporal succession between corresponding simple actions of the child and another person (as suggested, for example, by Holt and Piaget), and that the child acquires some disposition to respond to the other person's behavior with a similar act for which it already has a sensory-motor or representational schema (although not, perhaps, without the control of outcomes). But such a disposition would hardly account for the much broader range of contingencies under which children will change their behavior in the direction of the previously observed behavior of another person. In the case of imitation, children will very commonly reproduce programmatic sequences of behavior which are relatively novel for them, even when the model is no longer present.

It does not seem that a contiguity mechanism would effectively attach the child's replicative behavior to any kind of stimulus event in the course of observational learning, if the mechanism rested on the conventional requirement of a close temporal association between stimulus and overt response. The prototypical paradigm for observational learning is one in which the child is observing rather than performing during its exposure to the behavior of another person. On the other hand, if the contiguity concept is being applied to an association between receptive events—for example, between the child's perception of the external stimuli which elicit the other person's behavior and its own perceptual or cognitive "responses" in observing the behavior (Bandura, 1962)—then it is not clear as to how such an association would control the child's subsequent overt behavior. Perceptual contiguities would certainly determine the acquired power of specific external cues to elicit the cognitive structures which children use to represent the previously observed behavior of others. They would not provide, however, a mechanism for understanding how these representations would govern the child's overt performance, in part because they make no provision for affective control of behavior.

There are two other characteristics of observational learning which suggest that it requires changes of affective state to be associated with the observed behavior. First, observational learning is highly selective. For example, children do not imitate all of the behavior of the potential models whom they observe, even when external conditions may be appropriate. The types of behavior which they are most inclined to reproduce may reveal something about the affective prerequisites of observational learning. Secondly, observational learning may be very persistent. Children will sometimes show precise imitation of a social model repeatedly over long periods of time, when it does not appear that the fidelity of their behavior functions to produce reinforcing external consequences. Both of these characteristics of observational learning in general, and of imitation in particular, indicate that their behavioral products have reinforcing properties which derive from the affective value that becomes attached to the child's representation of another person's behavior. The role of affective value in observational learning is difficult to evaluate empirically, however, in part because of the vast range of behavior that children may reproduce, and in part because we know very little about the nature and magnitude of the value which a great variety of social stimuli may impart to the child's representations of the behavior of others. Nevertheless, experiments can sometimes be designed in such a way as to uncover the mechanisms of affective control over observational learning.

A number of theorists have proposed that the child's early experience of nurturance and affection establishes the positive affective value of the attributes of its social models, and thus fosters its generalized disposition to reproduce the attributes in its own behavior (Freud, 1933; Mowrer, 1950, Chapter 21; Mowrer, 1960b, Chapter 3; Sears *et al.*, 1957, Chapter 10; Whiting and Child, 1953, Chapter 11). Roughly formulated in the language of conditioning and learning concepts, the proposition may be described as follows:

Many attributes of the child's primary caretaker, and of other socializing agents as well, may become powerful stimuli for the induction of the child's pleasurable affect, as a result of their prior association with the child's experience of care, affection, and approval. The child is presumed to acquire a very broad disposition to reproduce these stimulus attributes of its nurturant models, particularly when the models are absent or their affection has been withdrawn, in order to provide itself with the secondary reinforcement value which the attributes have acquired. This disposition apparently is considered to have such strength and generalization that it extends even to the punitive reactions of parents (see, for example, Sears *et al.*, 1957, Chapter 10).

Common observation suggests that the earliest imitative behavior of the young child does show the stamp of the nurturant role of its primary caretaking agents. Some of the experiments which have been reported by Bandura and his co-workers have demonstrated that there are conditions under which young children are more inclined to reproduce the actions of a nurturant model than they are those of a neutral or competitive model (Bandura and Huston, 1961; Bandura, Ross, and Ross, 1963b). In a similar experiment, Mussen and Parker (1965) found that girls whose mothers characteristically maintained a high level of nurturance reproduced more of the mothers' behavior than did girls whose mothers were less nurturant. The findings of other more recent experiments also indicate that children are more inclined to imitate the behavior of either parental or peer models when they have had a history of nurturant or rewarding interaction with the model (Hartup and Coates, 1967; Hetherington and Frankie, 1967).

In other experiments, the nurturant or rewarding attributes of another person have been found to have no effect, an ambiguous effect, or even a disruptive effect, on the child's disposition to reproduce the person's behavior or judgements (Aronfreed, 1964; Bandura, Grusec, and Menlove, 1967b; Rosenhan and White, 1967; Sgan, 1967; Stein and Wright, 1964). Some of the evidence from these latter studies suggests that the disposition of children to reproduce the behavior or judgements of another person is more sensitive to continuity or withdrawal of the level of nurturance to which they have become adapted than it is to the sheer amount of nurturance that they have received from the person. However, only one of the five experiments which are cited immediately above is designed to assess the child's replication of the expressive or stylistic behavior of a model. As will be pointed out later, it seems very probable that nurturance is peculiarly effective in focussing the attention of children on the expressive aspects of another person's behavior.

It seems unlikely, for a number of reasons, that nurturance would have unique effects as a determinant of the affective value of another person's reproducible behavior. Experimental paradigms of socialization have been used to demonstrate that children acquire dispositions to reproduce verbal criticism of their own behavior (Aronfreed, 1964), and to behave sympathetically toward another person (Aronfreed and Paskal, 1966), under conditions which establish a close contiguity between the corresponding behavior of a model and the termination of the child's anxiety or distress. The effects which are obtained in these experiments are not contingent on first establishing the positive nurturant attributes of a model. On the contrary, the effects indicate that verbal criticism and sympathetic behavior acquire value and are reproduced on the basis of their function in reducing the child's aversive affective states. An affective context of nurturance would be expected to have a generalized effect, however, in establishing the positive or aversive value of other aspects of a model's behavior. The findings of two recent experiments (Grusec, 1966; Mischel and Grusec, 1966) do suggest that the nurturance of a model may facilitate the child's reproduction of critical verbal components of the model's punitive behavior. It is much more plausible to attribute this effect of nurturance to the salience or contrast of withdrawal of affection as a component of punishment, and to a consequent increment in the intensity of the child's anxiety, than it is to assume that nurturance somehow lends positive value even to a model's punitive behavior. The former interpretation of the experimental findings is entirely consistent with the correlational evidence, which we will examine later, on the effects of parental nurturance in naturalistic socialization.

Aversive control is only one kind of evidence of limitations on the role of nurturance as an affective base for imitation and other forms of observational learning. The range of the social stimuli which may attach positive value to the attributes of a model must be regarded as much more extensive than the stimulation that can be specified as nurturance or affection in any concrete sense. A great variety of social stimuli derive some of their affective power from their original relationship to the child's early experience of care and affection (Gewirtz, 1961; Rheingold, 1961). Once these stimuli have acquired positive affective value, they may also independently impart that value to the observed behavior of others. This class of stimuli would include gestures and expressive cues, verbal indicators of approval or praise, and many other kinds of positive social signals. The contiguity of these stimuli with the reproducible features of the behavior of a socializing agent would often be incidental to their occurrence as reinforcing outcomes of the child's own behavior.

Many social stimuli which we do not usually think of as being pleasurable may nevertheless have positive affective value for the child. A radical expansion of the common view of the range of stimulus events which have positive value for the child is suggested by Piaget's (1951) observations of the disposition of very young children to repeat the behavior of others in order to reproduce a great variety of inherent and external stimulus consequences. These consequences appear to have an interest value for the child that is unrelated to its experience of nurturance, and that may in fact require only the most minimal ingredients of experience in a social environment. It is conceivable that recent demonstrations of the facilitation of children's aggressive behavior by observation of the aggression of others

(Bandura and Walters, 1963a) also may rest partially on the child's pleasure in observing the vigorous forms of aggression which are directed against an object that is specifically designed to produce interesting effects.

The classes of social stimuli which may attach affective value to the observed behavior of others will also be greatly extended by the child's capacity for empathic or vicarious experience. Children may respond empathically, for example, not only to external cues which directly convey the affective states of others, but also to their cognitive representation of the affective experience that is implicit in the control of valued resources by others. Bandura *et al.* (1963b) found that another person's control of valued resources enhanced children's dispositions to make behavioral choices which corresponded to those of the other person. Some theoretical treatments of the concept of identification have argued that a model's control of valued resources is the central determinant of the child's disposition to adopt the model's attributes (Kagan, 1958; Maccoby, 1959; Whiting, 1960).

Because of the great range of social stimuli which acquire value for control of the child's behavior, it is easy to overestimate the extent of the role of imitation in socialization—particularly if it is judged on the basis of the general tendency of the child's behavior to become more and more like that of its socializing agents. There are many ways in which a child's behavior may be influenced by its observation of the behavior of others, without showing anything like the exactitude of matching that would correspond to imitative modelling. An increase in objective similarity of behavior, between child and socializing agent, does not require us to suppose that the child is learning through imitation (or that it is adopting the attributes of a model through more complex processes of the kind which are sometimes implied in the concept of identification). The observed behavior of others is an extensive source of informational cues and motivational stimuli. It will often serve to provide cues for behavior-contingent training, or to elicit dispositions which the child already has acquired in its past history of training. A child's behavior will therefore frequently be similiar to the observed behavior of another person, at the gross level of common choice among alternative acts, because it is under the established constraints of cues in the child's social environment, rather than because the other person's behavior serves as a model for changes in the child's behavioral repertoire.

Recent reviews by Campbell (1963) and Wheeler (1966) provide interesting analyses of the variety of paradigms of social influence which can induce an observer to match behavioral choices to those of another person. Thorpe (1963) has pointed out that different types of transmission paradigms are also required to account for the full range of social matching that one finds in the species-specific and learned behavior patterns of animals.

Miller and Dollard (1941) suggested, in their well-known conception of "matched-dependent" behavior, that imitative acts could be viewed as responses which had become attached, through repeated performance and external reinforcement, to the cues which were transmitted in the corresponding acts of another member of the same species. They demonstrated this conception of imitation in experiments with both rats and children. Their view of imitative learning has been criticized often on the grounds that it simply describes a form of behavior-contingent discrimination training in which the relevant cues happen to be socially transmitted (see, for example, Bandura, 1962). Thus, it does not seem to account for the more rapid kind of observational learning that so commonly produces significant changes in the child's behavior even when observation precedes the opportunity for performance and reinforcement.

An equally important deficiency of the conception of imitation as an externally reinforced behavioral correspondence, based on social transmission of cues, is that the relevant demonstrations usually appear to be restricted to the relatively gross matching of simple behavioral choices. They do not seem to extend very well, for example, to the human capacity for reproduction of the more precise structural sequence or topography of a model's behavior. And even when it may appear that behavior-contingent training does produce a close behavioral correspondence between observer and model, there is still the problem of accounting for the child's use of its observation to meet the criterion of behavioral precision that will be reinforced. Miller and Dollard appeared to have recognized this shortcoming to some extent in their alternative conception of imitative learning as "copying." But they did not carry this latter conception much beyond the suggestion that an imitator could also respond to cues of similarity or difference between his behavior and the behavior of the model.

Both of these limitations on the conception of imitation as a type of behavior-contingent training have a single fundamental point. The point is that the cues which are socially transmitted in the behavior of another person may elicit corresponding behavior from the child without the requirement that the child use the other person's behavior as a *model*. The cues which are transmitted in the behavior of others pervade all forms of social modification of the child's behavior. When the cues happen to be transmitted through another person's performance of the same behavior which they elicit from the child, their mode of transmission will very often not be essential to their function of providing information about the social environment and the consequences of the child's own behavior. There are many learning situations in which a simple correspondence between the child and another person, in the choice or general direction of their behavior, might just as well have been established through the mediation of nonsocial cues or through direct verbal instruction of the child in regard to the outcomes of its behavior (see, for example, Skinner, 1953, pp. 119–122). In the case of true imitation, however, the observed behavior of another person carries more than information about the external context and consequences of the child's behavioral choices. It functions also as a representation of the behavior to be performed by the child—that is, there are cues intrinsic to the structure of the observed behavior itself which quite literally serve as a model for the child. The fidelity with which children can reproduce the sequence and topography of the behavior of others is one of the characteristics of imitation which constrain us to infer that the model is represented and stored in a cognitive template.

We noted earlier that children may acquire imitative representations of another person's behavior when their observational learning is governed by the affective value of the observed outcomes of the behavior, as well as when it is governed by the affective value that is directly inherent in the behavior itself. In the case of observational learning which is governed by outcomes, the child's cognitive templates will show the most fidelity to those features of the model which it has observed to be criterial for the control of the outcomes. Thus, the child may learn to imitate accurately the structure of the sequential components of a model's behavior, if the structure is critical to the occurrence of social rewards or to successful negotiation of a task—as is illustrated, for example, in Poliakova's (1958) interesting report of children's observational maze learning. A recent report by Craig (1967) of the observational learning of a complex temporal maze by adults demonstrates a similar phenomenon. It is more unlikely, however, that the child will imitate the precise topography of the components in a model's behavior, if its observational learning is controlled by outcomes, because it is unusual for the reinforcing consequences of a social environment to be made contingent on the exact topography of behavior.

The problem of giving a precise topographical form to behavior, when the value of the behavior is established under the control of outcomes, becomes even more apparent in the case of behavior-contingent training without the assistance of observational learning. It is easy to imagine the difficulty of trying to establish, without the provision of a model, any significant amount of sequential structure or precise topography in a child's behavior. Actually, of course, the dispositions which the child acquires as a result of behavior-contingent training during socialization ordinarily have a wide latitude in the precise form which they may take. The established value of these dispositions is very much the same among a number of closely related but differentiable acts, because socializing agents have not made their reinforcement selectively contingent on the exact topography of the acts. It has been demonstrated that children can acquire strong dispositions to match the discrete actions of another person on the basis of direct social reinforcement which is combined with the opportunity for observational learning (Baer, Peterson, and Sherman, 1967; Baer and Sherman, 1964; Lövaas et al., 1966a; Metz, 1965). But these demonstrations do not show any marked similarity between child and model in the representation of an extended sequence or in the fine grain of behavior.

In contrast to the control of their behavior by outcomes, children sometimes use representational imitation with a fidelity that is well beyond what is required to elicit reinforcing consequences from their social environment. This phenomenon indicates that imitative behavior has acquired an intrinsic expressive value that is closely bound to the features of an original external model. It appears that variations in imitative behavior which are only grossly equivalent, in their fidelity to a model, are often not equivalent in their affective value. Their specific values seem instead to be determined by their fidelity to the precise features of the external model which were originally most closely associated with potentially reinforcing changes of affective state for the child. Even the simplest discrete choices among alternative acts may be shown to have acquired some intrinsic reinforcement value, as a result of the child's observation of another person's behavior, when experimental contingencies are arranged to permit inferences to be drawn about the locus of affective control over the child's behavior. In the absence of such contingencies, it is usually easier to discern that value has become directly attached to intrinsic correlates of the child's behavior if the behavior reproduces some distinguishable elements of structure or sequence in the behavior of a model.

Our survey of some of the boundaries of the phenomena of observational learning and imitation now makes it possible to draw more careful distinctions among the findings of a great number of experiments which demonstrate that the behavior of an observer can be influenced by the behavior of others. All of these demonstrations are effective in producing some control over the observer's behavior. But they fall into very different categories when we look closely at the nature of the contingencies which produce the control, and at the relationship between the observed and induced behavior. It becomes immediately apparent that the representational use of a model is a determinant of the behavioral effects which are obtained in only a limited number of these experiments. It is in fact difficult to ascertain, in some instances, the extent to which the obtained effects may be taken as evidence of any form of learning, since it often appears that they are the result of simple elicitation of the observer's well-established behavioral dispositions.

We might begin by pointing out that many of the behavioral effects which are interpreted as being attributable to the influence of a model are actually more properly described as the effects of a generalized social facilitation. Good examples of this type of effect can be found in the results of experiments which show that the aggressive play of children is facilitated simply by their observation of the filmed aggressive behavior of other people or of fantasy figures (Lövaas, 1961a; Mussen and Rutherford, 1961). Far from being evidence of a phenomenon that requires the child to use a model, these experiments demonstrate that the child can be induced to engage in one form of aggressive behavior by its observation of a totally different form of aggressive behavior. The facilitation of aggression in the absence of any necessary correspondence between observed and induced behavior is illustrated also in the findings of a great many similar experiments with adults (Berkowitz, 1965; Berkowitz and Geen, 1966, 1967; Lefcourt et al., 1966; Walters and Llewellyn Thomas, 1963; Walters, Llewellyn Thomas, and Acker, 1962; Wheeler and Caggiula, 1966; Wheeler and Smith, 1967).

The paradigms which are used in some of the experiments which are cited above provide cues which signal the appropriateness or consequences of the observed aggression. But none of the experiments is designed to show that the observed aggression itself exercises any kind of discriminative control over the form of the induced aggression. Indeed, in many of these experiments, the test for induced aggression provides no opportunity for the modes of aggression which the subjects have observed. The subjects' potential mode of aggression is determined by situational supports, which are specifically provided for that purpose, and the observed aggression acts only as a generalized motivational or eliciting stimulus for the subjects' own aggressive dispositions. Even when there is a correspondence of modes and targets between observed and induced aggression—for example, in the observation and use of verbal aggression toward the same person, as described in the experiments which are reported by Wheeler and his co-workers—it is only the subject's general level of aggression that is being assessed.

The facilitation of aggressive behavior by the observation of another person's aggression bears more than a casual resemblance to the phenomena of social facilitation of human behavior in crowds (Brown, 1954) or in the performance of tasks (Allport, 1924; Dashiell, 1935). Piaget (1951) has pointed out that a nonspecific social facilitation of behavior is present in very early infancy as a forerunner of imitation. It is also interesting to note that many studies of animal behavior have demonstrated facilitative effects of the presence or activity of one animal on the behavior of another (Harlow and Yudin, 1933; James, 1960; Scott and McCray, 1967; Simmel, 1962; Weiskrantz and Cowey, 1963; Zajonc, 1965). The resulting behavioral correspondence is usually much more marked than the correspondence which is typically seen in the social facilitation of human aggression. The effects are particularly strong in the case of feeding behavior.

It is characteristic of social facilitation that it produces what appears to be an immediate motivational effect on a well-established pattern of behavior, rather than a behavioral change that has the characteristics of learning (Zajonc, 1965). The evidence indicates, in fact, that learning is often disrupted by the motivational effects of social facilitation. For example, the feeding behavior of birds is highly sensitive to social facilitation (Bayer, 1929; Hake and Laws, 1967). But this sensitivity actually interferes with their observational discrimination learning in a feeding situation (Klopfer, 1961). Studies with humans and other primates also suggest that social facilitation produces motivational control over established behavioral dispositions rather than informational control over the learning process. Ader and Tatum (1963) found that human avoidance training was more often disrupted than it was facilitated when subjects were required to learn in the presence of another subject who also experienced but could not control shocks. Miller and Murphy (1956) found that the performance of monkeys on discrimination and oddity problems was more accurate when they were tested in pairs than it was when they were tested individually. But the monkeys first had received a substantial amount of individual training and also continued to perform alone on an intermittent basis.

In contrast to social facilitation phenomena, the behavior-contingent choice matching which Miller and Dollard (1941) described in their "matched-dependent" paradigm is very much under the discriminative control of the specific cues in the behavior of another organism. Their demonstration of how an animal could be trained to make correct choices, by using the cues which were transmitted in the concurrent choices of another animal, has been repeated successfully in other experiments with animals (Bayroff and Lard, 1944; Church, 1957a, 1957b; Solomon and Coles, 1954). The distinguishing characteristics of this paradigm are the occurrence of the behavioral match in the presence of the relevant cues, the gradualness of the course of learning, and the locking of a specific choice to specific cues (as opposed to the representation of alternative act-outcome contingencies, which is often apparent in true observational learning).

Miller and Dollard's use of their choice paradigm to produce behavioral matching in children also has been repeated (McDavid, 1959, 1962; Stein and Wright, 1964; Wilson, 1958). And essentially the same paradigm has been used to induce adults to match their choices to those of another person (Kanareff and Lanzetta, 1960; O'Connell, 1965; Rosenbaum and Tucker, 1962; Schein, 1954). The course of modification of behavior is ordinarily more rapid in human subjects than it is in animals. And there is much reason to think that the human subjects are taking advantage of their ability to give a cognitive representation to the contingencies among their cues, their choices, and the outcomes of their choices—particularly in view of the fact that their choices are sometimes made after the relevant cues have been terminated. For example, Miller and Dollard found that children typically learned to match the choices of another person in only three or four trials. However, even the matching paradigms for human subjects still maintain a very close temporal relationship between the occurrence of the cues and the choices. The contingencies of these paradigms generally are not arranged to permit the inference that the matching effect is attributable to any process other than the direct control of specific choices by concrete external cues.

We already have pointed out that behavior-contingent choice matching is a form of training that usually produces only a gross correspondence in the direction of choice. The complete arbitrariness in the relationship between the behavior that is learned and the behavior that transmits cues is brought to light in the often overlooked fact that Miller and Dollard were able to train different groups of subjects (both rats and children) to make either the same or opposite choice, with equal facility, in response to the cues of the choice which they had observed. The same arbitrary option has

been demonstrated for adults by Rosenbaum and Tucker (1962). The ir-
relevance of the form of behavior in this type of paradigm is also illustrated
by the choice matching that has been produced in experimental demonstrations of the control of cooperative behavior by reinforcing outcomes. Many
of these demonstrations actually do not even give their human adult subjects the opportunity to observe one another's behavior directly (Deutsch
and Krauss, 1960; Kelley *et al.,* 1962; Sidowski, Wyckoff, and Tabory,
1956).

The matching of discrete acts under the control of reinforcing outcomes
also has been used to impose a requirement of cooperative integration on
the already learned behavior of animals. Crawford (1937–38) was able to
superimpose a form of social coordination on the learned behavior of two
chimpanzees. A more interesting case, for our purposes here, is an experiment that was reported by Skinner (1962), which captures nicely the absence of any representational match and the stimulus-bound quality in this
type of learning. Skinner trained two pigeons to peck simultaneously for
food in a discrimination task, while they were in an adjacent side-by-side
orientation. When he then reversed their placement in the training com-
partments, they immediately assumed an identical orientation with respect
to one another, facing away from the discriminative stimulus panel, and
continued their pecking movements without any target.

Recently, there have been some impressive demonstrations of the effectiveness with which direct reinforcement by food and verbal approval can
be used to induce children to match their overt actions to those which are
displayed by another person or a puppet (Baer *et al.,* 1967; Baer and Sherman, 1964; Lövaas *et al.,* 1966a; Metz, 1965). These demonstrations do
not merely produce matching of choices. They reveal that a substantial
amount of fidelity to the form of another person's behavior can be built
into the child's behavior through the techniques of shaping by contingent
outcomes. The gradualness with which the children acquire their dispositions to reproduce observed behavior in these experiments suggests that
there is at least an initial period during which they do not use the behavior
as a representation of the actions to be performed, but rather use it as a
source of cues for movements which only slowly approximate the criterion
in a trial-and-error fashion. The same pattern of learning is apparent in
normal, retarded, and autistic children. The absence of the facilitation of
learning by a cognitive representation of the required behavior is especially
clear in some of the interesting techniques which Metz (1965) and Baer *et
al.* (1967) have used with autistic and retarded children. These investiga-

tors found that their subjects could learn more readily to reproduce some of the behavior which they had observed if they were first put through the required movements by external physical guidance. On the other hand, the final performance of the children, in all of the studies which are cited above, showed clear evidence of the effects of observational learning that was based on cognitive representation of the acts which had been observed. The children arrived at the point where they would often quickly and accurately match the behavior which they observed on the first trial of a new task. There was little evidence, however, of the representational imitation of sequential or finely structured behavior.

Some of the best examples of behavioral matching which requires cognitive representation are to be found in laboratory studies of observational discrimination learning and problem-solving in monkeys. The findings of many of these studies show quite clearly that learning is facilitated by various arrangements which give the monkey repeated opportunities to observe the performance of a peer (Darby and Riopelle, 1959; Riopelle, 1960; Warden, Fjeld, and Koch, 1940). The Japanese reports of "cultural transmission" of feeding habits among monkeys (Imanishi, 1957; Itani, 1958; Kawamura, 1963), and other reports of the behavior of larger primates in naturalistic or home settings (Goodall, 1965; Hayes and Hayes, 1952; Washburn, Jay, and Lancaster, 1965), also suggest striking instances of representational matching in observational learning. This kind of facilitation of the learning process also has been demonstrated for cats (Adler, 1955; Herbert and Harsh, 1944).

One of the criteria of true observational learning, which distinguishes it from the matching and direct reinforcement of simple choices, is that the learning process be more rapid and efficient than could be expected if the subject were to acquire the same performance through behavior-contingent training which is nonrepresentational and based on the immediate presence of social cues. A closely related and even more important criterion is a performance which permits the inference that the learner is not bound to fixed cues in the observed behavior—that he must be using a cognitive representation of the behavior and of its contingent outcomes in the environment. The time intervals between the opportunities for observation and performance should be long enough to minimize the possibility that the learner is able to perform accurately merely by maintaining an orienting response toward critical stimuli in the environment. This criterion is met in many instances by a design that does not give the learner an opportunity to perform until after he has observed a long sequence of another subject's learning or established performance. Moreover, the context of description of the observer's performance, in many of the reported demonstrations of observational learning in animals, makes it clear that the observer employs the capacity for a representation of contingencies. The most convincing evidence is found in the ability of some animals to take account of the outcome of an observed act in producing adaptive variations of their own behavior, so that they are not bound to a fixed relationship between external cues and their own choices. For example, one typical situation is that in which a monkey must choose among two or more locations, in order to make a response that will uncover food, when the correct location remains constant between observation and performance. When the monkey who is being observed has made an error, the observing monkey is able to take the error into account as it subsequently makes its choice (see, for example, Riopelle, 1960).

It seems quite clear, then, that monkeys are capable of observational learning that requires some cognitive representation of alternative contingencies between observed acts and their outcomes. On the other hand, one can certainly not say that they necessarily display imitation in their observational learning. It is necessary to take into account the relationship between the form of behavior that they observe and the form that they produce. Most experiments require only that the monkey use a cognitive representation of the general direction of behavior with which to engage its environment. Learning is revealed by the accuracy and speed with which the monkey approaches the correct location at which to make a response. When it has correctly engaged the stimulus scene, the specific form of its behavior may be irrelevant. In the type of experiment which is described above, for example, both the observed and the observing monkeys ordinarily use their hands to uncover the food. However, by the criteria which are employed to identify correct performance, the observing monkey might later just as well use its teeth or its tail. That the monkey does in fact use its hand is more likely to be the expression of unlearned manipulative dispositions than of any imitative learning of a specific form of behavior in the course of observation.

Some studies of observational learning have required the observing animal to use manipulative and even sequential behavior that seems to have more representational fidelity to the form of behavior which has been observed (Adler, 1955; Herbert and Harsh, 1944; Warden et al., 1940). Even in these cases, however, the imitative properties of the learned behavior are limited to fairly simple operations upon the environment (for example, pushing a pedal or turning a knob). The learning does not appear to require a structural representation of the components or topography of an extended pattern of behavior. Much the same point might be made, though with somewhat less force, about experiments in which observation of another person's learning or skilled performance of movement through a maze, together with observation of the outcomes of correct and incorrect choices, has been shown to facilitate the subsequent learning of the maze by both children and human adults (Craig, 1967; Poliakova, 1958). These experiments were cited earlier as demonstrations of the observational learning of the sequential components of a performance under the control of external outcomes.

Observational learning through a representational match provides a useful background against which to view the effects that have been obtained in a large number of experiments which show that the sheer observation of the behavioral or judgemental choices of others will often elicit corresponding choices from the child (Hartup, 1964; Hetherington, 1965; Rosenblith, 1961; Rosenhan and White, 1967; Sgan, 1967). These experiments do not employ paradigms of behavior-contingent training. Nor are they designed to show that the child has learned by imitation. The effects which are obtained are rather clearly the effects of social elicitation of established behavioral or cognitive dispositions which the child brings into the experimental situation. The inferences which may be drawn from the effects are much like those which may be drawn from other kinds of demonstrations of children's conformity to immediate social influence in the absence of explicit reinforcing outcomes (Abelson and Lesser, 1959; Harper *et al.,* 1965; Iscoe and Williams, 1963; Jakubczak and Walters, 1959). Parallel demonstrations of social conformity, in which the observer's behavior comes quickly under the control of discriminative cues in another person's behavior, have been carried out with adults (Bryan and Test, 1967; deCharms and Rosenbaum, 1960; Epstein, 1966; Walters, Bowen, and Parke, 1964).

Two other recent experiments (Hartup and Coates, 1967; Hetherington and Frankie, 1967) have interesting features which appear to confirm that the effects obtained in many demonstrations of children's choice-matching are attributable primarily to the children's established dispositions toward social conformity. The findings of both of these experiments include some evidence of children's imitation of the incidental expressive behavior of models. The findings also include, however, some effects which indicate that the children's conformity to simple behavioral choices was responsive to the prevalent character of their total past experience of interaction with the person whose choices they were observing. For example, Hartup and Coates found that children who generally had positive interactions with their peers were more likely to be influenced by the acts of sharing of the peer with whom they had the most rewarding experience than they were to be influenced by the acts of a peer with whom they had no rewarding experience. In contrast, children were more likely to follow the sharing behavior of a nonrewarding peer than they were to follow the behavior of a rewarding peer if they generally experienced a low incidence of rewarding interactions with their peers. Hetherington and Frankie found that the behavioral choices of children who were confronted by discrepancies in the choices made by their two parents were influenced both by the warmth and the dominance which respectively characterized each parent's behavior.

In all of these studies of social influence, it is difficult to assess the nature or extent of the occurrence of any learning. The observed behavior of others functions as the source of cues which signal the appropriateness and perhaps the potential approval of the child's choices among different objects, verbal judgements, or distributions of valued resources. It seems quite clear that the child's behavior is controlled by the affective value of information from its social environment. It is also clear that the child must be using some cognitive representation of the relationship between its own choices and the choices which it has observed, in order to bring its behavior so rapidly under the control of social information. But there is no interesting sense in which the observed behavior of another person can be said to serve as a *model* for the child's behavior. The effect that is obtained in the child's matching of behavioral choices does not require the control of a representation of any specific features of the form of the observed behavior. The same kinds of effects are apparent when children simply are told about the choices or preferences of others (Bandura and Mischel, 1965; Duncker, 1938).

Some recent investigations have provided striking illustrations of the extent to which observation of the behavior of others can influence the child's verbal expression of evaluative or linguistic cognitive structures. The effects of the social observation appear to be strongest in the case of cognitive structures which are having either a waxing or waning influence on the child's evaluative judgements or habits of speech. For example, Bandura and McDonald (1963) first identified two groups of children whose verbalized judgements of the magnitude of various transgressions were respectively dominated, though not exclusively so, by their orientations toward either the intentions or the consequences of an act (Piaget, 1948). It was then possible to produce sharp changes in the direction of a child's judgements by having it make each individual judgement just after it had heard an adult make a judgement that was discrepant with its own dominant orientation. The findings of a similar study by Turiel (1966), in which more complex criteria of moral judgement were employed, also indicate that the child's verbal judgements can be moved in the direction of either the evaluative structures which it has recently acquired or the evaluative structures which it has moved beyond in its cognitive development.

In a demonstration which may have required children to give more representation to the form of the behavior that they observed, Bandura and Harris (1966) were able to induce children to increase their relatively infrequent use of passive sentence constructions. Their technique included having each child listen repeatedly to the use of the passive construction by an adult, direct reinforcement of the child's use of passive constructions, and instructions which were intended to give the child a problem-solving set. In contrast, facilitation of children's already common use of prepositional phrases was maximized by the combination of direct reinforcement with a problem-solving set. Exposure to the constructions of an adult had no additional facilitative effect.

One does not suppose that the procedures which were used in the two experiments which are described above would in themselves produce new evaluative structures for the judgement of transgressions, or that they would result in the acquisition of new grammatical structures for the passive transformation. The experiments are interesting rather because they reveal some of the ways in which exposure to the judgements or speech of others may enhance the child's overt expression of cognitive capacities which have only either a rudimentary or a vestigial status. Much the same effect on children's moral judgements can be obtained, for example, when children are exposed to direct training in which they are rewarded or corrected by an adult who also simply indicates the correct choices to be made (Crowley, 1968).

A number of experiments have shown that children's observation of the rewarding or punitive outcomes of the behavior of others will elicit or suppress their own corresponding behavior (Bandura, Grusec, and Menlove, 1967a, 1967b; Rosekrans and Hartup, 1967; Walters, Leat, and Mezei, 1963; Walters and Parke, 1964a; Walters, Parke, and Cane, 1965). We will examine these findings more closely in our later analysis of empathic and vicarious experience. But it should be noted here that, in all of the ex-

periments which are cited, the effect of observation of the outcomes of another person's behavior is restricted to a choice or general direction in the
subsequent behavior of the observer. The findings indicate that the subject's choice of whether to perform or suppress particular acts is influenced
by the affective value of the observed outcomes of the acts for another person. There is no evidence, however, of any representational use of the specific form of the observed behavior. Bandura *et al.* (1967a) did require
children to engage in a sequence of interactions with a dog, which were like
those that they had observed in the behavior of another child, as an index
of vicarious extinction of fear. But the sequential acts were individually
specified by direct instruction, and their performance was not guided by the
more precise form of the acts which had been observed. Considerably more
learning by observation is to be found, though again without any evidence
of representational imitation of the structure of behavior, in experiments in
which the learning of simple verbal or motor tasks by children or adults
has been shown to be enhanced by prior observation of outcomes which
indicate the correct or incorrect choices of another person (Ditrichs,
Simon, and Greene, 1967; Kanfer and Marston, 1963; Marston, 1966).

Another way of looking at the problem of how to use the concept of a
model is to examine a type of experiment in which observation of the behavior of adults or peers influences the criteria or timing of the child's allo-
cation of its own rewards (Bandura and Kupers, 1964; Bandura and Mischel, 1965; Bandura and Whalen, 1966; Mischel and Liebert, 1966). Marston (1965) has reported a similar experiment with adults. The paradigm
that has been employed most frequently is one in which a child observes
another person play a bowling game with a varying quality of performance.
For each discrete performance, the other person either takes or does not
take some candies or tokens of reward, in accordance with criteria which
are made explicit for the child. The criteria are verbalized aloud by the
other person, in the context of references to the deservingness of the performance. Some children observe the application of high criteria of performance, while others observe the application of low criteria. The child is
then permitted to play the game and to control its own rewards. Observations are made of the extent to which the child has been influenced by the
criteria which it has seen applied to performance in the game—particularly
of whether it will limit its rewards by adhering to high criteria. Generally
speaking, the influence is apparent and effective.

An account of the predominant effects of this type of paradigm on the
child's behavior does not require the use of the concept of a model. The

child's behavior in the performance of the game itself is not shown to be influenced by the behavior of the previous performer. Nor, with the possible exception of the experiment that is reported by Bandura and Kupers (1964), is there any evidence of an effect on the specific form of the child's behavior when it takes rewards. The effects appear to be mediated almost entirely by the provision of social information that engages the child's established values with respect to the control of reward by performance. Of course, the use of this information would require the child's cognitive representation of the performance-outcome contingencies which are appropriate to the situation. But it would not require the child to use the behavior which it has observed as a representational model for its own behavior.

There is a substantial amount of evidence which indicates that sheer information about appropriate values controls the effect of the child's observation of the self-imposed performance criteria of another person. For example, a number of studies have shown that the criteria which children use in rewarding themselves are as sensitive to the information that is provided in previous direct training as they are to the information that is provided in the previously observed self-rewarding behavior of others (Bandura and Whalen, 1966; Liebert and Ora, 1968; Mischel and Liebert, 1966). In the direct training paradigms, the criteria of reward are externally imposed on the child's own performance, but the explicit verbalizations which are used to communicate the criteria are the same as those which are used in the observational paradigms (except for the reference to the performer). Liebert and Ora (1968) found that children more often violated the performance criteria which they had observed previously when they themselves later had high subcriterial performances than they did when they had low subcriterial performances. This pattern of behavior suggested that the children were using their cognitive capacities to construct an extension of the rule that was implicit in the information which they had received. But it was not a reflection of behavior that they actually had observed.

Bee and Colle (1967) have reported findings which clearly suggest that the phenomenon which is observed in this type of experiment is heavily dependent on verbal elicitation of the child's application of established values to a specific situation. They found that children were not influenced by the self-imposed performance criterion of another person, when the verbalizations of the criterion omitted only the reference to the deservingness of the performance. McMains and Liebert (1968) also found that the adherence of children to the performance criteria which they had observed was highly sensitive to immediate situational information. When the children were

successively exposed to the inconsistent self-imposed criteria of two different people, they conformed to the criteria which they had observed most
recently. Bandura *et al.* (1967b) found that children would more readily
reward themselves in accordance with the observed high performance criteria of an adult if they also had observed social reinforcement of the
adult's use of the criteria. The children's conformity to the high criteria of
the adult was disrupted, however, by conditions which transmitted information that was contrary to application of the high criteria—for example,
by simultaneous exposure to a peer who used lower criteria, or by the nurturant behavior of the adult toward themselves.

Imitation through the representational use of a model does appear to be
one of the determinants of the behavioral effects which have been demonstrated in three other types of experiments which are summarized below.
Close examination of the findings of most of these experiments reveals,
however, that it is difficult to evaluate the extent to which behavioral correspondence between child and model is attributable to the acquired representational value of imitative acts. Most of the experiments do provide the
child with the opportunity to reproduce structural or sequential components of the model's behavior. Moreover, the behavior which is displayed by the children in some of the experiments seems to have an intrinsic expressive value that is independent of reinforcing external consequences. But even under these conditions, the reported descriptions and
analyses leave much uncertainty, in a number of cases, about the innovative features of the child's behavior and about its topographical fidelity
to the model.

It is generally the case that the analyses of the findings in experiments on
imitation give insufficient attention to the frequency and fidelity of the discrete components of behavior which are being taken as evidence of imitative learning. There is a heavy use of compound indices which throw together without distinction elements of behavior which would be very
different in their representational requirements—for example, the choice of
a color and a highly specific pattern of movement. As a result, there is
often a considerable question as to how much of the observed behavior is
being elicited from the child's established repertoire and how much is being
acquired by imitation. The problem of interpretation is not one of whether
the children would show the same behavior spontaneously, without the eliciting cues which are apparent in another person's behavior (it is usually
clear that they would not). The problem is rather one of whether the children have acquired new behavioral dispositions, and of whether these dis-

positions have acquired some intrinsic value which is derived at least initially from their having been representations of an external model.

The extent to which children have acquired representations of a model's behavior is especially difficult to estimate in the findings of the group of interesting experiments which Bandura and others have designed to demonstrate the effects of the observation of aggression on children's subsequent expression of their own aggressive dispositions in play situations (Bandura, 1965a; Bandura, Ross, and Ross, 1961, 1963a, 1963c; Hicks, 1965; Kuhn, Madsen, and Becker, 1967; Rosekrans and Hartup, 1967). The aggressive behavior of the children in these experiments shows some striking similarities to the behavior of the person whom they have observed (who is almost always an adult). The similarities may include evidence that a model's expressive mode of aggression has acquired some intrinsic value for the children. The evidence is uncertain, however, because both the situation and the child's behavioral predispositions seem to provide pleasure in the performance and inherent consequences of the aggressive acts which have been observed. The appropriateness and pleasurable vigor of the potential play aggression would be apparent to the child, not only from the cues which are transmitted in the observed behavior, but also from the presence of a highly attractive target for aggression (a very large inflated doll that is specifically designed to invite physical aggression and to provide a maximal response). It is especially interesting to note the finding by Kuhn *et al.* (1967) that frustration did not enhance, and in fact tended to suppress, children's performance of observed aggression in this type of setting.

It seems very probable that much of the aggression which is observed in these experiments is prepotent in the children's behavioral repertoires, and that its performance by the children does not require any substantial amount of learning through the representational use of a model. The aggressive acts of punching or kicking, for example, are not really novel forms of behavior for children. Although the occurrence of these acts of physical aggression may have become relatively infrequent, as a result of suppression and the availability of alternative forms of aggression, it is clear that they often can be released by appropriate situational cues. The more general releasing influence of observed aggression is also indicated in other findings of the experiments. When the full range of the children's aggressive behavior is presented in the treatment of the observations, it becomes apparent that aggression which is classified as nonimitative has an incidence at least as high as, and often higher than, the incidence of aggres-

sion which is classified as imitative. The representational status of the behavior in the imitative category would be easier to assess if analyses of the
individual components were presented separately and with more attention
to the fidelity of the components to the observed behavior. It would be interesting to know, for example, whether the children's aggression reflects
the more specific expressive motor patterns of the model, and also whether
their aggression corresponds to the model's aggression in being directed
against particular aspects of the target. More discriminate information
about the relative incidence of the child's reproductions of specific physical
and verbal components of aggression would also be useful to an assessment
of the extent to which different components may have been prepotent in the
child's repertoire. Bandura (1965a) makes the observation in one report
that children reproduce the verbal components of observed aggression with
a much lower frequency than they do the physical components. In what
appears to be the only report which specifically indicates the frequency of
imitative verbal aggression, Rosekrans and Hartup (1967) found that children reproduced virtually none of the aggressive utterances of a potential
adult model.

There are other experiments which are more effective demonstrations of
imitation through the representational use of a model, since the children
reproduce with some precision the expressive and relatively idiosyncratic
features of the behavior which they have observed. Bandura and Huston
(1961) found that children for whom a relationship to a nurturant adult
model had first been established were more inclined to imitate the model's
expressive task-irrelevant behavior than were children whose model had
assumed a non-nurturant role. Mussen and Parker (1965) have verified
this finding in an experiment in which the levels of nurturance which characterized the models had been established over a much longer period of
time. Mothers acted as models for their own daughters. And the girls more
readily adopted the expressive behavior of highly nurturant mothers than
they did the behavior of less nurturant mothers.

Bandura et al. (1963b) reported that children were more disposed to
repeat some of the unusual behavior patterns of adults who had controlled
and dispensed nurturant resources than they were to repeat the behavior of
adults who had subordinate or consumer roles. Some of the behavioral
effects which were reported in this last experiment may possibly have been
attributable to the children's empathic or vicarious experience. The experiment included conditions under which children did not directly experience
nurturant or rewarding behavior from another person, but rather observed

such behavior being directed toward a third person. Findings from a number of other experiments also indicate that the nurturant or rewarding attributes of either an adult or a peer model facilitate the child's disposition to reproduce the incidental motor and verbal features of the model's behavior (Hanlon, 1964; Hartup and Coates, 1967; Hetherington and Frankie, 1967). The experiment which was reported by Stein and Wright (1964) appears to be the only one in which the child's imitation of a model's expressive behavior was not facilitated by the model's nurturance toward the child.

A third type of experiment has focussed on aversive control of the child's reproduction of a model's behavior. For example, the author (Aronfreed, 1964) has reported an experiment in which children learned to apply a new self-critical label to their own actions by reproducing a specific verbal component of the punishment to which they had been exposed. Other investigators (Grusec, 1966; Mischel and Grusec, 1966) have replicated and attempted to extend this phenomenon. Experimental paradigms of socialization also have been used to demonstrate aversive control over the child's observational learning of sympathetic behavior (Aronfreed and Paskal, 1966). In general, these experiments on aversive control of observational learning employ a relatively discrete criterial act, rather than a pattern of behavior which has sequential or expressive features. The intrinsic representational value of the criterial act is therefore not apparent in any detailed fidelity to the internal structure of the model's behavior. The value of the act is instead demonstrated by comparisons among the effects of different sets of experimental contingencies which are arranged to show that the performance of the act has some independence of external outcomes, and that it is controlled primarily by the original temporal relationship between the model's performance and reduction of the child's anxiety or distress.

The findings of recent experimental studies of imitation include some very interesting and neglected evidence that clarifies the role of the child's attentional dispositions and cognitive capacities in the mechanisms of imitative learning. The evidence points to a competitive relationship between the child's representation of the expressive features of a model's behavior and its representation of the features which are instrumental to the control of outcomes. The facilitation of a child's representational imitation by its experience of nurturance from a model has been demonstrated repeatedly with young children of nursery school or kindergarten age, in experiments which we already have examined. In every one of these experiments, the model's nurturance facilitates the child's imitation of expressive behavior which is incidental to the model's control of performance in a task. Although the constraints on the performance of the task vary among the different experiments, there are always at least informational outcomes which indicate the accuracy or effectiveness of the model's performance. Some of the experiments have set the model's performance in a context of intentional observational learning, and then also have assessed the effects of the model's nurturance on the child's performance in the same task (Bandura *et al.,* 1967b; Bandura and Huston, 1961; Hanlon, 1964; Mussen and Parker, 1965). But the nurturance of the model does not appear to facilitate the child's observational learning of the task-directed aspects of the model's behavior. On the contrary, there are suggestions in some of the findings that nurturance may actually disrupt the child's task-oriented observational learning of contingencies between performance and outcomes.

It may not be surprising that the nurturance of a model has very different effects on the young child's dispositions to acquire, respectively, the expressive and instrumental features of the model's behavior. As every kindergarten teacher discovers, a climate of affection and pleasurable expressive activity quickly reaches a point of diminishing return when it is necessary for the child to engage in observational learning under the control of discriminate outcomes. However, our understanding of imitative learning can be broadened somewhat if we look further into the respective determinants of the young child's orientations toward the expressive form and the instrumentality of a model's behavior. In particular, there is more general evidence which indicates that young children have a limited capacity for the effective screening of task-relevant from task-irrelevant information.

Adults will use extensive representational rehearsal of task-relevant information which they have been explicitly instructed to learn and retain on an intentional basis (Dornbush and Winnick, 1967; Postman, 1964). But the findings of recent experiments with children indicate that there is a gradual developmental increment in the ability of children to separate relevant from irrelevant information in the course of intentional learning (Hagen and Sabo, 1967; Maccoby and Hagen, 1965; Siegel and Stevenson, 1966). As a result, the proportion of learning that is incidental to successful performance in a task shows a decline with increasing age. It appears that young children show less motivational and attentional persistence than do older children in a learning task which is governed by criteria or outcomes of performance. Some investigators of this phenomenon have adopted Broadbent's (1958) analysis of information channels, and have suggested that overloads of the young child's limited information-processing capacity may be responsible for its relatively ineffective separation of relevant and irrelevant information.

The important point, for our purpose here, is the possible extension of these findings to the phenomena of observational learning and imitation in children. The findings imply that young children may be more disposed to reproduce the expressive features of a model's behavior—those features which are incidental to the behavioral criteria of an effective outcome-controlled performance—in part because they give more attention to the model's expressive behavior, and in part because they have only a limited capacity for the representation of the discriminative control of the model's performance by both cues and outcomes. These inferences in turn suggest the possibility that the child's attention to a model's behavior, and also its cognitive representation of the behavior, may have different potential sources of affective control which are reflected, respectively, in the imitation of expressive behavior and in the observational learning of instrumental or task-oriented behavior. Imitative learning of expressive behavior appears to be controlled by the affective value of the behavior itself; whereas observational learning of instrumental behavior seems to be controlled by the value of external outcomes or criteria of performance.

Bandura and his associates have shown that children's overt representations of either the expressive or the task-oriented aspects of a model's behavior can be facilitated by instructions which focus their attention on the appropriate elements of behavior (Bandura et al., 1966; Bandura and Harris, 1966). A potential model's nurturance toward a child would direct the child's attention to many expressive features of both positive and aversive affective value in the model's behavior. It would also maximize the child's disposition to give a cognitive representation to the model's expressive behavior, and thus to exercise some control over its own affectivity. Parker and Nunnally (1966) have shown that stimuli which have been associated with reward enjoy an advantage in the selective attention of children. The findings of an experiment which has been reported by Grusec and Mischel (1966) provide some support for the expectation that this advantage would also produce a facilitative effect of nurturance on the child's cognitive representation of a model's expressive behavior. These investigators obtained a fairly direct assessment of the formation and retrieval of cognitive representations by avoiding a reliance on spontaneous imitative performance and instead asking children to recall and reproduce the actions of a model. They found that children who were the recipients of nurturance from their models were better able to recall the subsequent expressive behavior of the models than were children whose models had assumed a nonnurturant role, even though strong external incentives were offered for reproduction of the actions of either model. The effect of nurturance extended to the recall of expressive behavior which the model had used in criticizing and delaying the child's play activity—a finding which suggests that nurturance may produce a generalized enhancement of the child's attention to both positive and aversive affective expression in the model's behavior.

The control of children's imitation of expressive behavior by the affective value that is inherent in the behavior is also indirectly suggested in the finding by Bandura *et al.* (1966) that positive external incentives, which were introduced before the observation of a model, did not facilitate children's recall of the model's expressive behavior. Ross (1966) has reported another kind of evidence which suggests that the inherent affective value of a model's behavior facilitates the young child's incidental learning of the expressive components and interferes with its intentional learning of the task-oriented or performance components. She found that nursery school children who were judged by their teachers to be highly dependent showed more incidental learning of a model's task-irrelevant expressive behavior than did children who were judged to be relatively independent. In contrast, the independent children showed more intentional learning of task-relevant behavior. This finding is in accordance with the expectation that the nurturant attributes of a model would facilitate a child's representation of the model's expressive behavior. Highly dependent children would be expected to be more oriented than less dependent children toward the nurturance and attention of their potential adult models (such an orientation is, in fact, a major determinant of the rating of dependency.) Bandura and Huston (1961) also found some evidence which suggested a greater incidence of expressive imitation among highly dependent children.

We may conclude that children are highly attentive to the expressive behavior of their models, and that the young child's experience of nurturance from a model facilitates its disposition to represent the model's expressive actions in both cognition and behavior. The nurturant attributes of a model are not unique, however, in their affective control over the child's attention. The punitive or otherwise aversive attributes of a model will also elicit the child's attention to expressive features of the model's behavior. They may be particularly likely to capture the child's attention when they occur in a broader context of nurturance.

In general, it appears that young children are very sensitive to the changes of affectivity which are directly transmitted in the behavior of their socializing agents. Their sensitivity to the concrete expressive cues in the behavior of their potential models may reflect the fact that their own behavior has only begun to come under the control of more symbolic cognitive and verbal processes. Accordingly, affective control of the young child's behavior will tend to be heavily vested in the child's representation of the cues and outcomes which are directly transmitted in the expressive features of either the verbal or nonverbal behavior of others. The behavior of older children comes more under the affective control which can be attached to symbolic cues and outcomes, and to their representation of the abstract criteria for extended sequences of behavior (Lewis, Wall, and Aronfreed, 1963; McCullers and Stevenson, 1960). A developmental decline in children's affective and cognitive orientation to the expressive behavior of other people is undoubtedly the source of the common impression that young children imitate more extensively than do older children.

Although direct external reinforcement of the child's overt behavior is not required for observational learning, behavioral dispositions which are acquired initially through observational learning may be maintained selectively by the reinforcing or suppressive consequences of their overt expression. Much of the behavior that a child learns through observation may have the reinforcing outcomes which are inherent in the social or nonsocial effects that it necessarily produces in the external environment. For example, the effects of a child's imitative aggression on the object of aggression may have an already established affective value for the child, as a result of its past experience of the reinforcing consequences of aggression. Reward and other forms of direct social reinforcement will also exert selective control over the occurrence of behavior that the child has acquired through observational learning. Bandura (1965a) has reported a cleverly designed demonstration of the use of external incentives to induce further behavioral evidence of what children have retained from their observation of another person's aggressive actions, after the children first have had an opportunity to reproduce the actions on their own initiative. Grusec (1966) showed that termination of punishment could be used to increase the probability of children's self-critical reactions to their transgressions, after the reactions first had been acquired on the basis of observation of a model. These findings confirm what is obvious to common observation: that imitative behavior is jointly determined by the intrinsic value of the child's representation of a model and by the total reinforcement structure of specific situations.

A considerable amount of the behavior which children can learn by observation may be inappropriate to their prescribed social roles. Moreover, the fidelity of some of their imitative behavior is quite incidental to the aims of their socializing agents. The behavior will therefore sometimes be extinguished or suppressed by the nonreinforcing and punitive reactions of other people. Many of the cognitive templates which children acquire from their observation of models must be stored, perhaps for long periods of time, until appropriate external conditions of motivation and reinforcement are present. The intrinsic affective value of behavioral dispositions which are acquired through observational learning cannot be maintained, however, with an indefinite independence of external outcomes. Nor are these dispositions insensitive to the information that is provided by external social cues. The behavioral products of observational learning are continually supported by direct external reinforcement, and also by the child's further experience of the association between the observed behavior of others and its own potentially reinforcing changes of affective state. And the value of the behavior will continue to be dependent on the stimulus control of the external environment.

The fact that some forms of imitative behavior seem to have an intrinsic value that is partially independent of their instrumentality in producing external effects suggests one other possible determinant of observational learning and imitation: that children gradually acquire a generalized disposition to replicate the behavior of others, which is based on both the intrinsic and external reinforcement value of the behavioral products of their past observational learning. The generalized value of the behavior that could be produced by such a disposition might be attached not only to precise imitative reproduction of a model, but also to any acts which roughly corresponded to the acts of others. This kind of generalized disposition would still be sensitive, however, to the specific affective context in which the observed behavior of others occurred. Examples of this phenomenon may be present in recent demonstrations of behavior-contingent shaping of children's imitative dispositions (Baer *et al.,* 1967; Baer and Sherman, 1964; Lövaas *et al.,* 1966a; Metz, 1965), in which the repetition of a small subset of behavioral matches is maintained without reinforcement, in the context of a larger set of matches which are continuously reinforced. The implications of such a disposition for a general account of socialization deserve more attention than can be given to them here.

EMPATHIC AND VICARIOUS EXPERIENCE

The terms empathic and vicarious sometimes are used more or less as though they were synonyms (for example, Bandura and Walters, 1963a). The two terms could be usefully distinguished, however, in a way that conforms to their somewhat different connotations in ordinary usage. *Empathic* might be used to refer to an individual's affective experience when it is elicited by cues of a corresponding affective state in the expressive behavior of another person—for example, by facial or gestural cues which are directly expressive of pleasure or distress. *Vicarious* might be the more appropriate term when an individual's affective experience corresponds to what he himself would feel under conditions which he perceives through cues that provide information about how an external event impinges upon another person—for example, cues which are observed in another person's preparatory or orienting reactions, or in the consumption of a valued resource. The two forms of experience will often be interwoven, of course, since an observer frequently perceives both the immediate impact of external events upon another person and the expressive cues which transmit the person's affective reaction to the events.

The application of the concepts of empathic and vicarious must be restricted to the elicitation of an observer's affective response by *social* cues. Without this constraint, the application would be so broad and indiscriminate as to be of little value. For example, the concepts would be used too broadly if they were applied, without further criteria, to a demonstration that one child's behavior had been influenced by its observation of another child's attainment of rewards. There would be no provision for a distinction between the observing child's affective response to the reward contingency itself and its response to the perception of another person's experience.

The criteria which are suggested here for both empathic and vicarious experience emphasize the affective response of an observer, rather than the perceptual-motor effects which have sometimes been emphasized in other conceptions (for example, Krus, Werner, and Wapner, 1953). The criteria require only a similarity between the observer's affective state and the affectivity that the observer perceives (or cognizes) in another person's experience. They do not require an identity of affective experience between the observer and another person. Nor do they require that the observer perceive himself to be in the other person's role (cf. Mowrer, 1960b, p. 115). The exact quality of an affective state is a function of its cognitive context. And the context will often not be transmitted with high fidelity from the actual experience of one person to the empathic or vicarious experience of another. For example, the empathic response of a young child to the positive affective cues which are emitted by its mother may be relatively undifferentiated, in comparison to what may be the highly specific affective experience of the mother. Even between individuals of comparable cognitive complexity, empathic or vicarious transmission may produce only a rough correspondence of affective experience, because social cues frequently can be read with only partial accuracy. A child may respond with vicarious positive affect upon seeing the affection given to a sibling. But its affective experience may be qualitatively different from its corresponding experience as the direct recipient of affection.

The looseness of these constraints on cognitive matching does not limit empathic and vicarious experience to a gross correspondence between two people in the general direction of their affective states. Since the specific quality of an affective state is determined by its cognitive housing, empathic or vicarious experience will require some correspondence between the cognition of the observer and the cognition of the person who is being observed. In some instances, the correspondence may be quite close. The fact that another person's experience can be given a cognitive representation will often make it difficult to draw an empirical distinction between empathic and vicarious mediation of an observer's affective states. The types of cues which are criterial to the identification of the two forms of experience may be represented in cognition even when they are not directly perceived. For example, a child's perception of another person's handling of a highly valued object may elicit not only its vicarious experience, but also its empathic experience in response to a cognitive representation of the other person's affective expression (even though expressive cues are not directly observable). Likewise, an adult might be relatively indifferent to certain kinds of events, and yet might experience vicariously the impact of the events on a child, if he were able to represent to himself the child's affective experience.

Very early in the course of their development, children begin to show evidence of pleasurable or aversive affectivity in response to social cues which carry information about the affective experience of other people. Some years ago, Escalona (1945) reported an experiment which suggested that the juice preferences of infants could be changed as a result of their empathic responses to the affective cues in the behavior of their caretakers. However, it is usually difficult to identify truly empathic or vicarious control of behavior. A child's affective response to another person's expressive cues, or to the cues of the person's behavioral engagement of external events, may be partially attributable to the child's own direct experience of the positive or aversive properties of the cues. Such a phenomenon might occur quite commonly because of some generalization from the child's own direct past experience of the relevant stimuli—for example, the expressive cues may be components of the social rewards or punishments which the child has experienced previously. Or the observed cues of another person's experience may be perceived as signals which portend events of corresponding affective value to be directly experienced by the child (particularly when the child's behavior may have been the source of the other person's observed experience).

To the extent that children experience social stimuli as having direct consequences for themselves, the concepts of empathic and vicarious are not required to account for the affective value of the stimuli. The concepts are applicable only to those components of the child's affectivity which are elicited by its perception of the affective experience of others—that is, to those components which are independent of the child's perception of social stimuli as having a direct impact upon itself. The application of this criterion obviously will be highly dependent on the child's cognition of concrete stimulus events. It is of some interest that the criterion of empathic experience is not fully met, for example, in experiments where animals have been shown to produce various response indices of aversion to the distress cues which are emitted by other animals (Church, 1959; Miller, 1961; Miller, Caul, and Mirsky, 1967). These experiments examine the behavioral effects of a prior association between observed distress cues and the direct experience of pain by the observing animal, in situations where the cues might well retain the value of signals which have directly aversive consequences for the observer.

The establishment of a child's empathic and vicarious dispositions might be thought of as being in itself one form of internalization, since these dispositions enable the control of the child's behavior to become somewhat independent of its direct experience of social reward or punishment. The origins of empathic and vicarious dispositions in the child's early experience are therefore of considerable interest in an outline of the mechanisms of socialization. The basic mechanism for the attachment of a child's affective response to the perceived experience of another person was suggested many years ago by both Allport (1924, p. 235) and Humphrey (1922). It is essentially a conditioning mechanism that rests on a close and repeated association between cues which convey the experience of others and stimulus events which have direct affective consequences for the child. This social conditioning process will be illustrated here by the paradigm for establishing the empathic transmission of positive affect. The reader can then easily construct for himself the corresponding paradigm for the aversive case and the paradigms for vicarious transmission.

Socialization provides many contingencies which would attach a child's empathic affective response to the expressive cues which signal another person's positive affective state. For example, certain kinds of pleasurable events may be directly experienced simultaneously by both the child and another person, and may thus occur in close contiguity with the other person's expressive cues of positive affect, with the result that the child's own affectivity becomes conditioned to the expressive cues. But a much more common basis for the necessary contingencies would be the high probability of coincidence between the positive affectivity of socializing agents and their disposition to behave in ways which directly induce corresponding affectivity in the child. This coincidence is effectively present in the child's earliest relationships to its caretakers. Parents are more likely to respond to their children with increments of affection and approval when their own behavior is under the control of positive affect. The affective states of the parents, and the changes in their behavior toward the child, may be elicited by the child's own behavior or may be entirely independent of it. In either case, the crucial association is between the expressive affective cues of a socializing agent and the direct experience of pleasurable events by the child.

Expressive cues may be initially subordinated, in the child's perception, to the total complex of social stimuli which is transmitted in the behavior of a socializing agent. As the cues become increasingly discriminable to the child, however, they can acquire their own distinct capacity to elicit its affectivity, under conditions where they are no longer perceived by the child as having direct consequences for itself. The empathic value of the cues may then be maintained by occasional repetition of the contingencies through which it was originally acquired. The importance of early social experience in the establishment of empathic responsiveness is suggested in the finding by Miller *et al.* (1967) that the distress cues of another monkey were a much more effective warning signal for the avoidance behavior of feral monkeys than they were for the behavior of monkeys who were artificially reared in social isolation.

The most direct attempts to demonstrate empathic or vicarious experience have used peripheral autonomic indices of the arousal of an observer's anxiety or distress in response to cues of pain or distress from another person (or animal), or in response to cues which are being used as objective indicators of the magnitude of the painful stimulation that another person experiences (Bandura and Rosenthal, 1966; Berger, 1962; Haner and Whitney, 1960; Lazarus et al., 1962; Miller et al., 1967). Another relatively direct approach has been the assessment of the generalized arousal effect of another person's pain cues on the observer's reponses in a simple reaction time task (DiLollo and Berger, 1965). These demonstrations are not designed to show how empathic and vicarious experience function to reduce the requirements of direct reward and punishment in the control of social behavior. However, attempts to examine the control of empathic or vicarious experience over overt behavior have been made in a great number of experiments with children (Bandura, 1965a; Bandura et al., 1967a, 1967b; Bandura et al., 1963c; Jones, 1924; Rosekrans and Hartup, 1967; Walters et al., 1963; Walters and Parke, 1964a; Walters et al., 1965). In these experiments, the child's behavior is shown to be influenced by its observation of another person's behavior and of the consequences of the behavior. The general strategy of the experiments assumes a demonstration of the child's empathic or vicarious experience of the outcomes of another person's behavior when the child's observation of the outcomes has no immediate consequences for itself, but does result in subsequent facilitation or suppression of its own behavior.

In a few of the studies which are cited above, the effects of the sheer observation of another person's behavior may be more important than the effects of observing any explicit outcomes. For example, the well-known study by Jones (1924) showed that a child's fearful behavior could sometimes be eliminated by placing the child, together with another child who was not afraid, directly into the fear-provoking situation. In a much more effective demonstration, Bandura et al. (1967a) have shown that children who fear dogs can be induced to approach and engage in physical contact with a dog, even without the immediate situational support of a fearless child's behavior, if they simply have observed another child's progressively more intimate contacts with the dog on earlier occasions. The experimental conditions of these demonstrations make it difficult to infer that the behavior of the observer is being influenced by the affective value of outcomes of the observed behavior. The observed behavior itself might well elicit affective or behavioral dispositions which are incompatible with the observer's original avoidance reactions—for example, pleasurable feelings which have been associated with the observer's own past experience in handling other pets. A large component of social facilitation, much like that which has been demonstrated in similar experiments with animals (Angermeier, Schaul, and James, 1959; Davitz and Mason, 1955), may therefore be included in the effect of reduction of the child's avoidance of the feared object.

Most of the studies which have been cited above do demonstrate effects which clearly go beyond the social facilitation that might be expected merely on the basis of the child's observation of another person's behavior. The effects are usually specific to the consequences of the observed behavior for the other person. Many of the effects are obtained in paradigms where the child's behavior is under some degree of constraint as a result of its past socialization or of prohibitions which are given in the situation. Since the behavioral tests are often made in the absence of external surveillance, or at least in the absence of external evaluation, the effects are relevant to an understanding of how social observation elicits the child's internalized control over its behavioral dispositions.

The findings of the experiments which have been reported by Walters and his associates (Walters et al., 1963; Walters and Parke, 1964a; Walters et al., 1965) indicate that a child's violation of a prohibition on the handling of a forbidden toy may be suppressed by its previous observation of the punitive outcomes of another child's violation. There is less evidence for a facilitative effect that is specific to observation of the rewarding outcomes of another child's violation. Bandura and his co-workers (Bandura, 1965a; Bandura et al., 1963c) have demonstrated similar suppressive effects on the aggressive behavior of children who have observed the punishment of the corresponding aggressive acts of adult models. Wheeler and Smith (1967) found that observation of the censure of another person's aggression also had some suppressive effect on the subsequent aggressive behavior of adult observers. Bandura et al. (1967b) have reported that children who observe the self-imposed performance-reward criteria of an adult are more likely to apply the same criteria to their own performance if they also have observed that the adult receives social approval for use of the criteria.

Recent summaries of the findings of this type of experiment appear to assume that a rapid form of observational learning, based on the observer's empathic or vicarious experience of reward and punishment, is required to account for the experimental effects (Bandura, 1965b; Kanfer, 1965). The criteria for empathic and vicarious experience which have been outlined here would not permit their presence to be inferred, however, merely from evidence that a child's behavior had been influenced by its observation of the outcomes of another person's actions. The affective value of the information that is carried in the observed reward or punishment of another person's behavior would be sufficient in itself to elicit or suppress the child's corresponding behavioral dispositions, without the requirement that the child respond to social cues which convey the affective experience of the other person. Moreover, it is by no means clear that the experimental effects require any significant amount of learning on the child's part. These demonstrations of the influence of social observation on the child's behavior do reveal the child's capacity for cognitive representation of information from its environment. But they do not necessarily provide evidence either of learning or of empathic or vicarious experience.

The importance of the simple transmission of information, as a determinant of the effects of observing the outcomes of another person's behavior, is clearly indicated in the findings of other experiments, in which the learning or performance of children has been shown to be sharply affected by their prior observation of the actual or simulated behavioral choices of another child or an adult, in tasks which require varying degrees of verbal or motor complexity and integration (Bruning, 1965; Ditrichs et al., 1967; Kobasigawa, 1965; Poliakova, 1958; Rosekrans, 1967). In these demonstrations, the child has the opportunity to observe the occurrence and magnitude of outcomes which indicate the correctness or effectiveness of another person's behavior. Rewarding outcomes in the form of candy or verbal approval are used most frequently. The same types of effects have been obtained with adult subjects when they are given information through observation of the outcomes of another person's performance on a task (Craig, 1967; Kanfer and Marston, 1963a; Lewis and Duncan, 1958; Marston, 1966). The ambiguity in the interpretation of these studies, as in the interpretation of the other studies which we have examined, arises primarily from the difficulty of making the inference that empathic or vicarious experience occurs. This difficulty could be resolved if there were available an overt behavioral index of the affective value which the social cues of another person's experience have for the observer during the period of observation.

Much the same difficulty of interpretation is apparent in the conflicting results of experiments with both adults and children on the question of whether the mere observation of another person's aggression, without observation of its consequences for the person, will strengthen or reduce the observer's own aggressive dispositions (Bandura *et al.*, 1963a; Berkowitz and Geen, 1966, 1967; Feshbach, 1961; Rosenbaum and deCharms, 1960; Wheeler and Caggiula, 1966). Comparisons among the results suggest that the observation of aggression does have generalized motivational effects. But the behavioral expression of these effects seems to be determined in part by the arousal of anger in the observer before the period of observation, and in part by the correspondence between the observed aggression and the potential aggressive behavior that the test situation permits to the observer. The results also suggest that the observer's subsequent aggression is sensitive to social cues which provide information about the appropriateness or permissibility of aggressive behavior.

A general conclusion that may be drawn from all of the conceptual and empirical distinctions which have been made here is that empathic or vicarious affective control of overt behavior might be examined more effectively if social cues were used as contingent outcomes of the observer's own overt performance of an act. It would then be possible to demonstrate the reinforcing or suppressive effects of the cues, even though they had no directly positive or aversive consequences for the observer. Two examples of such demonstrations will be presented in a later chapter, under the description of paradigms which are designed to study the mechanisms of the socialization of altruistic and sympathetic behavior.

🌿 CHAPTER FIVE 🌿

POSITIVE CONTROL
OF
CONDUCT

Anyone who has observed socialization at first hand can hardly fail to be impressed with the extent to which the conduct of children is shaped by rewards and other socially transmitted positive outcomes of their overt behavior. These outcomes most frequently take the form of reinforcing events which are directly experienced by the child. But a child's empathic or vicarious affective response to the effects which it perceives its actions to have upon others can also sometimes mediate the positive control of its behavior. Behavior-contingent channels of social learning are not, of course, the only source of positive control of conduct. Another important source lies in the pleasurable affective contexts in which children observe the behavior of others, including those contexts in which the observed behavior may serve as a model for imitation. Both of these sources of positive control contribute to internalization through the affective value which they may attach to the intrinsic perceptual and cognitive correlates of the child's own behavior.

The selective positive social reinforcement of certain forms of conduct will often tend to increase the relative effectiveness of punishment in the suppression of other forms, when it happens that both the reinforced and the punished acts serve the same motivational dispositions. In general, the emergence of the child's entire repertoire of internalized behavior, in a particular area of conduct, will be attributable to both positive and aversive control. It is nevertheless possible to abstract the positive components of internalization from the socialization matrix and to examine them independently.

Many forms of conduct which eventually come under the control of complex evaluative decision-making processes may be differentiated out of broader behavioral dispositions which have been established very firmly by the child's early experience of the pleasurable contingencies of a social environment. Positive social reinforcement can be seen to make a very substantial contribution, for example, to the learning and internalization of the kind of behavior that may be described as giving or sharing. The rudiments of giving and sharing ordinarily occur with high frequency in the repertoire of the infant and young child. Young children frequently hold out or pass their food, their clothes, and their playthings to their caretakers. There are likewise many episodes in which they may bring something that another person needs or pick up an object that the person has dropped. Children also actively give their affection to others. Socializing agents tend to selectively reinforce all of these forms of behavior with either explicit approval or increments of attention and affection. One effect of their reinforcement is the attachment of some positive affective value to the intrinsic correlates of the behavior itself. This intrinsic value then becomes the foundation for more specific and intentional forms of conduct such as altruism or generosity. It should be noted, however, that there is often some ambiguity about the extent to which conduct that has positive consequences for others is actually internalized. Since it most often occurs in a context where another person is present, it may be sustained by the child's anticipation of increased affection or approval for itself.

Honesty is another area of conduct that has early rudiments which are heavily supported by positive social reinforcement. Young children have considerable early experience, for example, with the consequences of behavior that is oriented toward possession. They are often confronted with choices between objects which are their own and objects which belong to others. The distinctions to be made among such objects do not initially require evaluative concepts of property. The child needs only to discriminate the stimulus features of its own toys, of the things which it is permitted to handle, or of the portion of food set at its place. Its parents frequently will respond with approval or other rewards when its behavior is directed toward objects which they consider to be appropriate. The internalized derivatives of the parents' reinforcement may be apparent quite early in socialization, when the young child shows signs of pleasure in being able simply to identify its own possessions or in knowing which objects it is permitted to touch. The child's early experience with self-report is another example of how the rudiments of honesty are fostered by direct social reward. Children commonly are asked, as soon as they are verbal, to report on their activities. Parents often give praise or affection to a child for an accurate report, in part because of the sheer functional value of correct information, and in part because they sometimes intentionally wish to support truthfulness itself.

The high probability of selective positive reinforcement that is associated with the forerunners of altruism, generosity, and honesty does not fully account for either the speed or the extensiveness with which these socially valued forms of conduct often become clearly identifiable in children's behavior. Once such behavioral dispositions have been acquired by the child, they appear to proliferate rapidly in the direction of specific acts and social objects which were not originally at the focus of direct positive reinforcement. For example, young children usually quickly extend their sharing or altruistic dispositions to include appropriate behavior toward siblings, peers, animals, and dolls. Yet the reinforcing reactions of these objects of their behavior may not be so predictable or so powerful as those of a parent. It seems unlikely that the rapid spread of many forms of conduct which are acquired relatively early in the course of socialization can be attributed entirely to the shaping of the child's overt behavior by reinforcing outcomes, even when allowance is made for the effects of such phenomena as stimulus generalization and behavioral drift. The breadth of these forms of conduct is more probably under the control of the child's cognitive representation and imitative reproduction of whole classes of related acts which it has observed in the behavior of its nurturant caretakers. Altruistic and generous behavior may well have a significant advantage in imitative learning, in comparison to other forms of conduct, because their appearance in the behavior of a model is often closely associated with their directly pleasurable consequences for the child.

In recent years, there have been a great many experimental studies of the effects of positive social reinforcement on the learning and performance of children (see the review by Stevenson, 1965). Very few of these studies bear directly on the socialization of conduct, and even fewer provide any evidence that is relevant to mechanisms of internalization. Walters and Brown (1964) have shown that positive reinforcement of a child's physical aggression against a large doll can facilitate the child's immediately subsequent aggression against a peer in a different situation. Lövaas (1961b) used positive reinforcement to increase the incidence of children's verbal aggression against a doll. The effects of the reinforcement also were evident when the children subsequently were given the opportunity to use physical aggression against the doll. Bandura (1965a) has demonstrated that positive external incentives may be used to induce children to perform the aggressive behavior of a model whom they have observed previously. However, none of these experiments is addressed to the problem of how the control of aggressive behavior becomes internalized.

Some evidence of internalization is demonstrated quite often in situational assessments of the suppression of behavior that is under a social prohibition—for example, in assessments of the conformity to rules which either children or adults may show in the absence of external surveillance (Burton, Maccoby, and Allinsmith, 1961; Grinder, 1962; Kimbrell and Blake, 1958; Lefkowitz, Blake, and Mouton, 1955; Sears, Rau, and Alpert, 1965, Chapter 6). Although the suppression that is observed in these situations undoubtedly has a large component of aversive control, it may also be under the positive control of the effects of the subject's past experience of the rewarding consequences of conformity. In fact, such situational observations of conformity to explicit prohibitions cannot be used to draw inferences about underlying mechanisms of internalized control. It is not possible to estimate the relative contributions which positive and aversive affective control make to the internalized value of the conforming behavior. The same limitation of inference is present in observations of the influence of social example on a child's sharing or charitable behavior (Rosenhan and White, 1967), or on its evaluative judgements of conduct (Bandura and McDonald, 1963; Turiel, 1966), when there is not sufficient evidence to indicate that the child's behavior or judgement is specifically under the control of positive affectivity.

A part of this problem of inference is nicely illustrated in the findings of the recent experiment by Hartup and Coates (1967). These investigators found that, among children who were accustomed to a generally high incidence of positive interaction with their peers, the observed generosity of a specific peer had a strongly facilitative effect on the subsequent generosity of children who had much positive interaction with that peer, but only a mild effect on the generosity of children who had no positive interaction with that peer. The direction of the difference between the two effects was reversed, however, for children who generally experienced a low incidence of positive interaction with their peers. Since the experimental test situation was one in which the generous peer was close at hand, and in which the child would almost certainly have perceived that its choices could be observed, it is obvious that the influence of the behavior of peers on the second group of children may have been primarily under the aversive control of fear of social disapproval or rejection.

Cooperation (and competition) is a type of social behavior that has often been shown to be malleable to positive social reinforcement, but without much evidence that the behavior can be brought under internalized control. Many experiments have demonstrated that rewards which are controlled by specific contingencies of social interaction can be used to establish and maintain cooperative behavior or sharing between children (Azrin and Lindsley, 1956; Fischer, 1963; Weingold and Webster, 1964), between human adults (Deutsch and Krauss, 1960; Kelley et al., 1962; Sidowski, Wyckoff, and Tabory, 1956), and between animals (Boren, 1966; Mason, 1959; Nissen and Crawford, 1936). The findings of a few of these studies indicate that the induced cooperative behavior may have some temporary stability when external reinforcement is withdrawn (during extinction procedures). But none of the studies provides evidence that cooperative behavior has acquired any intrinsic value that makes it partially independent of the subject's anticipation of external rewards which have been available previously—in contrast to the kind of internalized affective value that appears to govern behavior which is sustained, for example, by an individual's empathic or vicarious response to its consequences for another person. We will examine this problem in more detail in our later analysis of altruistic and sympathetic behavior.

Surveys of the child-rearing practices of parents provide some limited information about the effects of direct parental reward on the child's internalization of control over its social behavior. However, the reported correlations between the use of explicit rewards by parents and indices of the child's behavior may also reflect the hidden effects of the child's observational learning and imitation of the parents. In a number of surveys, the frequency or magnitude of parental reward that is given specifically for the child's independence and initiative have been found to show a positive correlation with various indices of the child's achievement motivation and performance (Crandall, Preston, and Rabson, 1960; McClelland, 1955; Rosen and D'Andrade, 1959; Winterbottom, 1958). In contrast, the more general disposition of parents to reward their children with verbal approval and affection does not appear to show a consistent direction in its relationship to the children's honesty or responsibility outside of the home (Bronfenbrenner, 1961; Burton *et al.,* 1961; Grinder, 1962; Sears *et al.,* 1965, Chapter 6). The contrast between the two sets of findings may be attributable in part to differences in the specificity with which the relevant surveys assess the parents' application of rewards to particular areas of the child's behavior. However, the contrast may also reflect with some accuracy a difference between the two areas of conduct in the extent to which the effects of reward are determined by the complementary effects of punishment. Many parents may use punishment earlier and more intensively in their control of conduct that is relevant to the child's honesty or responsibility than they do in their attempts to exercise control over the child's achievement dispositions.

The effects of social experience on the internalization of positive affective control over behavior are more consistently apparent in the extensive body of evidence which Mischel and others have gathered on children's choices between immediate and delayed rewards. The basic paradigm for this evidence is one in which the child must choose between an immediate small reward and a delayed larger reward. Choices of the delayed reward cannot, of course, be regarded as behavior that is internalized in the sense of being independent of external outcomes. But choices of delayed reward are an indication that the child controls its behavior with some freedom from immediately available incentives, and that its control rests on internalized representations of incentives which are relatively remote in time. Mischel (1958, 1961a, 1961b, 1961c) began this line of work with observations of children in West Indian subcultures. These observations suggested that children's choices of immediate or delayed rewards were determined by the extent to which the conditions of their socialization reinforced their tolerance of delay and their exercise of active control over the occurrence of rewards. The importance of the children's more generalized dispositions toward internalized maintenance of behavior over time, without the support of immediate external reinforcement, was also suggested in a number of related findings. For example, choices of the delayed reward were more frequent among nondelinquents than among delinquents, and were more characteristic of responsible than of irresponsible children. Choices of delayed rewards were also correlated directly with the children's accuracy in time statements, directly with their scores on a measure of orientation toward achievement, and inversely with their acquiescence to social influence.

Subsequent experimental studies which have used North American children as subjects have provided further evidence that choices of delayed rewards are a function of the child's more generalized expectation of being able to successfully predict and control the available rewards in its social environment. Metzner (1963) found that children more frequently made voluntary choices of delayed reward when their own performance would control the occurrence of reward than they did when they would be required simply to wait for the reward. Mischel and Gilligan (1964) observed that children who chose delayed rewards were slower to cheat and cheated less, in a game of skill, than did children who chose immediate rewards. Mischel and Staub (1965) found that children who had been given an experience of successful performance on a task were more willing to choose delayed rewards which would be contingent on their subsequent performance, in preference to immediate noncontingent rewards, than were children who had been given an experience of failure. Mischel and Grusec (1967) have shown that children's choices of uncertain delayed rewards increase in frequency with increasing probability of reward, and decrease in frequency with increasing interval of delay. Bandura and Mischel (1965) have used an adult's verbalizations of the relative predictability and value of immediate and delayed rewards to produce shifts in children's initial preferences. Mischel's (1966) recent review cites other evidence that the positive control of delayed rewards over a child's behavior is a reflection of the child's more general anticipation of being able to predict and produce a rewarding environment.

The use of the effects of direct social reward to examine mechanisms of internalization can be illustrated by a method that is employed in one segment of a series of experiments which are presently being conducted by the author. The subjects are eight- to ten-year-old boys and girls, and the experimental agent of socialization is an adult male. In the socialization paradigm, each child is required to choose repeatedly, over the course of ten training trials, between a highly attractive small toy and a relatively unattractive toy. The pairs of toys vary over trials. The child's task is to pick up and describe one of the toys on each trial. Initial instructions make it clear that reward will be contingent on the child's choices. But the instructions do not specify the contingency. The agent rewards the child with verbal approval (*Good!*) and candy whenever it chooses the unattractive toy, but gives no reaction when the child chooses the attractive toy. For one group of children, reward is given as soon as the child's hand reaches for an attractive toy. For a second group of children, reward is given only after the child already has picked up the toy. In an immediately subsequent test situation, the agent leaves the room on the pretext of an apparently time-consuming errand. The child is left alone with another pair of toy objects, under conditions of complete privacy which are carefully designed to convey that there is no prospect of reward or even of external knowledge of the child's behavior. Hidden timers record the occurrence and latency of the child's handling of each of the two test objects.[1]

In the training paradigm which is described above, the children typically choose the attractive toys for two or three trials, and then shift to consistent choices of the unattractive toys. The learning process is quite rapid for all of the children in this relatively simple discrimination situation, and there is accordingly no significant difference between the immediate and delayed reward groups in the number of errors which occur during training. The interesting effects occur during the test for internalization, when the opportunity for social reward has been withdrawn. The vast majority of children pick up and handle the unattractive test toy before they pick up

---

[1] The effect is reliable for both boys and girls, and there is no difference between the sexes in its magnitude. Forty children, equally divided by sex, are used in each of the two experimental conditions.

the attractive test toy. This pattern of behavior occurs among virtually all of the children who have been trained under immediate reward. The effect of the timing of reward for previous choices of unattractive toys is even more apparent in the latencies with which children pick up the toys after the agent has left the scene. Children who have been rewarded immediately upon reaching for unattractive toys during training pick up the unattractive test object more quickly than do children who have been rewarded only after they already have picked up the unattractive toys during training.

The effect of immediacy of reward in this experiment occurs in the speed with which the children make a choice that falls within a previously rewarded class of choices, after learning already has taken place, and when external sources of reward clearly have been withdrawn. The greater effectiveness of the immediate reward is in general agreement with the findings of many other experiments in which delayed reward has been shown to be less effective than immediate reward in facilitating children's performance (Setterington and Walters, 1964; Terrell, 1964; Walters, 1964; Ware and Terrell, 1961). In this case, however, the effect is not apparent during the learning process—a finding that is consistent with an earlier report by Hockman and Lipsitt (1961) of no delayed reward effect on children's learning of a simple discrimination. It should also be noted that the requirement of picking up the unattractive toy may have compensated for the lack of immediate reinforcement, during the delayed reward training paradigm, by maintaining the child's orientation toward the stimulus object which was associated with reward. There is other evidence that maintenance of a goal orientation may bridge a delay in the occurrence of reward. Fagan and Witryol (1966) have found that the effects of immediate and delayed reward on learning can be made more equivalent by instructing children to maintain an orientation toward the locus of reward during the interval of delay.

It does not appear that the experimental effect which has been described here can be attributed merely to differences in the external incentive value which the unattractive toys acquired for the children. Lipsitt and Castaneda (1958) found that stimuli which were associated with immediate reward acquired more positive incentive value for children than did stimuli which were associated with delayed reward. During the training paradigms of the present experiment, however, the delayed reward was actually closer in time to the point of the child's maximal contact with an unattractive toy (the point at which the toy was picked up) than was the immediate reward, because the immediate reward was given as the child only initiated its choices. The experimental effect therefore provides some support for the inference that the intrinsic correlates of an immediately rewarded act acquire more control over the child's positive affectivity than do the intrinsic correlates of an act that has received delayed reward. The magnitude of the positive affective value that would become conditioned to the behavioral or representational precursors of a previously rewarded act would be expected to be a function of how early the reward originally occurred in the course of the onset and performance of the act.

Experiments with adult subjects have shown that a number of parameters of direct external positive reinforcement, for performance in various kinds of learning tasks, will facilitate the accuracy or effectiveness of a subject's own administration of reinforcing events during his continued performance on the same task (Kanfer, Bradley, and Marston, 1962; Kanfer and Marston, 1963b; Marston and Kanfer, 1963). Although these experiments are interesting demonstrations of the capacity of human subjects to administer their own external reinforcements, the findings cannot readily be used to draw inferences about mechanisms of internalization. The self-reinforcement situation is essentially one in which the subject merely assumes control over the occurrence of a concrete external event. The external event retains the same significance, as an indicator of correct performance in a task, that was originally given to it by direct social instruction. And there is no evidence that value becomes independently attached to any intrinsic correlates of the performance. The self-reinforcement test situation appears to elicit the subjects' already established dispositions to provide themselves with reinforcing external information about their behavior, rather than to establish the internalized value of the behavior itself.

There are somewhat different problems associated with the inferences which may be drawn from studies in which either direct training or observation of another person's behavior is shown to influence the performance criteria to which children adhere when they subsequently exercise their own control over the administration of their rewards (Bandura and Kupers, 1964; Bandura and Whalen, 1966; Liebert and Ora, 1968; Mischel and Liebert, 1966). The children are usually alone, or are at least free of any explicit external control, in the situations which are used to test for the effects of training or observation in these experiments. And the children's exercise of some internalized control over their behavior is indicated in the fact that they often maintain high performance criteria in rewarding themselves, even though their choice of criteria does not appear to be under direct external constraint. However, as was pointed out in the last chapter, the findings of these experiments may be largely attributable to elicitation of the child's already established cognitive structures for the evaluation of performance-reward contingencies. The total pattern of results suggests that the children are engaged in making decisions about how to utilize available rewards, and that they choose from among alternative options in their system of values.

Bandura and Perloff (1967) have shown that children may choose and maintain very high criteria for themselves, when they are permitted to exercise complete private control over the evaluation and reward of their own performances, even though they have not been exposed to the influence of either direct training or social observation. The external information that is provided for children in other experiments which utilize the paradigm of self-controlled reward, either through the imposition of criteria on their own past performance or through their observation of the criteria used by others, appears to act simply as a situational selector among alternative criteria within the range prescribed by their evaluative dispositions. The influence of immediate situational cues on the children's evaluative decisions is clearly suggested in the sensitivity of their decisions to the inconsistencies which are observed in other people's application of the criteria (Bandura, Grusec, and Menlove, 1967b; McMains and Liebert, 1968), and also in their sensitivity to slight changes in the evaluative terms which are used to verbalize the criteria (Bee and Colle, 1967).

It is interesting to note that the effects which are obtained in these experiments may also reflect a component of prohibitive and aversive control over the performance criteria which the children use in the test situation, even though the children are administering rewards to themselves. The direct training paradigms, for example, are not structured so that the child is rewarded for its own applications of the appropriate criteria. Permission and prohibition are instead directly imposed on the child's use of available rewards as a function of its performance. Moreover, the verbalizations which the child hears, in the context of either direct training or observation of another person's self-imposed criteria, include explicit evaluations of subcriterial performances as being not deserving of reward. The aversive aspect of such a paradigm is reflected in the finding by Bandura and Kupers (1964) that some children, when they were applying the criteria to their own performance, also repeated the self-critical as well as the self-approving comments which they previously had heard used by another person. Some external prohibitive constraint may also be present in the visibility of the supply of candy or tokens with which the child rewards its own performance. From the child's point of view, frequent use of the supply without regard to its performance may provide an external marker of violation of the previously imposed or observed criteria.

We reviewed in the last chapter a number of experiments in which the nurturance of a model was shown to facilitate children's imitation of the model's expressive behavior. Generally speaking, the expressive modes which are used in these experiments do not fall within the range of behavior that is ordinarily treated as conduct. An exception is the finding by some investigators that the nurturance of a model facilitates a child's learning of the self-critical application of the verbal components of the model's punitive behavior (Grusec, 1966; Grusec and Mischel, 1966; Mischel and Grusec, 1966). However, as we will later note in a more extended analysis of self-criticism, this type of effect of the nurturant attributes of a model is probably mediated by facilitation of the model's aversive control of the child's behavior, rather than by facilitation of the model's positive control.

Another group of experiments, to which we can give more attention here, has focussed on the effects of the child's observation of the consequences of another person's actions for that person, when the child is immediately given an opportunity to behave in the same way. These experiments have in common their assessment of the effects of social observation under conditions in which the child's own behavior is not rewarded and cannot readily be attributed to the expectation of reward. The child's behavior often is observed in a setting that is apparently private. As was pointed out earlier, however, it is not possible to determine from the findings of such experiments whether the effects are the result of the child's empathic or vicarious experience of the outcomes of another person's behavior, or whether they simply reflect control of the child's behavior by the affective value of information about its possible consequences.

It has turned out to be quite difficult to show that the behavior of children can be influenced significantly by their observation of the rewarding outcomes of another person's behavior. The difficulty seems to stem in part from the use of behavior that is well provided with its own reinforcing consequences and does not require the additional support of more explicit social reward. For example, Bandura, Ross, and Ross (1963c) found that children who had observed the aggressive behavior of an adult were more likely to show similar behavior, when subsequently given the opportunity to do so, if they had also seen the behavior rewarded rather than punished. Rosekrans and Hartup (1967) found that children who had observed only rewarding consequences of an adult's aggressive behavior subsequently displayed more corresponding behavior than did children who had observed only punishment of the aggression or children who had observed both reward and punishment on different occasions. The findings of these experiments did not make it clear, however, whether the difference in the effects of the observed consequences of aggression was produced by the facilitative effect of reward or by the suppressive effect of punishment. The difference might well have been localized entirely in one of these two possible effects. In a subsequent study, Bandura (1965a) found no difference, in the behavioral effects of observation of an adult's aggression, between children who had seen the aggression rewarded and those who had seen it followed by neither reward nor punishment.

When these findings are taken together with the relatively negligible amount of aggressive behavior that is shown by children who are not exposed to an aggressive model, they suggest that the children's aggression may have been facilitated by the sheer motivational and informational impact of observing another person's aggression. When the social environment is structured to support the inherent reinforcement value of a specific form of behavior (for example, when it provides an attractive object of aggression), then it may be difficult to obtain any further control over the behavior through the positive affective value of observed or anticipated external rewards. This inference also is confirmed by the findings in Rosekrans' (1967) demonstration of preadolescents' adoption of the strategic actions which they have observed in the filmed presentation of a peer's performance at a game. When the behavior has less support from its inherently reinforcing consequences, then it may be more susceptible to facilitation by the child's observation of the social reward of another person's corresponding behavior—as, for example, in the case of sharing behavior (Doland and Adelberg, 1967). Other examples of the facilitation of children's behavior by their observation of the rewarding consequences of another person's corresponding behavior can be found in the recent reports by Bandura et al. (1967b) and by Ditrichs, Simon, and Greene (1967).

The same conclusions may be drawn from the findings of studies, which have been reported by Walters and his co-workers, of the effects of children's observation of the outcomes of another child's violation of a prohibition on the handling of attractive toys. Walters, Leat, and Mezei (1963) found that children were more likely to violate such prohibitions, when it appeared that they were free of surveillance, if they had seen another child rewarded for doing so than if they had seen another child punished. However, in subsequent studies in which some groups of children observed violations without social consequences for the violators (Walters and Parke, 1964a; Walters, Parke, and Cane, 1965), there proved to be no differences in counter-suppressive effects, during the tests for internalized suppression, between children who had seen violations rewarded and those who had seen violations followed by no consequences. Stein (1967) also has reported that children are more likely to commit an inherently attractive but prohibited act if they first see another child merely commit the act without any consequences.

❧ CHAPTER SIX ❧

ALTRUISM
AND
SYMPATHY

Altruistic and sympathetic behavior are identified more accurately by the conditions under which they occur than they are by the specific forms which they may assume. Although the identifying criteria for these two types of conduct can be made quite distinct, it sometimes happens that one act will meet both sets of criteria. Both altruistic and sympathetic behavior may be acquired through either behavior-contingent or observational learning. And their mechanisms of acquisition engage both positive and aversive affective control. But their socialization is always dependent on the prerequisite establishment of the child's capacity for empathic and vicarious experience.

It is often assumed that altruistic acts are independent of their reinforcing consequences for the actor (see, for example, Durkheim, 1951, pp. 217–240). If this assumption were taken quite literally, the criterion that it would impose on altruistic behavior would be inconsistent with the more general theoretical constraints which we find necessary to an account of socialization. From the point of view of a conception of socialization that is grounded on affective as well as cognitive control of the child's behavior, we must assume that an altruistic act is responsive to the affective value of its anticipated outcomes, and that it often has reinforcing consequences for the actor. The control of altruistic behavior cannot be an exception to the mechanisms which appear to govern all other kinds of social conduct. Nor is this assumption contradicted even by the fact that an altruistic act may have directly aversive consequences for the actor, since the performance of the act can always be taken to indicate that its total outcome structure is preferred to the outcomes of an alternative act. Irwin's (1961) analysis of the concept of preference could be extended here in order to illustrate how the outcomes of an altruistic act might be directly aversive to the actor, and yet might be preferred to the outcomes of another act that was not altruistic.

The assertion that an altruistic act must be sustained by its consequences for the actor does not commit us to the view that altruism is simply another manifestation of the rules which govern the mutual exchange and distribution of social resources. Such a view has been espoused in some analyses of social behavior (Gouldner, 1960; Homans, 1961; Thibaut and Kelley, 1959). But when we say that an act displays altruism, we assert that the choice of the act, in preference to an alternative act, is at least partly determined by the actor's expectation of consequences which will benefit another person rather than himself. This assertion does not imply that the consequences for the other person will have no affective value for the actor. Nor does it imply that an altruistic component of behavior can be maintained without reinforcing consequences. An act may have reinforcing consequences without having directly beneficial outcomes for the actor. The reinforcement of the act may be mediated either by its concretely visible consequences for another person or by the actor's cognitive representation of such consequences. For example, as a result of earlier social conditioning, people may come to experience altruistic pleasure in response to their own actions, through their capacity to represent to themselves the effect which their actions will have on another person (even when the effect may not be directly observable). The affective value of such cognitive representations may also be determined by the more complex normative and self-evaluative systems which people can apply to the consequences of their behavior for others.

Regardless of whether the effects of an act on another person are directly observed or are given a cognitive representation, they can function as reinforcing outcomes for the actor to the extent that their affective value is transmitted through the actor's empathic or vicarious experience. Empathic or vicarious control of behavior is in fact a requirement of the truly altruistic act. The initial establishment of altruistic dispositions in the young child takes place when the child's empathic or vicarious experience permits certain forms of its behavior to be reinforced by the visibly pleasurable or distress-reducing consequences which they have for others. As the cognitive capacities of the child expand in the course of development, the affective value that can be carried by representational cognition becomes an increasingly available source of potential support for its altruistic behavior. But even when the child can give extensive cognitive representation and evaluation to the consequences of its behavior, the altruistic component of the behavior is still dependent on the child's capacity for empathic or vicarious experience. Since the altruistic property of an act is defined in part by the absence of directly beneficial consequences for the actor, it may always be regarded as being under some degree of internalized control. Of course, an altruistic act may be said to have an even more highly internalized status when its empathic or vicarious reinforcement is mediated by a cognitive representation that does not require its consequences for others to be directly observable.

There has been an interesting recent development in the use of the concept of altruism by ethologists who have argued that natural selection favors a certain amount of behavior that has beneficial consequences for another member of the same species (Hamilton, 1964; Wynne-Edwards, 1962). The general line of argument is that there may be some adaptive advantage in the evolution of unlearned behavioral dispositions which are altruistic in the sense that they benefit others, even at some disadvantage to the individual—for example, alarm calls at the approach of predators (Maynard Smith, 1965)—particularly if the donor and the recipient of the advantage have a close genetic relationship. Comparative psychologists also occasionally have speculated that there might be certain innate dispositions toward the acquisition of altruistic behavior, which are especially visible at the highest phylogenetic levels (Hebb and Thompson, 1954; McBride and Hebb, 1948)—as evidenced, for example, in reactions to the distress of others. Campbell (1965) has suggested that human beings also may have strong unlearned altruistic dispositions, particularly toward others whom they perceive as similar to themselves, and that these dispositions have been selected for their adaptive value in meeting environmental stresses. There also have been other advocates of the view that human beings are innately endowed with altruistic dispositions (Holmes, 1945; Montague, 1950). It seems that Darwin (1871, Chapter 4), too, was of the opinion that altruism had some instinctive basis in man.

It is not unreasonable to suppose that there may be inherited dispositions to behave, or to learn to behave, in ways which favor the survival of other members of a species. Nor is it inconceivable that some of the behavior patterns of the higher animals, such as grooming or retrieval of the young, might be primitive forerunners of the altruism that is sometimes seen in human behavior. But the application of the concept of altruism to these forms of behavior does not shed much light on the more highly internalized altruistic acts of which human beings appear to be capable. The usefulness of a concept of altruism is lost if we simply apply it to any behavior of an animal that benefits another member of the species. We would then have to apply the concept to the extensive grooming behavior of many primates (DeVore, 1965), even though the grooming is reciprocal and is sometimes a source of edible insects for the groomer. Likewise, retrieval, cleaning, and other kinds of close contact with the young may have directly experienced pleasurable (or distress-reducing) consequences for the female adults of some species. The concept of altruism can be better employed, in reference to a distinct phenomenon, if we use criteria which restrict it to the situation in which the behavior of one individual is shown to be controlled by either the direct observation or the cognitive representation of its consequences for another individual. Human beings may have a unique capacity for this type of control over their behavior. However, one would hardly want to treat altruism as being anything like a species-specific phenomenon in humans. It shows the great variation of occurrence and form that we can only attribute to corresponding variation in social experience.

Aside from a few attempts to use verbal self-report as an index of a generalized attribute or trait of altruism (Cattell and Horowitz, 1952; Friedrichs, 1960; Turner, 1948), most of the empirical work that might be regarded as having any relevance to altruism consists of direct observation of dispositions to share possessions with peers or to extend aid to them. The findings of a number of studies have confirmed the common observation that children manifest such dispositions in ways which are determined by their developmental status, by the social cues in a specific situation, and by the occurrence of direct external reinforcement (Doland and Adelberg, 1967; Fischer, 1963; Gottschaldt and Frühauf-Ziegler, 1958; Handlon and Gross, 1959; Hartshorne, May, and Maller, 1929; Hartup and Coates, 1967; Lenrow, 1965; Murphy, 1937; Rosenhan and White, 1967; Ugurel-Semin, 1952; Wolfle and Wolfle, 1939; Wright, 1942). Similar dispositions are apparent in the actions of adults when they are given the opportunity to behave in ways which produce beneficial consequences for another person (Berkowitz and Daniels, 1964; Berkowitz and Friedman, 1967; Darlington and Macker, 1966; Goranson and Berkowitz, 1966; Schopler and Matthews, 1965). A great many studies also have been conducted as attempts to demonstrate analogous dispositions in other primates (Crawford, 1941; Mason, 1959; Mason and Hollis, 1962; Masserman, Wechkin, and Terris, 1964; Miller, Banks, and Ogawa, 1963; Nissen and Crawford, 1936; Yerkes and Learned, 1925). And corresponding demonstrations have been attempted with rats (Holder, 1958; Ulrich, 1967).

None of the studies which are cited above is directly addressed to the question of how either humans or animals originally acquire the kind of empathic or vicarious responsiveness to social cues that would provide a potentially altruistic motivational base for their dispositions to share or to give aid. Moreover, with the exception of the studies which have been reported by Lenrow (1965) and by Rosenhan and White (1967), it is difficult to determine the extent to which the observed behavior is under the control of altruistic expectations. It appears almost invariably that the behavior is reinforced by explicit rewards, is elicited by the implicit incentive of social approval, or is a cooperative effort to produce a mutually beneficial set of outcomes for both self and other. For example, Holder (1958) found that rats could be trained to perform acts which had the effect of aiding another rat, when both learning and maintenance of the acts were rewarded with food. Ulrich (1967) designed an experiment to show that rats could be trained to cooperate in order to escape jointly experienced electric shock. In the study that was reported by Fischer (1963), the sharing behavior of children was continuously reinforced by material reward or verbal praise. Virtually all of the other studies of children and human adults have been carried out under conditions in which it would not be possible to separate the altruistic component of the observed behavior from the subjects' expectations of social approval.

Daniels (1967) has described an experiment with human adults that illustrates quite well the problem of engaging an altruistic component in cooperative or sharing behavior which has been established by direct reward. The experiment shows that the facilitation of cooperative behavior by large monetary gains breaks down when the contingencies permit subjects to take advantage of one another. Some experiments on the cooperative behavior of monkeys in feeding situations also have generated interesting examples of the difficulty of putting such behavior on an altruistic footing, when it is no longer instrumental to the provision of food for a hungry animal. Boren (1966) designed a paradigm in which two pairs of monkeys were trained to a pattern of cooperative behavior such that each animal's operation of its own lever would produce food only for the other. The monkeys were permitted visual, auditory, and tactile contact, and therefore had available the social cues for empathic or vicarious experience. Mutual exchange behavior was stable under the constraints of an alternation procedure which made it highly probable that each monkey would eat and press the lever intermittently. The exchange soon deteriorated, however, when the monkeys were shifted to a free-responding situation which made it more likely that either monkey could continually receive food without pressing its own lever. Horel, Treichler, and Meyer (1963) found that it was extremely difficult for the hungry member of a pair of monkeys to induce its already satiated mate to perform previously learned behavior that would produce food for the hungry monkey, even though the hungry monkey was the dominant member of the pair. It appeared that the hungry monkey had to use some coercion and direct physical guidance in order to induce the satiated monkey to perform the required behavior.

Experiments which have focussed on the reactions which monkeys show to the distress of others are equally difficult to interpret as demonstrations of altruism. For example, R. E. Miller and his collaborators (Miller *et al.,*

1963; Miller, Caul, and Mirsky, 1967) first have trained monkeys to avoid shock in response to nonsocial cues, and then have observed that one monkey will respond to the distress cues of another in order to avoid shock to both itself and the other. Masserman *et al.* (1964) found that monkeys would suppress the act of pulling a chain if it produced visible distress (through electric shock) in another monkey, even though the same act also produced food for themselves. But their monkeys also could obtain food by pulling another chain that did not produce distress in another monkey. Both of these types of experiments demonstrate the point that the altruistic character of an act remains indeterminate unless the performance of the act can be shown to be empathically or vicariously controlled by its consequences for others. The experiments were designed in such a way that the subjects might have been acting to avoid stimulation (either shock or distress cues) which they experienced as directly aversive to themselves.

A comparison of the findings of two closely related experiments with rats is a particularly instructive confirmation of the fact that acts which reduce another individual's distress need not be empathically or vicariously motivated, but may rather be controlled by the directly aversive properties of the distress cues for the observer. Rice and Gainer (1962) found that rats would press a bar in order to lower a suspended and distressed peer significantly more often than they would press a bar in order to lower a plastic block. But Lavery and Foley (1963) showed that the bar-pressing behavior appeared to be comparably reinforced by the termination of white noise and by the termination of recorded distress squeals. Clearly, the rats in the earlier experiment might not have been reacting empathically to cues which they perceived as signals of another animal's distress, but might rather have been reacting to their own directly aversive experience of the distress cues. In a later experiment, Rice (1964) did in fact find that rats showed evidence of fear in response to the observed distress of a peer, even when they were exposed only to recorded squeals of distress. These findings are similar to an informal observation that was made some years ago by Lorenz (1934), who noted that a jackdaw was as likely to attack him if he were holding a wet black bathing suit as it was if he were holding another jackdaw.

One way of demonstrating the learning of altruistic behavior is suggested in an experiment that has been conducted by the author with the collaboration of Vivian Paskal (Aronfreed and Paskal, 1965). Six- to eight-year-old girls and an adult female agent of socialization were used in the experiment. The experiment was designed first to attach the child's empathic positive affect to cues which expressed a corresponding affective state of the agent, and then to establish the altruistic value of an overt act that the child could use instrumentally to produce the agent's expressive cues. During the initial socialization paradigms, the agent sat very close to the child and demonstrated the operation of a choice box that was automated to dispense a small candy as the outcome of the operation of one lever and a three-second red light as the outcome of the operation of another lever. Each outcome was programmed, however, only to a randomized sixty per cent schedule, so that the occurrence of an outcome would be unpredictable on any single trial. During the demonstration, the child simply watched while the agent varied her choices equally between the two levers over the course of twenty trials. The agent showed no reaction when her choices produced no explicit outcomes. Nor did she show any reaction when her choices produced candy. But when the agent's choices activated the red light, she showed one of three patterns of reaction which represented variations in the contingencies between her expressive cues and her behavior toward the child. These variations were designed to support the inference that the reinforcement value of the expressive cues, when they were used as outcomes of the child's own subsequent choices among alternative acts, was attributable to their conditioned elicitation of the child's empathic affective experience.

In the basic experimental paradigm, the children were exposed repeatedly to a very close temporal association between the agent's expressive cues of pleasure and their own direct experience of the agent's physical affection. Whenever the agent's choice between the levers activated the red light, the agent smiled while staring at the light, and at the same time uttered one of four exclamations in a pleased and excited tone of voice. All of the exclamations were roughly equivalent to: *"There's the light!"* Immediately following these expressive cues, the agent used one arm to give the child a firm hug, and simultaneously turned toward the child and inclined her head with a very broad direct smile. This affection was dispensed as though it were the spontaneous correlate of the agent's pleasurable reaction to the red light. Children in one control paradigm were exposed only to the agent's expressive affective cues, while children in another control paradigm were exposed only to the agent's affection.[1]

---

[1] Fifty-seven girls were used in the basic experimental paradigm. Thirty-seven girls were used in the control paradigm in which no physical affection was given to the child. Thirty-one girls were used in the control paradigm in which the agent did not emit expressive affective cues in response to the light.

The effects of the three paradigms were then immediately tested in a common performance task, during which the child herself operated the choice box over a great many trials. The red light on the face of the box, which originally had served as a potential outcome of the agent's choices, was now deactivated on a pretext. The agent sat across from the child, facing the rear of the box, with her gaze fixed on another red light that was visible only to her. The presence of this auxiliary light was made known to the child, who was told that it would go on whenever she chose the light-producing lever. The child was also told that she could keep all of the candy that came out of the box (although it was not to be consumed until the task was completed). During the task, the agent showed no reaction when the child chose to produce candy for herself. But whenever the child chose to operate the lever which produced the red light, the agent would smile at the light and exclaim *"There's the light!"*. She thus emitted the same expressive cues which had been used to convey her pleasure in two of the three initial paradigms. The performance task placed the child, then, in a situation where her empathic and altruistic dispositions could be tested by her repeated choices between an act that produced candy for herself and an act that produced only observably pleasurable consequences for another person.

The conjunction of the expressive cues of the agent with the child's direct experience of affection, during the basic experimental paradigm for empathic conditioning, had a substantial effect on the children's choices during the test for altruism. Children who were exposed to this conjunction were significantly more willing to forego candy than were children whose earlier experience had included only an association between the red light and the agent's expressive cues of positive affect (without physical affection). They also showed significantly more altruism than did children who previously had been exposed only to physical affection in association with the red light (without the compound of expressive affective cues that was used by the agent during the test task). The majority of the children who had been exposed to the basic social conditioning paradigm actually chose to produce the light for the agent more frequently than they chose to produce candy for themselves; whereas children from both of the control groups typically chose the candy-producing lever more frequently. In accordance with a distinction that was made earlier, it would appear that the altruistic behavior of the children in the experimental group was reinforced through empathic experience, but that it might also have been partially supported by vicarious experience. The children were able to see the agent's expressive affective cues during the test, but they were also able to see cues which indicated the agent's orientation toward maximizing her perception of the red light (for example, staring at the light).

The procedures which were used to establish and demonstrate the value of the agent's affective cues, for the children in the basic experimental group, were a specific application of a more general sequence of procedures that has been used in other settings to establish and test the acquired positive reinforcement value of a "neutral" stimulus. In this case, the expressive cues and the child's direct experience of affection were paired within the contingencies of a Pavlovian conditioning paradigm, during which the child was an observer—that is, the pairing was not contingent on the child's performance of a criterial overt act. The findings of a number of experiments with animals appear to confirm that the positive secondary reinforcement value of a stimulus can be acquired under Pavlovian contingencies which do not require the pairing with an unconditioned stimulus to be produced by the subject's overt behavior (Ferster and Skinner, 1957; Kelleher and Gollub, 1962: Knott and Clayton, 1966; Stein, 1958). But the distinguishing feature of the index of secondary reinforcement value which was used in the performance test for altruism was that it employed expressive cues which apparently had acquired empathic affective value for the children in the conditioning group.

The contingencies within the three initial paradigms, and their relationship to the contingencies of the performance test, were constructed with the intent of eliminating the possibility that differences among the groups in their test behavior could be attributed to differences in the children's perception of the agent's expressive cues as approval of their choices. Since the agent's affective cues were not contingent on the children's overt behavior during the initial paradigms, but were made contingent on the overt choices of all groups during the test, the experimental effect cannot easily be attributed to the children's perception of the cues as evidence of direct social approval. Finally, it is interesting to note that the effectiveness of the agent's cues of pleasurable affect, in the reinforcement of the altruistic choices of children in the experimental group, appeared to be as great during the second half of the test trials as during the first half. The apparent resistance to extinction of the value of the expressive cues might have been partly attributable to the inconsistent scheduling of both the cues and the agent's affection, with respect to the choices on which these events were contingent during the conditioning and test situations. The findings of other experiments with children suggest that the independent maintenance of the acquired positive secondary reinforcement value of a stimulus event can be prolonged by inconsistent scheduling of the event during extinction, and that it also can be enhanced by an original association of the event with a "primary" event that was used as an inconsistent outcome during acquisition (Myers and Myers, 1963; Myers, 1960; Myers and Myers, 1966).

Midlarsky and Bryan (1967) recently have reported an interesting replication and extension of this experimental demonstration of the socialization of altruism. Using essentially the same conditioning and control paradigms as those which already have been described, they also included two additional paradigms. One of these additional paradigms used a backward conditioning sequence, in which the agent's physical affection toward the child preceded her expressive cues of pleasurable affect. The other additional paradigm was a control paradigm in which neither expressive cues nor physical affection was associated with the appearance of the light. In the subsequent task that was employed as a test for altruism, only half of the children from each of the initial paradigms were provided with the agent's expressive cues as the outcome of choices which they previously had observed to be associated with the occurrence of the light. The other half of the children produced no reaction from the agent when they made such choices. During the performance test, children from both the forward and backward conditioning paradigms more frequently made the choice with which the agent originally had produced the light than did children from any of the control paradigms. Thus, the two groups for whom the agent's positive affective cues and physical affection had initially been paired, as contingent outcomes of a light-producing choice, were the ones who were most inclined to repeat that same choice when they had an opportunity to do so, and thereby to forego an alternative choice that would have produced candy for themselves. A second interesting finding was that the effect of the conditioning paradigms was markedly facilitated by the agent's expressive cues of pleasure in response to the children's altruistic choices during the test, but was also apparent when the agent did not display the expressive cues.

Midlarsky and Bryan interpret their findings as a disconfirmation of the view that the socialization of altruism requires empathic or vicarious experience to act as a medium of reinforcement. On the basis of the altruistic test behavior of the children from their backward conditioning paradigm, they argue first that contingencies of the type that would condition acquired reinforcement value were not required in order for the agent's expressive cues to support the child's altruistic behavior. This argument rests on the untenable assumption that the expressive cues could not acquire additional positive value for the child if they followed rather than preceded the child's experience of physical affection. Although there is considerable question about the conditions under which backward conditioning occurs (Kimble, 1961), there is also a large body of evidence that points to the reality of the phenomenon (Razran, 1956). Backward conditioning might be especially viable when physical affection and expressive affective cues are blended together in close succession in the experience of a highly cognitive organism—particularly in view of the possibility that the positive affectivity which is aroused by a quick hug may reach its highest magnitude after the hug is terminated.

Secondly, Midlarsky and Bryan argue that contiguity between expressive cues and physical affection was not a crucial determinant of their experimental effects, on the grounds that the effects remained constant across the test trials regardless of whether or not the agent's expressive cues were used as a reinforcing outcome of the child's altruistic choices. But their own evidence would appear to contradict this argument. The effects of the conditioning paradigms were significantly greater when expressive cues were used during the test than they were when the cues were not used. Moreover, children who had been exposed only to expressive cues during the demonstration paradigm did not show the high level of altruism that characterized the behavior of the conditioning groups during the test. It is hardly surprising that a distinct effect of the conditioning paradigms would be apparent even in the absence of any concrete expressive cues from the agent during the test. One would certainly expect that the acquired positive value of the cues, and their consequent empathic reinforcing properties, could operate through the child's capacity to give them a cognitive representation whenever it made an altruistic choice.

Midlarsky and Bryan used a second test of altruism which also indicated that the agent's expressive cues had acquired empathic reinforcement value during their conditioning paradigms. Immediately at the end of the first test, all of the children were equated on the number of candies which they possessed, and then were given the opportunity to make an anonymous donation of some of their candy to a fictitious unfortunate child. Children who had been exposed to the original conditioning paradigms were significantly more altruistic than children who had been exposed to the control paradigms, but only when the agent's expressive cues had been used as reinforcing outcomes of the child's altruistic choices during the first test. This finding leaves little doubt that the expressive cues did acquire some empathic value as a result of conditioning. Their reinforcing properties during the first test were an effective determinant of the children's generalization of altruistic dispositions to the second test. The fact that the generalization took place across rather different situations, and was not dependent on the presence of the original object of altruism, suggests also that the altruistic behavior of these children was under the internalized control of their cognitive representations of the consequences of their actions for others.

In the type of experiment that has been described here, the value of an altruistic act is established for the child by providing a situation in which the act will be performed and then reinforced by an outcome that can elicit the child's empathic affective response. The more general paradigm for the acquisition of an altruistic component of behavior consists of two basic prerequisites: first, the attachment of potentially reinforcing empathic or vicarious changes of affectivity to social cues which transmit information about the experience of others; second, the establishment of the instrumental value of overt acts for which such social cues are contingent outcomes—initially through their external occurrence as visible indicators of the experience of others, and subsequently through their cognitive representation by the child. The acquired behavioral form of an altruistic disposition does not require, however, a repeated performance by the child under the control of reinforcing outcomes. Altruistic acts also often may be acquired by imitative modelling or by related forms of learning which utilize the child's observation of the behavior of others and its capacity to store the information that is transmitted in the consequences of their behavior.

There are some interesting similarities and differences between a concept of altruism and a concept of sympathy. Sympathy has a more restricted affective base than does altruism. But its behavioral expression can be supported by a greater variety of reinforcing outcomes. Although the concept of sympathy may be used with a number of different connotations, there is one meaning of the concept which has a particularly direct relevance to social conduct. It is the use of sympathy to refer to a disposition to relieve the distress of others. This disposition appears to be displayed universally throughout the primate species (DeVore, 1965)—most notably, though not exclusively, in the behavior of mothers toward their offspring. Many attempts to define sympathy have made reference to a broad set of affective and cognitive dispositions which function in a highly generalized way to produce empathic and vicarious experience (Allport, 1954; Asch, 1952, pp. 171–172; Heider, 1958, pp. 277–282; McDougall, 1908, pp. 150–

179). These broad definitions give very little attention to the nature and origin of overt sympathetic behavior as a reaction that is specific to the observed or anticipated distress of another person.

As in the case of altruism, empathic or vicarious experience must be inferred as a prerequisite of sympathetic behavior. An act that has the effect of relieving another person's distress would obviously not be sympathetic, for example, if it were motivated primarily by the actor's own direct experience of the same distressful events. An act is truly sympathetic only to the extent that it is elicited through the actor's empathic or vicarious affective response to the actual or anticipated distress of another person. We already have noted that a concept of altruism cannot properly be applied to the findings of those experiments in which animals merely have been shown to perform actions which relieve the distress of another animal (for example, Miller *et al.,* 1963, or Rice and Gainer, 1962). The experiments are carried out under conditions where the performing animal might well experience the observed distress cues as having the value of aversive events which impinge directly upon itself. For the same reason, the results of these experiments do not permit the inference that the animals are behaving sympathetically.

The requirement of perceived distress emphasizes, in accordance with common understanding, that sympathetic behavior is controlled by an aversive affective state. An act that is intended to give pleasure to another person might well be described as altruistic, but it would not ordinarily be described as sympathetic. However, the conditions of reinforcement of sympathetic behavior are in another sense less restrictive than those for altruistic behavior. A person's sympathetic behavior may be altruistic to the extent that its anticipated reinforcing consequences are limited to the reduction of empathic or vicarious distress which the person will experience when another person is relieved or protected from distress. Recent experiments with college students appear to demonstrate such altruistic components in sympathetic behavior (Buss, 1966; Schopler and Bateson, 1965), as do the experiments which Lenrow (1965) and Rosenhan and White (1967) have conducted with children. But even though sympathy itself requires the capacity for empathic or vicarious experience of distress, overt sympathetic behavior is also often under the control of the individual's anticipation of direct social reward or of subsequent reciprocity from another person. Observations of the behavior of children in naturalistic settings clearly illustrate that sympathetic behavior cannot always be assumed to be altruistic (Isaacs, 1933; Murphy, 1937). Children will often aid their peers, or show solicitude toward them, because they anticipate social approval or the mutual benefits of cooperation in a shared difficulty. The internalized status of a sympathetic act may therefore vary in accordance with the extent to which its motivation and reinforcement are independent of external outcomes which are directly experienced by the actor.

This analysis of sympathetic behavior requires the socialization of the behavior to have two basic components. First, the child must acquire empathic or vicarious affective sensitivity to the cues which serve as indicators of another person's experience of distress. Secondly, the child must acquire specific forms of overt behavior which are instrumental to the reduction of the other person's distress.

When the required contingencies of social conditioning have established the young child's empathic and vicarious dispositions toward sympathy, then overt sympathetic acts can become part of its social behavior in a number of ways. Certain behavioral dispositions which the child already has acquired—for example, giving affection or sharing possessions—may be further shaped into sympathetic behavior when they are subjected to the selective contingent reinforcement of external outcomes which are associated with the relief of another person's distress. These reinforcing outcomes may take the form of observable cues which indicate relief of distress for another person, since the child's affective response to such cues may be a reduction of its own empathic or vicarious experience of distress. Or the reinforcing outcomes of sympathetic behavior may take the form of approval, affection, or other direct social rewards for the child. Both of these types of outcomes can produce an attachment of potentially reinforcing affective value to the intrinsic correlates of the child's sympathetic behavior, so that the maintenance of the behavior is no longer entirely dependent on either its observable consequences for others or its direct consequences for the child. After the child has had some opportunity for the direct observation of social cues of distress and relief of distress in other people, then the changes of affectivity which motivate and reinforce its sympathetic behavior may come under the more internalized control of its cognitive representation of the consequences of its actions.

The shaping of sympathetic behavior by reinforcing outcomes is not the only channel of learning through which the behavior can acquire internalized value. Indeed, because sympathetic dispositions often appear to emerge with remarkable suddenness and accuracy in the overt behavior of the young child, behavior-contingent learning alone would not appear to give a very plausible account of their acquisition. The early initiation and rapid spread of sympathetic dispositions toward peers, pets, and representational figures such as dolls, point to an important contribution of imitative modelling and other forms of learning based on observation of the behavior of others. Opportunities for observational learning would occur whenever the child observed the sympathetic behavior of others in conjunction with its own experience of potentially reinforcing changes of affective state. A powerful base for this kind of learning is provided, as a necessary consequence of caretaking, when the young child is the recipient of the actions with which socializing agents reduce its own direct experience of distress. But the affective value of relief of distress may also become attached to the observed sympathetic behavior of a model when the child's empathic or vicarious experience is elicited by its perception of the experience of others to whom the model's actions are directed. Even the child's opportunities to observe how others relieve their own distress may contribute to its learning of sympathetic behavior through empathic or vicarious experience.

All of these opportunities for observational learning may attach an intrinsic affective value, which corresponds to relief of distress, to the child's cognitive representation of a model's sympathetic behavior, and therefore to the cognitive correlates of its own emerging repertoire of sympathetic acts. The child can then reduce the empathic or vicarious distress that it experiences, in response to the perceived distress of another person, by reproducing the model's sympathetic behavior. Since the child's cognitive representations of a sympathetic act, and of its consequences, have already acquired some internalized affective value as a result of the observational learning process, the reinforcement of a performance of the act will tend to be at least partially independent of its immediately observable consequences. It is also possible that the child's sympathetic behavioral dispositions can acquire some generalized intrinsic value as a result of observational learning that does not necessarily produce imitation of the same behavior that has been displayed by a model. Lenrow (1965) found that the verbal expression of sympathy among both children and adults, and the performance of concrete sympathetic acts by children, were correlated with the extent of their actual or role-played previous experience as the recipient of other forms of sympathetic behavior under conditions of distress.

The author and Vivian Paskal recently have conducted a study which used experimental paradigms of socialization to examine the mechanisms for children's learning of sympathetic behavior (Aronfreed and Paskal, 1966). The paradigms were designed first to condition the children's empathic reactions to the observed distress of another person, and then to have them observe the sympathetic actions of an agent who relieved their own distress. The experiment was carried out with seven- and eight-year-old girls and a female socializing agent. The experimental design was a sequence of three separate and immediately successive phases of socialization, the last of which gave the subject an opportunity to respond sympathetically to the distress of another child. The conditions of socialization were varied within specific phases to create five distinct sequences or experimental groups. During each phase of any sequence, the child was engaged in the classification of a number of small toy replicas of real objects. She was instructed to classify each toy in accordance with whether she thought it most appropriate for a house, a dog, or a school. Twelve discrete classification trials were used in each of the three phases, and the toys were changed between phases. The child indicated her classification of each toy by pushing down one of the three levers on a choice box. Since the middle lever was used for the dog category, and the toys were selected so as to make its use inappropriate, it was ordinarily chosen very infrequently or not at all. This arrangement made it possible to treat choices of the middle lever as being irrelevant to the classification task, and to use them as an index of sympathetic behavior during the third (test) phase of the various experimental sequences.

The prototype for the learning of sympathetic behavior was the first of the five experimental sequences. It may be used as the reference point for a description of the basic design of the three phases within any of the sequences. The first phase was designed as a paradigm of the original acquisition process for conditioning a child's empathic affective response to expressive cues which indicate the distressful experience of another person. The contingencies for conditioning were introduced through a temporal contiguity between the observable distress cues of the socializing agent and the child's own direct experience of distressful stimulation. Both the child and the agent wore earphones, on the pretext of monitoring occasional noise from within the choice box. The agent told the child that the noise in her own earphones would be louder than the noise in the child's earphones. Among the twelve classification trials, there were six on which the child heard a highly aversive loud noise through her earphones. The noise lasted for seven seconds. It did not begin until well after the child had made her choice, and was actually confined to the intertrial interval that followed the child's classification of a toy. The noise was not contingent on the child's choice, and its pattern of occurrence across trials was unpredictable. Three seconds before the onset of the noise, the agent began to show cues of distress by placing her head in her hands (apparently because of the noise in her own earphones). The agent's distress cues were continued until the noise terminated.

The second phase of the first sequence was designed to maximize the distress-reducing value of the agent's sympathetic actions toward the child. During the second phase, the agent wore no earphones and showed no evidence of distress. She used another choice box to indicate her own classification of each toy, just after the child had classified the toy. She also told the child that she might be able, while she was using her own choice box, to turn off the noise that the child would still occasionally hear through the earphones that she continued to wear. When the child had completed the classification of each toy, the agent would appear to think for two or three seconds, with her hand poised above one of the two outer levers in the array of three on her choice-box. These outer levers were marked to represent house and school, and they were clearly the only correct choices for almost all of the toys. The agent did finally choose one of these two levers on six of the twelve classification trials. But on the remaining six trials, the child began to hear the highly aversive noise through her earphones at this point. The noise again was unrelated to the child's previous choice and unpredictable across trials. The noise lasted for only three seconds, since the agent moved fairly quickly to push the middle lever on her choice box. This action terminated the noise. At the same time, the agent said that she was choosing the middle lever in order to turn off the noise. She thus clearly gave up for the moment the task of making a correct classification, so that she would be able to reduce the child's distress.

The third phase of the first sequence was designed to test whether the child had acquired a disposition to reproduce the observed sympathetic actions of the agent. The child was given opportunities to reduce her empathic distress, in response to another child's distress cues, by performing the same act which the agent had used previously to reduce the child's own direct exposure to the noise. The third phase also was designed so that elimination of the other child's distress cues would be a potentially reinforcing event that was contingent on the subject's behavior. This procedure made it possible to exercise some control over the subject's actions through external events which would provide both empathic motivation and reinforcement for her behavior.

At the beginning of the third phase, another girl was introduced as a new subject. Actually, the new girl had been a subject previously, and she had been subsequently trained to the role of a more or less innocent dummy, who was to emit distress cues at critical junctures in the test phase of another subject's socialization. The primary subject now was given the adult agent's earlier role of using the second choice box to classify each toy, following its classification by the dummy. The dummy wore earphones, of course, but the subject did not. The agent now sat as an observer behind the subject. On six of the twelve classification trials, the dummy and subject simply made their successive choices. On the remaining six trials, the dummy placed her head in her hands, in response to a low signal from her earphones, at the point where the subject was about to make her choice. This distress cue was the same as the one that the agent had emitted earlier during the first phase. If the subject made the sympathetic choice of the middle lever—the choice which the agent had made to reduce the subject's distress during the second phase—the dummy would immediately raise her head and thus terminate her distress cues, in response to the termination of the low signal in her earphones. But if the subject made a nonsympathetic, task-oriented choice of one of the two outer levers, the dummy would not terminate her distress cues until five seconds after the subject had made her choice (so that such a choice would not be reinforced to any significant extent).

It can be seen that the entire first sequence was designed first to condition emphatic distress, then to maximize the potential intrinsic reinforcement value of the child's representation of the agent's sympathetic actions, and finally to provide external social stimuli which would empathically motivate and reinforce the child's overt reproduction of the sympathetic behavior. The remaining four experimental sequences represented a variety of controls on the specific contingencies which were employed in the three phases of the first sequence. The second sequence differed from the first only in that the agent's distress cues were not paired, during the first phase, with the aversive noise that the child heard. The noise occurred at the same six intertrial intervals at which it had occurred for the first sequence. But the distress cues were emitted only during the noiseless intervals which followed the remaining six trials. This sequence exposed the children, then, to the same frequencies of occurrence of noise and distress cues as had been used in the first sequence, but without the temporal contiguity that would be required for the conditioning of empathic distress.

The third experimental sequence also replicated the first, with the exception that the noise which the child heard during the second phase was sharply reduced to a very mild intensity. This sequence was designed to minimize the potential distress-reducing value of the agent's sympathetic behavior toward the child, so that it would be ineffective in establishing the child's disposition to reproduce the behavior. The fourth and fifth experimental sequences were again identical to the first sequence, except that two levels of reduction of social cues were introduced during the third phase. These last two sequences were designed to examine the extent to which the sympathetic behavior of the subjects was controlled by concrete external distress cues. In the fourth sequence, the dummy wore earphones during the third phase, but she emitted no distress cues. In the fifth sequence, the dummy did not even wear the earphones.[2]

The results of this experiment were a striking confirmation of the distinct contributions of both empathic conditioning and observational learning to the acquisition of sympathetic behavior. During the first two phases of all of the sequences, all of the children were highly task-oriented in their classification of the toys. Across the twelve classification trials of either phase, the children typically chose the task-inappropriate middle lever (classification in the dog category) only once or twice. During the third phase, however, the choices of the children in the basic first sequence moved to a marked preference for the middle lever. Half of the children from the first sequence chose the middle lever on six or more trials—and it will be recalled that the dummy emitted distress cues on only six trials. Almost all of the remainder of the children from the first sequence chose the middle lever four or five times, which represented a sizeable increment in the frequency of their use of it. Of course, in choosing to perform this sympathetic act, the children forfeited the opportunity to make a correct classification. In contrast, children from all of the other four sequences continued to show a strong task-orientation during the test for sympathetic behavior. Although some of these children showed a tendency to increase the frequency of their choice of the middle lever, in response to the dummy's distress cues, the frequency distributions of their choices were quite similar to the corresponding distributions for the first two phases. When the five groups of children from all of the sequences were compared with respect to the shifts of frequency of choice of the middle lever, between the first two phases and the test phase, there was a powerful and highly reliable difference between the effect of the first sequence and the effect of any other sequence. With one notable exception which we will

[2] The numbers of children used in each of the socialization sequences were: first sequence—twenty-six; second sequence—twenty-one; third sequence—twenty-one; fourth sequence—seventeen; fifth sequence—seventeen.

examine shortly, the groups of children from the second through the fifth sequences were very similar in the distributions of shifts in the frequency of their choices of the middle lever.

The difference between the effects of the first and second sequences clearly indicates that the empathic experience of distress must be established as a base for sympathetic behavior. When the distress cues of the agent and the children's own direct experience of distress were not associated under the precise contingencies of a conditioning paradigm, during the first phase of the second sequence, the children showed little evidence of sympathetic behavior during the test phase. They did not act to relieve another child's observable distress, even though they previously had been the recipients of a sympathetic act that was now readily available for their use. Apparently, sheer information about the experience of another person was not sufficient to elicit their reproduction of the previously observed sympathetic behavior of the agent. Their sympathetic behavioral dispositions seemed to be dependent on a reinstatement of the affective experience under which the agent's behavior had originally acquired value for them.

The fact that the third sequence produced little sympathetic behavior during the test phase indicates that the sympathetic dispositions of children from the first sequence were not determined merely by their earlier observation of the actions of the agent, even though these actions were directed to their own welfare. Nor was their sympathetic behavior controlled only by their knowledge that reproducing the actions of the agent would reduce another child's distress. During the first phase of socialization, children from both the first and third experimental sequences were exposed to contingencies which were designed to condition their empathic response to the distress cues of another person. But during the second phase of the third sequence, the agent's sympathetic acts toward the children terminated only a mild noise, in contrast to the highly aversive noise which they terminated for the children in the second phase of the first sequence. The difference between the effects of the first and third sequences therefore seems to be attributable to a difference in the acquired potential values of a sympathetic act for reduction of the children's empathic distress during the test phase. It appears that an important determinant of the observational learning of sympathetic behavior was the change of affectivity which the children originally experienced in conjunction with their observation of the agent's sympathetic actions toward themselves.

The relative ineffectiveness of the fourth and fifth sequences in producing sympathetic behavior demonstrates the specific function of distress cues as elicitors of the children's acquired sympathetic dispositions during the test phase. When the dummy did not emit distress cues, the children did not repeat the acts with which the agent had previously reduced their own distress. The control of the affective value of sympathetic behavior by the children's observation of distress cues was also clearly confirmed by inspection of the pattern of test trials on which children in the first sequence chose the middle lever. The increments in the frequencies of their choice of the middle lever were almost entirely confined to the six trials on which the dummy emitted distress cues. It seems clear that the reinforcement value of the imitative dispositions which the children had acquired, as a result of their exposure to the sympathetic actions of the agent, was under the affective control of their empathic experience of distress. The sympathetic behavior of the children in the first sequence did not represent merely a generalized disposition to repeat the previously observed actions of another person.

In the earlier analysis of observation learning and imitation, it was pointed out that the intrinsic representational value of an imitative act is often easier to discern if the act has some topographic fidelity to the structure of the model's behavior. However, even an act that is a relatively discrete choice, as in the case of the sympathetic act in the present experiment, may be identified as having a component of intrinsic representational value, when experimental contingencies are arranged to make this representational component apparent. The design of the experiment does permit some of the comparisons which can be made among the effects of different sequences to be used as evidence that the sympathetic behavior of children in the first sequence had a component of value that was independent of its reinforcing control over the termination of observable distress cues.

Although external distress cues obviously exercised significant control over the sympathetic behavior of children in the first sequence, through the elicitation of their empathic distress, other comparisons reveal that their behavior was not entirely determined by the reinforcing effect of termination of these cues. For example, the experience of children in the third sequence provided the necessary information about the distress-reducing consequences of choosing the middle lever, and also gave them the motivation and opportunity to reduce their empathic distress by terminating another child's external distress cues. Yet these children did not show a significant increment in their disposition to choose the middle lever during the test phase. Apparently, this act had acquired a certain amount of additional intrinsic value for the children in the first sequence, who had previously observed the agent's sympathetic performance of the act in direct association with the reduction of their own relatively intense distress. It is the effect that cannot be attributed to the control of external distress cues which suggests that part of the value of the sympathetic act was inherent in its being a representation of an earlier external sample of behavior.

The behavior of the children in the fourth sequence, during the test phase, gave an indication of another component of representational control over the value of sympathetic behavior. These children showed discernible increments in the frequency of their choice of the middle lever, despite their fairly strong task-orientation. Their increments were in fact closer to the large increments shown by children in the first sequence than were the increments for any of the other control sequences. Moreover, they chose the middle lever significantly more often than did the children from the fifth sequence, in which the dummy wore no earphones. Of course, since there were no observable distress cues from the dummy during the fourth sequence, the children distributed their choices of the middle lever more or less randomly among the twelve test trials. Since their behavior was independent of any exposure to distress cues, it seems probable that their sympathetic acts were controlled by their cognitive representation of the distress-reducing (or distress-avoiding) consequences of their actions for another child who was wearing the earphones. Their behavior suggested that the cognitive representation of the outcomes of a sympathetic act is another potential source of the mediation of its internalized affective value.

Some additional evidence of the role of cognitive representation was obtained from introspective reports which many of the children gave during a verbal inquiry that directly followed the experimental session. In the three sequences in which the dummy emitted distress cues, almost all of the children perceived the cues as indicators of loud noise in her earphones. A substantial proportion of the children's reports did not reveal, however, a clear recognition that their choice of the middle lever would have relieved the dummy's distress. Among the children in the first sequence, reported awareness of this contingency was a very reliable predictor of maximal sympathetic behavior. Among the children in the second and third sequences, reported awareness of the contingency was unrelated to their behavior.

🌿 CHAPTER SEVEN 🌿

BEHAVIORAL
SUPPRESSION

Suppression is a term which is commonly applied to the passive restriction of active behavior. Socialization does include some paradigms of learning which require that children learn to suppress active behavior in order to avoid punishment. However, children generally engage their social environment quite actively, and they must therefore usually learn to avoid punishment even when their behavior is in a continuous stream of activity. Of course, their active behavior will often have a complementary or alternative relationship to another active form of behavior that is being punished and suppressed.

Children also acquire a certain amount of internalized aversive control over their behavior through socialization that corresponds more closely to laboratory paradigms of active avoidance learning. For example, they may learn to initiate one among several alternative forms of behavior, in appropriate stimulus situations, on the basis of their experience with the aversive consequences of failure to make an active choice among the alternatives. Passive inactivity as well as acts of commission might therefore be said to be subject to suppression. And behavioral suppression could be broadly defined to include any reduction in the probability of one form of behavior, relative to the probabilities of other forms, as a result of punishment or other avenues of aversive learning. Nevertheless, it is the suppression of an active form of behavior which can be used most effectively to illustrate the internalization of aversive control over social conduct.

Some recent experiments on the effects of early experience have used special conditions of rearing to immunize certain species of animals against the development of their natural aggressive dispositions toward the members of other species (Denenberg, Hudgens, and Zarrow, 1964; Kuo, 1960). Ethologists have noted that the aggressive behavior of some animals seems to be forestalled or attenuated by "submission" signals from another member of their species, with the implication that the effect of the signals is strongly determined by unlearned predispositions (Lorenz, 1966: Marler, 1968). These observations indicate that the aggressive behavior of animals can be eliminated or prevented by both the predetermined and the acquired capacity of social stimuli to elicit incompatible or competing forms of behavior. The variation in dispositions toward aggression that we observe across human societies (as described, for example, in Whiting and Child, 1953) suggests that the early social experience of children may also establish alternative dispositions which curtail the development of aggression.

The arrest of the development of a behavioral disposition, or the social elicitation of incompatible forms of behavior, is quite different from the kind of suppression of well-established behavior that can be produced under aversive control. The concept of suppression is most useful when it is restricted to the effects of punishment and other forms of aversive control in reducing the overt behavioral manifestation of dispositions which are already prepotent in a specific situation. A possibly better example of how social experience can produce behavioral suppression in animals may be found in studies of the effect of defeat on the aggressive behavior of mice (Scott, 1958). The effect appears to be especially strong when defeat occurs at an early age (Kahn, 1951). But even in the case of this phenomenon, there is some ambiguity about whether aggressive dispositions are merely suppressed or are completely arrested in their development.

A number of different lines of investigation have established the variety of conditions under which the active avoidance behavior of animals may persist, for substantial periods of time, when punishment is no longer the consequence of failure to avoid (Kelleher, Riddle, and Cook, 1963; Melvin and Smith, 1967; Sidman, 1955; Sidman, Herrnstein, and Conrad, 1957; Solomon and Wynne, 1954). Studies of the effects of punishment on the behavior which animals have learned in order to obtain food have shown that suppression of active forms of behavior can also remain stable over significant periods of time, during which punishment is no longer an outcome of the suppressed behavior (Boe and Church, 1967; Hake, Azrin, and Oxford, 1967; Whiting and Mowrer, 1943), or during which the animal has been removed from the punishment situation (Boroczi, Storms, and Broen, 1964; Masserman, 1946).

Most of the experiments which have shown that punishment can make a contribution to children's learning employ discrimination paradigms or other tasks of a type which are not well suited to a demonstration of behavioral suppression (Brackbill and O'Hara, 1958; Nelson, Reid, and Travers, 1965; Spence, 1966; Stevenson, Weir, and Zigler, 1959). In the paradigms which are used most commonly, the child is required simply to make a correct response to a discriminative stimulus. The incorrect punished response does not have an independent motivation of its own. With the exception of some recent experimental studies of the internalization of behavioral suppression, which will be described later in this chapter, there has been very little empirical work on the use of punishment to suppress the overt manifestations of a motivated behavioral disposition in children. Hollenberg and Sperry (1951) found that punishment had only a mild and temporary suppressive effect on children's aggression in doll play. Lövaas,

Schaeffer, and Simmons (1965) have used electric shock as punishment, however, to produce a highly effective suppression of some of the characteristic behavior of autistic children. Other investigators have shown that deprivation of candy can be used as an effective suppressor of either the dominant or the cooperative behavior of children (Blum and Kennedy, 1967; Weingold and Webster, 1964).

Outcomes which generally are assumed to have an aversive value do not always have suppressive effects on motivated behavior. It is not uncommon to observe, for example, that mild punishment of an early component in a sequential pattern of motivated behavior may actually facilitate a child's learning and performance of the behavior, when the pattern is still uncertain and punishment can serve as a signal that a specific performance will produce other outcomes which are highly valued by the child. The findings of a number of experiments with animals have shown that discrimination learning can be facilitated not only by the use of electric shock as an outcome of incorrect responses, but also by the use of shock as an outcome of correct responses (Curlin and Donahue, 1965; Fowler and Wischner, 1965; Holz and Azrin, 1962; Muenzinger et al., 1952; Prince, 1956). These findings suggest that punishment of mild intensity sometimes may have significant cue properties which facilitate learning because they focus the subject's attention on relevant discriminative stimuli or because they provide additional information to confirm the correct response.

In all of the experiments which are cited above, punishment for the correct response has the informational value of an association with the reward of food for a hungry animal. Moreover, comparisons within and among the experiments clearly indicate that the informational value of the punishment is salient only at mildly aversive intensities. At more highly aversive intensities, punishment appears to facilitate discriminative control over learning only when it is applied to the suppression of nonrewarded (incorrect) behavior; intense punishment tends to interfere with learning when it is applied to rewarded (correct) behavior. In two of the experiments (Muenzinger et al., 1952; Prince, 1956), a single substantial intensity of shock as an outcome of correct responses facilitated learning only when the animals had first become adapted to the shock. Similar effects have been observed in other experiments (Murray and Nevin, 1967; Sandler, 1964), in which punishment has been introduced into the learning or maintenance of rewarded sequences of behavior which animals are free to perform without the control of explicit discriminative stimuli. Intense punishment has the more common effect of suppression of the behavior, even though performance continues to be rewarded. Punishment of mild intensity, or punishment that is introduced very gradually, tends to facilitate the performance of the behavior. The context of sequential behavior in which these effects occur suggests the possibility that mildly aversive outcomes may acquire positive reinforcement or incentive value, as well as informational value, when they are followed by rewarding outcomes of sufficiently high magnitude.

Punishment that is directly contingent on a particular class of overt acts is not the only source of aversive control which can produce behavioral suppression. The occurrence of a stimulus that has been repeatedly associated with a noxious event will independently suppress the well-established behavior which an animal has learned in order to obtain food, even though neither the stimulus nor its noxious correlate has been selectively contingent on the animal's behavior (Estes and Skinner, 1941; Kamin, 1965). This phenomenon commonly takes the form of a more generalized suppression of ongoing behavior in the presence of the stimulus. It can be attributed to the conditioned aversive affective value which has become attached to the stimulus. The behavioral suppression may be highly persistent when attempts are made to extinguish the value of the suppressive stimulus by eliminating its association with the noxious event—particularly if the noxious event has been used inconsistently in the original establishment and maintenance of the value (Wagner, Siegel, and Fein, 1967). Under certain conditions, a conditioned aversive stimulus may still retain a generalized suppressive effect after an interval of years during which it has not been tested (Hoffman, Selekman, and Fleshler, 1966). Conditioned aversive stimuli also have been shown to suppress behavior when they are given the function of secondary punishers—that is, when they are used as selective outcomes of a specific form of behavior (Hake and Azrin, 1965; Seligman, 1966).

All of these findings from paradigms for the conditioning of aversive affective value in animals have an obvious parallel in the socialization of children. Many kinds of social cues will acquire a generalized and durable aversive value for children, as a result of their intermittent association with noxious or painful experience. The cues will acquire some of their value because they have served as warning signals of the occurrence of a potential punishment. Other components of their value may be established by their association with the child's experience of aversive events which are not contingent on its behavior. These social cues can then act as conditioned suppressors of the child's ongoing or incipient behavior, without the immediate support of explicit forms of punishment. Once the aversive value of certain significant classes of social cues has been established, the cues may actually assume a more extensive role than that of direct punishment in the control of the child's behavior.

Although the socialization process generates a number of distinguishable contingencies for the establishment of aversive control over a child's behavior, the most important original source of these contingencies is the type of learning situation in which the child's overt behavior results in punishment. A wide variety of aversive stimulus events which are socially transmitted may produce suppression when they are contingent on a child's behavior. As was pointed out in Chapter Four, the range of these aversive outcomes goes beyond the more obvious categories such as physical punishment and explicit disapproval or rejection of the child. The disruption of pleasurable activity, the withdrawal of anticipated rewards, and other sources of frustration, are also potentially suppressive outcomes of a child's behavior. In addition, the behavior of socializing agents transmits a multitude of milder stimulus changes which cannot be described as punitive, but which nevertheless can function as suppressive outcomes of the child's behavior, because of their previous association with other events of established aversive value. For example, changes in another person's tone of voice or facial expression may acquire the function of conditioned suppressors.

It is useful to subsume under the concept of punishment all of the types of aversive outcomes which can produce suppression of the behavior on which they are contingent. Some of the forms of punishment which are embraced by such a broad concept will have an aversive value that is entirely acquired. Other forms of punishment may have certain components, such as abrupt physical contact or vocal stimulation of a high magnitude, whose value is highly predetermined by the child's unlearned dispositions. But the early experience of the child probably results in the attachment of some conditioned anxiety to specific stimulus components of virtually all forms of punishment. Even physical punishment may have elements of aversive value which are the product of the conditioning of anxiety that was originally elicited by such events as loss of physical support or withdrawal of a mother's presence.

The precise effects of punishment learning cannot be predicted from only a knowledge of the contingencies between the child's behavior and the occurrence of punishment. In the socialization of the child, punishment seldom produces a generalized suppression of behavior. It is typically the case that suppression of one overt form of the child's behavior enhances the probability of occurrence of other active forms of behavior. These alternative forms of behavior may be reinforced not only because they avoid punishment, but also because they produce rewarding social outcomes. The prediction of a child's internalized choice of conduct in a particular stimulus situation would therefore require a knowledge of the past history of its experience of both punishment and reward for the relevant behavioral alternatives in similar situations. Experiments with animals have demonstrated that punishment makes a more effective contribution to the maintenance of learned behavior when it has been used in paradigms which also provide positive reinforcement of nonpunished alternatives to the punished behavior (Boe, 1964; Solomon, 1964; Whiting and Mowrer, 1943). Failure to capture the interaction between the effects of punishment and reward undoubtedly accounts in part for the ambiguous findings of some of the surveys which have attempted to assess the relationship between the disciplinary practices of parents and the suppression of socially prohibited behavior by their children (Burton, Maccoby, and Allinsmith, 1961; Grinder, 1962; Sears, Rau, and Alpert, 1965, Chapter 6). The distinct role of punishment in producing internalized aversive control of the child's behavior can be separated out, however, in experimental paradigms of socialization which eliminate variation in the effects of positive reinforcement.

Among the different types of interaction between positive and aversive control of the child's behavior, probably the most important determinant of the suppressive effect of punishment is the positive incentive or reinforcement for the punished behavior itself. Common observation reveals that it is often difficult to produce suppression of behavior which has highly valued positive outcomes for a child. Most of the behavior that is exposed to punishment in the course of socialization also has positive reinforcing consequences of either unlearned or acquired value for the child. And in many instances, the reaction of a parent to a child's behavior may be a source of simultaneous reward and punishment. There is consistent evidence from studies of animal learning that the effectiveness of the suppression which is produced by punishment is inversely related to the magnitude, frequency, and immediacy of positive reinforcement of the punished behavior, and also to various indices of the strength of the motivation that is relevant to the positive reinforcement (Brown, Anderson, and Brown, 1966; Church and Raymond, 1967; Ferraro, 1966; Martin, 1963; Miller, 1959). The results of other experiments indicate that punished behavior is most sharply suppressed when the punishment is well removed in time from the point at which the behavior receives positive reinforcement

168CHAPTER SEVEN

(Akhtar, 1967; Holz and Azrin, 1963; Williams and Barry, 1966). This last finding suggests that the positive affectivity which is induced by reward may actually arrest or attenuate the aversive affectivity which is induced by punishment. The same inference is supported by the findings of experiments which have examined the effects of the interaction of positive and aversive intracranial stimulation (Buckwalter *et al.,* 1967; Olds and Olds, 1965).

Observations of children in both naturalistic and experimental situations confirm the expectation that the effectiveness of their suppression of socially prohibited and punished behavior will be inversely related to the strength of their positive motivation for the behavior. For example, Liebert and Ora (1968) have placed children in a situation where they could privately adhere to or violate the prohibition that was implied in the imposition of a high performance criterion on their self-administration of token rewards. Children for whom the tokens represented a highly valued positive incentive violated the prohibitions more frequently than did children for whom the tokens represented no additional incentive. The same type of relationship appears when well-established socialized dispositions, rather than the controlled incentives of a specific experimental situation, are used to assess children's positive motivation for prohibited behavior. Mischel and Gilligan (1964) found that the extent to which children cheated in a task of skill was directly related to an index of the strength of their need for achievement. Pearlin, Yarrow, and Scarr (1967) have observed that the children who are most likely to cheat in achievement tasks are those who experience the greatest pressure for success from their parents.

There is also some more indirect evidence that the suppressive effect of potential punishment is stronger when the child's behavioral dispositions are relatively free of its anticipation of the immediately pleasurable consequences of its actions. Mischel (1961a) found that children who were identified as delinquent more frequently chose an immediate smaller reward, in preference to a delayed larger reward, than did children who were not identified as delinquent. The findings of Mischel and Gilligan (1964) indicated that children's dispositions to cheat were inversely related to their dispositions to choose delayed rewards. Livson and Mussen (1957) found that children who were most persistent at a task for which reward was delayed were also least aggressive in their nursery school setting. Grim, Kohlberg, and White (1968) also have found that attentional persistence at a task is inversely related to cheating.

Some of the findings which are summarized above clearly imply that a child's orientation toward delayed rewards supports its maintenance of suppression of punished forms of behavior which may have more immediately rewarding outcomes. But it does not appear that the facilitative effect of an orientation toward delayed reward on the suppression of punished behavior can be attributed merely to a reduction in the intensity of the positive affective arousal that might be associated with the anticipation of an immediately pleasurable outcome at a behavioral choice point. Other evidence suggests that both the maintenance of behavioral suppression and the orientation toward delayed reward are closely related to the temporal span of the child's cognitive representation of anticipated outcomes of its behavioral choices (Brock and Del Giudice, 1963; Mischel, 1961a). Brock and Del Giudice found, for example, that children who were most likely to steal money from an experimenter also showed the shortest temporal span in their construction of stories.

A theoretical conception of the role of punishment in the establishment of internalized behavioral suppression was set forth in some detail in our earlier analysis of the mechanisms of socialization (see the analysis of behavior-contingent aversive learning in Chapter Four). Here only an abbreviated version of the conception is required in order to introduce the rationale of the design of a series of experiments. Any form of behavior may be defined as a transgression for a child when it has become discriminably associated with punishment that is sufficiently aversive to produce some degree of behavioral suppression. The punishment is always a social constraint on the child's behavior, even though it may not occur in a verbal context that would provide the child with a cognitive structure for evaluation of the transgression. One effect of the punishment is to condition anxiety directly to the discriminative behavioral cues and cognitive representations which are intrinsically correlated with the transgression (for example, to the child's cognitive representation of an actual performance of the transgression). The subsequent elicitation of anxiety by the intrinsic correlates of transgression is then the source of the motivation for the child's suppression of the transgression in the absence of potential agents of punishment. The anxiety may become attached to the child's intentions, and to other cognitive or behavioral precursors of the transgression, as well as to the intrinsic correlates of an overt performance of the transgression.

Punishment of a child's transgression will usually not produce a generalized passive suppression of behavior, but will instead facilitate the appearance of active behavioral alternatives to the transgression. Behavioral alternatives to transgression acquire a value that corresponds to reduction or inhibition of anxiety, in part because of their effectiveness in avoiding or terminating punishment (or warning signals), and in part because they arrest the anxiety that has already become attached to the intrinsic correlates of an incipient or ongoing transgression. Anxiety-reduction thus becomes directly conditioned to the behavioral and cognitive correlates of an act which is not punished. And the child's nonpunished behavior receives the reinforcement that is inherent in anxiety-reduction, even though it may have no reinforcing external consequences.

This conception of the internalization of punishment learning is an extension of the two-process conceptions of aversive learning which have been formulated largely on the findings of experiments on the avoidance behavior of animals (Mowrer, 1960a, Chapter 2; Solomon and Brush, 1956). These conceptions make a fundamental distinction between two processes which interact in the control of aversive learning. The first process is the Pavlovian conditioning of anxiety to either external cues or the intrinsic stimulus correlates of behavior. The second process is the reinforcement of behavior which is instrumental to the reduction of the anxiety. One way of testing the applicability of such a conception to the internalization of behavioral suppression is to examine the effect of the timing of punishment within as well as beyond the components of a punished act. The use of such an experimental design as an approach to the mechanisms of internalization was first suggested by R. L. Solomon (Mowrer, 1960b, pp. 399–404).

THE TEMPORAL LOCUS OF ANXIETY

Variation in the timing of punishment is particularly well suited to the problem of uncovering the mechanisms through which children internalize their control of behavioral suppression. When any form of conduct acquires some independence of social surveillance and external outcomes, it does not also become free of the control of external cues. The aversive value that punishment attaches to an act is rarely (or perhaps never) indiscriminate with respect to the external conditions under which the act occurs. The affective consequences of the onset, performance, or termination of the act, and of the behavioral alternatives to the act, continue to be governed by a stimulus complex that includes both internal and external cues, even though the child's behavioral choices may no longer be controlled by external reinforcing outcomes. In order to isolate the component of anxiety that has become attached to the discriminative cues and cognitive representations which are intrinsically correlated to punished behavior, it is therefore necessary to vary the temporal relationship between these intrinsic correlates and the occurrence of punishment, while the temporal position of external situational cues remains relatively constant.

Any act may be thought of as having a number of sequential intrinsic components. These components include intentions or other precursors of the act, motoric or cognitive correlates of the initiation and performance of the act, and corresponding intrinsic correlates which extend beyond the point of completion of the act. If internalized behavioral suppression requires the mediation of anxiety by the intrinsic correlates of a transgression, then the temporal locus of the original punishment should be a potentially powerful determinant of the point at which subsequent suppression will be motivated most effectively. Punishment at the point of a child's initiation of a transgression would attach maximal internalized anxiety to the intrinsic correlates of transgression which are present at that point. Conversely, punishment that follows the child's completion of a transgression would attach a greater intensity of anxiety to the intrinsic correlates of completion. Of course, the point of maximal intensity of anxiety could be varied more widely, within the course of punished behavior, if the behavior had sequential components with some duration in time. In short, the timing of punishment would be expected to determine the point at which Pavlovian conditioning mechanisms would attach the greatest intensity of anxiety to the sequential intrinsic correlates of punished behavior. And to the extent that behavioral alternatives to the punished behavior are motivated by anxiety (and reinforced by anxiety-reduction), they would have a greater probability of being elicited by the initial components of an incipient transgression if punishment originally occurred at the onset of the transgression, even though the child may no longer perceive any risk of punishment.

It is a well-established finding that the suppressive effect of punishment is a function of the immediacy with which the punishment follows the punished act. Experiments with animals in a variety of learning paradigms have shown that the strength of behavioral suppression falls off quite rapidly with increasing delay of punishment (Baron, 1965; Bixenstine, 1956; Camp, Raymond, and Church, 1967; Kamin, 1959; Mowrer and Ullman, 1945). Banks and Vogel-Sprott (1965) have observed the same difference between the effects of immediate and delayed punishment on the learned performance of human adults. The findings of an experiment that was reported by Azrin (1956) may be especially relevant to the effect of the timing of the inconsistent punishment contingencies which children commonly experience in the course of socialization. Azrin used punishment that was scheduled to occur in either a fixed or variable interval pattern, and found that immediate punishment was more effective in suppressing the behavior of rats than was delayed punishment.

The indices of suppression which have been used for investigations of the effects of timing of punishment generally are based on the performance of nonperformance of a single active form of punished behavior, rather than on the subject's choice among active forms of behavior under the control of discriminative stimuli. But Walters (1964) found that immediate punishment was also more effective than delayed punishment in facilitating the discrimination learning of children, in a situation where correct choices were rewarded and incorrect choices punished. In all of the experiments which have been cited, the timing of punishment was varied only across points which followed completion of the punished act. The timing was not varied within the components of the act. Other experiments have shown, however, that suppression is most effective when punishment follows closely on the initiation of punished behavior (Bolles and Warren, 1966), and also that the sequential components of punished behavior are differentially suppressed in proportion to the closeness with which they precede the occurrence of punishment (Rachlin, 1967).

The theoretical analysis which has been outlined here, for the effect of the timing of punishment on the internalization of behavioral suppression, was initially confirmed by an experiment in which nine- and ten-year-old boys were the subjects and a male experimenter took the role of the socializing agent (Aronfreed and Reber, 1965). Each child was confronted with a discrimination learning task during which he had to choose between two toys on each of nine training trials. A different pair of toys was used on each trial, but each pair consisted of one toy that was highly attractive and another that was relatively unattractive. All of the toys were small replicas of common objects in the child's environment. The child was instructed to pick up the toy in each pair that he wished to tell about, and then to describe its function at the agent's request. He was told also that certain toys were *"only supposed to be for older boys,"* and that he was not supposed to choose these toys. But he was given no further explanation of this constraint.

On each trial, the child was permitted to pick up the unattractive toy, and to describe its function, without any punishment. When he chose an attractive toy, however, the experimental agent punished his choice with verbal disapproval: *"No!—that's for the older boys."* In one experimental paradigm, the agent always administered punishment just as the child was reaching for an attractive toy and before he actually touched it. In a second experimental paradigm, the child was permitted to complete the transgression of picking up the attractive toy before the agent administered punishment (roughly two or three seconds after the toy had been lifted). The agent simultaneously expressed his disapproval and removed the toy from the child's hand, where it was being held and displayed in accordance with the instructions. There was also a control paradigm in which children were never given the opportunity to pick up toys or to experience explicit punishment. They were instructed only to point to the toy of their choice, and both toys were simply removed without comment when they pointed to the attractive one.

During the training trials, all of the children initially preferred the attractive toys. But the children in the two experimental groups shifted their choices to the unattractive toys after only one, two, or three punishments. And they consistently chose the unattractive toys thereafter. It was evident that the children discriminated easily between the two classes of toys, and that they quickly perceived the association between the choice of an attractive toy and the occurrence of punishment. Yet despite the narrow range of variation in the speed of learning, the children who were punished at initiation of a transgression suppressed their attractive choices after significantly fewer punishments than did the children who were punished at completion of a transgression. This finding was in accordance, of course, with the expectation that the suppressive effect of punishment would be a function of its temporal contiguity to the initiation of a punished act. The more dramatic effect of the timing of punishment appeared, however, during a common test for internalization that directly followed both of the punishment paradigms. This test was designed to convey that the child was entirely free of surveillance and of any risk of punishment. Two test objects were introduced as the first pair of toys in another choice task. Again, one toy was highly attractive and the other was unattractive. The agent then left the room on a pretext that would obviously take him far from the scene, and the child remained alone for five minutes within a protective nest of room-divider screens. The criterion of internalization was the observation of whether the behavioral suppression that had been acquired during training was still effective in the absence of the agent of punishment.

When the agent returned to the experimental room, he was able to observe a covert marker which indicated whether or not the child had picked up or handled the attractive toy. There was a much smaller incidence of transgression during the test among children who had been punished at initiation of transgression than there was among children who had been punished at completion of transgression, even though the former group actually had received fewer punishments during the training. Among the thirty-four children who had been punished at initiation of transgression, twenty-five did not handle or pick up the attractive test toy. But among the same number of children who had been punished at completion of transgression, only ten refrained from transgression during the test. The behavior of the children from the control paradigm made it clear that the highly reliable difference between the two groups of children from the punishment paradigms, in the effectiveness of their internalized suppression of punished behavior, was attributable to variation in the timing of punishment and not to the difference in the opportunity to pick up attractive toys during training. Twenty children in the control paradigm had no opportunity to pick up any toys during their training. Yet almost all of them picked up the attractive test toy. As is often true in naturalistic socialization, restriction of opportunity to transgress was insufficient, without explicit punishment, to produce internalized suppression of the children's dominant behavioral dispositions.

These basic findings have been more powerfully replicated and broadened in a recent extensive series of experiments (Aronfreed, 1966). Except for certain minor modifications, the procedures were fundamentally the same as those which already have been described. The age range of the subjects was widened to include children who were eight to ten years old. Boys and girls were used in equal numbers in each punishment training paradigm. The children were exposed to ten training trials, and the punishment was expanded to include deprivation of candy (that had already been given to the child) as well as verbal disapproval. In the paradigms which simply varied the timing of punishment, there was no reference, during either instructions or punishment, to certain of the toys being appropriate only for older children. The child was told that there were some toys which it was not supposed to choose, and that it would be punished if it chose these toys. But the agent gave no further cognitive structure with which the child could identify the punished choices or account for the constraint on its behavior. The learning situation was reduced essentially to choices and outcomes. During the test for internalization, the agent remained out of the room for ten minutes. A covert monitoring system recorded not only the occurrence of transgression, but also the amount of elapsed time (latency) since the agent had left the room.

Forty children were used in each of four paradigms which represented variations in the timing of punishment for choices of attractive toys: punishment when the child reached for the toy, punishment when the child completed the act of lifting the toy, punishment after the child had held the toy aloft for six seconds, and punishment after the child had described the toy's function in response to the agent's inquiry (roughly twelve or more seconds after the child had lifted the toy). Comparisons across these training paradigms indicated that suppression of attractive choices tended to appear more slowly with increasing delay of punishment—a tendency that was in accordance with the expectation that more immediate punishment would have a facilitative effect on performance in a discrimination learning task. Paradigms which represented adjacent values of timing of punishment were not reliably different, however, in the number of punishment (error) trials which were required to produce suppression, because all of the children were able to learn fairly rapidly the discrimination between attractive and unattractive toys. Regardless of the timing of punishment, all of the children undoubtedly had the benefit of their cognitive representations of the contingency between attractive choices and the occurrence of punishment. The absence of a significant effect of the timing of punishment on the speed of learning also has been observed in other experiments which have used the punishment of a social agent to produce discriminative suppression in the behavior of either children or dogs (Parke and Walters, 1967; Solomon, Turner, and Lessac, 1968; Walters, Parke, and Cane, 1965).

The more striking effect of the timing of punishment was apparent in the strength of behavioral suppression when the agent of punishment was absent during the ten-minute test for internalization. Latency of transgression was used as an index of suppression during the test situation, and no transgression at all was treated as a maximal latency. The strength of internalized suppression was a direct function of the immediacy of punishment during training. The earlier was the punishment during training, the stronger was the internalized suppression during the test. This experimental effect was quite powerful and was reliably sensitive to differences between each two adjacent values on the parameter of timing of punishment. The findings have been completely replicated with both male and female socializing agents, and also with certain variations of the agent's pretext for leaving the room. Separate analyses of the findings for boys and girls showed that the experimental effect was essentially the same for the two sexes.

The effect of the timing of punishment on children's internalization of behavioral suppression has been largely confirmed by the findings of other investigators who have adopted the same general experimental design (Parke and Walters, 1967; Walters et al., 1965). The same effect also has been demonstrated in experiments with dogs (R. L. Solomon, in Mowrer, 1960b, pp. 399–404; Solomon et al., 1968). These experiments have shown that punishment upon a puppy's approach to a forbidden food will produce more prolonged suppression, during a subsequent test in which the punitive agent is absent, than will punishment after some of the food has been consumed. The role of the timing of punishment as a determinant of the strength of internalized behavioral suppression provides strong support for the view that the suppression is under the control of the intensity of the anxiety that has become attached to the discriminative cues or cognitive representations which are intrinsically correlated to a transgression. The fact that the timing of punishment so markedly affects the internalized persistence of a complete suppression of transgression, when the locus of punishment has been varied within the sequential components of the punished act, indicates even more specifically that suppression of the initiation of transgression is controlled by the anxiety that becomes attached to the intrinsic correlates of the incipient act.

The close relationship between the timing of punishment and the effectiveness of internalized suppression also provides some indirect support for the hypothesis that nonpunished behavioral alternatives to a child's transgressions are reinforced by the anxiety-reducing value that becomes conditioned to their intrinsic correlates. There was more direct confirmation of the operation of an anxiety-reduction mechanism in some additional findings from the experimental series which used four variations in the timing of punishment. During the common test for internalization which followed all of the punishment training paradigms, the covert monitoring system recorded the latencies with which the children picked up both the attractive and unattractive test toys. The latencies with which the children picked up the unattractive toy tended to be inversely related to the delay of punishment during training, just as in the case of the latencies for picking up the attractive toy. The more immediate had been the punishment of attractive choices during training, the longer was the elapsed time before a child would pick up the unattractive toy during the test (although differences between paradigms which represented adjacent points on the timing parameter were not always reliable).

There appeared to be some generalization, then, of the suppression that had been induced by punishment of the children's choices of attractive toys. But the overwhelmingly typical test behavior of all of the children was nevertheless a pattern of picking up the unattractive toy before picking up the attractive toy. This last finding was in sharp contrast to the findings of other independent tests which had been used to ascertain that the children did in fact prefer the attractive toy. It pointed quite clearly to the possibility that nonpunished choices of unattractive toys might have acquired anxiety-reducing reinforcement value for the children in the course of the training paradigms.

Further analysis of the differences among the contingencies of the four punishment training paradigms suggested that the reinforcement of a child's nonpunished choices, through a mechanism of anxiety-reduction, might well have been highly sensitive to signals which were created by the consistency of a fixed temporal locus of punishment. During the early phase of any discriminative punishment learning, when a child has not yet fully decoded the external information that will enable it to distinguish between punished and nonpunished behavior, it will necessarily experience some anxiety in connection with any behavioral choice that it is about to make. And the reduction of the child's anxiety after a nonpunished choice will initially be dependent on external cues which have acquired the value of signals of the avoidance of punishment. The occurrence of these signals of punishment-avoidance will therefore enhance the suppression of the child's transgressions by serving to reinforce nonpunished behavioral alternatives.

The findings of some recent experiments in the animal laboratory clearly support the expectation that a stimulus will acquire the capacity to inhibit or attenuate anxiety when it functions as a signal that the animal will not be subjected to electric shock (Rescorla and LoLordo, 1965; Weisman *et al.,* 1966). Under the conditions of naturalistic socialization, the occurrence and timing of social signals of punishment-avoidance will often have an unpredictable relationship to the timing of punishment. But the four punishment paradigms of the experiment that has been described here were constructed in such a way that the child always received its first signal of punishment-avoidance, as an outcome of its choice of an unattractive toy, at precisely the same point in time at which its choice of an attractive toy would have been punished—for example, when the child's hand arrived at a toy without punishment in the first paradigm, when the child was asked to describe a toy after picking it up in the second paradigm, and whenever the child would have been punished for an attractive choice in the remaining paradigms. To the extent that anxiety-reduction came to be attached to signals of punishment-avoidance, the reinforcement of a nonpunished choice would be expected to be inversely related to the delay between the initiation of the choice and the occurrence of the signals. There would thus be a delay-of-reinforcement effect for nonpunished choices, which would be parallel to the delay-of-punishment effect for punished choices, across the four variations of timing in the training paradigms.

The variability in the timing of external signals of punishment-avoidance, across the original four training paradigms, suggested a more explicit test of the role of anxiety-reduction in the strengthening of internalized behavioral suppression. Forty additional children were exposed to a modification of one of the original paradigms. In the modified paradigm, the timing of punishment was maintained at a locus of six seconds after the child had lifted an attractive toy (the third value on the original timing parameter). But the signal of punishment-avoidance now occurred at an earlier point—the point at which the child had just lifted an unattractive toy. The effect of this paradigm on the children's behavior during the test for internalization confirmed the expectation that an early signal of punishment-avoidance would strengthen internalized suppression by providing greater reinforcement of the behavioral alternatives to transgression. The children showed the usual test choice pattern of first picking up the unattractive toy. Moreover, the latencies with which they picked up the unattractive toy were comparable to the latencies for the children from the original third paradigm that served as the baseline for the timing of punishment (in which the punishment and the signal of punishment-avoidance were equally delayed). However, the children who had been trained under the early signal of punishment-avoidance showed more prolonged suppression of the transgression of picking up the attractive test toy than did the children from the original baseline paradigm. Although the monitoring system did not provide information about the duration of the children's handling of the two test toys, it is reasonable to suppose that the children who received the early signal of punishment-avoidance during training may have spent more time in handling the unattractive test toy before they picked up the attractive toy. In any case, the pattern of behavior which these children showed during the test does support the view that behavioral alternatives to transgression acquire internalized reinforcement value as a result of the anxiety-reduction which becomes conditioned to their intrinsic correlates.

Variation in the timing of punishment is clearly a useful artificial device for teasing out the mechanisms of the internalization of behavioral suppression. The effect of the timing of punishment supports a conception of the internalization process which is grounded on the conditioning of the excitation and inhibition of aversive affectivity to intrinsic correlates of the child's behavior. But common observation suggests that the timing of punishment can hardly be a crucial determinant of the effectiveness with which children internalize their behavioral suppressions under naturalistic socialization. Of course, the social environment generates many sources of aversive control over a child's behavior. Once a child has had some experience with direct and explicit punishment of a specific form of behavior, the role of punishment in suppressing the behavior can easily be displaced to social cues which have acquired secondary aversive value through their previous association with the punishment. A child's incipient or ongoing transgressions will frequently be brought under the control of social warning signals which are emitted in the behavior of others. However, even when this extension of aversive control is taken into account, it is obvious that parents and other agents of socialization will have few opportunities to arrest the course of a transgression before it is committed. The mobility of young children increases radically during their early development, and their behavior comes to be under increasingly distant surveillance. Their experience of punishment will therefore necessarily have its greatest density of occurrence after transgressions are socially perceived as having been already committed.

It can be seen that an account of the effectiveness of naturalistic socialization in producing internalized behavioral suppression presents the same

problem as does an account of whatever internalized suppression was produced by the experimental paradigms in which punishment was delayed to
various points in time beyond the initiation of an attractive choice. The
problem is essentially one of finding a route by which the intensity of the
internalized anxiety that is mobilized at the point of an incipient transgression can be sufficient to motivate any suppression of the initiation of the
transgression, despite the fact that punishment for earlier transgressions
has not been encountered by the child until the transgressions already have
been committed.

Naturalistic socialization has a number of features which would govern
the occurrence of punishment and anxiety in such a way as to guarantee
effective internalized suppression, without requiring that parents be able to
anticipate the point at which a transgression will be initiated. For example,
the patterning of the temporal contingencies between a parent's punishment
and a child's behavior will often be determined by the duration or intermit-
tency of the behavior. Parents frequently punish after a discrete act that the
child already has committed but is about to repeat. Their punishment can
therefore attach substantial anxiety directly to the intrinsic correlates of an
incipient transgression, even though the punishment is not elicited until a
transgression has been visibly committed. This pattern of contingencies
was not present, however, in the experimental paradigms which controlled
the timing of punishment, since there the transgression was a discrete
choice that could not be repeated on a single trial. Naturalistic socialization
also often has the advantage of introducing punishment into the midst of a
sustained transgression which has continuity rather than sequentially different components in its behavioral topography. The intrinsic discriminative
cues and cognitive representations which are directly correlated to such a
continuous topography would tend to be relatively uniform between the
point of initiation of a transgression and the later point at which punishment may attach anxiety to the transgression.

The delayed punishment that is characteristic of naturalistic socialization is also made more effective by punishment-avoidance contingencies
which reinforce suppression even after a transgression has been committed.
The relatively weak internalized suppression that was produced by the
longer delays of punishment in the experimental paradigms may have been
partially attributable to designed constraints on contingencies for the
avoidance of punishment. In the experimental paradigms, a child's suppression was instrumental to the avoidance of punishment only when it
prevented the occurrence of a transgression. Once the child had initiated

the choice of an attractive toy, it was given no opportunity for a corrective suppression. Consequently, suppression could not acquire much value for reduction of the anxiety that was becoming attached to the occurrence of committed transgressions in the course of training. Under naturalistic socialization, it is also sometimes true that suppression loses its instrumentality for punishment-avoidance when the child already has committed a transgression. However, parents often modulate their punitive behavior in ways which permit the child to avoid or reduce punishment by suppressing an ongoing or repeated transgression. The child's behavioral suppression can therefore acquire some intrinsic anxiety-reducing value even when it does not initially prevent the occurrence of a transgression.

In the full context of a parent's characteristic habits of discipline, a child's internalization of behavioral suppression would also be determined by the interaction between the timing of punishment and a number of other regularities in the parent's behavior. For example, Burton *et al.* (1961) found that young children whose mothers reported that they intervened before their children had touched a forbidden object were actually somewhat more likely to transgress, in a controlled situation which was designed to test private conformity to an externally imposed rule, than were the children of mothers who reported that they punished after their children were already playing with the object. This finding must be evaluated, however, in the light of closely related findings from the same study, which suggested that the children who were most prone to transgress were also those whose mothers more generally gave relatively close supervision to their activities. It is by no means clear that a mother's disposition to arrest potential transgressions is an index of the readiness or vigor of her punitive reactions to the child's committed transgressions. On the contrary, there is evidence to suggest that parents who supervise their young children closely enough to constrain opportunities for transgression may also be less punitively oriented to the actual occurrence of transgression (Davis and Havighurst, 1946; Kohn, 1959; Maccoby and Gibbs *et al.*, 1954). The children of these parents may have quite limited experience with the more intense and suppressive forms of direct punishment, because their parents are using preventive and verbal socialization more extensively, with the aim of inducing what will eventually be a more internalized governor of conduct. It is also possible that their parents are more highly selective in the active suppression of very specific kinds of socially prohibited conduct, and that they broadly encourage their children's exploratory and manipulative dispositions, with the result that the children show relatively little generalized behavioral suppression in novel or unfamiliar situations (such as those which are commonly designed as tests of children's private conformity to the rules of a game).

A mechanism of stimulus generalization might be considered as a more general route by which the punishment that follows completion of a transgression would also attach some anxiety to the self-produced behavioral cues which are intrinsically associated with initiation of the transgression. Punishment that occurs after the completion of an act would attach maximal anxiety to the intrinsic correlates of the act which are immediately present at that point. But there might be some similarity or overlap among the sequential discriminative cues which are inherent in the different behavioral components of the punished act. And a certain amount of anxiety might consequently generalize to the intrinsic cues which are associated with the behavioral precursors or initiation of the act. However, the backward generalization of anxiety from a completed to an incipient punished act, across the sequential intrinsic correlates of the act, would provide only a weak and temporally narrow basis for an account of the effectiveness of delayed punishment in producing internalized suppression, if it were mediated only by perceptual information from motor components of the act. The generalization would be limited by the differences among the specific cues at different points in the motor sequence. An even more severe limitation is apparent in the contingencies of naturalistic socialization, where punishment most frequently occurs long after the point at which the inherent perceptual-motor traces of a punished act would still be present. Under these conditions, the traces could not provide a bridge for the movement of anxiety to the point of initiation of subsequent transgressions.

When punishment does occur after the initiation of a transgression, but while later intrinsic stimulus components of the transgression are still present—for example, during the course of a transgression—then the intensity of the anxiety that becomes attached to the intrinsic cues of an incipient transgression should attenuate across a generalization gradient. Of course, the similarity among the sequential discriminative cues which are embedded in a punished act, and the corresponding generalization of anxiety from the exact locus of punishment, would tend to be dependent on the temporal distance between specific cues, since the topography of the act would change as it moved from initiation to completion. When the relevant cues are sufficiently close to one another, the anxiety that generalizes to the cues of the incipient act may sometimes retain enough intensity to motivate subsequent suppressions of the act before it is committed. The operation of such a phenomenon is suggested in the findings of an experiment that was conducted by Walters and Demkow (1963), in which children were punished for transgression at one of two temporal positions which cut a rather fine difference into the intrinsic topography of the punished act. These investigators used reaching for a toy and touching a toy as their two contrasting loci of punishment. This variation of timing undoubtedly would have produced a substantial amount of overlap between the gradients of generalization of anxiety which were derived from two points of punishment which were so closely adjacent. And in a subsequent test of internalized suppression of the punished behavior, there was in fact only a tenuous difference in favor of the children who had been punished at the earlier point.

All of the considerations which have been outlined here point to one conclusion: that mechanisms for the conditioning of affectivity give only a partial account of the internalized suppression which can be induced by punishment that occurs over a wide spectrum of temporal relationship to the punished behavior. It appears that the internalized control of behavior which is produced by even the simplest forms of punishment training cannot be understood unless a central place is assigned to the representational function of the child's cognitive capacities. Cognitive representation eliminates any requirement that the internalized mediation of affectivity be monitored by the discriminative cues which are intrinsically available in the topography of the child's overt behavior. Changes of affectivity can be carried much more effectively by cognitive structures which assume the function of a common intrinsic representational bridge across the entire sequence of behavioral and external cues that unfolds as a punished act is initiated and completed.

The medium of language is the most discriminant channel of communication through which the social environment can provide the child with cognitive structures for the representation and evaluation of its behavior. It is the cognitive structures which are transmitted in the verbal communication of socializing agents, rather than the cues which are immediately inherent in overt behavior, which are the most powerful and extensive mediators of internalized affective control over the child's behavior. Language is the foundation of cognitive capacities which are not restricted to the direct or concrete representation of acts and their consequences. The capacity for symbolic representation makes abstract concepts and standards available to the child. These concepts and standards can be used to make complex discriminations within and among large classes of behavior, along cognitive dimensions which represent the properties of the behavior, the consequences of the behavior for the child or for others, and the external conditions under which the behavior may occur. The child's experience in a social environment is the generator of the development of these abstract representations. It is also the source of the affective values which become attached to different points along their cognitive dimensions.

Verbal communication is the pervasive feature of socialization that so greatly dilutes the potency of the timing of punishment as a determinant of internalized suppression. The verbal medium of socialization makes it possible for the locus of internalized anxiety to become independent of the original temporal relationship between a punished act and the occurrence of punishment. Behavioral or motivational precursors of a transgression can be given verbal and cognitive representations by both the socializing agent and the child, in direct conjunction with the occurrence of punishment, at points in time which are well beyond the termination of the transgression. These representations can then intercede to elicit conditioned anxiety and suppression before subsequent incipient transgressions are committed, since they can move relatively freely across specific behavioral and environmental cues. The intensity of the anxiety that is available to motivate the child's internalized suppression therefore does not require monitoring by the discriminative cues which are inherent in the actual performance of the transgression.

The power of cognitive structure in the child's internalization of control over its behavior can be demonstrated in the effects of a number of extensions of the punishment learning paradigms which were used in the experimental series that was described earlier (Aronfreed, 1966). The differential strength of internalized suppression that was induced by the original four variations in the timing of punishment was a product of paradigms in which children were given no cognitive structure for the representation of the criteria of transgression or of its relationship to punishment. In the extension series, however, one among several variations of a basic cognitive structure was verbally injected into each of a number of different paradigms. All of the paradigms had as their common baseline for the timing of punishment a delay of six seconds after the child had lifted an attractive toy (the third value of the original four variations in timing). Equal numbers of boys and girls were again used in each paradigm. And the basic procedure remained essentially the same as that used in the original timing paradigms. But the adult socializing agent added to the instructions, and to the administration of each punishment in the course of training, a verbal statement which transmitted a cognitive structure that focussed on the relative ease and difficulty of describing the two types of toys. The child was told initially that it would be punished when it chose toys which were *"hard to tell about"* and therefore appropriate only for older children. And the agent made a corresponding statement about the difficulty and appropriateness of the child's choice in direct conjunction with the occurrence of each punishment.

During the test for internalized suppression which followed training, observations were made of the occurrence and latency of the transgression of picking up the attractive toy. Among the forty children who were exposed to punishment training in the context of this kernel cognitive structure of ease versus difficulty, there was a marked facilitation of suppression during the test for internalization, in comparison to the suppression that had been shown by children who were trained in the original baseline timing paradigm (in which the delay of punishment was identical, but without the provision of any cognitive structure). Although this finding is based on punishment learning and pertains to the internalized maintenance of learned behavior, rather than to the learning process itself, it is in general agreement with the findings of experiments in which the verbalization of labels or concepts has been shown to facilitate children's transfer of discriminations learned under the control of rewarding outcomes (Kendler, 1963; Reese, 1966).

Another twenty children were then exposed to the same cognitive structure in a paradigm in which the verbal transmission of the structure did not occur in direct conjunction with punishment. The cognitive structure was verbalized instead in the intertrial interval that followed each punished choice, so that it actually occurred at ten to twelve seconds after the punishment. This paradigm also produced reliably stronger suppression, during the test for internalization, than did the original baseline timing paradigm which provided no cognitive structure. However, the strength of the internalized suppression was reliably less than that produced by the paradigm in which the agent verbalized cognitive structure in direct association with the occurrence of each punishment. The pattern of findings clearly supports the inference that cognitive structure facilitates the child's internalized suppression of punished behavior to the extent that the structure has become a conditioned monitor of anxiety. It appears that the anxiety which punishment attaches to cognitive representations can operate to suppress incipient punished behavior, even though socialization originally transmits both the punishment and the representations after the behavior has been committed.

Some even more striking findings emerged from additional paradigms in which the basic cognitive structure of ease versus difficulty in describing the toys was further elaborated to focus on the child's intentions. In the first of these paradigms, the experimental agent stated during the instructions, and in direct conjunction with each punishment of an attractive choice, that the child was being punished for *wanting* to pick up a toy that was appropriate only for description by older children. This paradigm again produced reliably stronger internalized suppression, among the forty children who were exposed to it, than did the original baseline timing paradigm which provided no cognitive structure. But the focus on the child's intentions did not produce reliably stronger suppression than that produced by the paradigm which used only the kernel cognitive structure of ease versus difficulty.

It was then noted that in all of the paradigms which had been designed up to this point, the verbal instructions had emphasized the contingency between punishment and picking up (or wanting to pick up) certain toys. In the paradigm in which the agent had verbalized a cognitive focus on the child's intentions, the intended behavioral component (picking up), as well as the intention itself, therefore already had occurred when punishment was administered at the point where the child had been holding a toy for six seconds. Accordingly, another twenty children were used in a paradigm which converted all verbal communication, during both instruction and administration of punishment, to an emphasis on *telling* about the toys and on *wanting* to tell. This variation was designed in such a way that the relevant intention (wanting to tell) would be present at the point of punishment, still six seconds after the child had lifted an attractive toy. But the intended behavioral component of telling would not yet have occurred. The verbalization of a cognitive focus on the child's intentions now did produce reliably stronger suppression, during the test for internalization, than had been produced by the verbalization of the kernel cognitive structure which made no reference to intentions. Children who received their punishment training under these conditions in fact most commonly showed complete suppression of the transgression of handling the attractive test object. The frequency of complete suppression was equivalent to the frequency for children who had been punished immediately upon reaching for attractive toys in the first of the original four paradigms which varied only the timing of punishment.

Finally, one other variation of a verbalized focus on intentions was carried out with twenty additional children. The cognitive structure that was verbalized to the child in this last paradigm again represented punishment as the consequence of wanting to tell about toys which were appropriate choices only for older children. Punishment was actually administered, however, after the child already had told about an attractive toy, so that now both the intention and the intended behavioral component of telling had occurred before the punishment (as in the first attempt to construct a training paradigm that focussed on intentions). Once again, the focus on the child's intentions had no specific effect on the strength of suppression during the test for internalization. The strength of internalized suppression was no greater than that produced by the kernel cognitive structure of ease versus difficulty.

Apparently, the verbal representation of a child's intention facilitates internalization of behavioral suppression only when the occurrence of punishment is closely and distinctly linked in time to the intention itself. A verbalized focus on intention seems to contribute little to internalized control of behavior, beyond the general mediational properties of any cognitive structure, when punishment does not separate intention from performance of the intended behavior. The strength of the internalized suppression that can be produced, when punishment is directly associated with the child's intentions, is another kind of evidence that suppression is highly sensitive to the intensity of the anxiety which becomes attached to intrinsic precursors of punished behavior. The evidence is also of considerable interest because of the special place that is given to intentions in accounts of the child's acquisition of moral judgement (Kohlberg, 1969; Piaget, 1948).

The child's capacity for cognitive representation also enables it to acquire dispositions toward suppression which are not originally dependent on the effectiveness of its own behavior in the avoidance of punishment. Socialization provides many opportunities for children to learn selective suppression of certain forms of behavior through their observation of the behavior of others. Some observational learning of this kind may actually occur through the child's imitative reproduction of the punitive reactions which socializing agents show toward its transgressions.

The opportunity for the use of an agent of punishment as a model of suppression is particularly evident in the case of acquired control over aggressive behavior. Many investigators have pointed out that models of aggression often may be provided for the child in a parent's punishment of transgression (Bandura and Walters, 1959, 1963b; Miller and Swanson *et al.,* 1960; Sears, Maccoby, and Levin, 1957, Chapter 7). Conversely, one might expect that a parent's punitive behavior would sometimes provide a model for the suppression of aggressive behavior. Parents frequently exercise obvious restraints on their aggressive dispositions in the course of re-acting to their children's behavior. Some of their punitive and mildly aggressive reactions may acquire potential intrinsic value for the child because they come to mark the termination of the anticipatory anxiety that follows a transgression. The child's imitative tendencies may then lead it to reproduce these reactions and their acquired anxiety-reducing value when its anxiety is subsequently elicited either by its own incipient aggressive behavior or by the behavior of others. Accordingly, the child's disposition to control its aversive experience through imitation would produce learning of some of the more socially permissible forms of aggression and a corre-sponding facilitation of the suppression of socially prohibited forms.

There are other kinds of imitative control of internalized suppression which may not even require the child's direct experience of aversive events. The stimulation of a social environment will often elicit a child's empathic or vicarious anxiety in ways which are not contingent on its own behavior. For example, the child may observe aggressive or threatening interactions between adults or peers. It then also has the opportunity to observe models whose actions may terminate such interactions and so eliminate the exter-nal source of its anxiety. These actions may represent the suppression of socially prohibited forms of behavior and the performance of more socially desirable behavioral alternatives. And to the extent that the actions of the models are effective in terminating the observed interactions which have elicited the child's anxiety, they may acquire an intrinsic value that the child can reproduce through imitation when it is subsequently a direct par-ticipant in similar interactions.

One other important contribution that imitation may make to inter-nalized suppression should be noted here. Children often independently react to their own transgressions by reproducing the verbal criticisms which they have already experienced as part of the punishment that is used by their socializing agents. The internalization of self-criticism is the most common specific instance of the child's broader tendency to reproduce cer-tain components of punishment which have first acquired reinforcement value as signals for the termination of its anticipatory anxiety following a transgression (see the discussion of self-criticism in the later analysis of Reactions to Transgression). However, socializing agents are extremely variable in the temporal positions at which they use their verbal punish-ment. They frequently use verbal criticism as a warning signal that more aversive consequences will follow, particularly if the child carries out an incipient transgression or continues an ongoing one. Their criticism may therefore also serve, at least initially, as an anxiety-arousing verbal cue which elicits the child's suppression of punished behavior. As the criticism becomes internalized by the child, its original dual signal function may well become collapsed to the single function of anxiety-reduction, since it gradually comes to be followed so closely by the effective suppression of incipient transgressions. One sometimes sees direct evidence in the overt verbalization of very young children that their internalized use of parental warning signals, even before they have committed a transgression, serves to reduce their anxiety through its rapid mediation of suppression.

A variety of recent experiments are interesting demonstrations of the control of internalized suppression by the child's observation of the punitive consequences of the behavior of others. These experiments were also cited in Chapter Five as attempts to demonstrate facilitation of children's performance of specific acts through their observation of the rewarding consequences of another person's performance of the acts. But the evidence for the suppressive effect of observed punishment is more impressive than the evidence for the facilitative effect of observed reward.

In the experiments which were reported by Bandura, Ross, and Ross (1963c) and by Walters, Leat, and Mezei (1963), children observed the aggressive behavior of an adult or the violation by another child of prohibitions on the handling of toys. When they were then given the opportunity to engage in the same behavior, in the apparent absence of surveillance, they were less likely to do so if they had seen the behavior punished than if they had seen it rewarded. These two experiments did not actually separate the suppressive effect of observed punishment from the possible facilitative effect of observed reward, since they provided no baseline for assessment of the extent to which observation of another person's behavior in itself might have elicited corresponding behavior from the child, without whatever effect might have been introduced by the child's observation of the consequences of the behavior. However, a further study by Bandura (1965a) and additional studies by Walters and his co-workers (Walters and Parke, 1964a; Walters et al., 1965) are clearer demonstrations of the internalized suppression that can be induced by the child's observation of the punishment of another person's actions. In these later studies, children who saw the behavior of another person punished showed more suppression of the same behavior than did children who saw the behavior occur without either punitive or rewarding consequences. Similar effects have been obtained in the behavior of adults who observe the punishment of another person's aggressive actions (Lefcourt et al., 1966; Wheeler and

Smith, 1967).

The findings which are summarized above leave no doubt that children have cognitive equipment which they can use to translate the observed punitive consequences of another person's behavior to the control of their own actions. It is interesting to note Rosekrans' (1967) recent finding that children who had observed a long sequence of another child's task-oriented behavior, and who had also seen the other child exposed to verbal punishment at the end of the sequence, showed suppression only of the observed component of behavior which had just preceded the punishment. This finding suggests that the timing of punishment can be a significant determinant of behavioral suppression even when the child's anxiety must become attached to its cognitive representations through observation rather than direct experience.

The concept of a model is not required, of course, to account for a demonstration that suppression of a child's behavior can be induced by its observation of the punishment that another person receives for the same behavior—particularly since what the child observes is the performance rather than the suppression of the behavior. The suppressive effect of the child's observation of punishment, in the experiments which have been described, is more generally interpreted as evidence of the child's capacity for empathic or vicarious experience (see, for example, Bandura, 1965b, and Kanfer, 1965). This interpretation is open to question. It is certainly possible for empathic or vicarious experience to be the source of the anxiety that is required to motivate suppression. The child's affective response to the aversive consequences of its actions for others, as well as to its observation of the aversive consequences of another person's behavior, may have much the same effect as its direct experience of punishment in producing internalized behavioral suppression. But the fact that the child suppresses behavior for which another person has been punished cannot in itself warrant the inference that empathic or vicarious experience mediates the effects of observation. As was pointed out in the earlier analysis of empathic and vicarious experience (Chapter Four), the observed consequences of another person's behavior may influence the child's choice among its already established behavioral dispositions through other kinds of social transmission of affective and informational values. It is not necessary to assume that the child experiences an affective state which corresponds to what it perceives as the experience of another person, or that it has acquired any new behavioral dispositions as a result of observation.

DISCRIMINATION AND CONTROL OF OUTCOMES

The burden that may be imposed on the effectiveness of punishment training, when it does not have the cognitive support of a verbal medium of socialization, can be demonstrated in the findings of another experiment, in which six- and seven-year-old boys were exposed to either mild or intense punishment in paradigms which required discriminations of varying complexity (Aronfreed and Leff, 1963). This experiment also was designed to examine the effects of punishment training on internalized behavioral suppression. The adult socializing agent was a male, and the procedure was similar in many respects to the procedure that was used in the experiments which already have been described.

The child was required to choose between two small toys in pairs which varied over ten training trials. The toys within each pair were roughly comparable in attractiveness, but they differed consistently in other properties which the child might use as cues to distinguish between punished and nonpunished choices. When the child made a punished choice, punishment was administered at the point where the child had just touched the toy. When the child made a nonpunished choice, it was permitted to pick up and describe the toy. Two groups of children were confronted with a relatively simple discrimination between red and yellow toys. Choices of the red toys were punished. Two other groups of children were confronted with a complex and difficult discrimination between toys which represented passive containers and toys which represented objects having an active internal mechanism. Choices of toys of the latter class were punished. None of the groups were provided with any verbal communication of a cognitive structure which could be used to represent the discriminate properties of the two types of toys or the relationship between choice and punishment.[1]

The simple and complex discrimination groups were further subdivided into paradigms in which the children experienced either a low or a high intensity of punishment for incorrect choices. The agent's punishment was compounded of verbal disapproval, deprivation of candy, and the sounding of a buzzer which could be varied in loudness in order to control the intensity of punishment. It was apparent that even the children in the simple discrimination groups were not able to distinguish between punished and nonpunished choices quite as readily as were the older subjects in the experiments which had varied the timing of punishment. These six- and seven-

[1] Thirty-six children were used in each of the simple discrimination groups, and forty-three children were used in each of the complex discrimination groups.

year-old boys committed more errors before arriving at fairly consistent correct performances (choices of the yellow toys) than did the eight- to ten-year-old children who had been required to choose unattractive toys in other types of paradigms (even when the older children had been given no explicit cognitive structure for the representation of the required discrimination). The difference in the speed of learning may have been attributable in part to the older children's greater spontaneous use of appropriate verbal labels of concepts. Incidental observations of the children's behavior in the different paradigms also suggested, however, that an association between punishment and the attractiveness of a toy was more consistent with their expectations than was an association between punishment and the color of a toy.

Despite their initial difficulty with the simple discrimination, most of the children clearly showed an increase in the frequency of their correct choices of yellow toys as the ten training trials progressed. Intensity of punishment had no effect on the speed with which they learned the required discrimination.[2] But among the seventy-two children who had been trained in the simple discrimination paradigms, under either low or high intensity of punishment, forty-two had suppressed choices of the red toys to the point where they were making three or four correct choices in the last four trials. In contrast, the performance of the children in the two complex discrimination paradigms did not improve in the course of training. Of course, they made significantly more punished choices than did the children in the simple discrimination paradigms. But they also showed little evidence of any gradual learning of the discrimination between passive containers and objects having an active internal mechanism. For example, only twenty-five of eighty-six children attained a performance criterion of at least three correct choices in the last four training trials.

A common test for internalized behavioral suppression followed each of the four training paradigms. The agent left the room on a pretext. And the child remained alone with a single pair of toys which were respectively similar in some of their properties to both of the types of pairs which had been used during training. One of the toys had red surfaces and represented an object with an active internal mechanism, so that it would be similar to toys which the children had been punished for choosing in either the simple or complex discrimination training. This test toy also was made highly at-

---

[2] Parke and Walters (1967) also have reported that intensity of punishment had no effect on the performance of children in the simple discrimination learning paradigm which they employed in one of their experiments.

tractive, in order to increase the probability of transgression. During the test for internalization, the children who had been trained in the simple discrimination paradigms were more likely to show complete suppression of any handling of the attractive toy if they had been exposed to intense punishment than if they had been exposed to mild punishment. Only fifteen of thirty-six children transgressed after they had experienced intense punishment; whereas twenty-seven of thirty-six children transgressed after they had experienced mild punishment. But the children who had been given training in the complex discrimination paradigms were actually more likely to transgress during the test if they had been exposed to intense punishment than if they had been exposed to mild punishment. Only eighteen of forty-three children transgressed after they had experienced mild punishment; whereas thirty-one of forty-three children transgressed after they had experienced intense punishment. It can be seen that the proportionate frequencies were almost exactly the reverse of those which were obtained for the simple discrimination groups. These effects of variation in the intensity of punishment were highly reliable for both the simple and the complex discriminations.

The findings which are summarized above clearly indicate that intensity of punishment was not the only determinant of the motivation and reinforcement for internalized behavioral suppression. The experimental effect in the simple discrimination paradigms was hardly surprising, since an extremely loud and aversive sound had been used as the intense punishment. Under the assumption that internalized suppression is motivated as a function of the intensity of the anxiety that becomes attached to the intrinsic correlates of punished behavior, intense punishment would be expected to produce more effective suppression. Apparently, however, the greater effectiveness of more intense punishment obtains only when the child is able to distinguish between punished and nonpunished behavior. The usual suppressive effects of punishment may be disrupted in unexpected ways if learning requires a discrimination that the child cannot resolve.

Our first clue to an account of how behavioral suppression might actually be undermined by intense punishment, when the child is confronted with a difficult or insoluble discrimination, is the observation that nonpunished behavioral alternatives could not acquire discriminate anxiety-reducing value under such conditions. The inability to exercise any control over the potential outcomes of its behavior in a punishment learning situation may have the effect of maintaining a high level of aversive affectivity in the child. For example, in the complex discrimination paradigms of the experiment, the child would experience not only the anxiety of the immediate anticipation of punishment following a choice, but also the more prolonged anxiety and frustration which are associated with unpredictable punitive outcomes. Since the outcomes remain unpredictable, neither class of choices acquires any consistent reinforcement value through avoidance of punishment. Inhibition of anxiety therefore cannot become selectively attached either to the child's behavioral dispositions or to its cognitive representation of external informational cues. As a result, a generalized aversive value is likely to become attached to the very act of making a choice.

When punishment itself has only a mild intensity, the inability to make correct choices and avoid punishment may nevertheless be sufficiently aversive to motivate a child's nonselective suppression of any active choice. In the experimental setting, of course, the child must pick up one toy or the other on each trial, so long as it remains within the constraints of the training task. But the child may actually be learning not to try to make a choice. During the test situation, when the agent is absent, the child is no longer required to pick up a toy. Its suppression of the handling of the attractive test toy may then reflect a more general behavioral disposition which is dominated by the aversive value that has become associated with any active engagement of the toys.

When a child is exposed to intense punishment, it may react very differently to its continuing inability to predict the consequences of its actions. Its disposition to attempt any correct choices may be suppressed by the aversive experience of being unable to exercise discriminate behavioral control over the reactions of socializing agents. But it may also learn to engage in active and relatively indiscriminate behavior in order to reduce the intense anxiety that has become attached to its anticipation of an intense and unpredictable punishment. Under conditions where a child must repeatedly experience intense anticipatory anxiety, the anxiety may come to be more aversive than the punishment itself. To the extent that punishment acquires the value of a signal that terminates anticipatory anxiety, it may then serve as a reinforcing outcome for any active commitment of behavior. In the complex discrimination paradigm of the experiment, for example, the active behavior of picking up either toy may reduce the child's intense anxiety regardless of whether it produces or avoids punishment. And during the test situation, when the child's anxiety is elicited again by the potential transgression that may be committed in the act of picking up an attractive toy, the act itself may be the most effective way in which the child can reduce the anxiety.

This entire analysis suggests, then, that a child's punished and nonpunished behavioral dispositions may sometimes be maintained simultaneously in areas of conduct where its social experience has attached intense anxiety to its potential transgressions, but where the child has not been able to discriminate information that will predict the consequences of its behavior. What the child may learn under these conditions is that both the punitive and nonpunitive consequences of its behavior are effective markers for the termination of its anticipatory anxiety.

The findings of other recent experiments also provide evidence that the effectiveness of internalized suppression is a function of the intensity of anxiety which is discriminately associated with punished or prohibited behavior. Leff (1967) has confirmed the finding that intense punishment produces stronger internalized suppression than does mild punishment, when children are given training in a simple discrimination paradigm of the type which has been described. Schachter and Latané (1964) reported that the administration of chlorpromazine, a drug which appears to depress sympathetic activation in the autonomic nervous system, increased the incidence of cheating among college women. The findings of the experiments which have been conducted by Parke and Walters (1967) are particularly relevant to the interaction between the effects of intensity of punishment and ease of discrimination. Close examination of their methods and results reveals that the effectiveness of internalized suppression was directly related to intensity of punishment when children were given clearly discriminable alternatives, but that the effect of intensity was obscured when punishment was arbitrarily assigned to the child's acts in such a way as to deprive it of discriminant cues.

In the types of experimental paradigms which have been described in this chapter, the usual effect of intensity of punishment on the strength of internalized suppression was actually reversed, when children were exposed to conditions of learning in which they were unable to discriminate the cues that signalled the consequences of their behavior. There is no reason to expect that this remarkable reversal will always occur when socialization confronts the child with an insoluble discrimination. Intense punishment and difficult discrimination will also undoubtedly sometimes interact to produce a generalized suppression of all of the child's relevant behavior, or to motivate the child to seek additional social information for the control of its behavioral choices. The experimental paradigms probably had specific properties, in their range of punishment intensities and in their constraints on the child's behavioral choices, which added a significant com-

ponent of anxiety-reducing value to behavior that was intensely punished
but poorly identified by the child. Nevertheless, the fact that there are conditions under which intense punishment may facilitate the child's subsequent engagement in punished behavior, while mild punishment is relatively more effective in producing internalized suppression, has some very
interesting implications for a more general understanding of the aversive
control of socialization.

Common observation of children's reactions to punishment will not
make it seem so surprising that they may occasionally acquire temporary
or even permanent equivalent dispositions toward punished and nonpunished behavior, when their own motivations constrain their behavioral
options, and when learning requires information for which they do not
have an adequate cognitive representation. Under these conditions of learning, children do sometimes behave as though avoidance of punishment has
less value for them than does the establishment of those consequences of
their actions which they cannot predict. Their behavior certainly suggests
the inference that the intensity of their anticipatory anxiety adds an increment of motivation to any active behavioral choice with which they can
produce an external event that will terminate the anxiety, even though that
event may sometimes be the occurrence of punishment.

There is also a very sizeable amount of experimental evidence which indicates that the crucial determinant of the effect of punishment learning is
the predictability and control of the aversive and nonaversive consequences
of alternative forms of behavior. It appears that the aversive properties of
punishment itself are primarily important as the base for the conditioning
of anxiety to external cues or intrinsic correlates of behavior. Once conditioned anxiety has been established, the direction of learning seems to be
determined by the relative effectiveness with which specific forms of behavior produce any class of events that reduces or inhibits the anxiety. The
experimental evidence deserves some attention here, because it expands
our view of the contingencies of socialization which govern the child's
acquisition of internalized aversive control over its behavior.

Various indices of the effectiveness of aversive learning in the animal
laboratory have been shown to be directly related to intensity of punishment. Intense punishment is more effective than mild punishment in the
suppression of both discrete acts and behavior sequences which have been
originally established and maintained by reward (Azrin and Holz, 1966;
Boroczi et al., 1964; Camp et al., 1967; Church, Raymond, and Beauchamp, 1967; Hake et al., 1967; Rachlin, 1967). Intense punishment also

facilitates the concurrent and subsequent extinction of behavior from which rewarding outcomes have been withdrawn (Boe and Church, 1967; Estes, 1944) and the extinction of behavior that was originally instrumental to the avoidance of punishment (Kintz and Bruning, 1967; Seligman and Campbell, 1965). Many studies of active avoidance training have demonstrated the same functional relationship between effectiveness of learning and the intensity of punishment for failure to avoid (Boren, Sidman, and Herrnstein, 1959; Church, 1963; D'Amato, Fazzaro, and Etkin, 1967; Sandler et al., 1966). Greater intensity of punishment also has been shown to produce more suppression of the punished behavior of adult human subjects (Kaufman, 1964; Sidowski, Wyckoff, and Tabory, 1956).

It is characteristic of the findings which are cited above that they are based on learning situations in which relatively little informational load is placed on the subject's discriminative capacities. The value of alternative behavioral choices in these situations is not conditional on external cues which explicitly require discrimination. It is conditional at most on the presence or absence of one signal. In contrast, the effectiveness of learning often proves to be inversely related to intensity of punishment, at least within certain ranges of intensity, when the active control of aversive outcomes places a substantial burden on the subject's capacity to discriminate between different cues. A well-known example of this finding was reported many years ago by Yerkes and Dodson (1908), who observed that the punishment of incorrect choices facilitated the discrimination learning of rats within an increasingly narrow range of intensity as the apparent difficulty of the discrimination increased. Punishment that was more intense than the optimal range appeared to produce "emotional" responses which interfered with learning. More recent experiments with animals also have demonstrated an inverse relationship between intensity of punishment and effectiveness of learning in discriminative avoidance paradigms and in discrimination tasks which require the subject to learn behavioral choices which are both rewarded and punished (Curlin and Donahue, 1965; D'Amato and Fazzaro, 1966).

There are similar implications in the findings of some of the experiments which Spence (1956) and his associates conducted with groups of human subjects who had been identified on the basis of their own reports of their general dispositions toward anxiety. In simple tasks which required only a minimal use of discriminative cues in order to avoid noxious stimuli, the subjects who had been classified as being highly disposed toward intense anxiety learned more efficiently than those who had been classified as being less disposed toward intense anxiety. But in more complex tasks—even in those which required only a choice between two alternatives on each trial—the subjects who were more susceptible to intense anxiety showed a poorer performance. There is reason to think that the relatively poor learning of the more anxiety-prone subjects in discrimination tasks is partly attributable to their active use of their choices to reduce anticipatory anxiety rather than to control external outcomes. For example, Katahn, Blanton, and Gipson (1967) found that college students who had strong dispositions toward anxiety gave responses of a more vigorous amplitude than did students who had weaker dispositions toward anxiety, in an insoluble problem situation where they received unpredictable electric shocks for incorrect choices.

Poor learning or nonadaptive behavior have been noted quite often in experiments which have not varied the intensity of punishment systematically, but which have employed highly aversive outcomes of the active behavioral choices of animals in very difficult discrimination situations (Farber, 1948; Maier, 1949). Amsel and Ward (1965) recently showed that the learning of a relatively simple discrimination was also severely hampered after hungry animals had been first exposed to the frustrating experience of being unable to use the discriminative cues consistently in their attempts to obtain food.

There are a number of reported experiments, then, in which the aversive outcomes of incorrect behavioral choices appear to interfere with the learning of a difficult discrimination and even to disrupt any consistent use of discriminative cues in the exercise of active control over the outcomes. Incidental evidence in almost all of these experiments suggests that the lack of discriminative control over outcomes is in itself a source of aversive affective arousal of behavior which is irrelevant to the discrimination. The observations which are made in other kinds of experiments indicate even more clearly that a difficult discrimination is often a source of aversive affectivity which disrupts the learning process. Tighe and Leaton (1966) found that rats who had been trained to resolve behavioral conflicts under a simple discrimination frequently exercised the option to terminate their subsequent exposure to conflict in a difficult discrimination. Many investigators have noted that children who are being rewarded only for correct choices show lack of attention and other overt behavioral evidence of frustration when they are performing poorly in a discrimination task (Reese, 1963; Spiker, 1959; Steigman and Stevenson, 1960). The intensity of the affectivity that is elicited in a child under these conditions might well be sufficient to increase the difficulty of learning by interfering with the child's attention to relevant cues (Easterbrook, 1959; Kausler and Trapp, 1960).

The reports of most of the experiments which demonstrate poor discrimination learning, when the subject cannot quickly acquire control over the occurrence of aversive outcomes, also recurrently include formal and informal observations of two dominant patterns of behavior: a generalized suppression of active behavior or a nondiscriminate commitment to a single direction of active choice. In those cases where unavoidable or unpredictable punishment has been used, it is difficult to resist the inference that these two patterns are the subject's primary behavioral resources for the reduction of anxiety. When the motivation for learning or performance is entirely defined by aversive contingencies which cannot be brought under active discriminative control, we might suppose that a generalized suppression of active behavior could become effective in reducing anxiety, providing that failure to make an active choice is not punished. However, if the suppression of active behavior is also punished, then a quickly negotiated active choice might be expected to be more effective in the reduction of anticipatory anxiety, even though it may result in punishment. These expectations are in fact roughly confirmed by a comparison of the findings of two experiments in which human subjects were confronted with choices between two conflicting directions of overt behavior, both of which produced aversive consequences. Sears and Hovland (1941) did not require their subjects to make an active choice, and they found a high incidence of immobilization or blocking of both directions of behavior. But Smith and Epstein (1967) found that subjects who were required to make an active choice under these conditions typically made a single direct and uncorrected choice in only one direction.

There are a number of other respects in which objective contingencies for punishment-avoidance have only a limited utility when they are used to predict whether the prevailing behavioral resolution of aversive experience will be a generalized suppression or an active attempt to exercise some instrumental control over events in the environment. For example, it appears that animals sometimes acquire a marked disposition toward immobility between their successive exposures to inescapable electric shock, neither the onset nor termination of which is contingent in any way on their behavior—particularly when the duration of shock is so long that active attempts to escape have ceased well before the termination point (Brookshire, Littman, and Stewart, 1961; Pearl, Walters, and Anderson, 1964). In some instances, the inability to control the shock produces the more dramatic effect of a passive helplessness throughout the entire course of its administration (Maier, Seligman, and Solomon, 1968). This kind of preliminary exposure to uncontrollable aversive stimulation may enhance the later suppressive effects of punishment, when animals are placed in a learning situation where aversive outcomes are contingent on a specific form of active behavior (Kurtz and Walters, 1962; Pearl *et al.*, 1964). But the same kind of initial experience with inescapable shock may have disruptive and even crippling effects on the subsequent learning or maintenance of active escape or avoidance behavior (McAllister and McAllister, 1965; Overmier and Seligman, 1967; Seligman and Maier, 1967). Some investigators have shown that the experience of inescapable shock by newly weaned animals has adverse effects on their active escape or avoidance behavior in adulthood (Brookshire *et al.*, 1961; Denenberg and Bell, 1960).

The fact that animals can be immunized against these effects of inescapable shock on subsequent escape- and avoidance-training, if they are first given shock-escape training (Seligman and Maier, 1967), indicates the importance of their total past experience of the exercise of control over aversive stimulation. It is interesting to note also that the effects are sometimes less visible in avoidance behavior if the animal subsequently is able to learn an escape contingency and thus obtains some experience of control over shock. Brookshire *et al.* (1961) reported that the avoidance behavior which followed successful escapes actually was facilitated by the earlier experience of inescapable shock. However, Bloom and Campbell (1966) have found that even the maintenance of well-established avoidance behavior may be disrupted after a series of trials on which the absence of warning signals temporarily deprives animals of their original active control over shock-avoidance.

Most of the contingencies of punishment learning which occur in the socialization of the child are unlikely to produce a generalized disposition toward suppression of active behavior. The greater part of the child's aversive social experience occurs in situations where it continues to exercise some active control over the outcomes of its behavior. Even when it is unable to employ discriminations which would allow prediction of the contingencies between acts and outcomes, the child will still frequently have the experience of making active choices which successfully avoid punishment. Some of the child's active choices will also reduce its anticipatory anxiety even though they result in punishment. Under these conditions, it is still possible that extremely aversive punishments of some active behavioral choices will produce a generalized disposition toward suppression. An example of such an effect in the behavior of animals was apparent in Maier's (1949) finding that it was sometimes necessary to shock rats in order to induce them to make an active choice, when they were unable to use discriminative cues in their efforts to obtain reward and avoid punishment. However, when animals are given some control over at least the point of occurrence of a potential punishment, they more typically show fixation of a single direction of behavior when they cannot discriminate cues which would enable them to avoid punishment consistently (Farber, 1948; Maier, 1949).

Many investigators have shown that animals will persist in active behavior that produces shock or other aversive stimulation when punishment becomes the consequence of acts which were originally established by escape- or avoidance-training (Brown, Martin, and Morrow, 1964; Campbell, Smith, and Misanin, 1966; Melvin and Martin, 1967; Migler, 1963; Sidman and Boren, 1957; Solomon, Kamin, and Wynne, 1953). This effect is typically obtained in extinction situations where the persistent behavior appears to have the function of reducing anxiety by terminating the animal's exposure to cues which have been associated with punishment. Human subjects will consistently act to produce an immediate potential punishment when their alternative option is to await a punishment that has a substantial probability of occurrence but an uncertain delay (Badia *et al.*, 1966; Belanger and Sattler, 1967; Breznitz, 1967; D'Amato and Gumenik, 1960).

Our review of the importance of the control of outcomes in the behavioral resolutions of aversive learning gives more than a hint of what to expect when we are interested in the selective suppression of active behavior which is also governed by positive motivation and reinforcement. When aversive experience is made contingent on a specific form of independently motivated behavior, either with or without the provision of conditional external cues, then the occurrence of both reward and punishment can be predictably controlled when behavioral alternatives and conditional cues are discriminable. Suppression of the behavior should be an effective means of reducing conditioned anxiety under these conditions. But if aversive stimulation is not discriminably contingent on a specific form of active behavior, then selective suppression of the behavior would be unlikely to acquire any more anxiety-reducing value than its active performance. The results of experiments with animals do show that unavoidable and unpredictable shocks are ineffective for the suppression of food-rewarded behavior; in contrast, punishment of the behavior by contingent shock produces a selective suppression which can be brought under the close control of specific external cues (Hearst, 1965; Hoffman and Fleshler, 1965; Rachlin, 1967). A particularly interesting parallel to these results is the finding by Myer and Baenninger (1966) that the killing of mice by rats could be suppressed only by contingent shock, and that unavoidable (and unpredictable) shock would actually release the suppressed behavior.

Although human socialization presents some significant analogies to these paradigms of aversive learning in the animal laboratory, there are also important differences to take into account. Children occasionally may be exposed to aversive stimulation that is divorced from their own behavioral control. But their aversive social experience is far more commonly contingent on their behavior. Moreover, it is generally the case that a child's punished behavior is inherently pleasurable or that it produces other external consequences which are rewarding to the child. Accordingly, the socialization episodes in which the child experiences punishment are typically those in which its behavior exercises control over external events and over its own affectivity. Human socialization is very rarely directed to a generalized passive suppression of the child's behavior. It is directed rather to the suppression of some forms of behavior and to the reinforcement of other forms with which the child can actively engage its environment. And to the extent that the child can discriminate among behavioral alternatives and their consequences, and can thus predict and control the outcomes of its actions, socialization will be effective in producing selective suppression of specific forms of punished behavior.

It is when the child cannot discriminate sufficiently between punished and nonpunished behavioral alternatives, and loses predictive control over the outcomes of its behavior, that socialization becomes ineffective in producing selective suppression. Children are highly manipulative and exploratory creatures. Their behavior does not ordinarily show the immobility or freezing that sometimes characterizes the behavior of the animals which are most commonly used in laboratory investigations of aversive learning. When their motivations require active forms of behavior, and when they cannot identify the external or intrinsic signals of the punishment of their potential acts, their dominant dispositions are usually in the direction of active behavior which is at least relevant to their motivation, and which may reduce their generalized anticipatory anxiety by either avoiding or producing punishment. A demonstration of this point under a more simplified set of contingencies can be found in the report by Karsh and Williams (1964) of an experiment in which children were both rewarded and punished for a single act, when no active behavioral alternative was available to them. Under these conditions, where the children were unable to exercise active discriminative control over the punishment of reward-motivated behavior, the punishment was generally ineffective in producing suppression. When children have alternative behavioral options under the conditions of naturalistic socialization, but cannot discriminate the cues which signal the outcomes of their options, their choices may in some instances actually be biased toward behavior that is socially defined as a transgression, since it will often be the case that transgressions have their own reinforcing consequences in addition to the reduction of anticipatory anxiety that might accompany any choice.

We are now in a position to appreciate some of the broader implications for socialization of the finding that intense punishment may sometimes produce poor internalized suppression. It is apparent that punishment itself is an important generator of control over the child's behavior because it is the source of the motivational function of anxiety. But the child's acquisition of selective dispositions toward the suppression of specific forms of behavior is more precisely determined by the anxiety-reducing predictive control that it has been able to exercise over the external outcomes of its actions. This predictive control in turn rests upon the child's ability to discriminate and choose between punished and nonpunished acts. Accordingly, the intensity of a parent's punishment may often be only a weak determinant of the child's selective behavioral suppressions, beyond the point at which the punishment is sufficiently aversive to produce any suppression. The gain in the effect of intense punishment on behavioral suppressions which require only the simplest discriminations may be largely attributable to the more powerful reinforcement that is inherent in the reduction of more intense anxiety, when the child's control of external outcomes originally requires very little information-processing and easily becomes automatized.

If predictive control over the outcomes of its actions is a crucial determinant of the child's acquisition and internalization of selective behavioral suppression, we would expect the effectiveness of the suppression to be closely determined by the behavioral and cognitive resources for control which socialization has given to the child. The child-rearing practices of parents should facilitate selective suppression of punished behavior to the extent that they maximize the value of the behavioral interventions which the child can use to control the contingencies between acts and outcomes, and also to the extent that they provide the child with accurate cognitive representations of the contingencies. For example, punishment may establish more effective suppression of the child's behavior in some situations if parents also reinforce the child's attempts to find or produce alternative situations in which the behavior is permissible. They may also reinforce suppression more directly if they are disposed to withhold or attenuate their punitive reactions when the child introduces corrective modifications of a transgression that is already initiated. Of course, the child's behavioral control over aversive outcomes is always dependent on its capacity to discriminate among external cues, among acts, and among the consequences of acts. And the child's discriminative capacity will be a function of its cognitive equipment. It is therefore the verbal medium of socialization that is the most pervasive determinant of the child's ability to make active behavioral choices which are discriminative before the occurrence of an overt act. The verbalization of socializing agents escalates the child's discriminative capacity. It provides the child with representational and evaluative concepts which economically subordinate the information that is carried in a great variety of situational and behavioral cues.

The impact of cognitive representation on the establishment of predictive control over outcomes, and on the consequent effectiveness of the aversive learning process, is nicely illustrated in the findings of the experiments which Turner and Solomon (1962) conducted on the ability of college students to learn an active avoidance of intense electric shock. They found that avoidance learning was poor when the response to be trained had a very short latency and was highly reflexive, whereas learning progressed more easily when the correct response was a more voluntary act of longer latency. However, the learning of the subjects who were required to use responses of short latency improved considerably when they were given verbal instructions which conveyed that they could exercise control over the termination of shock. The findings clearly suggested that avoidance learning is facilitated by cognitive representations of act-outcome contingencies, and that more voluntary behavioral options permit more time for the operation of such cognitive representations.

The discriminative suppressions which children are required to learn in the course of socialization may be even more sensitive to the dominant behavioral dispositions which are elicited in aversive situations. Certain parental habits of discipline, such as direct physical or verbal attack upon the child, may produce a high incidence of aversive contingencies which are likely to elicit reactions that are similar to a "defensive reflex"—for example, withdrawal or flight from potential agents of punishment after a transgression has occurred. Such reactions would tend to detract from the effectiveness of the child's subsequent internalized suppression of punished behavior, because they would interfere with its learning of corrective reactions which could serve as behavioral options for the avoidance of punishment before the occurrence of transgressions. Moreover, the types of discipline which foster these reactions may be relatively barren in the verbal and cognitive representation of the behavioral controls which children might use to avoid transgression and punishment. Evidence in support of some of these expectations appears in the findings of surveys of the relationships between the disciplinary practices of parents and the social behavior of their children. The evidence will be summarized and analyzed in Chapter Eleven.

The availability of discriminable behavioral options for the control of punishment points to an interesting phenomenon that may arise on the borderline between the predictive control that can be exercised by suppression of a punished act and the control that can be exercised after the act has been committed. Our analysis of naturalistic socialization, and of the evidence from experiments, indicates that effective suppression of punished behavior will require the child to have predictive control over the potentially aversive outcomes of its behavioral choices before it commits an overt act. However, one might argue that the effectiveness of a child's suppression should be diminished by the control that it can exercise over the aversive consequences of a transgression that already has been committed. Children very commonly learn to react to their committed transgressions in ways which are instrumental to the avoidance or escape of punishment. And their reactions to transgression should gradually become effective in reducing the internalized anxiety that comes to be elicited by the very occurrence of a transgression, even in the absence of any surveillance or risk of punishment. It might therefore be expected that the socialization of the child's resources for control over the aversive consequences of committed transgressions would undermine behavioral suppression by attenuating the anticipatory anxiety that is associated with an incipient transgression.

An inverse relationship between the effectiveness of suppression and the availability of escape from the consequences of a punished act has been demonstrated in the animal laboratory. Mowrer and Viek (1948) found that rats showed less suppression of punished eating behavior if they had learned to escape the punishment, even though they were not able to avoid the punishment entirely. The relevance of their demonstration to the socialization of children was limited by the fact that their animals could control only the duration and not the occurrence of aversive stimulation, since the animals were exposed to shock regardless of whether or not they ate. More recently, Leitenberg (1967) has found that a punishment-escape contingency will reduce the effectiveness of suppression even when suppression has the outcome of a complete avoidance of punishment—a paradigm that corresponds more closely to the conditions of human socialization. However, these laboratory demonstrations cannot be generalized too broadly to socialization, because they pertain to only a limited range of the resources which children may acquire for the control of their aversive experience. Avoidance of the external aversive consequences of their behavior is not the only type of resource that children may use to reduce the anxiety that follows a transgression. They can also learn a number of other reactions to transgression which are more highly internalized forms of control over their anxiety. The anxiety-reducing value of many of these reactions will not necessarily bear a compensatory relationship to the value that suppression has acquired for the reduction of the anxiety which precedes a transgression.

If a child's social experience limits its acquisition of either behavioral or cognitive resources for internalized control of conduct, then both its suppression of punished behavior and its reactions to transgression will show an external orientation. For example, its suppression of punished behavior will tend to remain dependent on external surveillance and threat of punishment. And its reactions to a committed transgression will tend to be oriented to an external resolution of the transgression through either the avoidance or the occurrence of punishment. The child's behavioral suppressions may therefore be released when it perceives that it can avoid the potential punishment which might follow a transgression. Some evidence for such a phenomenon may be implicit in the finding by Burton *et al.* (1961) that young children who were more likely to violate the rules of a game, when it appeared that their behavior was not under surveillance, were also reported by their mothers to be generally more disposed toward confession than were children who showed greater conformity to the rules. Confession is an externally oriented reaction to transgression that is learned in part on the basis of its effectiveness in the avoidance of punishment.

In contrast, when the child does acquire more internalized monitors for the control of its behavior, its suppression of transgressions will become relatively independent of the probability of punishment. The child will also be more likely to respond to a committed transgression with self-criticism, reparation, or other reactions which are less oriented toward an external resolution of transgression. The availability of such reactions will not release the maintenance of the child's suppression of punished behavior, because both the suppression and the reactions to transgression have an anxiety-reducing value that does not remain bound to avoidance of punishment.

It can be seen, then, that patterns of socialization which only sensitize the child to external punishment will have some tendency to produce an inverse relationship between the effectiveness of suppression and the effectiveness of behavioral resources which the child may use to control its aversive experience after it has committed a transgression. But patterns of socialization which induce more internalized monitors of the child's behavior will tend to support a parallel relationship between the effectiveness of suppression and the anxiety-reducing value of the child's reactions to a committed transgression. The different directions of relationship between the anxiety-reducing value of suppression and the corresponding value of reactions to transgression may also be attributable to differences in the foundations which various patterns of socialization build for generalization between the appropriate forms of behavior. Most of the socialization of transgressions occurs after their commission. If the behavior of parents establishes contingencies which reinforce confession, flight from punishment, or other reactions which are directed to an external resolution of transgression, there will be very little in the way of generalization to the child's subsequent suppression of punished behavior. The form of such reactions is irrelevant to the facilitation of suppression. On the other hand, if parents reinforce the child's corrective modifications of behavior after a transgression, or if they establish the child's self-critical resources by their verbal evaluation of its choice between transgression and more desirable behavior, they are inducing reactions to transgression which will generalize to the child's control of incipient transgressions. Such reactions contribute to the child's subsequent suppression of punished behavior because they facilitate its choice of nonpunished alternatives to transgression.

It is possible that a history of poor discriminative control over punishment and anxiety is one of the determinants of the apparent failure of socialization to produce effective suppression of commonly prohibited acts in people whose behavior is classified as psychopathic. The designation of primary psychopath sometimes has been applied to a person whose behavior seems to be characterized by an absence of the usual sensitivities to the affective values of a social environment (Cleckley, 1950). In particular, such a person shows little evidence of the internalization of the anxiety that is ordinarily elicited by social punishment. Lykken (1957) used a questionnaire and an avoidance learning paradigm to compare subjects who had been identified as primary psychopaths in a prison population with control subjects who were not prisoners. He found that the psychopathic sample reported less disposition toward anxiety, showed less reactivity in their galvanic skin response to a conditioned stimulus that had been paired with shock, and learned less effectively to avoid punished behavior. Similar findings have been reported by other investigators (Hare, 1965; Painting, 1961). All of these studies also included a third group that consisted of prisoners who were identified as neurotic psychopaths. But the findings for the third groups do not appear to have a consistently predictable relationship to the findings for the primary psychopathic and nonprisoner control groups.

It has been suggested that primary psychopaths may be relatively insensitive to social punishment, and to the experience of anxiety, because they are constitutionally endowed with a low reactivity of the sympathetic nervous system. A limited constitutional capacity for the arousal of anxiety would certainly account in part for the lack of self-imposed behavioral prohibitions that seems so typical of people who are identified as psychopaths. Investigators of the effects of human handling on the socialization of dogs have noted that there are large variations among breeds in their affective reactivity to punishment training and in the effectiveness of the training (Freedman, 1958; Scott and Fuller, 1965; Scott, Shepard, and Werboff, 1967; R. L. Solomon, in Mowrer, 1960b, pp. 399–404). In the socialization of the child, however, there may well be cognitive determinants which are at least as important as the affective determinants of the kind of behavior that is classified as psychopathic.

Schachter and Latané (1964) also essentially confirmed Lykken's results when they found that, under the condition of having been injected with a placebo, the avoidance learning of psychopathic prisoners was inferior to that of nonpsychopathic prisoners. But when the same subjects received an injection of epinephrine (a sympathomimetic agent), the avoidance learning of the psychopathic group improved radically, while the learning of the nonpsychopathic control group was quite poor. They also observed that the psychopathic group showed *more* evidence of sympathetic reactivity to the epinephrine. Schachter and Latané summarize a variety of evidence to make the point that the experience of emotion is not simply correlated to the reactivity of the sympathetic nervous system. They argue that the arousal of affectivity is relevant to the control of behavior when it is given appropriate cognitive labelling. And they suggest that their psychopathic group is deficient in the awareness and discriminative labelling of affectivity, but may actually be highly susceptible to a poorly differentiated sympathetic arousal. Their interpretation of their findings implies that a high magnitude of affectivity is required in order to penetrate the emotional awareness of psychopaths, who may have acquired cognitive mechanisms which shut out their cues of sympathetic arousal. There is also the unstated implication that nonpsychopathic subjects may show poor avoidance under the effects of epinephrine because they are unaccustomed to affective arousal which they cannot coordinate to their cognition of discriminate situational cues.

Although this account of psychopathic behavior must be regarded as very tentative and partial, it does point once again to the child's discriminative control over aversive experience as the crucial determinant of the effectiveness of socialization in producing internalized behavioral suppression. There are many potential features of the behavior of parents which might produce an irreversible barrier to the child's recognition and cognitive representation of both the behavioral and situational cues to which anxiety should be discriminately attached as a result of punishment. For example, it may be that highly infrequent and inconsistent punishment of a child's prohibited behavior makes the behavior very resistant to suppression when it is later exposed to more consistent punishment, in part because the suppression is extinguished so often and so quickly during the initial socialization process. Such a phenomenon has been seen in the animal laboratory (Banks, 1967; Sandler, 1964).

It seems more likely, however, that poor discrimination in the attachment of the child's anxiety to appropriate cues and cognitive representations is primarily attributable to a verbal medium of socialization which is either impoverished or very discrepant with other kinds of information that the child receives from its social environment. There is evidence in the findings of both Lykken (1957) and Painting (1961) that psychopathic adults show a deficiency in the ability to shift their behavior away from the direction of punished errors and to take account of the information that is available in the outcomes of their previous choices. This evidence is in accordance with our earlier description of the expected effects of social experience which attaches indiscriminate anxiety to the child's behavioral options.

❧ CHAPTER EIGHT ❧

REACTIONS
TO
TRANSGRESSION

The suppression of punished behavior is not the only internalized product of socialization that emerges from the child's experience with transgression and punishment. The child's social environment provides not only contingencies for the reduction of the anxiety that becomes attached to an incipient transgression, but also a number of different contingencies for the reduction of the anxiety that follows a completed transgression. The former contingencies are the primary source of the reinforcement of behavioral suppression. The latter contingencies are the source of the establishment of a variety of internalized reactions to committed transgressions. These reactions are very commonly observed manifestations of aversive control over conduct.

When a child arrests an ongoing sustained transgression, or refrains from repetition of a discrete completed transgression, its behavioral suppression can sometimes be reinforced by the avoidance of punishment or by the termination of punishment which already has been initiated. However, the behavior of socializing agents is much more likely to establish a punishment-avoidance contingency for the child's suppression of an incipient transgression than it is for the child's introduction of suppression after a transgression has been committed. And for many classes of transgression, such as those which have irreversible consequences for others, the intervention of suppression will be irrelevant to the control of punishment after a transgression is socially perceived as having been committed. Consequently, the internalized anxiety that becomes attached to an act of transgression often cannot be reduced effectively by suppression if the transgression already has been completed, or if it has progressed to the point where its arrest will not prevent the occurrence of its harmful or undesirable consequences. In other instances, suppression of a transgression may be only poorly established because the child cannot discriminate the cues which identify a transgression until it has made a behavioral choice and observed the consequences. However, the child is not limited to belated suppression when it reacts to transgressions which it has committed. It is also able to acquire a repertoire of other reactions which become remarkably effective in reducing the anxiety that follows a transgression. These other reactions are acquired, during the course of socialization, because they make it possible for the child to exert some control over the course of its aversive experience.

The patterns of behavior with which a socializing agent reacts to a

child's committed transgressions establish the reinforcing affective consequences of a variety of behavioral options which may be exercised by the
child. These consequences initially are defined by social stimulus events
which have acquired anxiety-reducing value because they have come to
mark the termination of the anxiety that is associated with the child's experience or anticipation of the external aversive consequences of a transgression. Avoidance or termination of punishment are obvious examples of this
class of events. And the great number of social stimuli which can be associated with avoidance or termination of punishment greatly extends the class
of signals which may function to mark the resolution of a transgression and
the reduction of the child's anxiety.

We already have had occasion to cite a number of experiments which
demonstrate that a stimulus may acquire the value of an inhibitor of anxiety
for an animal, when it functions as a signal of absence or termination of
shock, and that it then can be used independently to reinforce the animal's
overt behavior (Dinsmoor and Clayton, 1966; Murray and Strandberg,
1965; Rescorla and LoLordo, 1965; Wagman and Allen, 1964; Weisman
et al., 1966). The experimental analysis of suppression which was presented in the last chapter suggested that children's behavioral alternatives
to transgression are sensitive to reinforcement by signals of punishment-
avoidance (Aronfreed, 1966). A considerable part of the internalized
value which is acquired by children's reactions to committed transgressions
also is based on their original effectiveness in the control of social signals
of punishment-avoidance. However, a large component of the reinforcement value of many reactions to transgression actually is acquired on the
basis of their instrumental control over the production rather than the
avoidance of punishment. It may seem paradoxical that an account of the
learning of reactions to transgression should rest on two kinds of contingencies of reinforcement which appear to be quite opposite to one another.
But the two kinds of contingencies are in fact reducible to the single effect
of termination of the anticipatory anxiety which occurs between the commitment and the resolution of a transgression.

Many of a child's socialized reactions to its own transgressions remain
dependent not only on reinforcement by external contingencies which reduce its anxiety, but also on the motivational value of external social cues
which elicit its anxiety. For example, Silverman (1967) compared children
who cheated in the apparent absence of surveillance with children who did
not cheat, and found that the cheaters were no more likely to volunteer
their services for a task—an opportunity that they might have used to

make amends for their behavior. Even the reactions which adults have to their transgressions often are initiated at least as much under external social control as they are under the control of internal monitors. Wallace and Sadalla (1966) found that adult transgressors whose actions became unexpectedly known to an experimental agent were more likely to volunteer for an unpleasant experience than were transgressors whose actions did not become known. Bem (1965) trained adult subjects to lie and to tell the truth, respectively, in the presence of two distinct visual stimuli; when he later required the subjects to give false reports of their attitudes in the presence of the two stimuli, he found that they showed more cognitive change in reaction to their dishonesty when they lied in the presence of the "truth light."

The criterion of internalization which can be applied most usefully to a child's reactions to its committed transgressions is that the elicitation of the reactions be independent of external surveillance or risk of punishment—in other words, that the anxiety which motivates the reactions be directly attached to the intrinsic correlates of the transgression itself. Many reactions to transgression which are internalized in this sense nevertheless continue to be dependent by their very nature on the reinforcement that is provided by external events which reduce the child's anxiety. For example, a child might behave in such a way as to bring its transgression to the attention of another person, in order to resolve the transgression by either punishment or forgiveness, even though it realizes that the transgression would not otherwise have been discovered. Of course, the external contingencies which reinforce the child's reactions to transgression will often attach their anxiety-reducing value directly to the intrinsic correlates of the reactions, with the result that the reactions themselves acquire some independent effectiveness in the resolution of a transgression. It should also be noted that the original contingencies which socialization provides for the child's control over the aversive consequences of a committed transgression are more closely determined by the general direction of the child's subsequent behavior than they are by the specific form of the behavior. Consequently, the behaviorally produced cues which are inherent in the child's learned reactions to transgression are relatively insignificant as discriminate mediators of an internalized reduction of anxiety. The child's cognitive representations of its reactions, and of their consequences, must carry most of the internalized value of the reactions.

The motivation for the child's internalized reactions to transgression is a function of the intensity of anxiety which is mobilized by the intrinsic correlates of a committed transgression. In some of the experiments which have been designed to examine the effect of the timing of punishment on the internalization of behavioral suppression, there also have been behavioral indices of the anxiety that followed the commission of a transgression during the test for internalization (Aronfreed and Reber, 1965; Solomon, Turner, and Lessac, 1968). For both children and dogs, the relevant behavior was more in evidence among subjects who had been punished after commitment of transgression during training than it was among subjects who had been punished at initiation of transgression. There is no reason to expect, however, that socialization will ordinarily produce an inverse or reciprocal relationship between the relative intensities of anxiety which become attached to a child's incipient and committed transgressions. Nor can it be expected that the internalized reinforcement value of suppression will be inversely related to the internalized value of the reactions which the child acquires to resolve a committed transgression. Since the verbal medium of punishment in naturalistic socialization can attach anxiety to cognitive representations which may bridge the entire course of the initiation and completion of punished behavior, the respective intensities of anxiety which precede and follow a committed transgression will often have a common source of internalized mediation and a common magnitude. As was pointed out in the previous chapter, it is the nature of the child's acquired resources for the control of its internalized anxiety which is the primary determinant of the direction of whatever relationship exists between the functional value of its behavioral suppression and the value of its specific reactions to committed transgressions.

The cognitive housing that socialization provides for the anxiety that becomes attached to a committed transgression determines the child's qualitative experience of the anxiety—for example, it determines whether the experience will correspond most closely to fear, to guilt, or to shame. The cognitive housing also introduces some selective bias into the relative effectiveness with which various specific reactions to transgression can acquire anxiety-reducing value. The motivational properties of the concept of anxiety may be used, however, to describe the generalized cases of the contingencies which are required for the establishment of all reactions to transgression. Both behavior-contingent and observational learning contribute to the child's learning of its reactions to transgression. Although the reactions are acquired primarily under the control of aversive social contingencies, the learning of some reactions may also be facilitated by the positive affectivity that is induced through direct reward or through the child's observation of certain relevant actions in the behavior of others.

We will analyze the socialization of four types of reaction to transgression: self-criticism, reparation, confession, and reactions which are oriented toward external punishment. There are very specific contingencies which differentiate the learning of these reactions and determine their relative preference in the child's repertoire. The evidence that bears on this differentiation is a compelling contradiction of those conceptions of conscience which assume that internalization is a unitary or integrative acquisition process.

It should be noted that the four types of reaction to which we will give our attention all acquire their anxiety-reducing value through the control that they exercise over the consequences of transgression, rather than by introducing any change in the cognition of the transgression itself. However, the child's increasing cognitive capacities also gradually give it resources for reducing the anxiety that may follow a transgression through control over its perception of the very nature or occurrence of transgression. For example, older children may attempt to justify a committed transgression by attributing to the victim certain characteristics which appear to legitimize the harmful consequences of the transgression. A number of recent experiments have demonstrated some of the conditions under which adults will attempt to justify their transgressions by derogation of the person who suffers the consequences (Glass, 1964; Lerner and Matthews, 1967; Walster and Prestholdt, 1966). People also may reduce the anxiety that follows a transgression by altering their cognition of its magnitude or of their own volitional control over its consequences—for example, when they minimize the consequences for the victim or deny their responsibility for the transgression (Brock and Buss, 1962, 1964). All of these cognitive alterations permit an individual to produce representations of his behavior, or of the consequences of his behavior, to which inhibition of anxiety has been attached as a result of his previous socialization. Social experience often will teach the child that the consequences of its potential transgressions for itself are less aversive when its behavior can be justified or explained in certain ways, or when the harmful effects of its behavior are minimal.

SELF-CRITICISM

Self-criticism is the most common form of a class of imitative reactions to transgression in which the child reproduces components of the punishment to which it has been exposed previously. Such reactions do not contradict our general conception of the types of changes in affectivity which are required to yield the effect of reinforcement. In order to understand the learning of self-criticism as a reaction to transgression, we must take into account the signal value of punishment and its temporal position with respect to onset and termination of the anxiety that has become directly attached to the intrinsic correlates of transgression.

When a child has had sufficient exposure to punishment for a particular act of transgression, it will begin to experience anxiety in anticipation of punishment, for substantial intervals of time following its commitment of the same transgression on subsequent occasions. Certain of the components of punishment can then acquire value as signals for the termination of the child's anticipatory anxiety, since they mark the end of the interval of anticipation. The acquired anxiety-reducing value of these components also is facilitated by the relatively short duration of many of the child's experiences of punishment, which results in a close temporal relationship between the components and the termination of the punishment—particularly when the small temporal variations are perceived in the context of the much longer period that often intervenes between transgression and the onset of punishment. Socializing agents very commonly include in their punishment the verbalization of labels or standards which are critically applied to the child's behavior. Their verbal criticism will therefore acquire some anxiety-reducing value for the child, as a result of its temporal relationship to the child's anticipatory anxiety. The child may then reproduce the criticism in response to its subsequent transgressions, even in the absence of socializing agents, in order to exercise its own control over the reduction of its internalized anxiety. It appears that the child actually comes to prefer a component of punishment to the experience of anxiety, when the component is reproduced under its own control.

It can be seen that self-criticism will have immediately reinforcing affective consequences as soon as it begins to be used by the child, because its intrinsic correlates already have acquired anxiety-reducing value as a result of their original presentation in the behavior of a model. Although children also may sometimes reproduce other components of social punishment, in order to reduce the anxiety that follows a committed transgression, it is generally the verbal components for which they are able to produce the most exact cognitive and behavioral representations. It would be more difficult, though by no means impossible, for children to represent components of their previous physical punishments with a high degree of fidelity to their original experience.

Young children occasionally verbalize their self-criticism aloud and make its anxiety-reducing function transparent—for example, when they show signs of distress after they have committed a transgression and then apparent relief after they have criticized themselves overtly. The nature of the motivation and the reinforcement for self-criticism tends to be obscured, however, once the reaction becomes firmly established and covert. It cannot be inferred with any validity from the introspection of adults, who may perceive that their self-critical reactions to transgressions sometimes precede their experience of anxiety. This perception of the order of experience may actually be attributable more to the immediate recognition of a transgression than it is to the immediate application of a critical label. Nevertheless, it is quite possible that a well-established self-critical response can precede the experience of anxiety. The findings of some experiments in the animal laboratory have suggested that certain forms of behavior which are established under aversive control can be maintained, once they have been acquired, with a latency that is shorter than the latency with which anxiety becomes fully elicited (Solomon and Brush, 1956). The same change in the function of anxiety may occur between the acquisition and the maintenance of self-criticism.

An experimental investigation of the mechanisms for the learning of self-criticism can serve as an illustration of a more general case of observational learning—the case of imitation that is based on the child's representation of those features of a model's behavior which have acquired value through their previous external occurrence in conjunction with the termination of anxiety. A few years ago, the author reported the results of a series of experimental paradigms which had been constructed to examine the socialization of self-criticism (Aronfreed, 1964). This experiment also provided an example of some of the techniques which could be used to demonstrate the intrinsic value of the child's imitation of even a simple discrete element of a model's behavior, when the contingencies of learning were arranged to permit inferences about affective control of the child's behavior. The experiment employed a variety of paradigms of socialization which were designed to specify the conditions under which a child would acquire the use of the label "blue" to refer to its own punished behavior, after it had been exposed repeatedly to an agent's verbalization of the label as a component of punishment. The experiment was conducted with nine- and ten-year-old girls as subjects, and with a female experimenter in the role of the adult socializing agent and potential model.

During the training phase of the experiment, the child was engaged in the task of guessing how many of four hidden dolls were looking at her on each of ten trials. When she had made her guess on each trial, she indicated it by pushing down the appropriate number of levers from among an array of four on a choice-box. In some of the experimental paradigms, the child was punished for the way in which she pushed the lever on five of the ten training trials. But there was no further specification of the nature of the transgression, so that the child in fact had no cues with which she could identify her punished behavior before it occurred. A buzzer was used as an external signal of the occurrence of the transgression, and it was artificially controlled so that the five transgressions occurred in an unpredictable sequence. The socializing agent's punishment consisted of sharp verbal disapproval (*No!*) together with deprivation of candy that already had been given to the child. When a transgression occurred, both the buzzer signal and the punishment were initiated immediately upon the child's operation of one of the levers. The signal and the punishment also terminated together, after a duration of roughly ten seconds.

Part of the agent's punitive reaction to each transgression was her use of the label "blue" to refer to the child's behavior. The temporal relationship of the label to the course of the transgression signal and punishment was varied across training paradigms. In one paradigm, the agent used the label just at the termination of signal and punishment, where it was expected to acquire maximal anxiety-reducing value for the child, in its position as a signal that marked the end of an interval of anxiety. In a second paradigm, the agent used the label at the very onset of signal and punishment, in a position where it was expected that the child's anticipatory anxiety would not yet have attained any substantial intensity. In a control paradigm in which no punishment was used, only the buzzer signalled the occurrence of the behavior that was labelled "blue," and the agent used the label as the buzzer terminated.[1]

The child was given no opportunity to verbalize during the training paradigms. But on the two test trials which immediately followed all of the

---

[1] The numbers of children used in each of the three training paradigms which have been described were: label at termination of punishment—twenty-seven; label at onset of punishment—twenty-four; control—twelve.

training paradigms, the situation was restructured so that the child could overtly verbalize the label "blue" to describe her transgression, in response to an open-ended question from the agent. On each of the two test trials, the buzzer was activated to signal a transgression as the child pushed down a lever. However, the agent temporarily suspended the punitive role that she had assumed throughout the training. She appeared preoccupied with other activities and casually asked the child: *"What happened this time?"* The verbal replies which the children made to this question revealed a very large and reliable difference between the two punishment training groups in their self-critical reactions to the test transgressions. Children who had been exposed to the label "blue" at the termination of signal and punishment used the label, in describing the transgressions which they had just committed, with a much higher frequency than did children who had been exposed to the label at onset of signal and punishment. Among the children who had been exposed to no punishment in the control paradigm, the use of the label "blue" during the two test trials was also very infrequent (the relative frequency was roughly equivalent to the low frequency of occurrence among children for whom the label had been used at onset of signal and punishment). These frequency patterns were apparent on either of the two test trials.

When additional groups of children were trained in the paradigm which placed the label "blue" at the termination of signal and punishment, the children almost invariably acquired the disposition to use the label in reference to their own transgressions. Further consecutive test trials for these children were then converted into extinction paradigms, in which attempts were made to eliminate their use of the label by removing punishment entirely, eliminating any verbalization of the label, or changing the temporal relationship of the label to the onset and termination of the transgression signal. The children's self-critical reactions appeared to have the same tenacity, however, that is commonly seen in the self-critical reactions which are acquired under naturalistic socialization. Ten children were used in each of three extinction procedures, and only two extinguished under each procedure. All of the remaining children continued to verbalize the self-critical label, whenever the buzzer signalled the occurrence of a transgression, in response to the agent's open-ended inquiry throughout the extinction trials or after the extinction trials had been completed.

Another interesting finding of the same experimental series appeared when a third punishment training paradigm was designed to examine the effects of the agent's nurturance and withdrawal of nurturance on the child's learning of self-criticism. During the agent's instructions to the child, and during the training trials on which transgressions did not occur, she showed both physical affection and verbal approval toward the child. When a transgression occurred, the agent withdrew her nurturance and administered punishment. The agent applied the label "blue" to the child's behavior at the onset of the transgression signal and punishment (where it was not expected to acquire anxiety-reducing value). The nurturance of the agent did not facilitate the disposition of the children to reproduce her critical label in their own description of their transgressions during test trials. The frequency of self-critical use of the label following the nurturance paradigm was comparable to the low frequency of its use among children who had been trained with the label in the same temporal position (onset of signal and punishment), but who had experienced no nurturance from the agent.[2]

The entire pattern of findings from this series of experiments demonstrated that the learning of self-criticism rests on aversive control of the child's imitative behavior, and not on an extension of the positive control which can be exercised by the child's observation of nurturant or affectionate models. Self-criticism apparently is acquired through the child's experience of the contingency between verbal components of a model's punishment and the termination of its anticipatory anxiety, rather than through generalization from the child's pleasurable experience with the model. This conclusion does not imply that the nurturance of socializing agents has no effect on the child's disposition to reproduce their critical or punitive behavior. But it does indicate that the child will imitate the punitive behavior of a model only to the extent that contingencies of aversive learning permit the behavior to acquire intrinsic representational value, and that the nurturance of the model can control this kind of imitation only to the extent that it has an effect on the aversive learning process.

The results of experiments which have been reported by Grusec (1966), and by Mischel and Grusec (1966), suggest that the nurturance of a model can facilitate the child's reproduction of the model's verbal criticism, when the criticism is given a temporal position at which it can coincide with termination of the child's anxiety. The facilitation would be expected on the basis of the context that nurturance may provide for the salience of punishment and for its effectiveness in producing anxiety. The findings of surveys of the relationship between the child-rearing practices of parents

---

[2] Twenty-six children were used in the nurturance paradigm.

and various indices of internalization in their children's conduct indicate that a certain minimal early experience of nurturance from socializing agents may be a prerequisite of children's more general dispositions toward sensitivity to the aversive properties of social punishment (See Chapter Eleven). The nurturance of socializing agents may therefore indirectly affect the child's internalization of any kind of aversive control over its behavior.

It is important to recognize that the interval between the onset of anticipatory anxiety and the occurrence of a specific component of punishment is the critical temporal determinant of whether the component can acquire anxiety-reducing value for the child. Such an interval is almost always present, of course, under the conditions of naturalistic socialization. And the critical evaluations of socializing agents consequently need not occur near the termination of punishment in order to acquire anxiety-reducing value. If the interval is sufficiently long, and if punishment is not too intense or prolonged, then verbal components which occur even at the onset of punishment may acquire value and be reproduced by the child when it experiences anxiety following a transgression. It is just this point that appears to have been demonstrated in the experiment that is described by Grusec (1966), in which children reproduced the verbal criticism that a socializing agent had used previously at the onset of a punitive reaction to the children's transgressions. The findings of this experiment were mistakenly interpreted as evidence that the learning of self-criticism was not controlled by anxiety-reduction—on the grounds that children reproduced a model's verbal criticism even when it did not coincide with termination of punishment. But the procedures of the experiment would have permitted ample time for the children's anticipatory anxiety to develop between the occurrence of transgression and the onset of punishment.

One other finding from the experiment in which the behavior of children was critically labelled as "blue" also suggests that a child's reproduction of a model's verbal evaluations must be under the control of the specific context of affectivity in which the child experiences the evaluations. In all of the paradigms which were described above, the agent used the label "red" in reference to the child's behavior in operating the levers, on all trials on which the behavior was not labelled as "blue." The label "red" was associated simply with the absence of punishment in the two basic punishment paradigms, but was associated with physical affection and verbal approval in the punishment paradigm for which the agent had assumed a generally nurturant role. After the first two transgression trials of the test situation which followed the training paradigms, the children were given one further trial on which they had the opportunity to use the label "red" to refer to their own behavior, in response to the agent's verbal inquiry when the transgression signal was not activated. Only a few of the children from any of the paradigms used the label "red." This finding provides another indication that the children who did reproduce the label "blue," after appropriate contingencies of training, had not acquired what was merely a generalized disposition to imitate the verbalization of the experimental agent. Their self-criticism apparently had acquired an intrinsic reinforcement value that was governed by the specific changes of affectivity which had been induced by their original experience of external criticism.

It may seem surprising that the label "red" was not reproduced during the test situation by children who had been exposed to it in the nurturant context of physical and verbal affection during training. However, these children had no positive external signal that was correlated with the duration of the rewarding consequences of their "red" behavior—in contrast to the buzzer that signalled their "blue" behavior on transgression trials. And the positive affective properties of an evaluative label that was associated with reward may have been difficult to establish for the child in a learning situation that was so heavily laced with punishment and anxiety. The failure of the children to use the label "red" confirmed the expectation that the evaluative properties of verbal labels would not be defined merely by their cognitive or informational status. The conditions of affectivity under which the child acquires the use of the labels must also be taken into account. It seems certain that children in all of the paradigms attained a clear understanding of the distinction between the "blue" and "red" labels, with respect to the consequences of the behavior which the labels described. But the affective correlates which would motivate and reinforce their overt verbal application of the labels to their own behavior appeared not to be present in equal degree for the two labels.

The findings of another experiment (Aronfreed, Cutick, and Fagen, 1963) can be used to further illustrate some of the distinctions which need to be drawn among the conditions of socialization which facilitate the child's disposition to apply verbal criticism to its own previously punished behavior. This experiment was carried out with nine- and ten-year-old boys. Male experimenters were used as socializing agents. The procedure engaged the child in a task in which he had to knock down some toy soldiers with a "pusher," in order to move a doll that represented a nurse to a position of safety. On each of ten training trials, the child was punished by

removal of some of the candies from a pile that was already in his possession. The initial instructions informed the child that it was important not to
knock down too many soldiers, and that candies would be removed in
proportion to the number knocked down. The agent varied the number of
candies which he removed from trial to trial, but always verbalized the relationship between the magnitude of punishment and the number of soldiers which were knocked down.

In two training paradigms, the agent used repeated verbal descriptions of
the child's aggressive behavior, along the dimensions of *careful-careless*
and *gentle-rough* toward the termination of each punishment. The verbalization of these dimensions also had been introduced during the instructions. In two other training paradigms, the agent made no reference to
these dimensions during either instructions or the administrations of punishment. Within each of the two pairs of paradigms which were thus designed to vary the cognitive structure that was given to the child, there was
another variation of the agent's behavior toward the child. The agent
assumed a nurturant role toward some children. He was solicitous toward
them, replenished their supplies of candy, and commented on his attempts
to make their task easier by changing the positions of the soldiers. Toward
the remaining children, the agent assumed a role that included none of
these forms of nurturant behavior. The experimental design equated the
frequencies of nurturant and non-nurturant roles within the training conditions of high and low cognitive structure.[3]

Following all of the four paradigms which were defined by the variations
in cognitive structure and nurturance, there was a common test trial on
which the nurse-doll appeared to break when it was pushed by the child.
The experimental agent, who seemed to be distracted while he was trying
to assess the damage, casually made nondirective verbal inquiries as to why
the doll broke. Children who had been punished in the context of the verbalized cognitive structures of careful-careless and gentle-rough significantly more often criticized their own behavior as being responsible for the
breaking of the doll than did children who had been punished without cognitive structure (even though they rarely used the specific critical labels
which had been employed by the agent). This finding indicated that the
agent's verbalization of explicit evaluative dimensions, in the course of the
administration of punishment, had a generalized facilitative effect on the
children's self-critical dispositions. But there were no significant differences

---

[3] Fifteen children were used in each of the four paradigms which were created by
the experimental design.

among the children, in the frequency of their self-critical references, which were attributable to variations in the agent's nurturance. Thus, although this experiment was not designed to uncover mechanisms of internalization, it did produce some evidence that a high level of nurturance from a socializing agent is not a prerequisite of the child's disposition to adopt the agent's critical evaluation of its actions.

The learning of behavior that functions to reduce anxiety is ordinarily thought to be originally dependent on avoidance of (or escape from) punishment or other forms of aversive stimulation. Hill (1960) has used this assumption to argue that children acquire self-criticism through behavior-contingent training in which overt self-critical verbalization effectively produces an external reinstatement of parental affection. Grusec's (1966) recent experiment shows that the frequency of a child's overtly verbalized self-criticism can be increased by direct reinforcement in the form of termination of punishment, once the child has already acquired the self-critical disposition through imitation of a model. But all of the experiments which have been described here, as well as some others (Bandura and Kupers, 1964; Kanfer and Duerfeldt, 1967), demonstrate that behavior-contingent training is not very plausible as the primary source of self-criticism. Under the conditions of naturalistic socialization, self-critical responses are generally not overtly apparent in the child's behavior, and so they cannot easily be subjected to contingencies of external reinforcement. Even when self-criticism does sometimes temporarily show itself overtly in the young child's behavior, its initial appearance seems to emerge with the speed and vigor of a response that already has had the benefit of considerable rehearsal and internalized reinforcement.

An account of the learning of self-criticism requires a mechanism that will permit social stimuli which the child can represent and reproduce to acquire some intrinsic value, through their original external occurrence in conjunction with anxiety-reduction, even though the stimuli are not originally under the immediate control of the child's behavior. Other kinds of confirmation of the existence of such a mechanism may be found in the results of certain experiments with animals (Dinsmoor and Clayton, 1966; Goodson and Brownstein, 1955; Murray and Strandberg, 1965; Wagman and Allen, 1964). The findings of these experiments show that stimuli which are associated with the termination of aversive experience can acquire independent reinforcement value, even though the animals in some cases have not been given the opportunity to control the occurrence of the stimuli with their own behavior during the initial conditioning.

It is not paradoxical that a reaction such as self-criticism, which reproduces components of external punishment, can be acquired and maintained
by children in response to their own transgressions. We already have noted
a wide variety of experimental findings which indicate that the behavior of
both humans and animals may be more sensitive to anxiety-reduction than
it is to punishment-avoidance, and that it may maintain its anxiety-
reducing value even when it results in punishment (Badia *et al.*, 1966;
Belanger and Sattler, 1967; Brown, 1965; D'Amato and Gumenik, 1960;
Melvin and Martin, 1967; Seward *et al.*, 1965; Sidman and Boren, 1957;
Solomon and Wynne, 1954). Of course, self-criticism and other self-
punitive reactions which children may acquire in the course of socialization
are not established originally as avoidance or escape reactions. Although
the motivation of these reactions to transgression is initially dependent on
the aversive properties of punishment, their reinforcement comes to be contingent on their reproduction of stimuli which represent the presence rather
than the absence of punishment. The child's disposition to imitate punishment may be limited, however, by the nature and intensity of a potentially
reproducible component of punishment, and also by the duration and intensity of the remaining punishment that follows the component. The behavior of extremely punitive socializing agents might well induce a child to
acquire avoidance or withdrawal reactions to transgression, rather than to
acquire reactions which reproduce components of the agent's punishment.

Self-evaluation has a special status in the economy of the child's internalized control over its behavior. Because of its cognitive and verbal properties, self-evaluation can mediate other internalized forms of conduct.
There is no reason to assume, however, that self-criticism is fundamental
to any other type of internalized reaction to transgression. The findings of a
number of surveys of internalized reactions to transgression indicate that
there is great variability in the extent to which these reactions require the
mediation of self-criticism (W. Allinsmith, 1960; Aronfreed, 1960, 1961;
Whiting, 1959). And experimental paradigms of socialization have been
used to show that self-criticism and reparation are acquired by children
through relatively independent contingencies of learning (Aronfreed, 1963).

REPARATION

The concept of reparation is applicable to a fairly broad class of reactions to transgression. Like many other reactions to transgression, reparation represents a directional change of behavior with respect to the transgressions by which it is elicited—it returns the child to a position within whatever boundaries of social constraint have been transgressed. But reparative reactions are different from confessions, expressions of remorse, or commitments to modify behavior in the future, in that they require the child to exercise a more substantial degree of active control over the resolution of a transgression. Reparation has a restitutive or corrective character which suggests that it is learned through the consequences of the child's transformations of the effects of its transgressions upon other people.

The kinds of reactions to transgression which may be classified as reparation can be distinguished from one another to some extent by the directness of their relevance to transgression. Some reparative reactions are addressed directly and concretely to the consequences of a transgression, while others are restitutive in only an indirect and symbolic sense. The most clearly discernible forms of reparation are those which have a directly corrective relationship to transgression. They quite literally repair the damage—as when a child returns something that it has taken, cleans up what it has spilled, or tries to fix what it has broken. Reparations which are geared with some precision to the harmful consequences of one's acts continue to be maintained as a significant part of the behavioral resources with which adults react to their transgressions. Berscheid and Walster (1967) found, for example, that women were far more likely to make exact reparation for the material consequences of their actions than they were to make either insufficient or excessive reparation. A simple reversibility of consequences is much less apparent, however, in acts of reparation for the more common social transgressions which do not have concrete material consequences. Thus, children often learn to make reparation for their acts of aggression by verbal or nonverbal reaffirmations of their affection for the target of the aggression. Their reparative actions may repair the affective state of another person in a figurative sense, but the corrective effects of their actions are not very tangible (even though they may be highly effective in producing reinforcing consequences).

Many forms of reparation are even more indirectly related to the consequences of transgression. Children may express affection or helpfulness toward those who have suffered the consequences of their actions, but in ways which are irrelevant to effecting any change in the consequences. Or they may try to make material reparation for transgressions which do not have material consequences; for example, they may attempt to relieve the anxiety that they experience in response to their acts of aggression by offering a toy or food to the person against whom they have aggressed. Highly indirect reparative reactions also can be seen in the behavior of adults. Wallace and Sadalla (1966) found that adult subjects were quick to volunteer for an unpleasant experience which was entirely irrelevant to their apprehended transgressions. In a similar experiment, Freedman, Wallington, and Bless (1967) observed that subjects who had been induced to commit transgressions showed more behavioral compliance to requests which were not directly relevant to the transgressions, despite the absence of any significant social pressure, than did subjects who had not committed transgressions.

Perhaps the most general characterization of all reparative reactions is that they have a corrective orientation. They are oriented either to the correction of the consequences of transgression or to the correction of information that the transgression may have transmitted about the attributes or intentions of the transgressor (either to others or to himself). Reactions which are directed to the benefit of those who have sustained the consequences of transgression seem to be the largest derivative category of the general class of reparation. Even those reparative actions which specifically correct material loss or damage are probably to be included in this broad category, since they are undoubtedly originally learned through the child's experience of the effects of transgression and reparation upon others.

The fact that different forms of reparation can be grouped together, around a concept of the general direction of their consequences for others, testifies to the power of the normative cognitive structures which human society can impose on the organization and control of large classes of distinct acts. It does not require us to suppose, however, that a child's learning of a reparative act necessarily rests on its having an explicit conception of the effects of its actions upon the welfare of others. Common observation indicates that children sometimes acquire reparative forms of behavior without any significant change in their cognitive resources for the evaluation of their behavior. One often senses that the reparative actions of children (and even of adults) are being carried out mechanically, apparently on the basis of their sheer anxiety-reducing value. They also sometimes follow so immediately upon the occurrence of transgression as to make it obvious that they could not be controlled by evaluative decision-making processes. It is therefore hardly surprising that reparative acts are so often irrelevant to the objective consequences of a transgression. One inference which we may draw from these observations is that guilt cannot be a prerequisite of reparative behavior. On the other hand, we would certainly expect that the child's learning and use of reparation would be facilitated by the evaluative operations of conscience, particularly by the kind of moral evaluation that is focussed on the consequences of its actions for others. As the child expands its cognitive resources for the evaluation of its behavior, it also becomes more capable of judging accurately the impact of the behavior on others. It can then intentionally select reparative strategies which are tailored to correct that impact.

Behavior which can be identified as being specifically reparative is usually not visible until the young child's social conduct is fairly well developed. But direct social reinforcement for the rudiments of reparative behavior begins to occur very early in socialization. A very important contribution to the learning of reparative actions is made by their gradual shaping from more unstructured forerunners in the child's behavioral repertoire. Reversibility of the direction of behavior, and of the direction of corresponding affective states, is built into socialization. There is ample opportunity for children to discover that sharp changes in the direction of their behavior, many of which represent acts that already have been firmly acquired as a result of other kinds of social experience, can also be effective in avoiding or terminating the punishment that may follow a committed transgression. The child's reactive expressions of sympathy or affection for the targets of its aggressive behavior undoubtedly receive this kind of direct reinforcement. When a child's aggressive behavior results in the loss of affection that accompanies any form of social punishment, its past experience may predispose it to express overt affection or concern for the person toward whom its aggression was directed, to the extent that its affectionate behavior has a history of elicitation of reciprocal affection from others. This example is prototypical, since it also illustrates the contribution that positive social reinforcement can make to the learning of reparative behavior. Reinstatement of affection is a social outcome that can reinforce the child's reparative actions through both the reduction of anxiety and the induction of positive affectivity.

Many other forms of behavior, in addition to affectionate or sympathetic behavior, can be brought into the child's repertoire of reparative reactions to transgression, after their rudiments have been established by the direct reinforcements which are associated with contingencies of reward or punishment. For example, even before the concept of honesty is woven into socialization, children have much experience with the interchange of giving and taking that occurs in their relationships with parents and peers. And giving often is reinforced by social reward or by termination of the sometimes aversive consequences of taking. Nor is it trivial to observe that curiosity may impel children to put back together the things which they have taken apart, or that discomfort may motivate them to call their soiled condition to the attention of their mothers, well in advance of the time when the instrumental value of corrective acts of responsibility becomes apparent to them.

The contingencies under which a child's reparative behavior may receive direct social reinforcement also contribute to the appearance of nonrational relationships between the behavior and the transgressions to which it becomes a reaction. Socializing agents do not necessarily make their reinforcement of the child's reparative actions contingent on their perception that the child comprehends the relationship between reparation and the consequences of its transgressions for others. Their responses to the child's reparative actions are probably at least as often contingent merely on whether the actions alleviate their own aversive reactions to the child's transgressions. As a result, children may find that reparative behavior is an effective means of avoiding punishment and later reducing their own internalized anxiety, without having any articulate cognitive representation of the effects of their actions upon others. Children may therefore learn to react to their transgressions with helpfulness or kindness, or other kinds of socially approved behavior, even though their reactions may be relatively indiscriminate and not even addressed to those who have been adversely affected by their transgressions. The learning of reparative reactions would tend to be facilitated, however, when they do have a directly corrective relationship to transgression, in part because they can then be mediated by the same cognitive dimensions of conscience which the child may use to evaluate the consequences of transgression, and also perhaps because they then have a greater probability of being reinforced.

Reparation does not seem to be called forth equally by transgressions in every area of social behavior. Its use seems to be closely related to the ease with which a transgression may be construed as having harmful consequences for others. Acts of aggression lend themselves very readily to this construction, and so do acts of dishonesty or damage to the property of others. In contrast, reparative reactions do not appear to be indigenous to transgressions in the area of sexual behavior, for example, or in the control of bodily functions. The control of these areas of behavior is much less amenable to a focus on the direct consequences of transgressions for others. Of course, the child's socializing agents may sometimes react even to transgressions in these areas in such a way as to convey that they are hurt, disappointed, or otherwise distressed, so that appropriate reparative responses might be acquired by the child. But such responses could not easily have the reciprocal relationship to transgression that gives reparative action its high probability of reinforcement in other areas of social behavior such as aggression.

It is simply unlikely that restraints on sexual exploration, or voluntary control over eliminative functions, would emerge with sufficient immediacy and visibility, following the occurrence of their corresponding transgressions, to be perceived as corrective reactions and reinforced as such by socializing agents. Where the consequences of the child's actions for others are more concretely visible, it can more readily acquire a specifically corrective act that will terminate or reduce the aversive reaction of the socializing agent who is in control of the situation. Where the consequences are less evident, the learning of reparative behavior may require that the socializing agent heighten their visibility for the child and convey the contingencies for their amelioration through the use of extensive verbal mediation.

The effect of direct social reinforcement on the learning of reparative behavior has been demonstrated in two closely related experiments (Aronfreed, 1963), the findings of which also point to the independent antecedents of reparation and self-criticism in the socialization process. In the basic procedure of both experiments, a child repeatedly engaged in the aggressive act of using a "pusher" to knock down some toy soldiers and a doll that represented a nurse, as part of its task of removing the nurse from danger. An adult male socializing agent repeatedly initiated one of two types of administration of punishment, on each of ten training trials, ostensibly for the excessiveness of the child's aggressive behavior. Punishment consisted of the deprivation of a variable number of candies from among a store that was already in the child's possession. In the case of some experimental groups, the agent overtly verbalized his decision about how many candies were to be taken away and then removed them, in apparent proportion to a concrete visible index of how much aggression had occurred (the number of toy soldiers that had been knocked down). Other groups of children were given active control over the resolution of their transgressions; they evaluated their own performances and then removed the number of candies which they judged to be appropriate. Regardless of the method of punishment, the deprivation of candy on each trial always terminated the agent's critical and punitive reaction. And for the children who administered their own deprivation, the removal of the candy was immediately followed by the agent's verbal approval (*Good!*).

Variations in the provision of cognitive structure were also introduced among the groups, in the context of the agent's initial instructions and of his verbal observations on the child's behavior on each trial. The agent described the child's performance along the dimensions of *careful-careless* and *gentle-rough,* during instructions and the course of each punishment, in order to produce a high degree of cognitive structure for some of the groups. A minimal amount of structuring was provided for other groups by having the agent restrict his verbalization to descriptive references to the number of soldiers knocked down. Immediately following the training trials, a common test trial was used to assess the child's reparative and self-critical dispositions. The nurse-doll broke on this trial, apparently as a result of the manner in which it had been pushed by the child. While surveying the damage to the doll, the agent casually verbalized a brief series of standardized open-ended queries. These queries were designed to elicit the child's perception of why the doll broke and its suggestions about what course to follow now that the doll had been broken.

The first of the two experiments which employed these procedures was carried out with ten-year-old girls. The second experiment was carried out with ten-year-old boys.[4] The same male experimenter took the role of the socializing agent in both experiments. In the first experiment, control over punishment and cognitive structure were parallel to one another within the experimental design. For example, one group of children was given both control over their own punishment and a high degree of cognitive structure. This group significantly more often volunteered methods of repairing the nurse, or suggested alternative ways of continuing the procedure, in reaction to their transgressions on the test trial, than did the group of children who were given no control over their punishment and only a minimal cognitive structure. The first group also significantly more often expressed self-criticism in their explanations of why the doll broke.

In the second experiment, the two variations of control over punishment

---

[4] The first experiment used fifty-seven girls from a school in a working-class residential area. The girls were assigned as equally as possible to two experimental conditions. The second experiment used sixty-eight boys from a school in a middle-class residential area. Seventeen boys were assigned to each of four experimental conditions.

and the two variations of cognitive structure were independently combined to produce four distinct paradigms. The results of this experiment now showed that the appearance of reparative dispositions, in reaction to the test transgression, was sensitive to variations in control over punishment during training, but not to variations in cognitive structure. Reparation was facilitated only by giving the child the opportunity to experience the reinforcing consequences of its own evaluation of its behavior and of its self-deprivation of candy. Conversely, the induction of self-critical dispositions was a function of the amount of cognitive structure that had been given to the child in the course of punishment, but was not sensitive to the amount of control which the child had over the evaluation and punishment of its behavior—a finding that confirms the evidence from other experiments which were described earlier. These findings indicate that direct external reinforcement of the child's active resolutions of transgression can induce more specifically reparative dispositions in response to subsequent transgressions, even when cognitive resources for self-evaluation are not explicitly provided for the child. However, although the experimentally controlled cognitive structure appeared not to have facilitated the induction of reparative dispositions, it seems certain that the children who generalized a reparative orientation from the training to the test situation would have required some cognitive representation of the direction and consequences of their behavioral control over punishment during the training.

As is true of any other form of conduct, the effects of direct external reinforcement on the learning of reparation undergo internalization when the changes of affectivity which motivate and reinforce reparative acts become attached to intrinsic correlates of the child's behavior. And because reparative dispositions encompass such a broad spectrum of specific forms of overt behavior, the cognitive representations which are associated with reparative acts are crucial to their internalized control. The child's control over directly experienced rewards and punishments is not, however, the only channel through which reparative reactions can be acquired and internalized. Reparative acts also can be acquired by behavior-contingent learning when they are reinforced by the child's empathic or vicarious experience of their distress-reducing or pleasurable consequences for others.

An equally important source of some of the more highly specific and transgression-relevant forms of reparative behavior which children acquire may lie in imitation and other types of observational learning. Many reparative actions emerge in the child's behavioral repertoire with the same saltatory appearance that seems to mark the first overt indicators of self-criticism. Some of these actions are very distant from any which would be expected to occur naturally in the child's behavior, and they are therefore unlikely to derive much benefit from a past history of direct reinforcement. Yet even their first appearance may show a highly tailored specificity to particular transgressions. Such sudden behavioral acquisitions indicate that past observational learning has made a contribution to the child's reparative dispositions.

Some of the forms of behavior which children learn from their observation of others can be brought into the service of reparation even though their value originally may have been learned in situations which were not defined by transgression and punishment. For example, the affection or sympathy which children often display in corrective reactions to their aggressive behavior may have been first learned in the context of their experience as the recipients of affectionate or sympathetic behavior from others. Most children have a wide range of experience of relief of distress—for example, when parents or others care for their injuries, or come to their assistance when they have broken or lost something. Their experience would tend to attach intrinsic value to highly specific acts of their social models, which they could then reproduce in situations where they experience empathic distress on being confronted with the consequences of their transgressions for others.

Children may also acquire reparative dispositions through their observational learning in socialization episodes which are specifically relevant to the resolution of transgressions. For example, reinstatement of a parent's affection often marks the resolution of a transgression. Under the motivation of the anxiety that is elicited by subsequent transgressions, the child might well reproduce the parent's affectionate behavior and direct it toward others. Certain types of corrective parental reactions to a child's transgressions may serve as even more direct models for the formation of reparative dispositions. Parents provide some of the foundations for socially desirable forms of conduct such as honesty, responsibility, or compassion, when they show a child how to return what it has snatched, clean up what it has broken, or be solicitous toward a playmate whom it has attacked. These resolutions of transgression acquire anxiety-reducing value for the child, and can subsequently be reproduced on its own initiative without external constraints.

CONFESSION

Confession is a much narrower type of behavior than reparation. But it also has multiple determinants. Confession is essentially a verbal report to another person of one's own wrongdoing. It has both verbal and nonverbal forerunners in the behavior that children use to seek out the presence and resources of socializing agents when they experience distress or anxiety. When a young child commits a misdemeanor, then shows evidence of discomfort, and finally runs to inform a parent of its behavior, the child's pattern of behavior bears an instructive comparison to its behavior when it cries to bring the parent because it is in distress for reasons which are unrelated to transgression. The similarity suggests that a child's learning of confession would be facilitated by its earlier experience of nurturance from its parents. It also suggests that a child's preferential use of confession as a reaction to transgression might be predictable from its parents' reinforcement of its dependent behavior. Support for these inferences can in fact be found in the data of some surveys which have focussed on confession as a reaction to transgression (Burton, Maccoby, and Allinsmith, 1961; Sears, Maccoby, and Levin, 1957, Chapter 10).

A natural channel of generalization tends to be established for the child between behavior that elicits parental caretaking or protective functions and the confession of wrongdoing. The generalization is supported in part by a considerable amount of overlap between those actions of the child which produce immediately aversive consequences for itself and those which come to be defined as social transgressions. For example, some kinds of behavior which are destined to be treated as transgressions will be brought to the attention of parents even before they are subjected to social punishment—as when a toddler who is not yet exposed to toilet training indicates to its mother its discomfort upon soiling itself.

The nurturant resources which parents use to relieve the distress of their children can account only for some of the predispositions which underlie confession. In order to understand the internalization of confession as a specific reaction to transgression, we must look to the control that confession exercises over contingencies of punishment. The first and most obvious example of this control is the potential effectiveness of confession in the avoidance or attenuation of punishment. Socializing agents place a certain amount of value on the child's self-initiated recognition and report of wrongdoing. They may not punish, or may use milder punishment, when the child confesses; whereas they may be more likely to punish, or to punish more severely, when they themselves must discover or confirm a transgression. Even the slightest discriminable bias in the direction of such contingencies may be sufficient, despite inconsistencies over time, to give confession an edge over alternative reactions such as not disclosing the transgression or avoiding the presence of others. One of the reasons why a small advantage in punishment-avoidance may favor confession is that the probability of observation or discovery by others may be quite high from the child's point of view—in part because the probability has been objectively high during early socialization.

Avoidance or attenuation of punishment not only establishes the anxiety-reducing value of confession, but also generates concurrent contingencies which may give some intrinsic positive value to confession. The child's use of confession frequently is followed by reinstatement of affection or other rewarding social outcomes which are sensitive to the child's initiative in reporting its transgressions. Consequently, confession may be reinforced by the induction of positive affectivity as well as by the reduction of anxiety. These multiple sources of reinforcement undoubtedly account for the fact that confession is so often closely bound to the child's expectation that it may be forgiven. Of course, the learning of confession is not entirely dependent on the child's direct experience of the actual outcomes of its behavior. Parents often use a verbal medium of socialization in such a way as to give to their children a very explicit cognitive representation of the contingent outcomes of potential alternative responses to a known or suspected transgression. For example, they may tell the child that confession will have less aversive consequences than will failure to confess, so that the child can discriminate alternative contingencies without having to test them with its overt behavioral choices. Socializing agents sometimes exert strong pressures toward confession on children, in part because they need information in order to respond appropriately when responsibility for transgression is ambiguous, and in part because they wish to foster the child's honesty. When confession is forced under very strong external pressure, however, it is not likely to come under the same degree of internalized control as does self-initiated confession.

Confession is a relatively externally oriented form of reaction to transgression, even after its motivation has become internalized, since it necessarily employs the medium of an external agent in the resolution of transgression. It is therefore easy to comprehend that another important source of the acquired value of confession lies in its function of producing punishment. Children will often experience some anxiety about the potential punishment of their transgressions even when there is no objective risk of discovery. And although parents are sometimes not inclined to withhold or minimize punishment when the child confesses, the child can at least reduce its anticipatory anxiety by bringing about the occurrence of the punishment. We see here another instance of behavior that can be reinforced by the value of certain components of punishment which have become signals for the termination of the child's anxiety, because of their temporal position in the resolution of transgressions. The contingencies which underlie this mechanism of reinforcement are in fact a point of kinship between confession and self-criticism. The distinction between the two reactions, from the point of view of their exercise of control over anxiety, is that confession can *produce* punishment, while self-criticism can *reproduce* punishment.

It can be seen that confession may have the peculiar advantage of not having its functional value reduced by what will necessarily be the child's experience of inconsistent outcomes. A certain amount of unpredictability in the external consequences of confession may in fact magnify its value for the reduction of anxiety. For the child can use confession with the expectation that it will resolve transgression either through the avoidance or the occurrence of punishment. And confession may then acquire some intrinsic value for anxiety-reduction, which becomes quite independent of the child's perception of external surveillance or knowledge of its transgressions. As in the case of self-criticism, however, the intensity and duration of punishment may determine its anxiety-reducing value for the reinforcement of confession. If confession is too often followed by extremely aversive consequences, the child may find more effective anxiety-reduction in escape or withdrawal from the presence of potential agents of punishment.

REACTIONS ORIENTED TOWARD
EXTERNAL PUNISHMENT

There are a variety of reactions to transgression which are entirely oriented toward explicit external markers of either punishment or punishment-avoidance. These reactions are acquired under two types of contingencies which correspond to those that control the learning of confession. The anxiety-reducing function of these reactions tends to remain more permanently dependent on concrete external events than does the anxiety-reducing function of confession. Nevertheless, reactions which are oriented toward external punishment do become internalized, to the extent that the anxiety which motivates them has become independent of external surveillance at the point of transgression.

This type of reaction to transgression takes one of its most interesting forms in behavior which provokes or seeks out punishment. The behavior is sometimes easily observable in the reactions which young children may show to their transgressions, when they commit a transgression and then act in such a way as to insure that socializing agents will recognize and punish the transgression. Adults may also sometimes respond to their own transgressions by testing the punitive reactivity of other people. The reinforcement of punishment-seeking behavior stems in part from the value that punishment may acquire for the reduction of the anticipatory anxiety that follows a transgression. Here, again, we see some communality with the contingencies which establish the functional value of self-criticism. The two types of reaction to transgression would have their acquisition selectively determined, however, by very different patterns of socialization. Self-criticism is the more probable outcome of those learning experiences which provide reinforcement of the child's use of its own behavioral and cognitive resources in the control and resolution of transgression. Punishment-seeking is more likely to be the result of social experience that reinforces the child's dependence on external control of behavior—particularly when the child cannot easily identify the discriminant cues which would enable it to distinguish between punished and nonpunished behavior.

Many of a child's most strongly motivated behavioral dispositions include multiple alternatives which straddle the borderline of transgression. The child's prediction and control of the reactions of socializing agents to these alternatives will often require fine behavioral and situational distinctions. When the distinctions are difficult to make, the child's repeated variations of behavior within a broad common class of acts, some of which already have been exposed to punishment, may serve to reduce its anticipatory anxiety about potential transgressions by producing either punishment or social signals of the absence of punishment.

Although punishment-seeking is a striking case of reactions to transgression which are oriented toward external punishment, other forms of these reactions are probably more common. This class of reactions also includes the avoidance of potential punishment and the punitive interpretation of the incidental actions of others or of impersonal fortuitous events. Such reactions are, like punishment-seeking, limited in the extent to which they can become internalized. The anxiety that motivates them can become intrinsically attached to transgression. But the anxiety-reduction that marks their reinforcement continues to require the occurrence of certain concrete external stimulus events. These reactions have been shown to have a wide spectrum of variation in frequency and form across different societies (Lambert, Triandis, and Wolf, 1959; Spiro and D'Andrade, 1958; Whiting, 1959). There is evidence that they constitute a sizeable segment of the internalized reactions to transgression of both children and adults in western society (Adorno et al., 1950; W. Allinsmith, 1960; Aronfreed, 1961; Heinecke, 1953). Surveys of children's rationales for refraining from social transgressions also suggest a substantial incidence, particularly among younger children, of a cognitive orientation toward the resolution of transgression through the occurrence or avoidance of punishment (Kohlberg, 1963a; Piaget, 1948).

As is the case with confession, the anxiety-reducing value that punishment can acquire is only one of two major sources of reinforcement for reactions which are oriented toward external punishment. These reactions are also reinforced through their partial success in avoiding punishment. Withdrawal from the vicinity of socializing agents, hiding the consequences of a transgression, and vigilance toward cues which portend punishment, are all examples of reactions to transgression which can be instrumental to the avoidance of punishment. The external event that marks the reinforcement of such internalized avoidance reactions to transgression is simply the absence of punishment.

Because of the uncertainty and inconsistency which necessarily attend absence of punishment as the reinforcing outcome of avoidance reactions to transgression, especially when the child still has only limited cognitive resources for the representation of external contingencies, the passage of a certain duration of time will often be required before an avoidance reaction reduces the child's anxiety. The anxiety-reducing value of sheer absence of punishment following a transgression, and the consequent instrumental function of avoidance reactions, will therefore be greatly curtailed for children when parents extend the tenure of their potential punishment well beyond the visible availability of the child. The anxiety-reducing value of avoidance reactions to transgression will also be attenuated by the parents' extensive use of a verbal medium of socialization. A verbal medium would give the child cognitive representations which could bridge the mediation of anxiety over longer spans of time after the occurrence of a transgression. Moreover, avoidance reactions will often compete at some disadvantage with more corrective reactions to transgression, such as reparation or confession, since the corrective reactions are likely to receive more immediate and consistent social reinforcement.

A child's preference for avoidance reactions to transgression will not be inversely related to its preference for reactions which utilize or seek out punishment in order to resolve the transgression. On the contrary, there ought to be a high coincidence of selective use of these two apparently opposite types of reaction, because of the intimate relationship between the contingencies which are the source of their establishment during socialization. Their relative anxiety-reducing values will be determined by the relative probability and consistency of their complementary contingencies of reinforcement. For example, after a child commits a transgression to which some internalized anxiety already has been attached, it may first attempt to avoid what it perceives as an impending punishment. But if the avoidance reaction originally was acquired under such an uncertain schedule of reinforcement as to sharply limit its anxiety-reducing value, then the child may subsequently seek out punishment in order to resolve the transgression. Such shifts of orientation are not at all unusual in the behavioral dispositions which children show in response to their transgressions (Aronfreed, 1961). Intensity of punishment would also affect the child's relative preferences for avoidance and punishment-seeking reactions. A high incidence of extremely aversive punishment might tend to favor the child's learning of avoidance reactions, even if the avoidance reactions were only infrequently successful.

🌿 CHAPTER NINE 🌿

FEAR, GUILT, AND SHAME

Some readers may find it remarkable that we have carried the analysis of internalized control over conduct so far with so little reference to concepts of morality and guilt. But the specific nature of the criteria of moral judgement, and the limited role of guilt in the control of human behavior, could not have been clearly described without our first having examined the larger variety of cognitive operations in the internalization process. We are now in a position to appreciate that representational and evaluative cognition do not always enter significantly into the mechanisms through which the child acquires internalized control over its social behavior. Moreover, it begins to become apparent that moral judgement is a rather special case of the broad range of functions which evaluative cognition does have in the control of the child's behavior.

Of course, the usage of concepts of morality and guilt in common speech is often so liberal as to erase entirely the interesting distinctions which can be made between different types of evaluative cognitive structures. For example, the term moral is sometimes used as though it were synonomous with behavioral conformity to social standards. And guilt has become a term that is used indiscriminately to refer to what are in fact a number of very different kinds of aversive affective experience. Any attempt to single out the criteria which separate moral judgement from other kinds of evaluative cognition will therefore require semantic constraints. However, the constraints which will be suggested here are not arbitrary. They follow from a more general conception of the dimensions of some of the different types of cognitive structures which can exercise evaluative control over conduct.

The variety of affective states which children may experience in response to their own committed transgressions are a particularly instructive point of departure from which to illustrate the utility of distinguishing among different kinds of cognitive structures for the evaluation of conduct. The main argument of this chapter will be that specific cognitive structures determine the child's qualitative experience of the aversive changes of affective state which socialization attaches to its recognition of its own transgressions. No one of these cognitive structures is a specific prerequisite of any one of the common behavioral reactions to transgression. All of the behavioral reactions to transgression can be acquired by children on the basis of external contingencies and more general cognitive representations which function to reduce the nonspecific aversive properties of a state of affective arousal (see Chapter Eight). As was pointed out earlier, this aversive state may be given the generalized designation of anxiety, in order to recognize its motivating properties and its initial relationship to punishment. However, the cognitive framework in which the affective state is embedded will not only determine the qualitative experience of the state, but will also sharply influence the relative probabilities of different forms of behavioral reaction to transgression.

The cognitive housings in which the anxiety that follows a transgression may occur are phenomena of central interest in the analysis of internalized control over conduct. They govern the child's perception of the classes of behavior which have been socially defined as transgressions. And they constitute an important part of the substance of the evaluative processes which we call conscience. There are at least three kinds of cognitive structures which can be usefully described in distinguishing among the aversive affective states that a child may experience in reaction to its transgressions. These structures correspond, respectively, to fear, guilt, and shame. The three types of cognitive structures are not mutually exclusive of one another. All of them probably occur to some extent in every society, even though their relative incidence across societies will vary with differences in patterns of socialization. Moreover, the child's affective reaction to a single transgression often may be determined simultaneously by more than one of these cognitive structures. The aversive state that follows a transgression may therefore be characterized as fear, guilt, or shame, or as any combination of these affects, to the extent that its experience is determined by cognitive components from each of the three relevant structures.[1]

---

[1] Any one of the three affective states might occur in response to the intentions or thoughts which precede action (particularly when intentions or thoughts are perceived as transgressions in themselves). Fear is perhaps the most likely of the three states to be experienced by an individual even before he perceives himself to have committed a transgression, since fear requires an anticipatory cognitive orientation toward the aversive consequences which the transgression may have for himself. In contrast, the cognitive structures which define shame and guilt make these concepts seem more appropriate when they are applied to a person's affective reactions to already committed transgressions. It is nevertheless possible, of course, that shame and guilt also can assume some anticipatory function in the control of behavior, if they become attached to the cognitive representation of prospective transgressions. But the fundamental differences among the three affective states can be examined most clearly when we consider them as reactions to completed transgressions.

FEAR AND GUILT

The aversive state which follows a trangression may be described as fear to the extent that its qualitative experience is determined by a cognitive orientation toward an external source of aversive consequences for the transgressor. The basic affective component of anxiety is channelled through a cognitive framework that focusses on the anticipation of these aversive consequences. The anticipated consequences may be any one of a great variety of forms of social punishment. Or they may be aversive events which are impersonal outcomes of transgression. It is interesting to note that the anticipation of being shamed or ridiculed can also be classified as one kind of fear, since it represents a cognitive focus on an external source of anxiety. Fear has been reported to be the dominant affective reaction to transgression in many societies (Mead, 1937, 1961; Whiting, 1959). Its predominance does not imply, however, an absence of internalization in these societies. It appears that the fear may be experienced in the absence of any explicit threat of punishment, and even in the absence of any substantial objective risk of punishment.

Fear would tend to have a high probability of association with the kinds of behavioral reactions to transgression in which the child avoids external agents of punishment, seeks cues which indicate the likelihood or intensity of punitive reactions by others, or even elicits punishment (particularly when punishment is perceived as unavoidable). But the cognitive structure through which fear is filtered does not in itself predetermine these externally oriented reactions or select among them. The relative probabilities of specific behavioral reactions to transgression will depend on their effectiveness in reducing the basic affective component of anxiety. And their instrumental value for the reduction of anxiety will in turn be a function of their past history of reinforcement, during the course of socialization, in the child's exercise of control over the aversive consequences of its transgressions. If punishment-oriented behavioral reactions to transgression tend to be associated with fear, the coincidence may be attributed to earlier social experience which supplies both the cognitive structure to support fear and the reinforcement contingencies to support punishment-oriented reactions. Under the appropriate contingencies of reinforcement during socialization, however, other reactions might also easily be acquired as fear-reducing responses.

Many reactions to transgression which are commonly taken as evidence of guilt in western societies—for example, confession or reparation—may be at least equally likely to occur in a cognitive context that corresponds more closely to fear. In contrast, it seems much more improbable that self-criticism would acquire value as a fear-reducing reaction, in part because it does not ordinarily have observable external consequences which can be used as signals for avoidance or arrest of punishment. Whiting's (1959) analyses of social control in different societies do in fact suggest a low inci-dence of self-critical dispositions in societies which are strongly oriented to fear of external agents of punishment. Another reason for the absence of self-criticism in a fear-motivated context is its history as a reaction that replicates components of the punishment which the child has experienced previously. The contingencies of learning which would induce such a repli-cative response may be very different from those which would only sensi-tize the child to the avoidance or engagement of external punishment.

The aversive state that follows a transgression may be described as guilt to the extent that the quality of the transgressor's affective experience is determined by moral evaluation of the transgression. This definition re-quires, of course, a specification of the criteria for moral cognition. Some efforts to characterize moral thought have been constructed around a very limited set of cognitive criteria, such as prescriptive or imperative judge-ments, which are either categorical or else take into account all of the pos-sible consequences of an act for anyone who might be affected by it (see, for example, Hare, 1952, or Kohlberg, 1969). Such definitions seem more appropriate to the special purposes of ethical theory than they do to a broader psychological conception of moral judgement. There is a more general core meaning of the term moral than can be abstracted both from common usage and from certain traditional distinctions which have been made in moral philosophy. The abstraction is one that designates evalua-tive cognition as moral when it makes reference to the consequences of an act for others. It is obvious that we apply our moral judgement very readily to certain classes of behavior, such as acts of aggression, whose conse-quences for others tend to be highly visible. Moral judgement seems much less appropriate to other areas of behavior, such as cleanliness or achieve-ment, where actions are less easily subject to evaluation in terms of their consequences for others. These areas of behavior may also be placed in a moral context, however, when social experience provides the child with appropriate cognitive structures.

To say that the evaluation of conduct is moral to the extent that it makes reference to the consequences of an act for others does not imply that moral cognition necessarily has a highly internalized orientation. The judgement of an act according to its consequences for others may occur in the context of any one of a number of broader cognitive structures. These broader structures translate the perceived consequences of the act for others into more specific evaluative schema which vary in their internal or external orientation. For example, an individual may judge his actions to be good or bad in accordance with their consequences for others. Yet his evaluation may reflect his expectations about how the consequences for others will produce directly positive or aversive consequences for himself. Alternatively, his moral evaluation of an act might represent its consequences for others in the cognitive context of the rules set down by authority, of the normative practices which make for effective social intercourse, or of the obligation to general principles concerning the welfare of others.

When a child is asked why it would be wrong to commit a certain act, and answers that the act would be wrong because it would hurt another person, we cannot therefore immediately infer the degree of internalization that characterizes the child's moral cognition. Further questioning may reveal the view that it is wrong to hurt others because of possible retaliation, or because parents disapprove of hurting others, or because people are not supposed to hurt one another, or because one should think of how others will feel. All of these rationales have the common element of reference to the harmful consequences of the aggressive act for others. But they are different in their implications for what Piaget (1948) has called the autonomy of the child's moral judgement. Conversely, if the child asserts that an act is bad because it will be punished, its evaluation of the act may still have some moral reference if it perceives that punishment is predicated on the harmful consequences of the act for others.

The perception of intentionality in an act is not required as an essential condition of moral judgement. Intentional acts may have a much higher probability of coming under the scrutiny of moral evaluation than do unintentional acts, because socializing agents are more likely to have reacted to the child's intentional acts in such a way as to induce cognitive salience of the consequences of the acts for others. Introspection and common observation clearly indicate, however, that people sometimes respond to their own actions with guilt or other expressions of moral evaluation even when the actions may have been unintentional. From the point of view of the conception of moral cognition that has been set forth here, the fact that older children give more attention to the intentional precursors of an act than do younger children (Piaget, 1948) may be an indication of developmental cognitive change in the direction of a more internalized orientation of moral judgement, rather than an indication of change in the moral character of the judgement. An increased use of the intentionality criterion in the moral evaluation of an act does not necessarily imply a sharpened cognitive focus on the consequences of the act for others. It may well be the case, however, that the child's evaluation of conduct does generally take on an increasingly moral character in the course of development, along with its greater sensitivity to intentions, as changes in social experience and cognitive equipment make older children more aware of the actual effects of their actions upon others.[2]

The distinctive qualitative properties of guilt may be regarded, then, as the experience of anxiety through the filter of the cognition of the harmful consequences of one's actions for others. Since moral cognition itself may have varying degrees of internal or external orientation, it follows that guilt is not necessarily a highly internalized affective state. Cognitive components of fear and guilt often may be blended together when the child perceives external punishment as the potential outcome of actions which have harmful consequences for others. A child's verbal report may give primary expression to one of the two kinds of affective experience, while it masks the presence of the other. It is therefore quite possible that the distinction between fear and guilt is not so sharp as it sometimes appears to be in the reports of cross-cultural surveys of different societies. We cannot know very much about the moral status of an informant merely on the basis of his assertion that some actions are bad because they may result in punishment. If he also perceives that the punishment is predicated on the harmful consequences of the actions for others, then his evaluation of the actions can be said to have some moral reference.

Certain forms of conduct may also be more ambiguous as indicators of fear or guilt than is commonly assumed. For example, a child's attempts to avoid punishment for a transgression do not exclude the possibility that it experiences guilt as well as fear. Conversely, reactions to transgression such as reparation or self-criticism can hardly be regarded as infallible indicators of guilt. Reparative behavior probably is facilitated by moral cognition, since reparation is generally directed to correction of the harmful

[2] The distinction that Piaget (1948) made between consequences and intentions as the foci of moral judgement does not bear directly upon the criterion of moral cognition that is being examined here. The types of questions which Piaget used to demonstrate a morality of consequences among younger children, for example, typically referred to material or impersonal damage. And there was no evidence that the children formed their responses to such questions on the basis of any conception of how the damage would affect other people.

consequences of an act. However, reparative actions undoubtedly also can be acquired by the child in a verbal and cognitive context of socialization that is oriented primarily to the avoidance of external punishment.

For reasons which already have been noted, self-criticism is unlikely to be a fear-oriented response. But neither is it to be equated with the experience of guilt, since the child's replication of the verbal components of earlier punishment may rest on evaluative processes which are not necessarily oriented toward the consequences of its actions for others. It is possible that the cognitive prerequisites of guilt are more likely to produce self-criticism than are other kinds of cognitive structures, because the child's moral orientation toward the effects of its actions upon others may tend to make its conduct more independent of the resolution of transgression through external punitive events. Accordingly, a response such as self-criticism, which utilizes a high degree of internal control over termination of the anxiety that follows transgression, may be more probable in the cognitive context of guilt than it would be in other evaluative contexts which do not have the properties of moral judgement.

GUILT AND SHAME

The aversive state that follows a transgression may be described as shame to the extent that its qualitative experience is determined by a cognitive orientation toward the visibility of the transgression. The essence of shame is a cognitive focus on the appearance or display of that which ought not to show. It is this cognitive focus which provides the sense of exposure or vulnerability to observation that is so intimately associated with shame.[3]

Guilt and shame cannot be fundamentally distinguished on a continuum of internal versus external orientation. The cognitive structure that produces the experience of shame can show the same variability on a continuum of internalization as has been described for the moral cognition that supports guilt. Common self-observation suggests that some of our actions result in the experience of shame even when they are unknown to others, because they expose to us what we feel ought not to be visible. Of course, the experience of shame in the absence of surveillance still requires the salience of the visibility of transgression, either to ourselves or to imagined significant others. There are also more objective indicators of substantial internalization among societies for which shame has been described as the dominant affective response to transgression. As an extreme illustration, Mead (1950) points out that the Ojibwa may commit suicide because of his shame about an act that has not been open to observation. Some of the descriptions of Japanese society (LaBarre, 1948) also suggest that shame and its behavioral consequences may be highly internalized. Nevertheless, since shame occurs under a cognitive focus on the visibility of transgression, it would tend to be a more externally oriented affective state than guilt. Guilt is more likely to be separable at least from the condition of external observation of transgression, because its cognitive focus is on the harmful consequences of an act for another person.

In view of the distinctions which have been made here, it is not surprising to find that there is much artificiality in attempts to dichotomize societies into guilt and shame cultures, on the presumed basis of the presence or absence of an internalized conscience (Benedict, 1946; Leighton and Kluckhohn, 1947). Even before such categorization became common, Mead (1937) classified the modal affective responses to transgression of

[3] The emphasis on visibility also is relevant to an understanding of how shame can become attached to observable attributes of a person as well as to overt acts which have been treated as social transgressions.

different societies in such a way as to imply that internalization was not essential to the distinction between guilt and shame. Since then, other analyses of guilt and shame (Ausubel, 1955; Singer, 1953) have indicated serious deficiencies in their respective characterization as internally and externally oriented affective states.

It is not even clear that guilt and shame can be distinctly identified in some of the phenomena which have long been cited as evidence of their presence. For example, Leighton and Kluckhohn (1947) asked Navajo and white American children to describe occasions when they would feel shame (their inquiry apparently did not include any explicit reference to guilt). They found that the white children more frequently mentioned "failure or inadequacy" and "bad behavior or aggressiveness," whereas the Navajo children more frequently referred to "embarrassment before others" and "making a poor personal appearance." They then classified the responses which were characteristic of the white children as evidence of "guilt," and assumed that these responses would require an internalized moral orientation. The responses which were more typical of the Navajo children were considered, in contrast, to be externally oriented reflections of "shame." It seems fairly obvious that this kind of categorization is questionable. The white children might surely have felt shame rather than guilt in response to some of the incidents which they mentioned, particularly in response to those which concerned failure or inadequacy. And even though the Navajo children may have been more sensitized than the white children to the visibility of their transgressions, their responses may well have been affected also by the moral perception of the unpleasant consequences of their actions for others.

The comparisons which Havighurst and Neugarten (1955) made among white children and the children of a number of American Indian societies gave more attention to the cognitive structures that lay behind their informants' normative statements about conduct. Their findings did not suggest that the Indian children lacked an internalized conscience. The Indian children appeared to have well-developed concepts of internalized responsibility, although they were perhaps somewhat more attuned to external control of conduct than were the white children. What seems to have been discerned in cross-cultural studies is a rather broad and imperfect distinction between western and nonwestern societies along the continuum of internal versus external orientation. Western societies are characterized by a marked orientation toward the individual's responsibility for active control and modification of his behavior, while many nonwestern societies seem to have a more externally oriented view of the determinants of conduct.

Some recent additional evidence of this difference between western and nonwestern societies appears in the report of an investigation by Mc-Michael and Grinder (1966). These investigators found that the frequency of dispositions toward active corrective reactions to transgression, among the children of various ethnic groups in Hawaii, was greater in the groups which had more exposure to the dominant values of the American mainland. It would be an oversimplification to reduce this difference to a contrast between guilt and shame, since each of these affective states can sustain a considerable range of internal or external orientation. It should also be noted that much of the external orientation that has been labelled as shame in nonwestern societies may actually consist of varieties of fear (Hallowell, 1949; Mead, 1961; Whiting, 1959). Shame and fear are probably more closely intertwined in many societies than either is with guilt, because a cognitive focus on the visibility of a transgression would tend to blend easily with a focus on its punitive consequences for the transgressor.

The experiences of guilt and shame are also often blended. The induction of shame during socialization could hardly leave the child without any perception of the effects of its behavior upon others, since an act must have at least some aversive consequences for socializing agents if they are to treat it as a transgression. From the descriptions of socialization in societies in which shame is reported to be the typical affective response to transgression, one can infer that the children often come to experience not only shame, but also what may be called guilt in connection with having brought shame upon their parents or upon a larger filial reference group (De Vos, 1960). Thus, the fact that Navajo children referred so frequently to exposure to observation, when they were asked to describe occasions of transgression (Leighton and Kluckhohn, 1947), may indeed have signified that shame was a salient experience for them. But more intensive examination of their thought processes might have revealed that the cognitive structures through which they perceived the transgressions also had some of the moral reference that would support the experience of guilt.

There are certain classes of transgression which seem to have a highly discriminate coincidence with the experience of either guilt or shame. However, these classes do not stand up under close inspection to the test of being criteria for differential prediction of the two affective states. For example, it sometimes has been suggested that guilt is associated with transgressions which are positive acts of commission, and that shame is associated with failure or defect (Piers, 1953). But there are many common occurrences of guilt and shame under conditions where such a distinction can hardly be definitive. We might imagine having heard that a neighbor has lost his child in a swift current after he made an unsuccessful attempt at rescue. If we are also told that the neighbor is very disturbed over his failure to save the child, we would immediately assume that he feels guilty, and not that he feels ashamed. And our assumption would almost certainly be correct. Obviously, it is the consequence of his failure for the child that has cognitive salience for him.

There are many other more ordinary occasions when people may feel guilt over actions which represent inability to successfully negotiate a task or to come up to a standard of performance, because they perceive that their failure causes disappointment or hardship to others. This kind of association of guilt with failures of performance requires some previous socialization in which failure has been treated in such a way as to emphasize its aversive consequences for others. Conversely, many transgressions for which guilt appears to be the primary reactive affect in our own society, and which are clearly positive acts of commission (for example, certain aggressive or sexual transgressions), may be more closely associated with shame in other societies. Even within our own society, a distinction between guilt and shame in terms of acts of commission versus failure or defect would turn out to be inadequate. A person might carry out selfish or aggressive acts purposefully rather than through failure of control, and yet later might feel shame at having visibly displayed childishness or pettiness.

Some of the illustrations which are used above can also serve to demonstrate the deficiencies in still another conception of guilt and shame. It might be thought that guilt is attached to volitional or intentional acts, while shame is attached to involuntary lack of control. But the man who feels guilty about not having been able to save his drowning child need not perceive himself as having committed an intentional transgression. There are many occasions on which we may experience guilt when we unintentionally harm or offend someone, because of the effects which we perceive our actions to have on the other person. And there are likewise times when we may experience exposure and shame in reaction to the unexpected visibility of intentional actions. It may nevertheless be true that guilt has a much higher probability of becoming attached to intentional acts than it has of becoming attached to unintentional acts. Intentional acts exercise more control and direction over behavior. They are therefore more capable of having aversive consequences for others, and they are more likely to have been treated by socializing agents in such a way as to emphasize these aversive consequences.

The same relative bias in the determinants of guilt and shame can be discerned in the distinction between positive acts of commission and behavior that represents failure or defect. Involuntary loss of control, failure, and defect are properties of a transgression which can only sometimes be construed as having harmful consequences for others. But these same properties can always be perceived as having made visible that which ought not to be permitted to show. Accordingly, transgressions which have such properties would have a higher probability of being associated with shame than they would of being associated with guilt.

The analysis of shame and guilt that has been outlined here suggests that the cognitive orientations which are respectively required for the two affective states might be constructed by the child, under appropriate conditions of social experience, around virtually any class of acts. However, not all forms of behavior would be equally amenable to the construction of either of the two orientations. Any act that can be socially defined as a transgression must have observable correlates which may be subjected to a cognitive focus on visibility. But not all transgressions can easily be subjected to a cognitive focus on their harmful consequences for others. We might accordingly expect that a great variety of behavior could be embedded in a cognitive context of shame, but that guilt would tend to be more selectively localized only in certain areas of conduct.

The difference in the extent of the behavioral applicability of guilt and shame may bear upon the fact that cross-cultural investigators often have been prone to find classes of transgression which elicit primarily guilt in our society and shame in nonwestern societies, but not to find transgressions which elicit shame in our society and guilt in other societies. We have noted that guilt can easily become attached to transgressions in such areas of social behavior as aggression, where the child's actions usually will have fairly concrete and observable consequences for others. In contrast, guilt might become attached only with considerably greater difficulty to behavior that is functionally related to cleanliness, for example, or to the ingestive and eliminative systems of the body. Transgressions in these latter areas of behavior could come to elicit shame quite readily, since they would lend themselves to a cognitive focus on the exposure of what ought not to be observable. But their aversive consequences for others would tend to be much less immediately apparent than would the consequences of aggressive behavior.

It is of some passing interest that there appears to be a marked neurobe-havioral bias in the determination of which classes of transgression are re-spectively correlated, at least in western society, to the cognitive structures of guilt and shame. It would seem that guilt tends to be restricted to behav-ior that is primarily controlled by voluntary neural mediation, whereas shame is very likely to become the dominant affective reaction to behavior that is more dependent on involuntary neural mediation.

Although some forms of behavioral reaction to transgression can be used as indicators of guilt or shame, with a certain degree of reliability, their criterial value is undoubtedly less than perfect. For example, an at-tempt to hide a transgression or its effects would be particularly appropri-ate to shame (though such a reaction would also be appropriate to fear). In contrast, a reparative reaction would be peculiarly appropriate to guilt. An individual might attempt, however, to correctively hide something that he has exposed about himself, with a cognitive focus on eliminating its offensiveness or embarrassment to others. Such a blending of shame and guilt again demonstrates that shame does not exclude the presence of moral evaluation of an act. There are other reactions to transgression which are probably equally likely as responses to either guilt or shame. For example, self-criticism may be just as frequently instrumental to the reduction of shame as it is to the reduction of guilt. The child's internalized replication of the verbal components of punishment that it already has experienced would be compatible with either affective state, since neither is character-ized by a cognitive focus on an externally punitive resolution of transgres-sion (in contrast to fear).

The terms which can be applied to the affective states which are the complements of shame and guilt also reveal something about their respec-tive cognitive structures. Pride would be the complement of shame. And pride is clearly an affect that is based on the exhibition or visibility of posi-tively valued behavior or attributes (see the analysis of pride by Levin and Baldwin, 1959). We do not appear to have an exact term for the comple-ment of guilt. But it would seem to be something like a feeling of virtue in perceiving that one's acts have beneficial consequences for others.

CHAPTER TEN

VALUES AND
SOCIAL EXPERIENCE

Most of our formal evidence concerning the evaluative dimensions of conscience comes from descriptive surveys of the verbal expressions of conscience among children in western society. These surveys frequently reveal certain changes in the substance and form of conscience which are correlated with advancing age. But the age-related differences in the cognitive structure of conscience also often appear when middle-class children are compared to working-class children of the same age. And the same changes with age are frequently not apparent among children of nonwestern societies. Moreover, comparable variations in the evaluative expressions of conscience can be discerned even among adults, both as stable features of their value systems and as reactions to radical changes in their social environment.

After we have examined the cognitive changes in conscience which sometimes occur as children advance in age, we will consider whether they require any conception of a developmental order of qualitatively distinct stages or types of morality. We will conclude that the acquisition of conscience can best be conceptualized as a continuous representation of social experience, even though it also may have cumulative structural features. We will then look at some additional evidence which indicates that the internalized transformations of social experience ordinarily produce structures of only limited integrative capacity for the organization of both conscience and conduct. Finally, we will consider some of the ways in which the constraints and incentives of a social environment may engage established evaluative structures in the control of behavior.

ACQUISITION OF VALUES

Developmental changes in the structure of conscience were highly visible in the results of the verbal inquiries which Piaget (1948 [1932]) conducted with children many years ago. A number of other investigators have replicated Piaget's original method of inquiry, and have partially confirmed some of his findings (Boehm, 1962; Caruso, 1943; Durkin, 1959a; Havenga, 1958; Lerner, 1937; MacRae, 1954). Using a very elaborate and detailed set of verbal probes into children's thought processes, Kohlberg (1963a, 1964, 1969) has made even more refined distinctions among a series of sequential changes in the form of children's evaluations of conduct. He describes changes which are more extended in developmental time, and in order of cognitive complexity, than those which are described by Piaget. The basic technique in all of these inquiries has been to elicit the child's verbalized rationale for the judgement of specific acts in hypothetical situations—that is, the child generally is not confronted with situations in which it must evaluate acts which have been committed in actuality by either itself or other people (although Piaget did examine children's conceptions of rules in the context of a game of marbles). This technique has the advantage of permitting an assessment of the child's evaluative judgements of many specific acts in a great variety of hypothetical situations.

The verbalized evaluations which children give in response to inquiries about their judgements of hypothetical acts most frequently are categorized as representations of moral thought. But their judgements actually represent evaluative operations along a number of different kinds of cognitive dimensions, many of which would not meet the narrower criteria that might be imposed on a conception of moral cognition. For example, it is apparent that only a quite limited proportion of the samples of evaluative thought which are obtained from the children could be classified as evidence of a moral orientation toward the consequences of an act for other people. Nevertheless, the types of judgement which do occur with the highest incidence, and their tendency toward an order in developmental time, are phenomena of very considerable interest. They provide the starting point for an understanding of how the child's social experience and cognitive capacities produce changes in the evaluative structures of conscience.

The general nature of all of the age-correlated changes in the expression of conscience might be described as a movement from an external to a more internalized orientation. The most representative specific changes, and the ones to which most attention has been given, are the following:

1. The young child at first judges the severity of transgressions with respect to their visible damage or harm. As the child becomes older, its judgements become more sensitive to the intentions of the transgressor.

2. Younger children tend toward the perception of "immanent justice"—the perception that punishment is impersonally ordained in the very performance of a transgression. The older child becomes more perceptive of how punishment follows from principles which take into account the consequences of a transgression for other people.

3. The young child judges the appropriateness of punishment by its severity rather than by its relevance to transgression. Younger children seem to perceive that the expiation of a transgression is proportionate to the magnitude of external retribution. The older child is more likely to recommend that the transgressor make restitution or that punishment be tailored to have reciprocity with the transgression.

4. The child first interprets rules as having a fixed and absolute legitimacy that is given by external authority. Gradually, the child comes to see that the application of rules may be relative to people and situations, and that rules are established and maintained through reciprocal social agreements.

5. When young children are asked to evaluate an act, they show a marked orientation toward its concrete consequences for the actor—that is, they judge an act to be good or bad by reference to its rewarding or punitive consequences. Kohlberg's (1963a) findings indicate that the evaluative judgements of older children follow from more abstract principles of conduct, and that the principles show an increasingly internalized orientation which is correlated to some extent with age. The principles which can be inferred from the children's verbalizations appear to show first an orientation toward conformity to the requirements of social approval and of maintenance of authority, then an orientation toward contractual obligation and the welfare of others, and finally an orientation toward the intrinsic rightness or wrongness of an act.

The first four of the changes in the expression of conscience which are described above were central trends in the observations which were made by Piaget. Although the changes were not firmly anchored to specific chronological points, there was some normative uniformity in the typical ages at which they appeared. Generally speaking, all of the changes began to be visible when the children were of grammar school age, and became characteristic of the children's judgements when they had reached an age of roughly between nine and eleven years. Piaget recognized that there were substantial individual differences in the timing and extent of the changes, even among children in his relatively homogeneous sample. Nevertheless, he was impressed by the appearance of a certain amount of synchrony, among the different sequences of cognitive change, in their movement toward a more internalized and less authority-centered moral orientation.

The fact that the various specific forms of cognitive change seemed to some extent to be yoked to one another suggested a more general transformation in the structure of the child's conscience—a transformation that was parallel to broader changes of cognitive structure which Piaget (1929) already had discerned in other areas of the child's thought. He described the changes in the orientation of conscience as a transition between two successive stages in the child's understanding of rules or principles of conduct, the first of which followed a very early period when the child appeared to be capable of expressing rules only in action. The kinds of evaluative judgements and justifications which children first verbalized were characterized as a moral heteronomy, oriented toward multiple sources of authority and external constraint, and based on the perception of rules as absolute objective realities. In contrast, the evaluative thought processes of older children were characterized as a moral autonomy, a more advanced stage in which their verbalizations revealed an internalized subscription to relativistic principles of social interaction and exchange. Although Piaget noted that there was much overlap in developmental time between the two types of conscience, even within the evaluative judgements of the individual child, he regarded them as sequential stages which were essentially discontinuous in their qualitative and structural features.

Kohlberg's systematic classification of children's evaluative rationales for the judgement of conduct also leads him to the conclusion that there are structural cognitive shifts in the development of conscience, and that the shifts produce sequential stages of moral orientation. A somewhat similar, though more roughly outlined, conception of sequential developmental types of conscience has been suggested by Peck and Havighurst et al. (1960), on the basis of their intensive idiographic assessments of individual subjects. Kohlberg's method of verbal inquiry tends to probe quite deeply into the child's thought processes, particularly into its capacity for abstraction in the application of principles of conduct. The different forms of verbalization of values which are elicited from children by this method appear to be highly sensitive to the child's cognitive complexity, to the breadth and economy of the concepts which it can apply across many specific situations, and to the resources of language which it has available for the very expression of its evaluative thought.

Kohlberg finds it necessary to organize the variations in children's verbal expressions of their values around six sequential and qualitatively distinct idealized moral types, which he represents as being on a developmental continuum. He argues that the moral thought of the child advances through the stages of the developmental continuum in a fixed order, with important transitions occurring well into adolescence. However, there are wide individual differences among children in the age at which specific stages appear, and in the extent to which the more advanced stages are attained. Thus, even among adolescents who may have acquired some of the most advanced form of moral thought, it will not ordinarily be the case that this form of thought is typical of the moral orientation at which their development stabilizes. Kohlberg's assertion of an invariant developmental order of moral principles is based in part on his application of scaling analyses of order to the basic categories or types into which he classifies the verbalizations of his respondents. The ordinal analyses do provide some evidence of an ordered sequence. Evaluative judgements of any given type are relatively unlikely to occur in the absence of judgements of the type that is considered to represent the immediately preceding stage on the developmental continuum.

It is very difficult to ascertain what acquisition processes are implied in theoretical conceptions which assign the organization of the child's conscience to developmental stages. These conceptions do not specify the mechanisms of transformation which give rise to the successive structures of conscience. To the extent that any conception of mechanisms of transition can be discerned, it appears to go not much beyond the suggestion that the forms of conscience arise from an interaction between the child's intrinsic dispositions toward cognitive change and its social treatment. Both Piaget's and Kohlberg's conceptions share the assumption that there are a fixed number and order of potential stages in the development of conscience. Of course, it is not assumed that changes in the structure of conscience unfold through purely maturational determinants which are independent of social experience. But neither is it suggested that variations in social experience might act as a generative source of variations in the form of the child's conscience. The stage conceptions appear rather to be based on the idea that social experience serves as a supportive catalyst for the natural emergence of successive forms in the organization of conscience.

Piaget (1948) views the transition to moral autonomy as a specific outcome of broader developmental changes in the child's cognitive structures—an outcome that is facilitated by the child's movement away from the constraint of authority-centered social interaction and toward the greater freedom of peer-centered interaction. Kohlberg (1963a, 1969) offers a more complex view of the sequential restructuring of a moral order that the child spontaneously integrates from the expanding varieties of social stimulation to which it is exposed, particularly from the successive roles which it is required or permitted to take. The undertone of these conceptions is unmistakeably that of Rousseau's *Emile*. The assumption seems to be that patterns of conscience necessarily evolve, through a fixed sequence of qualitative transformations, in the direction of what is considered to be socially desirable or "mature," provided only that certain common forms of social experience are available to the child. Failure of the sequence to reach its terminal point must be regarded as an arrest of the natural order of development.

There are a number of different kinds of empirical observations which place very serious limitations on the view that children acquire conscience through a fixed series of emergent cognitive transformations which are developmentally imposed on appropriate forms of social stimulation. Among the most important observations are those which have been made on children elsewhere than in Europe or the United States, and those which have been made on samples of children who differ in their socioeconomic status within western societies. These observations reveal differences which are related to variations in social experience that cannot simply be placed on a fixed developmental continuum. For example, many of the prominent features of an external orientation of conscience do not show the same decline with advancing age in other societies as they do in our own (Dennis, 1943; Havighurst and Neugarten, 1955; Jahoda, 1958; Najarian-Svajian, 1966; Whiting, 1959). In some cases, it seems clear that an externally oriented evaluative structure is the end result of acculturation.

Very substantial differences in the expression of conscience, which are as striking as those associated with changes in age, have been found to exist between middle- and working-class children in western society. The findings of almost all of the relevant surveys indicate that the shift from an external to a more internalized orientation of conscience, as the child advances in age, occurs more slowly among working-class children (Boehm, 1962; Boehm and Nass, 1962; Durkin, 1959c; Harrower, 1934; Johnson, 1962; Kohlberg, 1969; Lerner, 1937; MacRae, 1954; Medinnus, 1962). The changes of orientation in the working-class groups are in some cases quite small in comparison to what appear to be fairly large and stable differences between the two social classes. In certain of the studies, the analyses of the data show that a considerable part of the difference between classes remains even after intelligence has been taken into account. It is interesting to note that most of these findings are based on the same types of verbal inquiries which were introduced by Piaget (1948), who described his original French-speaking Swiss sample as a working-class group. It is possible that the socioeconomic characteristics of what Piaget considered to be a working-class sample had more in common with those of children who since have been categorized as middle-class in other surveys within western countries. However, there is evidence in some of the investigations which have been cited, as well as in others (Durkin, 1959b; Morris, 1958), that not all of the cognitive changes which Piaget perceived in his observations are necessarily to be found even in middle-class samples.

These socioeconomic and cultural differences in the expression of con-science among children indicate that specific patterns of socialization can siphon cognitive development into the formation of conscience along more than one channel. The same implication is carried in the findings of surveys of the values of older adolescents and adults. For example, some of Kohl-berg's (1964, 1969) descriptions of delinquent boys' rationales for the judgement of conduct are lucid illustrations of an external orientation. But the descriptions also suggest that the evaluations of conduct by delinquents are sometimes no less broadly structured and terminal than are those which follow from the more internalized orientation of their nondelinquent peers. McCord and Clemes (1964) have demonstrated large differences in the orientation of conscience among groups of adults who differ in their com-mitment to various religious, political, or other social institutions. The different types of orientation which characterized their adult samples can-not be ordered in any convincing way on a developmental continuum of changes in cognitive structure. Similar differences of orientation are appar-ent in the cross-cultural survey of values that was reported by Kluckhohn and Strodtbeck (1961).

The conception of a natural order of structural stages in the acquisition of conscience also leaves us without much understanding of the cognitive changes which can be induced by experience that does not occur over developmental time. It appears that values which are relevant to the control of conduct can be altered substantially when adults are placed under severe stress (Lifton, 1961; Schein, 1957). They also can be changed to some extent by persuasion, by a person's conformity to behavioral demands which are initially discrepant with his values, and by other fairly ordinary techniques of social influence (Brock and Buss, 1964; Kelman, 1965; Mills, 1958; Zimbardo, 1960). There are some especially interesting findings in the report by Suedfeld and Vernon (1966) of an experiment in which college students were isolated as part of the procedure of "sensory deprivation." Toward the end of the period of isolation, the subjects were forced to ignore the content of messages about a national group, and to make only one kind of judgement about the attitude that was implicit in the messages, in order to obtain the reward of another message. Tests of attitude toward the national group were conducted some weeks before and immediately after the experience of isolation. Subjects who had been identified as concrete in their conceptual structure appeared to have internalized the judgements which they had made under the external constraints of isolation. Subjects who had more abstract conceptual capacity generally did not continue to make the judgements which had been forced upon them during their isolation.

Experiments which demonstrate that brief exposures to social influence can induce changes in the expression of established values raise some searching questions about any assumptions concerning the development and stability of different evaluative structures—particularly when the induced changes are direct parallels or reversals of the changes in orientation of conscience which have been observed to occur as children become older. If we suppose that conscience can be restructured around different kinds of principles or rules which become successively available to the child, the principles must still be given a substance of cognitive dimensions, along which affective value may be assigned to specific acts in a way that takes account of their consequences and their situational context. It will not be surprising if the application of these evaluative dimensions to a particular class of acts is susceptible to immediate modification by social influence. But when episodic social experience produces what appears to be a shift in the very nature of the principles which are applied to the evaluation of conduct, then we are confronted with the problem that the operation of conscience can draw on the simultaneous availability of more than one type of evaluative structure. Recognition of this problem alerts us to the possibility that the fundamental cognitive and affective substance of values remains relatively unchanged after it has been established in the course of socialization, but that the values become subordinated to representation in various forms or structures which differ in their abstractness, complexity, and sensitivity to later social influence.

The results of some of the recent experiments which have been interpreted as demonstrations of observational learning in children also can be used to illustrate the problem that is posed for a conception of sequential stages in the orientation of conscience. Bandura and McDonald (1963) identified two groups of children who were respectively characterized by their dispositions to judge the severity of hypothetical transgressions with respect to either the intentions of the transgressor or the objective consequences of the transgression. Their subjects were distributed throughout all of the grades of an elementary school. It will be recalled that Piaget (1948) found an orientation toward intention in the judgement of transgression to be one index of children's advancement toward a more subjective and autonomous moral orientation. Bandura and McDonald exposed their subjects to a social interaction in which a child's own judgements of the severity of transgressions were interspersed with those of an adult whose verbalized rationales were contrary to its original evaluative dispositions. Regardless of whether the child originally had been oriented toward the intentions or the consequences of a transgression, it showed substantial shifts of judgement and corresponding justification in the direction of the adult's orientation.

Turiel (1966) has reported a similar experiment in which children were first classified in accordance with their responses to the extensive verbal inquiry that is employed in Kohlberg's system of moral typology. He found that exposure to an adult's verbalized orientation toward the judgement of conduct would induce children to shift their own evaluations. There were shifts of roughly comparable magnitude to principles of an abstractness and complexity which were either an order above or an order below the children's initially dominant orientations (although a tendency toward somewhat greater shifts in the direction of the lower order was in fact obscured by the questionable procedure of reducing the magnitude of change by the amount of change that occurred in a control group which was not exposed to social influence). However, the judgements of an adult produced relatively little shift in the direction of principles which were two orders of complexity beyond the children's initial orientation.

These effects of brief exposure to an adult's verbal expression of values reveal that the child's conscience is organized around multiple cognitive structures which can easily replace one another even at the same moment in developmental time—a finding that common observation would certainly compel us to expect. The effects cannot be dismissed as mere evidence of the child's ability to make verbal statements which will gain social approval. Since the children had to give appropriate justifications for their judgements, it is clear that they must have had available the required evaluative modes of thought in order to qualify as having shown a shift of orientation. Such observations suggest a very considerable question as to whether any evaluative structure is ever lost to the individual, even after cognitive development has run its course. It is obvious that the ordinary adult is capable of applying more than one kind of principle to the evaluation of conduct, and that many social cues may elicit modes of thought which function beneath the individual's cognitive capacity. For example, Walster (1966) found that college students attributed more responsibility to a specific person for an accident that had more severe consequences, when they could not readily make their judgements on the basis of the person's intentions.

We may conclude that while children may acquire successive structures for the elaboration of social values, as a result of their changing cognitive capacities, their new acquisitions generally displace rather than transform the structures which were previously available. Whatever transformation does take place is not so extensive or irreversible as to make it seem especially useful to think of conscience as being formed in stages or levels. A conception of stages would be more powerful if it referred to structural and functional entities which successively incorporated and eliminated one another. Of course, there may be some individuals whose cognitive capacity and social experience provides them with evaluative concepts which are sufficiently complex and yet economical to be broadly applicable to a great many areas of behavior and specific situations. Such individuals are less likely than others to be forced to utilize more concrete and limited principles of evaluation in order to accommodate to external pressures of authority or social approval. But the conscience of the ordinary person appears to operate through a number of alternative evaluative structures which vary in their abstractness and complexity. Even the person whose conscience is capable of operating at the heights of moral philosophy will often judge alternatives of conduct on less exalted ground because he is subject to constraints of information, intensity of affect, and decision-making time.

The role of sheer cognitive power in the operation of conscience is confirmed by a number of investigations which have shown that the orientation of conscience in children is independently correlated with their intelligence, in a direction that is parallel to its association with age (Abel, 1941; Boehm and Nass, 1962; Johnson, 1962; Kohlberg, 1964; MacRae, 1954). Recent surveys have demonstrated substantial correlations between conventional tests of intelligence and the complexity of the information which children can take into account in their judgements of conduct (Kellmer Pringle and Edwards, 1964; Whiteman and Kosier, 1964). Breznitz and Kugelmass (1967) have reported findings which clearly demonstrate that increasing verbal complexity is a central determinant of age-correlated changes in the child's ability to apply the principle of intentionality in its evaluation of the behavior of others. It is true that the principles which children verbalize in their evaluations of conduct may show some orderly association with their age even after the variance which is attributable to measures of intelligence has been eliminated. Kohlberg (1969) notes, for example, that allowance for scores on a test of intelligence still leaves a correlation between classification within his system of six moral types and the age of the child. However, standardized psychometric tests of intelligence are designed to make rather gross predictive distinctions, rather than to characterize the child's cognitive status with any precision. One wonders therefore whether any significant variation in principles of conscience would be apparent among children who, regardless of their age, had been identified as comparable in general cognitive capacity by techniques which were more sensitive to the specific operations of their thought processes (Inhelder and Piaget, 1958; Kessen and Kuhlmann, 1962).

It is distinctly possible that the changes in the principles which children apply to the evaluation of conduct are determined primarily by the increasing cognitive and verbal complexity which they can use to integrate their social experience, rather than by any shift in the substance of the values which are specific to conscience. The capacity for abstraction would necessarily be associated with the capacity for a more internalized orientation of conscience, at least at the point where the child becomes capable of employing principles of judgement which take into account more than the immediately rewarding or punitive consequences of an act. But if we were to make a distinction between the basic dimensions of value and the operators which are applied to the dimensions, it would not be necessary to assume that the dimensions themselves are transformed by advances in the child's cognitive capacity.

The changing complexity of the child, in the status of a verbal informant who is responding to the inquiries of an adult, does not require the inference of change in the fundamental affective values which may continue to determine the performance or suppression of specific acts of conduct. In our earlier analysis of the relationship between conduct and conscience (Chapter Two), we considered a seven-year-old child's evaluation of her own conduct. It was apparent that she had sufficient moral perception to be concerned about the potentially harmful consequences of her intended aggression toward her younger brother. She already had, then, the rudiments of a moral decision-making apparatus. We would certainly expect that she would acquire more complex forms of evaluation of conduct as she gains more abstract cognitive structures for taking into account finer discriminations among different acts, among their consequences, and among the conditions under which they may occur. She will acquire increasing cognitive complexity in many areas of thought other than conscience. But her increasing complexity need not be equated with increasingly moral transformations of conscience. She is already a basically moral creature, because her thought shows some of the fundamental properties of moral value.

Our analysis of the structure of conscience cautions us to expect that any universality in its acquisition will be found in the development of cognitive capacity rather than in the substance of values. There appear to be very sharp limitations on the generalizations which can be made from the sequence of principles of conduct that is sometimes found in the judgements which are made by children of different ages in western society. It may be that an increasingly abstract and internalized orientation of conscience would be apparent as children advance in age in any society. The development of their cognitive capacities might guarantee their acquisition of some evaluative principles which would be independent of the immediate anticipation of reward or punishment. But there is no reason to expect that these principles will have a uniform nature or order that transcends the child's rearing in a specific culture. Because self-direction is a central value in many western societies, some individuals in these societies may place a premium on using their cognitive capacities to arrive at principles of conduct which supersede any form of external normative constraint. In other societies, however, cognitive development may be used to elaborate highly abstract and complex formulations of very different principles of conduct. For example, Erikson's (1950) description of Yurok society makes it clear that this American Indian group continually restructures the values of cleanliness and economic exchange into the final abstract principles of an adult conscience.

We can see that there are many restrictions on the utility of a conception that proposes a universal sequence of stages in the structure of conscience. None of the restrictions gives us any reason to question the evidence that the acquisition of conscience has a genuine developmental thread. The child's changing conceptions of the rules of conduct undoubtedly do have certain structural and qualitative properties. And it seems certain that some types of cognitive structures are nested in the previous establishment of others. There is no pattern of socialization that can produce an abstract concept of justice, for example, in the young child who does not have the required cognitive capacity. The development of the child's cognitive capacities cannot in itself account, however, for the acquisition of either the form or the substance of conscience. Changes in the structure of conscience may require more general alterations in the operations of the child's thought processes—for example, an increasingly abstract and less egocentric direction of thought (Piaget, 1948). But we need also to know how the formal properties of the child's thought interact with the socialization process to become translated into the dimensions of conscience. The child's cognitive status cannot influence its evaluation of conduct without at the same time shaping its social experience.

The total body of knowledge that we have about both structure and change in the forms of conscience can be reasonably contained only by the view that the developmental sequence of the forms has antecedents in specific varieties of social experience. But we must also recognize the corollary proposition that cognitive development is an active determinant of experience. What appears to be required for an understanding of developmental changes in conscience is a conception that emphasizes continuity in the relationship between the child's cognitive structure and its social experience, rather than the kind of transformational discontinuity that is implicit in any conception of stages. However, our formulation of the nature of learning will have to be broadened and modified very considerably, in ways which are as yet uncertain, before we can uncover the mechanisms through which experience produces alterations in the evaluative structure of the child's conscience.

A number of speculative accounts of developmental pacing in social experience are set out below, in order to illustrate some of the possible avenues for the acquisition of new elements in the structure of conscience. Particular attention is given to changes in the child's cognitive status, and to corresponding changes in the expectations and the behavior of its socializing agents. Although the illustrations are drawn in general terms, not all of their details will be accurate with respect to socialization in nonwestern societies. Nor will the illustrations be equally applicable to socialization within different strata of the social structure of western society. Nevertheless, the illustrations may serve as a useful initial probe into the learning that underlies the child's cognitive representation of social experience.

Let us consider the decline in the perception of immanent justice as a first illustration of continuity in the shaping of the child's conscience by social experience. The mobility of young children is restricted, and they are under relatively close supervision. They do not yet have significant capacities for controlling the visibility of their transgressions or for taking corrective measures which may forestall punishment. Moreover, the cognitive status of the young child places limitations on its parents' use of a verbal medium of communication. It can therefore have only the most limited comprehension of the real causal chain of events in social punishment, the pivotal point of which is the aversive consequences of its actions for others. Clearly, the young child's experience would initially implant the perception that punishment follows automatically upon transgression. During the early years of socialization, the child also is exposed to punishment that has an immediacy which is required by its protective function. Sharp suppression of certain kinds of behavior often must be established quickly, on the basis of the child's capacity to be conditioned, and without its understanding of the actual mediating contingencies between actions and their consequences. After a few years of experience with the immediate aversive social and impersonal consequences of aggression, of touching dangerous objects, and of generally failing to regulate its behavior in accordance with its limitations, it is not surprising that the young child would come to see punishment as being immanent in action.

As the older child expands its behavioral and cognitive capacities, and becomes increasingly independent of external control, it will also become more able to perceive and exercise control over the chain of events that links transgression to consequences. Of course, the social environment does not necessarily support new forms of experience which are made available by changes in the child's capacities. The persistence of conceptions of immanent justice that is sometimes found among children of lower socioeconomic status, or among children of nonwestern societies, may be attributable to a sparse verbal context for socialization or to lack of reinforcement of the child's attempts to control the punitive consequences of transgression. Or perhaps some societies place a continuing emphasis on external surveillance and punishment, and also crystallize the child's perception that the consequences of an action are externally fixed and immutable—with the result that the child never acquires a cognitive focus on the actual effects of its actions upon others.

The criteria by which children judge the magnitude of transgression also can be traced directly to social experience. Young children cannot easily separate their behavior from their intentions. Nor can they effectively monitor the amplitude of their behavior. They will perceive themselves as having little control over the harmful or damaging consequences of their actions, because the magnitude of the consequences is so often not specifically intended. And they will accordingly perceive punishment to be more closely attached to consequences than to intentions. The reality of the young child's situation is that the extent of the harm or damage which is caused by its actions is in fact a discriminate cue, to both others and itself, as to whether punishment is called for and how severe it will be. Socializing agents have only limited expectations concerning the young child's understanding of the social definition of transgressions, and they are therefore not likely to be very attentive to its intentions in committing a transgression. And so it frequently turns out to be true that punishment is determined by how much damage has been done to property, how much of a mess the child has made, or how much pain or complaint result from its aggression.

In contrast, the capacities of the older child make it possible for the intentions and the consequences of its actions to be much more coordinate. As the child's cognitive power increases, socialization can employ an increasingly verbal medium in which intentions are easily represented. For example, when they enforce their broadened expectations on the conduct of the older child, many parents make it clear in their behavior that they do not punish for involuntary transgression. Older children also become more sensitive to intentions because their enhanced cognitive capacities facilitate their discrimination of the cues which indicate volition in the behavior of either themselves or others. Again, the extent and pace of these changes with age will be markedly affected by patterns of socialization. The practices of some social groups may exploit cognitive development so as to produce an increased sensitivity to the magnitude of the consequences of transgression rather than an increased sensitivity to an internal motivational governor.

The tendency of young children to apply rules absolutely and by reference to authority, and of older children to apply rules more relativistically and by reference to reciprocal social agreement, likewise fits their respective forms of social experience. As Piaget (1948) observes, the social behavior of the young child is bound to a unilateral power relationship in which the flow of information and resources is not reciprocal. The application and enforcement of rules by parents must necessarily often be arbitrary, because of the child's limited ability to evaluate actions for itself. What may be even more significant is that there are very few occasions, in the young child's experience, on which the rules of adults do not seem to work. Authority figures simply predict the outcomes of various courses of action much more accurately than the child does. Even without the contribution of social punishment, the child must have numerous exposures to the unpleasant consequences of exercising its own judgement instead of conforming to the rules of others. Indeed, parents often knowingly apply rules more broadly to the young child than is rationally warranted because they know that the child does not have the discrimination to protect itself. Parents are much more likely to permit older children to exercise their own application of rules. Older children move out into an extended network of social relationships in which they participate as equals, and in which their ability to predict the consequences of actions is more comparable with that of other participants. Moreover, their cognitive capacities permit socializing agents to transmit verbally a conception of the reasons for various standards of conduct, and allow them to perceive behavioral options which are based on multiple dimensions of value.

The types of punishment or correction of transgression which are specified by children of different ages also can be derived from the character of their social experience. Neither the cognitive status nor the experience of young children will support the perception of restitution or punishment in kind as an appropriate resolution of transgression. From the young child's point of view, all punishment must seem to be the inherent consequence of having transgressed rather than the socially prescribed correction for the nature of the transgression. Since the young child's resources for making restitution are quite restricted, it is more likely to experience retributive punishment than is the older child. Similarly, expiative punishment is much more available to socializing agents than is reciprocal punishment during the early years of childhood. One cannot readily give reciprocal punishment to a child who is being dirty or noisy, or to one who is showing aggression that cannot legitimately be returned by an adult. The older child's perception of restitution and reciprocity as appropriate consequences of transgression rests on its capacity and social support for initiation of its own resolutions of transgression. This particular shift in conscience is also facilitated by the older child's increasing exposure to relationships with others in which there is mutuality in the flow of social control.

The movement from evaluation of an act in terms of its immediate consequences for the actor, to evaluation in terms of broader principles of social desirability or obligation, is another kind of cognitive alteration that can be seen as the outcome of gradual change in social experience. This change is more sweeping, however, than the others which have been described above. And its specific antecedents in social experience may be more difficult to localize. Obviously, the use of broad principles of conduct to evaluate an act demands a degree of cognitive abstraction that is not required for evaluation in terms of the act's concrete external consequences. The young child undoubtedly judges actions in direct relation to external reward or punishment because these are the most reliable discriminanda available to it. But the formal features of cognitive development only begin to provide the necessary distinctions which need to be made here. It is not really apparent, for example, that there are such significant differences of cognitive status among those children who say that an act is bad because it will be seen and punished, those who say that it is bad because it violates the rules of authority, and those who say that it is bad because it disrupts social relationships. Yet the evaluative structures which lie behind these various statements may be quite different in their substantive dimensions. What we need to discern further are the particular forms of social experience which produce these different evaluative structures. While the dimensions of these structures may well be formed throughout the entire course of socialization, it is not inconceivable that their roots are laid in early patterns of social interaction in the home, the effects of which are not apparent until the child's cognitive and verbal equipment can make them articulate.

GENERALITY AND SPECIFICITY OF CHARACTER

The nature and extent of the developmental changes which occur in the structure of conscience have some interesting implications for the problem of generality versus specificity in the formation of character—a problem that turns our attention once again to the relationship between conduct and conscience. One of the indispensable supports for a conception of stages in the acquisition of conscience is the requirement of evidence that developmental transformations are producing an integrative consistency in the child's cognitive resources for the evaluation of conduct. The relevant evidence does in fact suggest that character is not composed entirely of specific and unrelated elements. But even when every allowance is made for the overlap of stages in developmental time, the evidence reveals nothing like the highly integrative structural transformations which would be required to make a conception of stages particularly useful.

The findings of a great many investigations indicate that there is a substantial amount of consistency in children's evaluations of various forms of conduct and their potential consequences, when the consistency is examined rather grossly from the point of view of a continuum of internal versus external orientation (Boehm, 1962; Durkin, 1961; Havighurst and Neugarten, 1955; Johnson, 1962; Kohlberg, 1963a, 1969; MacRae, 1954). Kohlberg's findings suggest that his elaborate system of classification of moral judgement is especially sensitive to certain consistencies in the rationales which children offer for their evaluation of conduct across different hypothetical situations. However, the consistency that Kohlberg finds seems to lie primarily in the cognitive power of the operators which children use in their application of values, rather than in the breadth of application of any particular set of dimensions of value. The reports of all of the investigations which have been cited make it clear that great specificity is found in comparisons among children's evaluative judgements in different areas of social behavior or in different situations within a single area of behavior. Moreover, the various components of the structure of conscience do not seem to hang together very well. For example, the developmental status of the child's perspective on immanent justice may be unrelated to and even discrepant with its orientation toward intentions or consequences in the judgement of magnitude of transgression (see particularly Johnson, 1962, and MacRae, 1954).

The integration of the evaluative operations of conscience also ought to be reflected to some extent in the relationships which are found among different aspects of conduct. But the organization of conduct gives no more reason to suppose that character is highly integrated than does the organization of conscience. The findings of the studies which were initiated by Hartshorne and May are the classic example of situational and behavioral specificity in the predictability of the child's internalized control of conduct (Hartshorne and May, 1928; Hartshorne, May, and Maller, 1929). Their observations showed that there was only very minimal consistency in the child's behavior across different situations which were designed to test honesty. With the exception of one finding of situational specificity in children's sympathetic behavior (Murphy, 1937), all of the later evidence appears to be based on internalized suppression of prohibited behavior and reactions to transgression.

Projective story-completion devices have been used to gather a considerable amount of evidence on the interrelationships among children's dispositions toward a number of different internalized reactions to their own committed transgressions. The author found that most of a sample of American children drawn from the sixth grade individually showed dispositions toward virtually all types of reaction to transgression (Aronfreed, 1961). A number of the reactions would typically appear in tandem with respect to a single transgression, as though one reaction were not in itself sufficient to resolve the transgression. But the story-completions did not indicate any predictable relationships among the dispositions toward different types of reaction. The multiple forms of reaction to a single transgression probably reflected the kinds of sequential contingencies which govern the flow of the aversive consequences of transgression during the course of socialization. The findings of other similar investigations also point to the absence of consistent dependencies among the child's dispositions toward various internalized reactions to transgression (Maccoby and Whiting, 1960; Sears, Rau, and Alpert, 1965, Chapter 6). However, it is interesting to note that Grinder and McMichael (1963) did find positive correlations among the dispositional frequencies of remorse, confession, and restitution, when they compared the story-completions of children from two cultural contexts which were very different in the extent to which their socialization practices would induce any form of internalized control over the resolution of transgressions (children of Samoan plantation workers were compared to children of American administrators). McMichael and Grinder (1966) have reported comparable findings for various Hawaiian ethnic groups who vary in the degree to which they have assimilated the values of the American mainland.

Some investigators have reported a limited amount of positive association between the effectiveness of the child's internalized suppression of
prohibited behavior and its internalized orientation in reacting to committed transgressions (W. Allinsmith, 1960; Heinecke, 1953). MacKinnon
(1938) reported the same finding for college students. But these findings
do not suggest that the incidence of any specific reaction to a committed
transgression is predictable from the effectiveness with which the transgression is suppressed. And the findings of a great many other investigations of
children's behavioral dispositions fail to indicate any consistent relationship between the extent to which they have internalized the suppression of
prohibited behavior and the types of reactions which they are likely to
show to their own transgressions (Burton, Maccoby, and Allinsmith, 1961;
Grinder, 1962, Grinder and McMichael, 1963; Rebelsky, Allinsmith, and
Grinder, 1963; Sears *et al.,* 1965, Chapter 6; Stein, 1967).

Because the assessments of reaction to transgression which are used in
these investigations are heavily biased toward projective devices such as
story-completions, inferences should be drawn from their findings with
some caution. Another limitation on the interpretation of their findings
arises from the fact that they assess generalized dispositions toward suppression and reactions to transgression rather than dispositions which are
discretely matched to specific potential acts. One might expect that more
consistent relationships would emerge between the relevant dispositions if
it were possible to employ extensive direct observations of the child's behavior, and if observations of suppression and reaction to transgression
were matched around specific acts. Even if there is only limited integration
of the child's cognitive structures for the evaluation of conduct, there are
other grounds for thinking that the child's internalization of behavioral
suppression should bear some relationship to its orientation in reacting to
its committed transgressions. For reasons which were outlined in some
detail in Chapter Seven, the functions of both suppression and reactions to
transgression in the control of punishment and anxiety would gravitate
toward a compensatory relationship in the child who has externally oriented monitors of conduct, but toward a more parallel and mutually facilitative relationship in the child who has a more internalized orientation.

The absence of strong dependencies among different components of
aversive control of the child's behavior is entirely consistent with the view
that social experience produces continuity in the internalized cognitive and
affective monitors of conduct. It is an oversimplification of the complexities of learning in a social environment to suppose that the strengths of the

different components of aversive control, or their relative probabilities of occurrence, will all be parallel functions of the frequency or intensity of the punishment that is experienced by the child (cf. Kohlberg, 1963b). All of the internalized behavioral derivatives of social punishment come from a common matrix of learning which attaches either anxiety or anxiety-reduction to their inherent and representational correlates. The different derivatives are not parallel in their incidence or strength, however, because they draw upon different behavioral elements and contingencies within the matrix. The absence of strong interrelationships among the derivatives might be pointed to in criticism of those theories of identification which assume that the child adopts a parental value system which integrates all aspects of its conduct. But the analysis of the relevant mechanisms of internalization in terms of an aversive learning process does not lead to the expectation that different features of conduct will be uniformly predictable from one or two parameters of punishment.

Even from a point of view that emphasizes the continuity of learning and change in social experience, it is rather surprising to find such minimal evidence of integration in character. Social experience must have some consistency. It cannot be specific to each act and to each situation. And most of the young child's social experience is heavily concentrated in its interaction with just a few socializing agents. Maller (1934) was able to use the techniques of factor analysis to show some evidence of a common factor of delay of gratification across the tests of honesty, cooperation, and persistence which were used by Hartshorne and May. And Burton (1963) more recently was able to show, through a similar careful analysis of situational components, that there was more consistency within the various observations which Hartshorne and May had made of children's honesty than there originally appeared to be. Perhaps even more consistency would be apparent in the organization of conduct if future studies were to give more attention to the origins of specific forms of conduct and to the specific external situations in which they are assessed.

The child's cognitive resources for generalization, as well as the common properties of its social experience in different situations, would make it implausible that different components of either conduct or conscience should be totally unpredictive of one another. But the integration of character may nevertheless make it possible for a specific form of conduct to have different probabilities of occurrence across a wide variety of stimulus situations. The discrepancies of internal versus external orientation which are observed in the structure of the child's conscience are attributable to the fact that different components of cognitive change have different antecedents in social experience. These antecedents will be partially independent in their developmental timing and in their impact on different areas of the child's behavior. On the other hand, the consistencies of orientation which do exist in the child's conscience indicate that socialization is sufficiently integrative to support some degree of consistency in cognitive structure and synchronization in cognitive change.

The limited integration that we find in character has suggestive implications for the phenomena which are sometimes considered to require a concept of identification. Identification is usually conceptualized as a process in which the child's evaluative cognition is broadly and fairly rapidly transformed by its adoption of the evaluative role of another person. However, the restricted generality of both conduct and conscience, and the gradualness and continuity which one observes in their development, do not point to a broad or rapid adoption of the evaluative role of models. It would seem much more accurate to describe the internalization of character as an even and highly differentiated series of behavioral and cognitive changes. It may be that identification is a useful concept for the description of a psychological process through which values are socially transmitted. But the nature of this process will have to be specified to a much greater extent than it now is, if we are to understand its function in the cognitive representation of social experience.

BEHAVIORAL ENGAGEMENT OF VALUES

The most significant barrier to an understanding of children's acquisition of values is the lack of a psychological theory of the nature of value. The concept of value can be used in more than one sense. For example, one can think of the value of an act as being inherent in the changes of affectivity which it produces for the person who performs the act, regardless of whether the changes of affectivity are externally mediated or intrinsically correlated to the act. It is also possible to think of the stimulation from a social environment in terms of distinguishable affective and informational values for the control of a person's behavior. However, when we speak of an individual's values, or of the value system of a society, we are thinking of relatively stable cognitive and affective dispositions which are not closely bound to specific acts or to the concrete presence of particular environmental events. These evaluative dispositions have a powerful cognitive base which can be used for the representation of a great variety of potential acts, of the conditions under which the acts may occur, and of the consequences of the acts. Of course, a person's resources of cognitive representation are applicable to the evaluation of objects as well as to the evaluation of behavior.

An initial and tentative conception of evaluative thought might treat it as a set of classificatory operations which employ a representational cognitive base that is both constructed and imposed upon the flow of information from a social environment. The representational base may be regarded as having structural properties to the extent that it has dimensions along which acts or events may be ordered, categories which are assigned by classification on more than one dimension, and other features which introduce sequence and hierarchy into evaluative operations. However, an evaluative structure is not merely a cognitive schema for the economical coding of information. It is the quality and magnitude of the affectivity that becomes associated with particular classifications which permit the structure to enter into the operations of value and to exercise some control over behavior.

Although virtually nothing is known about how children acquire the evaluative structures which enter into the control of their conduct, there is a certain amount of evidence that demonstrates the engagement of the evaluative operations of established structures by the variable requirements of a social environment. Almost all of the demonstrations of the social engagement of the child's established values are based on situations which elicit or constrain certain forms or choices of behavior under varying degrees of external control. The demonstrations are consistent in showing that the child's own resources for the assignment of value are called into play more extensively when external determinants of value are not in themselves sufficiently strong to control the child's behavior. In general, the relevant experimental effects appear to be produced by changes in the affective value that the child assigns to its behavioral options or to the consequences of its behavior, rather than by any change in the representational cognitive base of its evaluative operations. The effects have been obtained primarily under conditions in which the external determinants of the child's behavior have a large aversive component.

Some observations on children's behavioral expression of their aggressive dispositions can serve as the first illustration of a compensatory relationship between the external monitors of a child's conduct and the engagement of its already established internalized monitors. There have been a number of observational studies of the behavior of young children in free play situations where they have the opportunity to use dolls, toys, or other appropriate targets for the expression of aggression. Under the typical conditions of observation in these studies, an adult observer is immediately present in the play area. The observer is a relative stranger to the child, but is highly permissive and does nothing to constrain the child's aggressive behavior. When observations are made over two or more successive sessions, which are separated by at least a day, it invariably turns out that the children show a sizeable increment in the amount or frequency of aggressive behavior (Bach, 1945; Levin and Sears, 1956; P. S. Sears, 1951; Siegel and Kohn, 1959). The effect is quite apparent even though the observations are usually restricted to two sessions, and it is in marked contrast to the children's tendency toward decreased aggression after a session during which aggressive behavior has been punished (Hollenberg and Sperry, 1951). Hartup and Himeno (1959) found the increase of aggressive behavior over time to be discernible even within the limits of a single continuous observational session.

The tendency of a child's play to become more aggressive, as the child becomes acclimated to an unfamiliar but potential agent of constraint and punishment, suggests the possibility that there has been some release of the child's internalized suppression of its aggressive dispositions. We might well expect that a young child would limit its aggressive behavior during its initial exposure to an adult whose potential reactions to the behavior would be perceived as very uncertain. A certain amount of effective suppression

of aggressive behavior under these conditions would require the child to utilize its own internalized resources for the assignment of value. Quite possibly the child would evaluate its contemplated aggressive acts and their
possible consequences in such a way as to reduce its anticipated positive
affectivity or to increase its anticipated aversive affectivity. In contrast,
after the permissiveness of a relatively unknown agent has been established, the probable reactions of the agent will be perceived by the child
with a far greater certainty, and the child can then permit its aggressive
behavior to be controlled by prevailing external monitors. The child has
less need to subject its behavior to the control of its evaluative thought
processes, not merely because its aggressive dispositions require less suppression, but more generally because the nature and extent of external controls are explicit enough to determine the situational value of the
behavior.

If these inferences have some validity, we might expect opposite effects
to be apparent in the aggressive free play behavior of children who are not
under direct surveillance. In the absence of any constraint from an adult
agent, children might be expected to show a substantial amount of aggressive behavior initially. The possibility of punishment for their behavior
would not be salient for them. However, in the continued absence of any
external assignment of value to the behavior, the child's past experience
with the aversive consequences of its aggressive behavior—in other words,
its internalized anxiety—would tend to engage some of its own evaluative
resources toward the suppression of the aggressive behavior. Such a decrement in children's aggressive behavior over successive sessions, in the absence of an observer, has in fact been seen in the studies which were conducted by Siegel (1957) and by Siegel and Kohn (1959). Levin and
Turgeon (1957) reported a study which is a particularly effective demonstration of the point that the child's internalized suppression of punishable
behavior is engaged when the potential reactions of a socializing agent are
unknown rather than when they are familiar. These investigators observed
the aggressive behavior of children during a first play session in which the
only person present was an experimenter. During a second session, the
children showed an increase of aggressive behavior if their own mothers
were also present as observers, but showed a decrease of aggressive behavior if a total stranger was added as an observer. Apparently, they were
more inclined to rely on external control as a potential source of constraint
on their aggressive behavior, in the presence of an agent of control whose
dispositions were known to them, even though they had more experience of

punishment from their mothers than they would have had from a stranger.

A compensatory relationship between external constraint and the child's exercise of internalized control over its behavior is even more dramatically apparent in the findings of certain experiments which have been generated by Festinger's (1957) concept of cognitive dissonance. These experiments are fairly direct demonstrations of the changes in evaluative cognition which can be produced by different magnitudes of external constraint on the child's behavior. Their findings raise some interesting problems for a more general understanding of aversive control over the socialization process.

The basic assumption of the expectations which follow from the concept of dissonance is that a person will find it unpleasant or aversive to have two cognitions which are significantly discrepant or inconsistent with one another. He will therefore be motivated to change one or both of his cognitions so as to introduce more consonance or balance between them. Although the critical properties of the required inconsistency have not been given a formal definition, it appears that they are thought of as being more psychological than logical in nature. A very extensive body of experiments has been designed to test the validity of the concept of cognitive dissonance (Brehm and Cohen, 1962; Festinger, 1957; Festinger et al., 1964). These experiments appear to provide a considerable amount of support for the broader outlines of the concept. The types of experiments which were designed originally by Festinger and Carlsmith (1959) and by Aronson and Mills (1959) produced particularly seminal examples of dissonance effects under conditions of "forced compliance" or of additional information about the unrewarding consequences of a free choice.

Many of the most effective experiments which have grown out of the dissonance formulation have used forced compliance situations, in which an individual is constrained to engage in behavior that is unpleasant, effortful, or at least discrepant with his initial dispositions. The constraint may take any one of a variety of different forms of social influence or pressure, including the application of potential rewards or punishments. Under these conditions, it is presumed that the individual's cognitive representation of his behavioral commitment will be inconsistent with other representations in his evaluative cognition—for example, with the value that he actually places on his behavioral choice, or with attitudes which are contrary to those implied by the behavior. The dissonance that is produced by the inconsistency can then be reduced by a shift in the value that the individual assigns to his behavior, to its potential consequences, or to his reasons for commitment to the behavior. The magnitude of the dissonance that a person experiences, and the consequent magnitude of change in evaluative cognition, are assumed to be an inverse function of the amount of external justification or constraint that he perceives as a determinant of his choice of behavior. Thus, for example, the smaller the magnitude of the potential rewards or punishments which are used to induce the original behavioral compliance, the greater the amount of the dissonance that will be elicited by compliance.

Among the experiments which have used paradigms of forced compliance, a series that has been conducted with children is most directly relevant to the question of how social constraint engages the mechanisms for internalized evaluative control of behavior. The point of origin of the series was an experiment that was designed by Aronson and Carlsmith (1963). For each of the preschool children who were the subjects of this experiment, the experimental agent first obtained a relative order of attractiveness among five toys. The agent then left the room on a pretext, after telling the child that it could play with all but one of the toys. The prohibition of play was always placed on whichever toy the child's choices had given the rank of second most preferred. The prohibition was supported by the agent's verbalization of either a mild or a severe threat. Under the mild threat condition, the agent told a child that he would be "annoyed" if the child were to play with the forbidden toy. Under the severe threat condition, the agent stated that he would be "very angry" if the child played with the forbidden toy, that he would remove the toys and leave, and that he would think the child was a "baby." Covert observation of the children's behavior during the agent's absence indicated that none of the children, under conditions of either mild or severe threat, violated the explicit prohibition on playing with the forbidden toy. When the agent returned, he obtained a second ordering of the relative attractiveness of the five toys from the child. Children who had been exposed to a mild threat showed a significant decrement in the relative value that they assigned to the toy with which they had been forbidden to play; in contrast, children who had been exposed to a severe threat tended to increase the relative value that they placed on the critical toy.

The dissonance concept can be applied, in a fairly obvious way, to the finding of devaluation of the forbidden toy under the condition of mild threat. Given that both the mild and severe threats produce sufficient anxiety and uncertainty to suppress the prohibited behavior, the child's behavioral commitment to the prohibition would find less support in a mild constraint than in a severe constraint. Under the mild constraint, then, the child would experience more dissonance between its cognitive representation of its behavior and its representation of the justification for the behavior. And it could reduce the dissonance by devaluation of the attractiveness of the forbidden toy.

A number of investigators have repeated the essential design of this experiment, with some variation in the age of the subjects and in the nature of the threat, and have observed similar effects as well as some interesting extensions of the original findings (Freedman, 1965; Pepitone, McCauley, and Hammond, 1967; Turner and Wright, 1965). Freedman found direct behavioral evidence of the effect of mild threat in producing more persistence of the suppression of play with the forbidden toy, when the prohibition was lifted some weeks later. When the children were permitted to play with all of the toys, those who originally had been exposed to a mild threat showed a significantly lower frequency of attempts to play with the critical toy than did those who had been exposed to a severe threat. However, Freedman did not find a reliable difference between the mild and severe threat conditions in the immediate effects which they produced on the child's re-evaluation of the attractiveness of the critical toy. Pepitone *et al.* found that children who had been exposed to a mild threat showed an immediate decrement in the value of the forbidden toy after they had conformed to the prohibition. And when the prohibition was lifted, directly after the second evaluation of the toys, these children showed longer latencies and shorter durations of play with the critical toy than did children who had been exposed to a severe threat.

The experiments which have been cited all examine the evaluative cognitive changes which are produced when children must suppress prohibited behavior under varying magnitudes of aversive constraint. However, similar effects would be expected when children must make behavioral choices under the predominant control of rewards or other positive outcomes which have a socially determined variability of magnitude. Mills (1958) found that children who cheated on a task became more lenient in their attitudes of disapproval toward cheating, while children who resisted the opportunity to cheat became more severe. Mills attempted to control the motivation to cheat by introducing variation in the magnitude of reward for a high level of performance. The evidence suggested that the children became most severe in their disapproval when they resisted cheating under the condition of a high magnitude of potential reward for a good performance; whereas they became most lenient after cheating under the condition of a lower magnitude of potential reward. These findings would follow from the expectation that the child's cognition of the magnitude of reward for doing well would enter into the experience of dissonance as a component of justification for cheating. Of course, in this kind of temptation situation, the external social control of reward was being used primarily to influence a form of behavior (cheating) that already was under some suppressive and aversive constraint. The converse and very common case in socialization would be the use of potential rewards to produce behavioral commitments which are in accord with the desires of socializing agents.

Festinger and Freedman (1964) have summarized the general cases for the nature and direction of the evaluative cognitive changes which ought to follow from the dissonance formulation when reward or punishment are applied to the socialization of the child's behavior. The central point of their argument is that when the child makes a behavioral choice, under the control of either positive or aversive external constraints, the choice will be accompanied by larger corresponding cognitive changes in the child's values if the external constraints are relatively weak. The proponents of the dissonance concept have emphasized the changes of valuation which occur as a result of the cognitive inconsistency that follows a behavioral commitment. This emphasis on dissonance as a post-decision phenomenon treats the child's behavioral conformity to external constraints as a kind of cognitive trap into which it falls, with the consequence that it is suddenly confronted by the inconsistency between its actions and its original evaluative dispositions. The treatment therefore accords little attention to the problem of the affective and cognitive controls which must be exercised in order to produce a behavioral choice in the first place.

In the case of the experiments on the effects of threat, it is assumed that either a mild or a severe threat is sufficient to suppress the prohibited behavior, so that the child's own evaluative resources will not be called into play until its choice of suppression already is realized in its behavior. In fact, however, it seems highly unlikely that the quite different magnitudes of threat which generally have been used in the relevant experiments would produce equivalent behavioral results—a total conformity to a prohibition on playing with an attractive toy, in the absence of external surveillance —unless there were initially some reciprocal differences in the children's affective and cognitive reactions to the threats. The very fact that the mild threat does also suppress the prohibited behavior suggests that a shift in the child's evaluative cognition may be required in order even to initiate the suppression and to sustain it throughout the period of temptation. These considerations in turn give rise to an alternative interpretation of the experimental effects which is based on the engagement of the child's values in the very process of making a behavioral commitment under differential social constraints. The alternative interpretation may prove to be useful in resolving an apparent contradiction between the effects of threat and the effects of the actual experience of punishment.

As a first approach to an account of how mild and severe threats induce common effects on children's behavioral suppression of play with a forbidden toy, but distinct effects on their evaluation of the toy, we may note that explicit prohibitions are used in the experiments which have been cited. It must be clear to the children, regardless of the magnitude of the threat, that playing with the forbidden toy will, if the action is discovered, be perceived as intentional disobedience toward authority and incur the disapproval of the experimental agent. The common elements of willful disobedience and potential disapproval are probably the baseline for the equal effectiveness of mild and severe threat in producing suppression. In other words, either threat will elicit some anxiety about an incipient transgression, and will engage the children's well-established dispositions toward suppression. The children are already highly socialized creatures, and they have evaluative structures which pertain to prohibitive constraints on contact with attractive objects in their environment. There is no question about the discriminability of the forbidden behavior, and the children are familiar with the contingency between prohibited actions and their potential aversive outcomes.

However, although the threatened outcome of violation of the prohibition is specified to some extent, the children will experience much uncertainty about the resources which an unfamiliar external agent of control may have for surveillance or knowledge of their behavior. Despite the external threat, the actual occurrence of punishment for transgression will necessarily appear somewhat unpredictable to the children while the agent is absent. Under these conditions, it should be much easier for a child to suppress an incipient transgression, without any significant engagement of its already established evaluative resources, if it has been threatened with a very aversive outcome. Even though the child still places a relatively high value on the forbidden toy, it is in little danger of committing a transgression, because its cognitive representation of the potential external outcome induces enough anxiety to motivate suppression. One might well suppose that the child who is exposed to a severe threat does not even come close to transgression, so long as it still perceives a substantial probability of punishment. Its orienting reactions to the forbidden toy may be sufficient in themselves to elicit anxiety of an intensity that interrupts an incipient transgression.

In contrast, the child who is only mildly threatened is in much greater danger of actually committing the transgression and incurring the agent's disapproval, because its cognitive representation of the potential outcome, when it attends to the forbidden toy, may not elicit anxiety that is intense enough to motivate suppression. Such a child is likely to come much closer to an overt transgression and to experience more anxiety about its possible commitment of transgression, than is a child who has been exposed to a severe threat. A decrement in the value that the child places on the forbidden toy would be one of the ways in which its evaluative resources could be used to reduce its anxiety. The decline in the value of the toy would make it easier for the child to come to a behavioral commitment of avoidance of transgression.

Uncertainty about the nature of the threatened punitive outcome of a transgression should have effects which are similar to the effects of uncertainty about whether the threat will materialize, provided that a child can anticipate at least the intensity or magnitude of the outcome. Of course, if information about potential outcomes is too restricted, then it is not possible to distinguish between mild and severe threats. It is interesting to note that the threats which have been used in the experimental settings are often fairly vague in their specification of the agent's resources for punishment. For example, the warning that the agent would be annoyed if the child played with the forbidden toy, which Aronson and Carlsmith (1963) used as a mild threat, would not give the child much information about what to expect from a relative stranger. Some of the replications of their experiment have reduced even more the explicitness of the threatened punishments, with the use of a verbalized prohibition that emphasizes primarily the "naughtiness" of transgression. When information about the nature of potential punishment is sparse under conditions of both mild and severe threat, then the difference between the two conditions, in the extent to which suppression of the prohibited behavior requires adjustments of the child's evaluative predispositions, may not be as great as it would be if only the occurrence of the punishment were uncertain. Freedman (1965) used virtually no specification of the punishment that might follow from the agent's disapproval of a transgression, other than the implication of magnitude in the severe threat that the agent would be very angry. And unlike other investigators, he found no reliable difference between the effects of mild and severe threats on children's evaluations of the attractiveness of the forbidden toy.

The use of the dissonance concept to account for the valuational changes which children show under mild behavioral constraints assumes that the children need to justify their behavior after it has been committed. An emphasis on justification in the children's thought processes seems to imply that they are intentionally shifting their evaluative judgements to accommodate their behavior. For example, one might imagine that the children change their perception of the properties of a toy in such a way as to place it in a category to which they attach less positive value. However, while intention may enter into the decrement in value of a toy with which a child has been forbidden to play, it is not necessary to suppose that the decrement is volitional on the child's part. Even if it is assumed that the devaluation takes place within the process of commitment to avoidance of transgression, rather than after the commitment has been made, the lack of any requirement of volition is suggested by some further specification of the mechanisms which may mediate the control of the devaluation by the child's experience of anxiety. This additional specification also calls to our attention that the change in the attractiveness of the toy may be determined not merely by a decrement of positive affective value, but also by a heightening of certain components of aversive value.

In the experiments which have produced the devaluation phenomenon, the procedures for ordering the attractiveness of the toys make it obvious that the child is being asked how much it would like the activity of playing with the toys. The child is responding to the value of the toys as concrete objects of action. The child also is able to give a cognitive representation to the entire sequence of behavior that would culminate in playing with the forbidden toy during the period of prohibition—that is, to orienting toward, approaching, reaching for, touching, and finally playing with the toy. Some of the earlier components of this sequence actually may occur as motor correlates of cognitive representation, even though a child does not transgress. When the child is under the constraint of severe threat, its cognitive representation of the threatened punishment will elicit anxiety that is intense enough to interrupt its representation of the sequential components of an incipient transgression. Even at a very early point in the sequence, when the potential occurrence of punishment is still temporally distant, the aversive magnitude of the punishment may be great enough so that its representation disrupts the sequence. But when the child is constrained by a mild threat, the thought of punishment may not elicit sufficient anxiety to disrupt its sequential representation of the components of transgression until the cognitive sequence is closer to or localized on the final overt act. As a result, the child experiences maximal anxiety in close association with its representation of the overt behavior of playing with the forbidden toy. And the anxiety will add an aversive component to its evaluation of the toy, when it is asked once again to indicate how much it likes the toy— again in terms which focus its attention on the activity of playing with the toy.

To sum up this view of the devaluation phenomenon: the child likes the forbidden toy less after its play has been constrained by a mild threat than after it has been constrained by a severe threat, because there has been more opportunity under the mild threat for anxiety to attach aversive value to the child's cognitive representation of an actual behavioral engagement with the toy.

We have given little attention thus far to the enhancement of the value of the forbidden toy that occurred under severe threat in three of the four experiments which have been reported (Aronson and Carlsmith, 1963; Pepitone et al., 1967; Turner and Wright, 1965). This increment of value is not an effect that follows from the dissonance formulation, since it would not contribute to the child's justification for avoidance of transgression under any conditions. The investigators who have observed this increment have suggested that the child becomes satiated to some extent with the toys which it is permitted to use during the period of selective prohibition. Their suggestion implies that the increment in the value of the forbidden toy is an effect that is relative to a decline in the value of the remaining toys. This inference would appear to find some support in the fact that increments of the relative value of a single toy also occurred, in two of the experiments, when devices other than prohibition or threat were employed to prevent the children from playing with that toy. Of course, to the extent that a child becomes satiated with the toys with which it has been permitted to play, the satiation would produce a relative increment in the value of the forbidden toy under any magnitude of threat. Accordingly, an effect of devaluation of a forbidden toy under mild threat would presumably not be visible unless it were strong enough to overcome the effect of the child's satiation with the other toys.

Although it is reasonable to suppose that toys may undergo a decline in value, when children are permitted to play with them over certain periods of exposure, there are some limitations on the assumption of a satiation effect to account for the relative increment in value of a single toy with which the children are not permitted to play. For example, in the course of an extensive exploration of the effects of various constraints on a child's opportunity to play with a particular toy, Turner and Wright (1965) found an increment in the value of the toy when the experimental agent removed the toy on the pretext of repairing it, when the agent removed the toy and promised that it would be available later, and when the agent secretly removed and returned the toy. They found a decrement in the value of the toy, however, when the agent removed it with the statement that it would never be available for play, or with a statement which indicated only that it might be possible for the child to play with the toy later. The decrement of value under the latter two conditions is particularly interesting, because it seems to suggest a parallel to the effect of devaluation under mild threat. We have noted that prohibited behavior, and the environmental objects which the behavior engages, may acquire a component of aversive value, under the conditions of a mild threat, because the child's anxiety comes to be closely associated with its cognitive representation of an overt commitment of the behavior. On the same conceptual grounds, one might expect anticipatory frustration to attach some aversive value to the child's representation of an initially attractive activity (or object), when the child has been given information which explicitly conveys that it will certainly or at least very possibly be deprived of the activity.

The findings which Freedman (1965) has described point to another limitation on the possibility that a satiation effect could account for the relative gain in value of the single toy with which play had been prohibited by a severe threat. The gain may be attributed to a satiation effect only to the extent that the remaining toys, with which the child has played, do in fact undergo a decline in value. In all of the experiments other than the one that Freedman reported, the investigators obtained only a relative order of preference among the toys from their nursery or kindergarten subjects. And since the forbidden toy was the one that originally was second in attractiveness to the child, an increment in its value would be discernible only if it displaced the originally most attractive toy in the child's order of value. Accordingly, the relative increment in the value of the critical toy might be assigned either to an increment in its absolute value or to a decrement in the absolute value of the remaining toys. Freedman used older children as his subjects, however, and was able to obtain independent ratings of attractiveness for each individual toy on an arbitrary absolute scale. He therefore had available a distinct index of the absolute changes which occurred, between the ratings which were taken before and after the period of prohibition, in the value of the toys with which the children had played. This index showed substantial increments, under all experimental conditions, in the positive value of the toys which had not been prohibited to the children. The finding would appear to contradict the speculation that an increment in the value of a forbidden toy, of the kind that has been observed under the influence of severe threat in other experiments, is merely relative to the child's satiation with the toys which it has been permitted to use in its play.

Freedman's findings are interesting for yet another reason. He did not find that a severe threat produced an increment in the value of the forbidden toy. Instead, the toy underwent a significant decrement of value under conditions of both mild and severe threat. The source of this generalized decrement probably can be found in certain critical differences between Freedman's procedure and that of other investigators. Freedman placed a prohibition on play with the most attractive toy, rather than on play with the second most attractive toy. Moreover, as he notes, the most attractive toy for all of the children was a large and gifted robot, the value of which was incommensurate with the value of any of the other toys. During the period of prohibition, then, the children would have been strongly tempted to play with the forbidden toy, regardless of whether they were constrained by a mild or a severe threat. When prohibited from playing with a toy of such overwhelming attractiveness, all of the children would have been prone to cognitive representations which came very close to the overt behavior of playing with the toy. They would therefore have experienced considerable anxiety about their potential commitment of a transgression. Following the analysis that was outlined earlier, their anxiety would be expected to induce a decrement in the value of the toy through the attachment of an aversive component to their representation of the activity of playing with it.

The general finding of a decrement in the value of the forbidden toy, under the conditions of Freedman's experiment, also suggests indirectly a possible explanation of the increment in value that has been found under severe threat in other experiments, in which the children have been prohibited from playing with their second most preferred toys. Faced with the threat of a highly aversive outcome of a behavioral alternative that is *less* desirable than another alternative which it may freely choose, a child might experience uncertainty and anxiety about an inadvertent transgression for which the environment provides continuing opportunity—rather than, as might be true under a milder threat, anxiety about whether it could refrain from an intentional transgression. For example, in the case of the type of prohibition that has been used in the experiments, the children may have feared that they would mistakenly or accidentally have contact with the forbidden toy, in the course of playing with the other toys, or that the agent would wrongly perceive the occurrence of a transgression (since the children did play freely with the initially most attractive toy). This source of anxiety could be reduced by evaluative changes which would enhance the distinctiveness of the forbidden toy and set it even more apart from the other toys—in particular, by changes in the relative values which the children placed on their initially first and second most preferred toys.

In general, children may tend to give more attention to the inherently pleasurable aspects of behavior that has been prohibited, and may thus enhance that part of the value of the behavior which is not determined by the potential consequences of violation of a social constraint. The shift of value may in some instances be large enough to change the position of the behavior relative to that of other nonprohibited behavioral alternatives which initially were valued more highly, provided that the initial discrepancy in value is not too great. Of course, when the prohibited behavior originally has a higher value than any alternative (as in the case of the prohibition on play with the singularly attractive robot), then the behavior already may be more than sufficiently discriminate for a child to avoid it easily.

There is also an instructive problem to be found in the behavioral effects which were observed by Freedman (1965) some weeks after the children's experience of constraint, and by Pepitone et al. (1967) immediately after the children had made their second evaluation of the toys. When the original prohibition was lifted in both experiments, the children who had been constrained by mild threat showed less of a disposition to engage in play with the forbidden toy than did the children who had been constrained by severe threat. Since direct behavioral indices of play were not obtained before the period of prohibition, it was not possible to estimate how much of this effect represented changes which were attributable, respectively, to the mild and severe threats. However, to the extent that any kind of evaluative change made the activity of playing with the forbidden toy seem less attractive to the children who had been exposed to a mild threat, it would not seem that the effect could have been mediated by cognitive adjustments which were required in order for the children to justify behavioral commitments to which they were still bound (the requirement that is assumed in the dissonance formulation). When there was no longer a prohibition, and the children could play freely with all of the toys, there should have been no further constraint of any magnitude with respect to which they would have needed to justify their behavior in the new situation. Even though the children's free behavioral choices were being used concurrently as an index of the evaluative change that had occurred under constraint, one might suppose that the freedom itself would have produced some correction of the change.

The same problem can be seen even more acutely in the procedures which were employed by Aronson and Carlsmith (1963) and by Turner and Wright (1965). These investigators actually gave their subjects a short period of nonprohibitive play with all of the toys, immediately after the period of prohibition and just *before* they obtained a second evaluation of the toys, although they did not use the children's play as an index of change in values. With this sequence of events, most if not all of the children would have completed a behavioral engagement of play with the once forbidden toy before they were asked again to place relative values on the different toys. The question therefore arises as to how the second evaluation would have reflected any effect of dissonance—unless one wishes to make the burdensome assumption that the children's earlier commitment to the suppression of prohibited behavior produced changes of value which were then frozen or insensitive to the children's subsequent engagement in the same behavior.

The conditions under which the experimental effects were obtained may be somewhat less difficult to understand if we assume that the effects rested on evaluative changes which were required in order for the children to initiate and maintain their behavioral commitments under social constraints, rather than on evaluative changes which occurred after the commitments had been stabilized. For example, although the forbidden toy may have declined in value under a mild threat, as a result of the anxiety that was associated with the children's representation of the prohibited behavior of playing with it, there would have been no further generator of change in its value (in any direction) after the prohibition had been lifted. When the children were free to make their own choice of whether to play with the critical toy, variation in the perceived power and certainty of an adult agent's reactions would no longer be relevant determinants of their behavior. The children's evaluative representations of the various toys would remain stable, in the state which they had attained under prohibition, because there would be no additional source of systematic change in their relative affectivity. The very brief period of play would not have provided sufficient time for any substantial extinction of the acquired aversive components of the value of the critical toy.

In summarizing the implications of their experimental findings, Aronson and Carlsmith (1963) drew the inference that the use of a mild threat of punishment by socializing agents would be more effective than the use of a severe threat in the establishment of internalized control over the child's behavior. Aronson (1966) has argued even more specifically that the threat of severe punishment may produce more effective behavioral suppression than a mild threat only when the child's behavior is subject to external control, but that a mild threat will produce more *internalized* suppression of prohibited behavior because it generates permanent changes in the child's values. Festinger and Freedman (1964) have drawn the broader inference that the minimal constraints and justifications which can be used to induce desirable behavior will be the most effective source of the child's adoption of an internalized "moral" attitude toward the behavior—that is, of evaluative changes which will give the behavior an intrinsic value that is independent of external control. They point out that the dissonance formulation predicts greater internalization of control over behavior when the child is not well provided with reasons or explanations for external constraints.

Common observation as well as experimental evidence indicate some crucial gaps in a conception of the internalization process that predicts maximal effects from minimal external constraints and justifications. A first problem is that such a conception seems to make little allowance for the extensive verbal medium of socialization that would be required to establish the child's evaluative cognitive structures in the first place. One would suppose that the acquisition of these cognitive structures, and their representational economy for the child's internalized control over a wide range of its conduct, would be fostered by a rich rather than an impoverished diet of reasoning and explanation from socializing agents. It is difficult to imagine that the formation of conscience is facilitated by potential rewards and punishments which are just sufficient to influence the child's behavior, in a context of restricted transmission of the values which determine the outcomes of the behavior. And in the experiments which were described in some detail in Chapter Seven, it was clearly shown that punishment training paradigms produced more persistent internalized suppression among children when they were buffered by the verbal transmission of cognitive structures which provided some justification for prohibitions on the children's behavior (Aronfreed, 1966).

The experiments which have been used to examine the effects of mild and severe threats on children's evaluative cognition are in fact not demonstrations of an internalization process. They are rather demonstrations of the accommodation of the child's established evaluative dispositions to variations in the strength and contingent probabilities of external controls on its behavior. Close analysis of the experimental procedures indicates that the behavior of the children during the prohibition period, when they refrain from playing with the forbidden toy, is under internalized control only to the extent that it does not require immediate external surveillance, and not in the sense that it is free of the expectation of punishment for transgression. Despite the uncertainty that the children must experience about the potential outcomes of their behavior, they are given the prohibition in a verbal context which clearly implies that the agent will know if they commit a transgression. Since the agent specifies how he will react if the child plays with the forbidden toy, after it is already clear to the child that it will be alone in the room, the child can hardly fail to perceive the possibility that the external threat is supported to some extent by the agent's resources for knowing about or discovering a transgression.

Freedman (1965) employed an experimental control which indirectly confirms that the interaction between external and internalized monitors is the source of the differential effects of mild and severe threats. It will be recalled that Freedman found behavioral differences between mildly and severely threatened children, when the children were free to play with all of the toys many weeks after the original period of prohibition in the agent's absence. The children who had been exposed to a mild threat showed less disposition to play with the once forbidden toy. However, when the agent simply remained with the child during the original period of prohibition, there were not significant behavioral differences, during the later free play session, between children who had been exposed to mild threat and children who had been exposed to severe threat.

The dissonance conception does not give an entirely satisfactory account of the difference that Freedman found between the effects of his experimental and control conditions. Although the immediate surveillance of the agent may have made it easier for children in the control groups to resist playing with the forbidden toy, in view of what may have been their perception of certain punishment for transgression, their external justification for their behavioral commitment would still not be equivalent under mild and severe threat. Nor can it be assumed that the mere presence of the agent was in itself an overwhelming justification for conformity to the prohibition, regardless of the degree of threat, since the nature of the threats would have been very unlikely to give that much force to the agent's presence. In the case of the mild threat, for example, the agent stated only that "it would be naughty" to violate the prohibition. The behavior of children does not ordinarily suggest that they would find such a statement to be a compelling reason for honoring a prohibition, even when they are under the direct surveillance of adults. But if we suppose that changes in the child's evaluative cognition, in response to external threats, are primarily the consequence of the child's efforts to exercise the control that will produce an avoidance of transgression, it is easier to see why the direct presence of an adult would eliminate the function of such changes. Given that the authority and potential disapproval of a relatively unfamiliar adult are sufficient to enforce the prohibition, under either a mild or a severe threat, the child does not need to re-evaluate toys, behavioral choices, or outcomes, in order to arrive at a commitment to the prohibition. Because the child perceives certainty in the potential external outcomes of its actions, its representation of the outcomes can control its behavior without the engagement of its own already internalized evaluative resources.

Another and even more serious problem for an account of the effects of threat on children's internalized evaluative control of their behavior lies in unequivocal but apparently discrepant findings concerning the effects of punishment. It is in the resolution of this discrepancy that we can begin to find a key to the understanding of a critical distinction between the establishment and the engagement of values. Although it appears that mild threats are more effective than severe threats in the translation of external constraints to the control of children's behavior by internalized monitors, the opposite is clearly the case when we look at the effects of children's actual experience of varying intensities of punishment. Experiments which were described in Chapter Seven have shown that intense punishment is more effective than mild punishment in producing internalized behavioral suppression, provided that children can discriminate the punished behavior (Aronfreed and Leff, 1963; Leff, 1967; Parke and Walters, 1967). These experiments test the persistence of punishment-induced suppression with a criterion of internalization that not only eliminates surveillance, but also gives the child every objective support for the expectation that its actions will not have punitive consequences or even be known to others.

Casual observation of the socialization of young children certainly seems to confirm these experimental findings. If punishment is actually applied to a child's behavior, when it touches or plays with a forbidden object, one does not expect that mild punishment will suppress the behavior more effectively than will a severe punishment, or that mild punishment will produce a greater decrement in the value which the object appears to have for the child. On the contrary, it is very common to observe that mild punishment may act as a beacon which attracts the child's further interest in the objects and environmental effects toward which its punished behavior has been oriented. Conversely, it is usually the case that highly distressful punishments will produce subsequent behavioral evidence that strong aversive value has become attached both to the child's punished behavior and to the objects toward which the behavior has been directed. Quite aside from the evidence that is inherent in the suppression of the behavior, the child may show other signs that intense punishment has made a once attractive object a source of displeasure or anxiety. The very young child may suddenly turn away its head, or cry, or show other signs of distress, when it either intentionally or accidentally comes too close to an object with which it has had previously punished behavioral intercourse. This phenomenon can be apparent even when the child does not perceive the presence of an observer or potential agent of punishment. It cannot be assumed that the child's aversive experience under these conditions is entirely associated with cues of its incipient behavior, while the object itself maintains its initial attractiveness. As was pointed out in the analysis of the experiments on the effects of threat, it is not possible to abstract the value of objects in the environment from the young child's experience of activity in relation to the objects.

A compensatory relationship between external and internalized controls over behavior is a useful base from which to resolve the apparent discrepancy between the findings of experiments which have varied the magnitude of threat and the findings of experiments which have varied the intensity of punishment that the child actually experiences. The resolution requires, however, an appreciation of the fact that the constraint of potential external outcomes on the child's behavioral choices engages its internalized evaluative dispositions only to the extent that these dispositions are already established by the child's previous direct experience of similar outcomes. When the child has not yet been exposed to socially determined contingencies between a particular class of behavioral choices and their consequences, or when it is relatively unfamiliar with the contingencies, then directly experienced positive or aversive outcomes will have their maximal effects in the establishment of internalized affective and cognitive control over the child's behavior. The actual experience of the contingencies will

provide the child with cognitive representations of the relationships between acts and outcomes, and will attach various magnitudes of affectivity
to those representations. It is under these conditions that we would expect
to find evaluative and behavioral changes which correspond to reinforcement and punishment effects—that is, the direction and amount of change
would be coordinate to the magnitude or strength of outcomes. Even familiar rewards and punishments will tend to induce proportionate affective
components in the child's internalized evaluative dispositions, although
their effects may be negligible if they are highly redundant with respect to
the child's past experience.

In contrast, to the extent that a child's behavior is under the control of
its anticipation of the external outcomes of its actions, even before the
actual occurrence of the outcomes, the engagement of its already established evaluative resources would not be a direct function of the value of
the outcomes. On the contrary, the child's representation of the potential
external outcomes of its behavioral choices might be expected to engage its
internalized evaluative operators as an inverse function of the power of the
outcomes. When an anticipated external outcome exercises a powerful constraint on the child's behavior—that is, when the outcome is capable of
inducing a large change of affectivity—then the affective value of the
child's representation of the outcome would be more than sufficient to
make its behavior conform to the constraint. But when the power of a potential external outcome is only barely sufficient to constrain the child's
behavior, then its behavioral commitment to the constraint will often require its cognitive representations to provide sources of affective control
other than those which are originally inherent in the value of the anticipated outcome. These sources can only be found in the child's internalized
evaluative operators. Of course, the limiting case of this compensatory relationship is the one in which there is no perceived external constraint, and
the child's behavior is therefore entirely under the control of the dispositions which it has internalized on the basis of earlier socialization. Under
these conditions, the power of internalized control should be a direct function of the value of the rewards or punishments to which the behavior previously has been exposed.

When the anticipation of rewards or punishments does constrain the
child's behavior, there are a number of ways in which the child's already
socialized dispositions may accommodate to the constraint. Under the conditions of naturalistic socialization, children actually have available a variety of behavioral as well as evaluative adjustments which they can make to

expected social consequences of their actions. Moreover, some of these adjustments may be evoked not only by the child's anticipation of the outcomes of particular acts, but also in the very course of the direct experience of the outcomes. Children acquire an impressive behavioral repertoire of techniques for maximizing reward and minimizing punishment, even when they may not intend to conform to constraints with which they are familiar. For example, they may attempt to persuade socializing agents to remove aversive constraints, they may seek additional information about the conditions under which constraints apply, or they may alter the stimulus features of a situation so that they can obtain rewards or avoid punishments without conforming. When a child does show behavioral conformity to potential rewards or punishments which are relatively weak, there are a number of different directions of evaluative change which may support the conformity. Decrement in the perceived value of the inherently pleasurable consequences of an act (as, for example, in the case of playing with an attractive object) is only one of the possible resolutions of the requirement of behavioral conformity under weak external constraint. Other alternatives would be enhancement or reduction of the perceived positive or aversive social consequences of the act for either the child or other people.

The experiments in which children have refrained from playing with an attractive toy, during a period of prohibition, typically are designed in such a way as to sharply reduce the likelihood of a great many evaluative and behavioral accommodations which children ordinarily can make under more naturalistic conditions. Devaluation of the toy, under the constraint of a mild threat, is the evaluative adjustment which is most easily available to the children in the circumstances of the experimental setting. The procedure focusses their attention on the relative attractiveness of a set of toys in which the forbidden toy is embedded by its initial value. Because no reason is given for the prohibition, the children are not provided with cognitive representations of other possible consequences of violation, upon which their evaluative operators might otherwise work. And since the agent of threatened punishment is absent during the period of prohibition, cues associated with the agent's presence or behavior are not available as a base for change in the children's evaluation of the potential outcomes of their behavioral choices.

The results of Freedman's (1965) procedure, which was different in that the forbidden toy was extremely attractive in comparison to all others, clearly indicate that devaluation of the toy was not the only accommodation which could be made to support conformity to the prohibition under a mild constraint. Freedman found that his mildly threatened and severely threatened groups did not differ in the extent to which they devalued the highly attractive toy. However, when the prohibition was lifted some weeks later, the children who had been only mildly threatened were far less likely to initiate play with the originally forbidden toy. As Freedman notes, other kinds of evaluative shifts may have been responsible for the later disinclination of the mildly threatened children to play with the forbidden toy. Incidental observations of many of the children's hesitant or reluctant interaction with the critical toy, even though playing with the toy had become permissible, in fact indicated that the children might have exaggerated the potential aversive consequences of transgression in arriving at their commitment to the initial prohibition.

It would be interesting to have the results of experiments which are designed to test the conceptions which have been advanced here as an account of the relationship between the effects of the anticipated and the experienced outcomes of behavioral choices. Such experiments might attempt to examine changes in children's evaluation of the determinants and consequences of their behavior not only when they are subject to potential external outcomes which constrain their final overt commitment of an act, but also when the outcomes are contingent on precursors of the final act such as orienting or approach behavior. An equally critical type of experiment might compare directly the isolated or sequential effects of anticipated versus experienced outcomes of behavioral choices for the same children. Some relevant experiments of the latter type have been conducted with adult subjects, though without the opportunity to make comparisons within subjects. Gerard (1967) and Linder, Cooper, and Jones (1967) have found that the changes of evaluative cognition which adults show, in the direction of their behavioral commitments, are inversely related to the magnitude of anticipated outcomes in the form of positive incentives for the commitments. These results would follow, of course, from the dissonance formulation. However, when the same incentives were introduced for other subjects only as the outcomes of behavioral choices which already had been made, so that the subjects were not able to anticipate the outcomes beforehand, then cognitive change in the direction of choice was directly coordinate to the magnitude of the outcomes. An analogous pattern of findings appears in Watts (1966) report of an experiment in which the value of a decision was affected by an aversive outcome after the decision had already been made. The adult subjects showed the most justification of their decision, in response to the negative outcome, when they had been given information which enabled them to perceive the possibility of the outcome before they made their decision.

All of these findings provide some confirmation of the view that changes of value which are an inverse function of external constraints can occur as the individual produces and maintains the behavioral commitments which are induced by the constraints. The changes of value are not necessarily cognitive resolutions which arise from looking backward at discrepancies between choices which already have been made and the outcomes of those choices. There is other evidence which more indirectly suggests that changes of value are facilitated by the requirement of generating affective control over commitments to active behavior, and that they are not merely the consequence of discrepancies between a person's initial cognitive status and the information that is produced by the person's behavior. Janis and his collaborators (Janis and King, 1954; Janis and Mann, 1965) have found, for example, that people show more attitude change when they must overtly verbalize the communicative role of a person whose position is discrepant with their own than they do when they must simply read the discrepant communication.

Our detailed analysis of the effects of experiments which have constrained children's behavior with threats of varying magnitudes, and our comparison of these effects with those which are observed when children are exposed to different intensities of punishment, have been based primarily on evidence concerning aversive control of behavior. But the evidence opens a larger view of the internalized affective and cognitive dispositions which socialization both induces and utilizes in the control of conduct. It seems clear that these dispositions are more extensively brought into play when the value of potential external rewards and punishments is not in itself so great as to completely determine the child's behavior. And it will therefore often be true that very powerful external constraints are less effective than weaker constraints in evoking the exercise of internalized evaluative monitors which the child already has acquired. There is equally clear evidence, however, that relatively weak rewards or punishments cannot be expected to be more effective in the initial establishment of internalized control of the child's behavior. The promise of reward and the threat of punishment obtain their effects through dispositions which socialization previously has given to the child. And the strength or magnitude of rewards and punishments which are experienced by the child must always be regarded as a direct determinant of the power of the internalized affective residue which they leave in the child.

CHAPTER ELEVEN

CHILD REARING
AND
DISCIPLINE

There have been a great many surveys in which investigators have attempted to uncover consistent relationships between the child-rearing practices of parents and various indices of internalization in the behavior of their children. The assessments which are made in these surveys often are interpreted as evidence of the extent to which children have adopted the values of their parents. Although the findings of the surveys undoubtedly do reflect in part the contribution that socialization makes to the cognitive structures of conscience, the fact is that the vast majority of the surveys use indices of overt conduct in their assessment of the effects of variations in child-rearing practices. The indices are based almost exclusively on children's dispositions to suppress prohibited behavior and to react in a variety of ways to committed transgressions, usually under conditions where the objective risk of punishment appears to be negligible. Of course, both suppression and reactions to transgression are heavily determined by the aversive controls which are embedded originally in the behavior of socializing agents.

Direct observations of behavior, the reports of parents and teachers, story-completions, doll-play, and cultural customs all have been used to assess internalized control of conduct as the product of child-rearing. Some indices have been fairly specific—for example, self-blame for illness or suppression of cheating. But it is often the case that a number of different forms of conduct are thrown together in a broad index of internalization. Very few attempts have been made to relate different indices of internalization to the same array of child-rearing practices within a single survey. The multiplicity of methods and findings has resulted in a certain amount of inconsistency and difficulty in drawing inferences. Yet some of the correlations which have been found appear to be sufficiently replicable to warrant theoretical attention.

Punishment and correction are the components of socialization which have been studied in greatest detail as antecedents of the child's internalized control over its conduct. Although the focus on the disciplinary habits of parents is appropriate to the emphasis on the child's behavioral suppression and reactions to transgression, it represents some oversimplification of the socialization matrix in which these aspects of conduct are acquired. As was pointed out in an earlier chapter, the learning that takes place around the occurrence of the child's transgressions cannot be separated entirely from the positive affectivity which is associated with the behavior of parents in their roles as agents of social reinforcement and as models. For example, direct positive reinforcement would strengthen the child's suppression of punished behavior, and would enter into its learning of active behavioral alternatives to transgression. Positive reinforcement also would support the child's acquisition of corrective reactions to its committed transgressions.

The findings of the surveys which we are about to review have a limited value for an understanding of the mechanisms of internalization. They are limited not only by the usual constraints on the inferences which can be drawn from correlations, but also by the fact that the correlations represent the effects of unknown interactions of different types of learning paradigms. Nevertheless, the kinds of child-rearing variations which have been studied most extensively sometimes lend themselves to analysis in terms of affective and cognitive mechanisms of learning. And it is possible to discern some important areas of agreement between the findings of the surveys and the theoretical expectations which were set forth earlier in our analyses of behavioral suppression and reactions to transgression. The findings constitute, in fact, a rough naturalistic confirmation of the reinforcement contingencies and cognitive processes which already have been described as the foundations of internalized aversive control of conduct.

THE CLIMATE OF REARING

In order to examine the specific effects of discipline on the social behavior of children, it is necessary to first consider in some detail how the broader context of socialization may determine a child's reaction to discipline and the corresponding effectiveness of its internalized control over conduct. The available evidence offers no reason to think that any index of internalization will be related consistently to specific practices of care and feeding during infancy, or to the pace at which weaning and control of eliminative functions are introduced into the socialization process (W. Allinsmith, 1960; Burton, Maccoby, and Allinsmith, 1961; Grinder, 1962; Sears, Rau, and Alpert, 1965, Chapter 6; Whiting and Child, 1953, Chapter 11). But there is a substantial amount of evidence which indicates that the child's acquisition of an internalized orientation toward the control of its behavior requires a certain minimum of nurturance in the general climate of socialization.

Whiting and Child (1953, Chapter 11) compared a great many different societies with respect to the incidence of self-blame for illness, which they used as an index of an internalized orientation toward the control of conduct. Their cross-cultural comparisons suggested that self-blame was unlikely to be prevalent in societies which were very severe in their early socialization of the child—as reflected, for example, in the imposition of demands which were made too early to be met by the child's capacities. The same kind of relationship is implicit in the cross-cultural finding by Bacon, Child, and Barry (1963) that a high incidence of theft was more characteristic of societies which used extremely severe practices during early socialization.

Within the more confined variations of socialization in our own society, numerous investigators have found relationships which indicate that children's suppression of prohibited forms of aggression (McCord, McCord, and Howard, 1961), their responsibility in the performance of tasks (Bronfenbrenner, 1961), and their reactions to their own transgressions (Sears, Maccoby, and Levin, 1957, Chapter 10), are characterized by relatively weakly internalized controls when the children have experienced a high density of parental rejection or punitiveness. However, as we will see when we examine this and other evidence more closely, general constructs such as nurturance or severity are too gross to be useful, without finer analysis, to an account of the mechanisms for the child's internalization of control over its behavior. The findings of many surveys clearly contravert, for example, any expectation that a child's internalized resources for the control of behavioral suppression or reactions to transgression will be a direct function of the amount of nurturance that it has received from its socializing agents.

The nurturant behavior of parents has been given a great deal of attention in theoretical accounts of the child's internalization of control over conduct. This attention has been generated in part by the findings of the surveys which have suggested an association between unusually severe or harsh child-rearing practices and minimal internalization in the child's control of conduct. Although assessments of parental affection or "warmth" often are used as indices of nurturance, the concept of nurturance also is anchored to more specific features of the parents' behavior, such as responsiveness to the child's needs and the frequency with which it is given praise or approval. There is a sense in which nurturance may be regarded as the converse of severity, if we think of severe socialization as being lack of affection, neglect of the child's needs, imposition of demands beyond its capacities, and a high level of punitiveness. Surveys of child-rearing practices have generally not used nurturance, however, as a synonym for permissiveness or indulgence. In certain areas of the child's conduct, it is apparent that even nurturant parents will often apply strong pressures for social conformity (Sears *et al.,* 1957).

A great many theorists have taken the view that children acquire a highly generalized disposition to internalize control of their social behavior. Most of these theorists appear to assume that the nurturance of parents is a uniformly critical determinant of the child's acquisition of internalized behavioral controls, throughout a wide range of potential variation in the child's experience of nurturance. We have already examined some of the limitations of this assumption for a general account of the phenomena of observational learning and imitation. Its limitations for an understanding of the broader phenomena of internalized control over conduct are equally instructive.

Some writers seem to suggest that nurturance simply establishes the positive value of the parents as objects of the child's affection, and that the child begins to monitor its own conduct because it becomes concerned for the interest and welfare of others (for example, Ausubel, 1955, or Bowlby, 1947). But there also have been a number of attempts to construct more specific conceptions of nurturance as a general base for the mechanisms of internalization (Mowrer, 1950, Chapter 21; 1960b, Chapter 3; Sears *et al.,* 1957, Chapter 10; Sears *et al.,* 1965, Chapter 6; Whiting and Child, 1953,

Chapter 11). These formulations have as their common core the conception of a generalized process of identification, through which the child acquires the values as well as the behavior of its socializing agents. The formulations bear some resemblance to a view that was originally put forth by Freud (1933)—that the desire to reproduce and stabilize the properties of a "love object" is a major source of the child's identification with its parents (although it is interesting to note that Freud apparently viewed the punitive or threatening aspects of the behavior of parents as a more significant source of the child's motivation to internalize its control of conduct).

The most explicit formulation of a mechanism for the effect of nurturance on a generalized disposition toward internalization can be found in the very similar conceptions which have been advanced by Sears *et al.* (1957, Chapter 10) and by Whiting and Child (1953, Chapter 11). They observe that many attributes of the child's socializing agents, particularly of the mother, will acquire positive affective value for the child because of their association with its experience of care, affection, or approval. It is further presumed that the child will acquire a very broad motivation to reproduce these attributes, and that the motivation will be strongest when the affectionate presence of its potential models is absent or has been withdrawn. The child can thus induce and control its own pleasurable affective states with some independence of the presence of its socializing agents. Its disposition to replicate the attributes of its socializing agents is reinforced by the intrinsic positive value which the attributes have acquired. In order to allow such a disposition to account for the child's acquisition of values, it is apparently assumed that the disposition applies not only to the behavioral attributes of socializing agents, but also to the cognitive schemata which they transmit in their verbal evaluations of the child's behavior. The disposition also is presumed to generalize so broadly that it extends to the behavioral and evaluative aspects of the punitive reactions of socializing agents. In other words, it is assumed that children come to evaluate, suppress, and correct their transgressions, in ways which correspond to the previous reactions of their parents, as part of an acquired and powerfully generalized disposition to reproduce the role of a nurturant model.

A mechanism that permits the nurturant attributes of a model to facilitate the child's reproduction of the model's behavior is perfectly consistent with our earlier analysis of observational learning and imitation. The positive affective value that would be associated with much of the behavior of a nurturant model would be expected to become intrinsically attached to the child's cognitive representation and overt reproduction of the behavior. We have reviewed a number of experiments which demonstrate that the nurturance of a potential model toward a child does enhance the child's disposition to imitate the model's expressive behavior (Bandura and Huston, 1961; Bandura, Ross, and Ross, 1963b; Hartup and Coates, 1967; Hetherington and Frankie, 1967; Mussen and Parker, 1965). Other studies which have been conducted by Mussen and his collaborators have produced consistent evidence that children's preferences for the sex role of a parent, and their perceptions of their own attributes as being similar to those of the parent, are correlated with the amount of affection or warmth which they experience from their appropriate parental models (Mussen, 1961; Mussen and Distler, 1959; Mussen and Rutherford, 1963). The same kind of correlation was found in P. S. Sears' (1953) study of young children's preferences when they were asked to play sex-typed roles.

The body of evidence which is summarized above cannot be taken, however, as support for the view that all of the internalized products of socialization can be treated as more or less parallel derivatives of a generalized disposition to identify with nurturant models. The conception of a generalized process of identification does not account for important differences among specific forms of conduct and among their discrete antecedents in socialization. It does not specify, for example, the origins of various distinct internalized reactions to transgression, or their differential probabilities of occurrence under the influence of particular situational cues. The weakness of an overly generous view of the function of nurturance in socialization is, more generally, especially visible in any attempt to account for the very large contribution which punishment and anxiety make to the child's internalization of control over its behavior. There are both theoretical considerations and empirical findings which make it clear that the child's internalized aversive control of its behavior is not acquired in simple proportion to the magnitude or extensiveness of the nurturance of its socializing agents.

A basic conceptual difficulty arises from the assumption that a great variety of forms of control over conduct, many of which obviously have been acquired as a result of the child's experience of punishment or of other aversive external contingencies, are somehow internalized through the child's disposition to reproduce the evaluative judgements and the behavior of its nurturant models. The nurturant or affectionate presence of socializing agents is necessarily distinct from their punitive behavior in response to the child's transgressions. Even though children may acquire generalized dispositions to reproduce the attributes of their nurturant models, it hardly seems credible that such dispositions could be so pervasive as to include representations of their model's roles as agents of punishment. The problem is especially clear in the case of self-criticism, a reaction to transgression in which the child reproduces some of the verbal stimulus components of the punishments to which it has been exposed.

If the spread of effect of the pleasurable affectivity that is induced by the child's experience of nurturance were so indiscriminate as to encompass the punitive behavior of the source of nurturance, then any hypothetical gradient of generalization would yield the prediction that the child would still be more inclined to reproduce the nurturant behavior of a model than it would to reproduce the punitive behavior—since it is the nurturant behavior that originally would have been associated directly with the child's positive affective experience. One might therefore expect that the child would be more prone to reproduce the nurturant attributes of a parent than the punitive attributes even when it has just committed a transgression. It is presumably then under the duress of an affective state that is derived, at least in part, from its previous experiences of withdrawal of affection. Common observation contradicts such an expectation, of course, and reveals in other ways that a broad construct of identification with a nurturant model does not give a good account of why children also adopt the behavior and values which socializing agents show in the context of punishment.

The relationships which have been found in a large number of surveys repeatedly disconfirm the assumption that the nurturance of socializing agents is a uniformly functional determinant of a broad disposition which children acquire toward the internalized control of their behavior. The findings of many surveys indicate no consistent association between the nurturance of parents and various indices of their children's internalized orientation toward the control and correction of prohibited behavior (Grinder, 1962; Heinecke, 1953; Sears et al., 1965, Chapter 6; Whiting and Child, 1953, Chapter 11). Burton et al. (1961) found a restricted amount of positive association between the affection of parents and their children's inclination to confess transgressions. And as was noted earlier, the findings of other surveys indicate that children who have experienced rejection or extreme punitiveness from their parents are likely to show weak internalization on indices of responsibility, control of aggressive behavior, and reactions to transgression (Bronfenbrenner, 1961; McCord et al., 1961; Sears et al., 1957, Chapter 10). The correlations which are reported by Bronfenbrenner (1961) and by Burton et al. (1961) also suggest, however, that the children of highly nurturant parents show less responsibility and cheat more readily than do the children of parents who are more modal in their nurturance. The same direction of relationship is implied in the cross-cultural finding by Whiting and Child (1953, Chapter 11) that overall harshness of early socialization showed a limited positive association with the tendency of the members of a society to blame themselves for illness (it will be recalled that these investigators found, within the same cross-cultural data, a trend which indicated that self-blame for illness was distinctly uncharacteristic of societies in which early socialization was *extremely* severe).

The correlations which suggest that a highly nurturant climate of rearing may curtail a child's internalization of control over its conduct make a certain amount of sense when one considers that the indices of conduct which are used in the relevant surveys are primarily the products of the child's experience with transgression and punishment. A society which is very indulgent toward its children, and which imposes few demands or constraints upon them, might well induce relatively little anxiety or even perception of transgression in many areas of social behavior.[1] The less obvious and more interesting correlations, however, are those which reveal a positive association between the nurturance of parents and evidence of internalization in the conduct of their children. The range of nurturance over which these correlations appear points firmly to the inference that they are generated entirely by the effects of parental rejection or extreme punitiveness toward the child. To the extent that the presentations of the relevant data permit close inspection, it becomes apparent that the correlations are visible primarily when parents who give very little nurturance to their children are separated from all other parents.

What seems to be true is that a certain minimal intensity and focus of

[1] It should be noted that the indices of internalization which are used in different surveys vary considerably in the position which they might have on a hypothetical continuum of internal versus external orientation. At least in the case of those surveys which have been conducted on samples of children in the United States, the indices of internalization which appear to be inversely associated with a highly nurturant climate of rearing tend also to be based on aspects of conduct which are ordinarily often open to external observation—for example, responsibility or conformity to rules in the performance of tasks. It is therefore possible that the children of very nurturant parents are required to conform to fewer of the conventional constraints on their social behavior, but that they have no less of an internalized orientation than other children in those areas of their conduct where they have acquired suppressive and corrective controls. Certainly there is no reason to think that a highly nurturant climate would in itself interfere with a child's internalization of aversive control in areas of behavior where punishment has been introduced into the socialization process.

social attachment to nurturant figures are required in order for children to acquire effective internalized behavioral controls on the basis of their experience with punishment. Beyond these minimal prerequisites, however, the child's internalization of aversive control cannot be viewed as a generalized, continuous function of parental nurturance. The effectiveness of socialization in producing internalized aversive control appears to be governed only by a restricted range of variation in nurturance, around the threshold at which a durable positive attachment is formed between the child and its primary agents of socialization.

Many other kinds of evidence support the inference that a minimally nurturant base for social attachment is a prerequisite of the child's effective internalization of aversive control over its conduct. Surveys of delinquent groups consistently reveal that their parents are unusually punitive and rejecting (Bandura and Walters, 1959; Glueck and Glueck, 1950; McCord and McCord, 1958; McCord, McCord, and Howard, 1963). Absence of an internalized orientation and weakness of internalized controls on prohibited behavior often have been found to be associated with patterns of socialization which would tend to dilute the strength of the child's affective ties to specific agents of nurturance. For example, Whiting (1959) has summarized cross-cultural findings which suggest that there is less self-blame for illness among societies which are structured around an extended family than among societies which are structured around a nuclear family. Goldfarb (1945) found poor control over aggressive behavior among institutional children who had been deprived of consistent parental figures. Freud and Dann (1951) made the same observation among children whose early rearing took place in a concentration camp.

It is not difficult to understand why a substantial degree of attachment to nurturant socializing agents would be an essential condition for the effectiveness of any mechanism of internalization. Although human infants appear to have powerful unlearned dispositions toward attachment to their sources of social stimulation (Ambrose, 1961; Schaffer and Emerson, 1964), there is much evidence which indicates that the maintenance of their social attachments also requires the experience of consistent nurturance from their primary caretakers (Casler, 1961; Maccoby, 1969). Many of the complex social stimuli which are transmitted in the behavior of socializing agents can exercise control over the child's behavior because they have acquired the capacity to induce changes of affectivity. Their affective value is originally acquired as a result of contingencies which associated them with the child's experience of increments or decrements of nurturance and affection. The lack of a strong attachment to nurturant figures would therefore interfere with the establishment of either the positive or the aversive value of a great many of the social stimulus events to which children are exposed.

A deficit in the child's experience of nurturance would remove the foundation of the positive value that ordinarily becomes attached to much of the reproducible behavior of socializing agents, and would thereby reduce the child's disposition to imitate its potential models. This curtailment of the child's imitative dispositions would limit its resources for the internalization of the socially desirable forms of control over conduct which might be represented in the behavior of its models. The consequences of a deprivation of nurturance can perhaps be seen even more clearly, however, in the potential disruption of the effectiveness of behavior-contingent training for producing internalized control through either the positive or the aversive outcomes of the child's overt acts. The nurturant treatment of the child will be a crucial determinant of the power of the rewards and punishments which socializing agents transmit in their reactions to the child's behavior. For example, if parents have generally been affectionless or indiscriminately punitive, then there is very little basis for the establishment of the value of their behavioral resources for positive reinforcement and control of their children's behavior. Conversely, withdrawal of affection may have only negligible value as a component of the resources which socializing agents have for aversive control of the child's behavior, if the child does not experience the withdrawal against a background of sustained nurturant treatment.

Although withdrawal of affection is sometimes classified as a particular form of punishment, it is very probably a component of all forms of social punishment. And it may well be the component which is most durably effective in producing aversive control over the child's behavior. If a child has failed to acquire social attachment to a parent, or has become adapted to a high level of aversive stimulation in the parent's presence, then the element of loss of affection in the parent's punishment may not induce sufficient discriminant anxiety to motivate the child's suppression of transgressions or its corrective reactions to their occurrence. The absence of loss of affection as an effective medium of punishment also may orient the child to other components of punishment, such as physical attack or deprivation, which are less likely to permit its anxiety to become independent of external surveillance and threat. There is some support for this expectation in the finding by Sears *et al.* (1957, Chapter 10) that the frequency of the use of withdrawal of affection by parents was correlated with evidence of internalization in their children's reactions to transgression, but only for parents who were generally nurturant toward their children. It is also of some interest to note Freedman's (1958) finding that dogs who were prone to generalized aversive reactions to human handling, even though an attempt was made to give them nurturant treatment early in their development, failed to acquire internalized suppression following subsequent punishment training. These findings suggest that intense and continued aversive experience, early in the course of contact with a socializing agent, may have adverse effects on the child's internalization of aversive control because it reduces the effectiveness of the agent's punishment of specific acts.

Social attachment to agents of nurturance undoubtedly also is required in order to establish the child's empathic and vicarious experience as another channel through which socialization can produce internalized control of conduct. The child's sensitivity to the pleasurable or distressful consequences of its actions for others, and its sensitivity to the outcomes of the behavior of its potential models, will be dependent on its acquired capacity for affective response to social cues which indicate the experience of other people. Social cues originally acquire their empathic or vicarious value for the child through their association with a larger complex of stimulus events, some components of which must induce affectivity because they are directly experienced by the child. The directly experienced stimulus components in turn often have an affective value that is derived from their association with changes in the nurturance or affection of those to whom the child is attached. For example, if a mother were so lacking in nurturance that her withdrawal of affection had little aversive value for her child, then her affective cues of distress could not acquire much empathic value for the child as a result of their association with loss of affection.

The importance of a threshold of social attachment in the establishment of the child's internalized control over its behavior does not imply that nurturance beyond the requirements of such a threshold has no further effects on socialization. There are reasons to expect that a wide range of variation of nurturance and social attachment would have an early and lasting influence on the effectiveness of both the rewards and punishments which are transmitted in the behavior of parents and other socializing agents. The child's attention to many specific features of a socializing agent's positive or aversive reactions to its behavior would be determined by its past experience of the probability of nurturant interaction with the agent. The child's expectation of nurturance also may control its overt performance of behavior that originally has been acquired through behavior-contingent or observational forms of learning which were not dependent on its experience of nurturance.

In the case of aversive control of the child's behavior, the general level of nurturance to which the child has become adapted may establish the salience of punishment by contrast. The amount of contrast would tend to determine the magnitude of the child's experience of withdrawal of affection. Although nurturance does not appear to have had such an effect in some experiments on children's internalization of aversive controls (Aronfreed, 1964; Aronfreed, Cutick, and Fagen, 1963), the results of other experiments indicate that the effectiveness of punishment is sometimes enhanced by the nurturance which the child experiences from the agent of punishment. For example, some investigators have reported that children show more evidence of internalized suppression, or of self-criticism which reproduces the previous criticism of a socializing agent, after they have been punished by a nurturant agent than after they have been punished by a relatively neutral agent (Grusec, 1966; Mischel and Grusec, 1966; Parke and Walters, 1967). The results of Grusec's experiment suggested that a focus on withdrawal of affection was particularly effective as a medium of punishment. Discrepancies between the findings of different experiments may be attributable to the fact that other aversive components of punishment overshadowed withdrawal of affection in the experiments in which no effect of nurturance was obtained. Similar inconsistencies appear in the findings of experiments with dogs. Black, Solomon, and Whiting (1954) did not find that the effects of punishment training on internalized suppression were sensitive to the nurturance that was previously given to dogs by the agent of punishment. But Freedman (1958) did find some evidence of such an effect.

In summary, then, a substantial positive attachment to nurturant socializing agents, which emerges in varying intensities from the extended early dependence of children, appears to be required for the effectiveness of all of the forms of learning through which children acquire internalized control over their behavior. The nurturance of socializing agents is a crucial and general determinant of internalization, however, only up to a certain point—the point at which their behavior acquires powerful derivative properties for the induction of changes of affectivity in the child. Beyond that point, nurturance enters into the process of internalization only through the parameters of a variety of specific mechanisms of learning. In general, the child's experience of nurturance conditions the effectiveness of socializing agents to the extent that it determines the affective value of many more discrete features of their behavior and the corresponding control which they can exercise over the child's behavior.

AN ANALYSIS OF DISCIPLINE

The use of punishment by parents is ordinarily assessed as part of a broad variety of external controls which they exercise over the behavior of their children. These controls are collectively described as discipline, and they include positive as well as aversive contingencies. However, the evidence of the relevant surveys focusses most intensively on the variety of reactions which parents show to their children's transgressions, and on indices of conduct which represent children's suppression of prohibited behavior and reactions to transgression. Accordingly, the evidence must be analyzed primarily in terms of the impact of different types of discipline on children's affective and cognitive resources for internalized aversive control of their behavior.

It is a common practice to use two broad categories in the classification of the disciplinary habits of parents. The first category of discipline is usually characterized as being "psychological" or "love-oriented." One of the prototypes of this category is the kind of reaction to transgression in which parents explicitly emphasize their withdrawal of affection—for example, when they ignore or isolate the child, or otherwise indicate their rejection or disappointment. The first category of discipline also includes as another prototype, however, those reactions to the child's transgressions in which the verbal transmission of the parents' values is a dominant component—for example, reasoning, explanation, or other forms of evaluation which may accompany verbal disapproval of the child's behavior. Some surveys also have included inquiry into the child's motivation for its actions and direct attempts to initiate or reinforce the child's self-corrective reactions. Both of these latter types of parental response to transgression tend to be closely interwoven with the verbal transmission of values.

The second category of discipline consists of parental reactions to transgression which result in a relatively direct and concrete application of aversive stimulation to the child. The basic prototype of this category is physical punishment. But verbal assaults such as "screaming" and "bawling-out" frequently are treated as components of the second category. These parental reactions are as much attacks upon the child as they are communications of values. Ridicule or public shaming of the child also sometimes are classified as elements in this category. Techniques of discipline such as deprivation and restriction usually are not classified as belonging to either of the two basic categories, or are at least treated separately, in part because their other correlates in the parents' behavior appear to be highly variable.

It seems fairly obvious that the distinction between these two broad categories of discipline becomes rather gross when it is translated into the child's experience. For example, verbal assaults can transmit some features of the parents' evaluative standards, even though they are usually classified as direct attacks upon the child. Nevertheless, although some important information is lost in such a broad categorization, the disciplinary habits which are collected in each category do have significant common properties. These general properties can be usefully characterized, with reference to their impact on the child, when the two categories of discipline are respectively subordinated to the concepts of *induction* and *sensitization* (Aronfreed, 1961). Induction and sensitization are descriptive concepts which are designed to distinguish between two different patterns of learning that are nested in the disciplinary habits of parents. Analysis of the components of these two patterns of learning reveals why socialization can produce more than one direction of control over the elicitation and management of the anxiety that becomes attached to children's potential or committed transgressions. In particular, the two patterns of learning may be idealized as the respective sources of an internal or an external orientation in the child's acquired aversive control over its conduct.

The less directly punitive forms of discipline may be characterized as induction because they are likely to induce more internalized monitors of the child's anxiety, and of its instrumental resources for reduction of anxiety, in response to a transgression. For example, the anxiety that is elicited in a child by discipline that emphasizes a parent's withdrawal of affection is less dependent on the parent's continued presence or physical proximity, and is therefore more likely to become internalized, than is the anxiety that can be elicited by physical punishment or by other direct applications of noxious stimulation to the child. Discipline that relies on withdrawal of affection is in fact often made effective by separating the child from the parent's presence. Correspondingly, the parent who uses extensive verbal evaluation of the child's behavior and explanation of standards, without an aversive affective display that is so intense as to disrupt the transmission of information, is providing a medium of discipline that can expand the child's own cognitive resources for internalized control of its behavior. And if the child is made to focus attention on the intentions which precede its actions, or is reinforced for its own active corrections of its behavior, then it is more likely on subsequent occasions to exercise self-initiated controls over the anxiety that has become attached to its incipient or committed transgressions.⟩ The various components of the discipline which may be described as induction have in common, then, their tendency to make the child's control of its behavior independent of external contingencies.

In contrast, direct physical and verbal attack may be characterized as sensitization because they would tend merely to sensitize the child to the anticipation of punishment. Sensitization discipline reinforces children for their anticipation and control of the potential punitive reactions of other people. But it does not easily permit their anxiety, or the anxiety-reducing value of their suppression and reactions to transgression, to become independent of external monitors which signal their control over the avoidance or the occurrence of punishment.

The findings of a number of surveys have shown significant correlations between the type of discipline that is used by parents and various indices of their children's internalization of control over conduct. Although the reported relationships are restricted in their magnitude, they generally confirm the expectation that children will have a more internalized orientation when they have experienced primarily discipline of the induction type than when they have experienced primarily discipline of the sensitization type. The consistency among the different surveys provides some additional evidence of the validity of their findings, particularly in view of the fact that they vary considerably in where their specific indices of internalization might fall on a continuum of internal versus external orientation.

The children of parents whose disciplinary habits fall primarily in the induction category consistently show more internalization in their reactions to transgression than do the children of parents whose disciplinary habits fall primarily in the sensitization category (W. Allinsmith, 1960; Aronfreed, 1961; Burton et al., 1961; Heinecke, 1953; Hoffman and Saltzstein, 1967; MacKinnon, 1938; Sears et al., 1957, Chapter 10; Whiting and Child, 1953, Chapter 11). The evidence shows less uniformity in the relationship between parental discipline and the effectiveness of the child's internalized suppression of socially prohibited forms of behavior. But it usually indicates a relationship which is parallel to that found for reactions to transgression. The relationship is quite clear in surveys which have assessed children's control over their aggressive behavior—particularly over their physical aggression (B. Allinsmith, 1960; Chorost, 1962; Hoffman, 1960; Sears et al., 1957, Chapter 7; Sears, Whiting, Nowlis, and Sears, 1953). And it is further confirmed by the common finding that the parents of aggressive delinquents typically show a high incidence of physical and verbal attacks in response to their children's transgressions (Bandura and Walters, 1959; Glueck and Glueck, 1950; McCord *et al.*, 1963).

Less consistent evidence has been found in surveys which have used honesty or obedience as indices of internalization (Grinder, 1962; Sears *et al.*, 1965, Chapter 6). MacKinnon (1938) found a substantial positive association between the honesty of college students and their parents' reported use of discipline of the induction type. But Burton *et al.* (1961) have reported findings which appear to be opposite in their direction. The inconsistency among the findings concerning the child-rearing antecedents of honesty may be partially attributable to the fact that recent surveys assess children's cheating or disobedience in situations where a prohibitive rule is explicitly conveyed to the child by a social agent, and where there is consequently too high a probability that the child's behavior will be sensitive to its perception of external surveillance and risk of punishment.

The usefulness of the distinction between the induction and sensitization categories of discipline is also indirectly supported by findings concerning the correlates of other aspects of parental control over the child's behavior. For example, a number of surveys have suggested that the restrictiveness of parents has a positive association with their children's suppression of socially prohibited forms of aggression (Bandura and Walters, 1959; McCord *et al.*, 1963; Sears, 1961; Sears *et al.*, 1957, Chapter 7), and with their children's tendency to enforce prohibitions on others (Maccoby, 1961). Although it is not entirely clear what restrictiveness implies about how parents will respond to the actual occurrence of transgressions, surveys of social-class differences in child-rearing indicate that restrictiveness, in the sense of closeness of supervision, may be embedded in the context of induction patterns of discipline (Aronfreed, 1961; Bronfenbrenner, 1958; Davis and Havighurst, 1946; Kohn, 1959; Maccoby and Gibbs *et al.*, 1954).

Parents of higher socioeconomic status generally behave in ways which would tend to induce an internal governor in their children. Along with their relatively close control over their children's behavior, they use a verbal medium of discipline and much explicit withdrawal of affection. They also concern themselves with the intentions behind their children's actions. Parents of lower socioeconomic status tend to exercise less immediate control over their children's activities, and seem to give their attention primarily to the visible manifestations of transgression. Their discipline more frequently takes the form of direct attack, with less explanation of their punishment, and is therefore more likely to sensitize their children to the punitive consequences of transgressions. Children from the two major social classes in our society do differ in their evaluative expressions of conscience, and in the orientation of their internalized reactions to transgression, in ways which are predictable from their predominant experiences of discipline (Aronfreed, 1961; Boehm, 1962; Johnson, 1962; Kohlberg, 1968; Lerner, 1937). Cross-cultural comparisons suggest similar associations between orientation toward the control of conduct and the types of parental discipline which are characteristic of entire societies (Grinder and McMichael, 1963; Whiting, 1959).

The relationships between the disciplinary habits of parents and various indices of their children's internalized control over conduct pose an interesting problem for a theoretical account of the mechanisms of internalization. The entire body of findings which is summarized above often has been interpreted as evidence that punishment which is "severe" or intense will not be effective in producing internalized suppression of the child's behavior. But such an inference is inconsistent with the findings of experiments which clearly demonstrate that children will show more internalized suppression of punished behavior after intense punishment than they will after mild punishment, provided that they can discriminate between punished and nonpunished acts (Aronfreed and Leff, 1963; Leff, 1967; Parke and Walters, 1967). It is also inconsistent with extensive findings concerning the effects of intensity of punishment on behavioral suppression in the animal laboratory (Church, 1963). There is in fact no reason to suppose that physical punishment, or other very direct forms of punishment, are experienced by the child as being more painful or aversive than those forms of punishment which fall into a category of discipline that we have classified as induction. It is quite possible, on the contrary, that withdrawal of affection, which parents so often make the central feature of their induction discipline, is actually the most aversive component in the child's experience of any kind of punishment.

The problems which arise from assumptions about the severity of different forms of punishment are especially noticeable in respect to the disciplinary antecedents of the child's internalized control over aggressive behavior. In addition to the surveys which already have been cited, there are a number of other surveys in which it has been found that the children of parents who frequently use physical and other direct methods of punishment are more likely to be physically aggressive toward their peers than are the children of parents who tend to use induction discipline (Becker *et al.,*

1962; Eron *et al.,* 1963; Lefkowitz, Walder, and Eron, 1963). Levin and Sears (1956) found the same direction of relationship in the study of children's aggressive behavior during doll-play. In order to account for these findings, it sometimes has been suggested that the more direct forms of parental punishment actually serve as models for the child's own physical aggression (Bandura and Walters, 1959, 1963b; Miller and Swanson *et al.,* 1960; Sears *et al.,* 1957, Chapter 7). However, although the motivation and performance of children's aggressive behavior may be influenced by their observation of the aggression of others (as has been demonstrated in the reports of a variety of experiments which were analyzed in Chapter Four), it certainly is not clear that their typical aggressive behavior toward their peers would follow from observation of the aggression that is evident in the discipline of their parents. Moreover, the aggression of parents in the context of discipline is not merely observed by the child. It is also directed at and experienced by the child. And whatever disposition the child might have to imitate the aggression of parents could hardly be expected to negate the aversive and suppressive effects which the aggression would have as a punitive outcome of the child's own aggressive behavior.

A more plausible account of why the more "severe" forms of punishment produce weaker internalization of children's suppression of physical aggression may be found in the different conditions of learning which are implied in the conceptual distinction between induction and sensitization discipline. The more direct and aggressive forms of punishment may induce less internalized suppression of the child's aggression because they are more effective in sensitizing the child to external risk of punishment than they are in providing the child with internalized monitors for the control of its behavior. And in peer interactions in which the child is not subject to the external constraint of authority or superior power, its sensitization to punishment will not be sufficient to suppress its aggressive dispositions. This interpretation of the relationship between parental discipline and the child's control of aggression has the advantage of being applicable not only to one area of conduct, but also to other indices of the child's internalized control of its behavior, which show a parallel direction of relationship to the parents' use of induction or sensitization discipline. The more aggressive forms of discipline are commonly found to be associated with other kinds of evidence of minimal internalization in the child's control of conduct—for example, in its reactions to its committed transgressions. It seems more economical, then, to attribute their effects on the child's control of aggression to the same properties of sensitization to external punishment which appear to account for the more general weakness of internalized monitors in children who are exposed primarily to this type of discipline.

Our understanding of why induction and sensitization patterns of discipline generate different types of effective monitors of the child's conduct can be sharpened if we examine some of their specific components more closely. For example, the findings of a number of surveys indicate that the use of reasoning and explanation by parents is in itself correlated with evidence of internalization in their children's suppression of prohibited behavior and reactions to transgression (W. Allinsmith, 1960; Bandura and Walters, 1959; Burton *et al.,* 1961; Sears *et al.,* 1957, Chapter 10; Sears *et al.,* 1965, Chapter 6). These findings support the inference that a verbal medium of punishment gives the child representational and evaluative equipment which frees its behavior from the control of external social indicators of the potentially punitive outcomes of its behavior. The cognitive gain that is provided by the verbalized evaluations of socializing agents is also confirmed by the findings of a few surveys which have assessed relationships between parental discipline and the child's expression of values (Hoffman and Saltzstein, 1967; Kohlberg, 1969). The findings indicate that the children of parents whose disciplinary habits are induction-oriented show a more internalized and abstract orientation toward principles of conscience, when they are asked to verbally express and apply their evaluative standards to specific hypothetical actions, than do children of parents whose disciplinary habits are sensitization-oriented.

Withdrawal of affection also may make a special contribution to the more effective internalization that is produced by induction discipline, because of the contingencies under which it is usually experienced by children. Although loss of affection may be an aversive component of any form of punishment, once its value has been established by contrast with the parent's affectionate presence, many parents prolong their withdrawal of affection or use a verbal medium to focus their children's attention on it. These parents may regulate their punishment in ways which give the child options for the exercise of control over their behavior and its own anxiety. Parents who use induction discipline more generally have an orientation toward producing self-initiated control of conduct in their children. They may tend to reinstate their withdrawn affection only after the child has activated its own resources to evaluate, arrest, or correct its transgressions.

Parents who use sensitization discipline also will transmit loss of affection to their children. But their discipline is less likely to include contingencies which permit the child to exercise active control over the avoidance or termination of punishment. Sensitization discipline tends to subject the child to punishment that is immediate and focussed in time. It makes the avoidance or the occurrence of punishment, rather than any act of the child, the event that marks the resolution of a transgression. Under these conditions, the priority of avoiding or producing punishment would sharply curtail the probability that the child would acquire any self-corrective reactions to transgression.

This view of the different contingencies which are embodied in the two types of discipline finds some support in the findings of one survey which specifically included an index of children's self-corrective dispositions (Aronfreed, 1961). The mother's use of induction discipline was found to have a positive association with the child's internalized self-corrective reactions to its transgressions. In contrast, sensitization discipline was found to be associated with the child's tendency to perceive the resolution of a transgression in aversive external consequences which were beyond its control. Some findings from the recent survey by Hoffman and Saltzstein (1967) suggest, even more specifically, that withdrawal of affection in itself is not as effective in producing internalization of the child's reactions to transgression as are the parents' efforts to induce the child to reinstate affection by introducing active changes in its behavior.

There are also some other important differences between the contingencies of learning which respectively characterize induction and sensitization discipline. The loss and reinstatement of affection which are often at the focus of induction discipline would tend to maintain the affective and cognitive salience of transgression for the child, and would elicit anxiety of greater and more uncertain duration than the anxiety that would be elicited by more direct and quickly terminated punishments. Parents who use induction discipline predominantly also may be likely to hold their children responsible for transgressions long after their point of occurrence. The child's internalized anxiety, in response to subsequent transgressions, would therefore have a relatively long duration despite the absence of any cues of external surveillance. The more prolonged and variable period of anxiety would raise the probability that the child would make active attempts to reduce the anxiety rather than wait upon external events. The fact that induction discipline often does not require the immediate presence of the parent is another source of the child's disposition to use its own behavioral resources for the reduction of the anxiety that follows a transgression.

Parents whose disciplinary habits are primarily of the sensitization type may tend to react more narrowly in time to the transgressions which occur in their immediate presence. And their punishments may tend to expose the child to aversive stimulation that is more narrowly focussed in time. Sensitization discipline might therefore have the effect of sharply limiting the length of time during which the child would experience anxiety after its commission of a transgression that was not under direct surveillance.

🌿 CHAPTER TWELVE 🌿

SOCIAL ORGANIZATION
AND
THE DIRECTION OF CONTROL

We have had a number of occasions to observe that there are interesting variations of both conduct and conscience, along a continuum of internal versus external orientation, among different societies and among individuals who have different positions or roles within a society. These variations appear to show some striking parallels to variations in the more general orientation which people acquire toward the control of their social and physical environment. There is a large inference that may be drawn from the parallels, and it can be stated very simply: the orientation of both overt conduct and the evaluative operations of conscience will be coordinate to the broader direction and balance of control which characterize the individual's interaction with his environment. People will have an internalized orientation to the extent that they have control over their environment and over its determination of their own behavior. They will have a more external orientation to the extent that their behavioral choices are imposed upon them by events which are outside of their control.

Of course, the direction of control between the individual and the environment will not always be uniform across different dimensions of social organization or across different areas of social behavior. However, certain instructive abstractions can be made on the basis of distinctions which have to do with status, role, and the control that a society as a whole exercises over its physical environment. The particular kinds of distinctions which are especially useful for our purposes here are those which have to do with socioeconomic status, sex role, and technology.

Any dimension of status in a social hierarchy can be partially translated into orientation toward the environment. People who hold higher positions in the hierarchy have greater power to determine and evaluate their own actions, and also to act upon their external environment. People in positions of lower status must be relatively more responsive to externally controlled determinants and consequences of their actions. These differences in social experience should produce corresponding differences of orientation in the control of many areas of conduct. Any two groups which are significantly different in status, along a common dimension of stratification in the society, would also be expected to be different in the extent to which their behavioral and cognitive dispositions show an internalized or externalized orientation toward the control of conduct. However, attributes of status cannot be merely transient if they are to have any durable implications for an individual's orientation toward the direction of control. They must be sufficiently stable to generate some long-term consistency in the individual's interactions with his social environment. Conversely, the effects of the social experiences which are determined by a particular status over a long period of time may be resistant to subsequent changes of status. For example, in a society which is characterized by high mobility with respect to any specific dimension of status, an individual's orientation toward the control of conduct may be at least as much a function of the status of his family of origin as it is of his own status as an adult.

Where there are multiple dimensions of status, particularly in complex societies, the dimensions may not be translated equivalently into the matrix of social experience from which the direction of control over conduct is derived, either within or across different areas of conduct. Consequently, a person's orientation toward control in a particular area of conduct may be determined by social experiences which reflect unequally his positions on each of a number of dimensions of status. There appears to be much commonality, however, in the effects of various dimensions of status on the kind of social experience that determines the control of conduct. The commonality is suggested, for example, in the parallel relationships which have been found between a number of different criteria of status and the individual's internalized or externalized orientation in the control of aggressive behavior (Gold, 1958; Henry and Short, 1954). These relationships indicate that higher status is associated with a more internalized orientation.

Some of the ways in which socioeconomic status shapes the balance of control between the individual and his social environment are apparent in differences of experience between the middle and the working classes in western society. The requirements of middle-class occupations tend to foster considerable independence of immediate external supervision. And members of the middle class have substantial opportunities to realize their aspirations through the modification of their external circumstances. Middle-class individuals would therefore be likely to have reinforcing experiences in their use of behavioral and cognitive resources which act upon and control events in their social environment. The occupational roles of the working class are much less likely to support initiative or self-reliance. Their work is circumscribed within rather narrow limits by sources outside of their own control, in part because of its concrete material nature. And their opportunities for modifying their social environment tend to be more restricted.

These socioeconomic differences in control over the environment do appear to be paralleled by differences between the two major social classes in their orientation toward the control of conduct (Hyman, 1953). There is a large amount of evidence which consistently shows that the differences of orientation between the two classes are particularly salient in the child-rearing values and practices of parents (B. Allinsmith, 1960; Aronfreed, 1961; Bronfenbrenner, 1958; Davis and Havighurst, 1946; Kohn, 1963; Maccoby and Gibbs *et al.,* 1954). As was pointed out in the earlier analysis of the effects of parental discipline, the disciplinary habits of parents of higher socioeconomic status are oriented toward inducing an internal governor in their children, whereas the habits of parents of lower status are oriented toward sensitizing their children to the punitive consequences of their behavior. The difference between the two classes in their child-rearing dispositions provides a very important source of the parallel relationship between their specific orientations toward the control of conduct and their more general orientations toward control of the external environment. It is unlikely that any attribute of a parent's social status would have a lasting influence on a child's orientation toward the control of conduct unless the attribute were translated into the medium of socialization.

When children of the middle and working classes are asked to verbalize the criteria of conscience which they would apply to the evaluation of various acts, they reveal the kinds of cognitive orientations toward the control of conduct which would be expected on the basis of their parents' characteristic habits of discipline (Boehm, 1962; Harrower, 1934; Johnson, 1962; Kohlberg, 1969; Lerner, 1937; MacRae, 1954). Similar variations of orientation can be observed in the internalized control of behavior when specific forms of conduct are carefully separated from one another (Aronfreed, 1961). For example, middle-class children more frequently show dispositions toward self-criticism as a reaction to transgression. Working-class children are more likely to perceive the resolution of transgression in external punitive consequences for the transgressor, and are more likely to seek external sources of responsibility or justification for their actions. The same kinds of differences of orientation between middle- and working-class children have been observed in their attitudes toward authority (Tuma and Livson, 1960), their dependence on social reinforcement in achievement tasks (Douvan, 1956), and their interest in occupations which require supervisory responsibility (Maccoby, 1962). A disproportionate incidence of delinquency in certain elements of the working class also may be partially attributable to differences between the two classes in their orientation toward the control of conduct (see, for example, the analysis of delinquency by Cohen, 1955).[1]

The two sexes also differ in the dominant direction of control which they experience in their interactions with a social environment. This difference can be described to some extent in terms of status (Aronfreed, 1961; Parsons, 1953), but it appears to embrace somewhat broader features of masculine and feminine sex roles (D'Andrade, 1966). It seems to be a reasonably sound cross-cultural generalization that greater status and self-direction of action are associated with the masculine role. Men are permitted more control over their own behavior and over their external environment. In contrast, the feminine role calls not so much for self-reliance as it does for sensitivity and responsiveness to externally imposed events. A woman's activities in her primary roles of wife and mother are very much affected by the social status of her spouse. She does not have the same freedom of movement or decision-making power which attach to his more crucial occupational role. Moreover, the social tasks which represent a society's orientation toward acting upon its external environment are typically reserved for men. Women have greater responsibility for those tasks which represent the standing balance of control between the society and its environment.

Of course, the relative distance between the two sexes, on a continuum of internal versus external orientation, would be dependent on the extent to which their roles were differentiated in a given society. In the United States, for example, it is clear that even young children are very much aware of differences of activity and status between the two sexes (Brown, 1958; Lynn, 1959). Yet the differentiation between the two sex roles in our society appears to be somewhat less sharp than it is in many other societies (Murdock, 1937). The absence of a sharp differentiation in our society may account for the fact that sex differences in orientation toward the control of conduct are somewhat less striking than differences between the two major social classes. Nevertheless, the sex differences exist, and they fit the expectations which follow from the differential power and control which characterize the two sex roles. Hartshorne and May (1928)

[1] There are dimensions of socioeconomic structure other than status which are relevant to the socialization that produces an internal or external orientation in the child's control of conduct. For example, socialization practices which would tend to induce self-control and independence in the child appear to be somewhat more prevalent when the head of the family has an entreprenurial occupation than when his work is performed in a bureaucratic occupational setting (Miller and Swanson, 1958).

found that girls gave more verbalized expressions of conformity to socially valued norms than boys did. Many other investigators have reported that girls are more susceptible than are boys to external social influence (Harper *et al.,* 1965; Hetherington, 1965; King, 1959). Terman and Miles (1936) found that boys showed more orientation toward fixed principles of justice or fairness in their verbal judgements of conduct, while girls were more easily swayed by the values or opinions of others.

Boys are more honest than girls in their overt conduct in private temptation situations, and in their accuracy of report of their own social behavior (Barbu, 1951; Hartshorne and May, 1928; Kohlberg, 1963b; Terman *et al.,* 1925). The studies which are reported by Douvan and Adelson (1966) indicate that boys are more internally oriented, and that girls are more externally oriented, in their descriptions of situations in which they would experience concern over their own capacity for self-control. In both the middle and working classes, boys also are more internally oriented than girls in their reactions to transgression (Aronfreed, 1961). Boys are less dependent on various forms of external influence, less likely to display their reactions for social approval, and less likely to focus on external sources of responsibility or justification for their transgressions. There also have been consistent indications that girls are more prone than are boys to confess their transgressions (Aronfreed, 1961; Rebelsky, Allinsmith, and Grinder, 1963; Sears, Maccoby, and Levin, 1957, Chapter 10). Confession is a relatively externally oriented reaction to transgression. The sex difference in its frequency does not occur in Israel, for example, where there is reason to think that socialization of boys and girls is even more similar than it is in our own society (Luria, Goldwasser, and Goldwasser, 1963).

We have noted that differences between children of the middle and working classes, in their orientation toward the control of conduct, are independently predictable from the disciplinary habits of their parents. There is much less evidence of consistent relationships between specific rearing practices and the apparent sex differences in orientation toward the control of conduct. Barry, Bacon, and Child (1957) have shown that there is a consistent tendency, across many societies, to attempt to induce self-reliance in boys, and conversely to emphasize obedience and conformity to external demands in the socialization of girls. In our own society, it seems probable that girls generally receive less support for independence of action and thought than do boys. Hatfield, Ferguson, and Alpert (1967) found that mothers more readily rewarded their boys for independence, but were more disposed to reward their girls for conformity to external influence.

There are similar indications of a greater parental emphasis on conformity and obedience for girls than for boys in the findings which are reported by King (1959). These differences in socialization might possibly account for the external orientation which girls show in their heavy use of confession and in their sensitivity to the influence of others. The fact that there are not clearly demonstrable relationships between child-rearing and sex differences in orientation toward the control of conduct suggests again that the most visible and easily catalogued features of socialization do not really capture the reinforcement contingencies and cognitive infusions which are the basis of internalization.

An individual's orientation toward the control of conduct also may be affected by the general orientation of his entire society to its external environment. It often has been observed that people of western societies show more of an internalized orientation in their values, and in their control of their own behavior, than do the people of many less "advanced" societies (McClelland, 1961; Mead, 1953). Similar differences of orientation can be discerned even among western societies (Weber, 1930). An apparent correlation between technological development and internally oriented control of conduct suggests that internal versus external orientation may be influenced by the effectiveness of a society's control over its environment. However, technology would probably not be the only determinant of a society's orientation toward its environment. Other factors, such as a favorable ecological niche, might play an important role. Whiting (1959) has shown, for example, that nonwestern societies vary considerably among themselves in the extent to which social control is internalized. And it is by no means clear that those societies which show a more internalized orientation are always those which are more technologically advanced. Whatever the sources of a society's generalized orientation to its environment, the orientation must be culturally transmitted through socialization if it is to have any effect on the child's orientation toward the control of its conduct. Whiting's findings suggest that the transmission may be mediated in part through the effects of familial structure and interaction on the variety and intensity of the attachments between the child and its socializing agents.

BIBLIOGRAPHY

Abel, Theodora M. Moral judgments among subnormals. *Journal of Abnormal and Social Psychology*, 1941, **36**, 378–392.

Abelson, R. P., and Lesser, G. S. A developmental theory of persuasibility. In C. I. Hovland and I. L. Janis (Eds.), *Personality and persuasibility*. New Haven: Yale University Press, 1959. Pp. 167–186.

Ader, R., and Tatum, R. Free-operant avoidance conditioning in individual and paired human subjects. *Journal of the Experimental Analysis of Behavior*, 1963, **6**, 357–359.

Adler, H. E. Some factors of observational learning in cats. *Journal of Genetic Psychology*, 1955, **86**, 159–177.

Adorno, T. W., Frenkel-Brunswik, Else, Levinson, D. J., and Sanford, R. N. *et al. The authoritarian personality*. New York: Harper, 1950.

Akhtar, M. Increased resistance to punishment as a function of counterconditioning. *Journal of Comparative and Physiological Psychology*, 1967, **64**, 268–272.

Allen, V. L., and Crutchfield, R. S. Generalization of experimentally induced conformity. *Journal of Abnormal and Social Psychology*, 1963, **67**, 326–333.

Allinsmith, Beverly B. Directness with which anger is expressed. In D. R. Miller and G. E. Swanson *et al., Inner conflict and defense*. New York: Holt, 1960. Pp. 315–336.

Allinsmith, W. The learning of moral standards. In D. R. Miller and G. E. Swanson *et al., Inner conflict and defense*. New York: Holt, 1960. Pp. 141–176.

Allport, F. H. *Social psychology*. Boston, Massachusetts: Houghton-Mifflin, 1924.

Allport, G. W. The historical background of modern social psychology. In G. Lindzey (Ed.), *Handbook of social psychology*. Volume I. *Theory and method*. Cambridge, Massachusetts: Addison-Wesley, 1954. Pp. 3–56.

Ambrose, J. A. The development of the smiling response in early infancy. In B. M. Foss (Ed.), *Determinants of infant behaviour*. Volume I. London: Methuen, 1961. Pp. 179–196.

Amsel, A. Frustrative nonreward in partial reinforcement and discrimination learning: Some recent history and a theoretical extension. *Psychological Review*, 1962, **69**, 306–328.

Amsel, A., and Ward, J. S. Frustration and persistence: Resistance to discrimination following prior experience with the discriminanda. *Psychological Monographs*, 1965, **79**, No. 4 (Whole No. 597).

Angermeier, W. R., Schaul, L. T., and James, W. T. Social conditioning in rats. *Journal of Comparative and Physiological Psychology*, 1959, **52**, 370–372.

Argyle, M. Social pressure in public and private situations. *Journal of Abnormal and Social Psychology*, 1957, **54**, 172–175.

Aronfreed, J. Moral behavior and sex identity. In D. R. Miller and G. E. Swanson *et al., Inner conflict and defense*. New York: Holt, 1960. Pp. 177–193.

Aronfreed, J. The nature, variety, and social patterning of moral responses to transgression. *Journal of Abnormal and Social Psychology*, 1961, **63**, 223–240.

Aronfreed, J. The effects of experimental socialization paradigms upon two moral responses to transgression. *Journal of Abnormal and Social Psychology*, 1963, **66**, 437–448.

Aronfreed, J. The origin of self-criticism. *Psychological Review,* 1964, **71,** 193–218.

Aronfreed, J. The internalization of social control through punishment: Experimental studies of the role of conditioning and the second signal system in the development of conscience. *Proceedings of the Eighteenth International Congress of Psychology, Moscow, 1966.*

Aronfreed, J. The concept of internalization. In D. A. Goslin (Ed.), *Handbook of socialization theory and research.* Chicago: Rand-McNally, 1968, in press.

Aronfreed, J. The problem of imitation. In L. P. Lipsitt and H. W. Reese (Eds.), *Advances in child development and behavior.* Volume IV. New York: Academic Press, 1969, in press.

Aronfreed, J., Cutick, R. A., and Fagen, S. A. Cognitive structure, punishment, and nurturance in the experimental induction of self-criticism. *Child Development,* 1963, **34,** 281–294.

Aronfreed, J., and Leff, R. The effects of intensity of punishment and complexity of discrimination upon the learning of internalized suppression. Unpublished manuscript, University of Pennsylvania, 1963.

Aronfreed, J., and Paskal, Vivian. Altruism, empathy, and the conditioning of positive affect. Unpublished manuscript, University of Pennsylvania, 1965.

Aronfreed, J., and Paskal, Vivian. The development of sympathetic behavior in children: An experimental test of a two-phase hypothesis. Unpublished manuscript, University of Pennsylvania, 1966.

Aronfreed, J., and Reber, A. Internalized behavioral suppression and the timing of social punishment. *Journal of Personality and Social Psychology,* 1965, **1,** 3–16.

Aronson, E. The psychology of insufficient justification: An analysis of some conflicting data. In S. Feldman (Ed.), *Cognitive consistency: Motivational antecedents and behavioral consequents.* New York: Academic Press, 1966. Pp. 109–133.

Aronson, E., and Carlsmith, J. M. Effect of the severity of threat on the devaluation of forbidden behavior. *Journal of Abnormal and Social Psychology,* 1963, **66,** 584–588.

Aronson, E., and Mills, J. The effect of severity of initiation on liking for a group. *Journal of Abnormal and Social Psychology,* 1959, **59,** 177–181.

Asch, S. E. *Social psychology.* Englewood Cliffs, New Jersey: Prentice-Hall, 1952.

Asch, S. E. Studies of independence and conformity: I. A minority of one against a unanimous majority. *Psychological Monographs,* 1956, **70,** No. 9 (Whole No. 416).

Ausubel, D. P. Relationships between shame and guilt in the socializing process. *Psychological Review,* 1955, **62,** 378–390.

Ayer, A. J. *Language, truth, and logic.* (Second Edition) New York: Dover Publications, 1935.

Azrin, N. H. Some effects of two intermittent schedules of immediate and non-immediate punishment. *Journal of Psychology,* 1956, **42,** 3–21.

Azrin, N. H., and Holz, W. C. Punishment. In W. K. Honig (Ed.), *Operant behavior: Areas of research and application.* New York: Appleton-Century-Crofts, 1966. Pp. 380–447.

Azrin, N. H., and Lindsley, O. R. The reinforcement of cooperation between children. *Journal of Abnormal and Social Psychology,* 1956, **52,** 100–102.

Bach, G. R. Young children's play fantasies. *Psychological Monographs,* 1945, **59,** No. 2 (Whole No. 272).

Bacon, Margaret K., Child, I. L., and Barry, H. III. A cross-cultural study of some correlates of crime. *Journal of Abnormal and Social Psychology,* 1963, **66,** 291–300.

Badia, P., McBane, Bonnie, Suter, S., and Lewis, P. Preference behavior in an immediate versus variably delayed shock situation with and without a warning signal. *Journal of Experimental Psychology,* 1966, **72,** 847–852.

Baer, D. M. Escape and avoidance response of preschool children to two schedules of reinforcement withdrawal. *Journal of the Experimental Analysis of Behavior,* 1960, **3,** 155–159.

Baer, D. M. Effect of withdrawal of positive reinforcement on an extinguishing response in young children. *Child Development,* 1961, **32,** 67–74.

Baer, D. M., Peterson, R. F., and Sherman, J. A. Building an imitative repertoire by programming similarity between child and model as discriminative for reinforcement. *Journal of the Experimental Analysis of Behavior,* 1967, **10,** 405–416.

Baer, D. M., and Sherman, J. A. Reinforcement control of generalized imitation in young children. *Journal of Experimental Child Psychology,* 1964, **1,** 37–49.

Baldwin, J. M. *Mental development in the child and in the race.* New York: Macmillan, 1895.

Baldwin, J. M. *Social and ethical interpretations in mental development.* (Fourth Edition) New York: Macmillan, 1906.

Bandura, A. Social learning through imitation. In M. R. Jones (Ed.), *Nebraska symposium on motivation.* Volume X. Lincoln, Nebraska: University of Nebraska Press, 1962. Pp. 211–269.

Bandura, A. Influence of models' reinforcement contingencies on the acquisition of imitative responses. *Journal of Personality and Social Psychology,* 1965, **1,** 589–595. (a)

Bandura, A. Vicarious processes: A case of no-trial learning. In L. Berkowitz (Ed.), *Advances in experimental social psychology.* Volume II. New York: Academic Press, 1965. Pp. 1–55. (b)

Bandura, A., Grusec, Joan E., and Menlove, Frances L. Observational learning as a function of symbolization and incentive set. *Child Development,* 1966, **37,** 499–506.

Bandura, A., Grusec, Joan E., and Menlove, Frances L. Vicarious extinction of avoidance behavior. *Journal of Personality and Social Psychology,* 1967, **5,** 16–23. (a)

Bandura, A., Grusec, Joan E., and Menlove, Frances L. Some social determinants of self-monitoring reinforcement systems. *Journal of Personality and Social Psychology,* 1967, **5,** 449–455. (b)

Bandura, A., and Harris, Mary B. Modification of syntactic style. *Journal of Experimental Child Psychology,* 1966, **4,** 341–352.

Bandura, A., and Huston, Aletha C. Identification as a process of incidental learning. *Journal of Abnormal and Social Psychology,* 1961, **63,** 311–318.

Bandura, A., and Kupers, Carol J. The transmission of patterns of self-reinforcement through modeling. *Journal of Abnormal and Social Psychology,* 1964, **69,** 1–9.

Bandura, A., and McDonald, F. J. The influence of social reinforcement and the behavior of models in shaping children's moral judgments. *Journal of Abnormal and Social Psychology,* 1963, **67,** 274–281.

Bandura, A., and Mischel, W. Modification of self-imposed delay of reward through exposure to live and symbolic models. *Journal of Personality and Social Psychology,* 1965, **2,** 698–705.

Bandura, A., and Perloff, B. Relative efficacy of self-monitored and externally imposed reinforcement systems. *Journal of Personality and Social Psychology,* 1967, **7,** 111–116.

Bandura, A., and Rosenthal, T. L. Vicarious classical conditioning as a function of arousal level. *Journal of Personality and Social Psychology*, 1966, **3**, 54–62.

Bandura, A., Ross, Dorothea, and Ross, Sheila A. Transmission of aggression through imitation of aggressive models. *Journal of Abnormal and Social Psychology*, 1961, **63**, 575–582.

Bandura, A., Ross, Dorothea, and Ross, Sheila A. Imitation of film-mediated aggressive models. *Journal of Abnormal and Social Psychology*, 1963, **66**, 3–11. (a)

Bandura, A., Ross, Dorothea, and Ross, Sheila A. A comparative test of the status envy, social power, and secondary reinforcement theories of identificatory learning. *Journal of Abnormal and Social Psychology*, 1963, **67**, 527–534. (b)

Bandura, A., Ross, Dorothea, and Ross, Sheila A. Vicarious reinforcement and imitative learning. *Journal of Abnormal and Social Psychology*, 1963, **67**, 601–607. (c)

Bandura, A., and Walters, R. H. *Adolescent aggression*. New York: Ronald Press, 1959.

Bandura, A., and Walters, R. H. *Social learning and personality development*. New York: Holt, Rinehart, and Winston, 1963. (a)

Bandura, A., and Walters, R. H. Aggression. In H. W. Stevenson (Ed.), *Yearbook of the National Society for the Study of Education*. Part I. *Child Psychology*. Chicago: University of Chicago Press, 1963. Pp. 364–415. (b)

Bandura, A., and Whalen, Carol K. The influence of antecedent reinforcement and divergent modeling cues on patterns of self-reward. *Journal of Personality and Social Psychology*, 1966, **3**, 373–382.

Banks, R. K. Effect of pairing a stimulus with presentations of the UCS on the extinction of an avoidance response in humans. *Journal of Experimental Psychology*, 1965, **70**, 294–299.

Banks, R. K. Persistence to continuous punishment following intermittent punishment training. *Journal of Experimental Psychology*, 1966, **71**, 373–377.

Banks, R. K. Intermittent punishment effect (IPE) sustained through changed stimulus conditions and through blocks of nonpunished trials. *Journal of Experimental Psychology*, 1967, **73**, 456–460.

Banks, R. K., and Vogel-Sprott, M. Effect of delayed punishment on an immediately rewarded response in humans. *Journal of Experimental Psychology*, 1965, **70**, 357–359.

Barbu, Z. Studies in children's honesty. *Quarterly Bulletin of the British Psychological Society*, 1951, **2**, 53–57.

Baron, A. Delayed punishment of a runway response. *Journal of Comparative and Physiological Psychology*, 1965, **60**, 131–134.

Barry, H., III, Bacon, Margaret K., and Child, I. L. A cross-cultural survey of some sex differences in socialization. *Journal of Abnormal and Social Psychology*, 1957, **55**, 327–333.

Bayer, E. Beiträge zur Zwei Komponententheorie des Hungers (Contributions to a two component theory of hunger.) *Zeitschrift für Psychologie*, 1929, **112**, 1–54.

Bayroff, A. G., and Lard, Katherine E. Experimental social behavior of animals. III. Imitational learning of white rats. *Journal of Comparative Psychology*, 1944, **37**, 165–171.

Becker, W. C., Peterson, D. R., Luria, Zella, Shoemaker, D. J., and Hellmer, L. A. Relations of factors derived from parent-interview ratings to behavior problems of five-year-olds. *Child Development*, 1962, **33**, 509–535.

Bee, Helen L., and Colle, H. A. The origin of standards of excellence: Modeling vs. direct reinforcement. Paper presented at the meeting of the Society for Research in Child Development, New York, March, 1967.

Belanger, R. M., and Sattler, J. M. Motive to achieve success and motive to avoid failure as a capacity to tolerate uncertainty in a pain-producing situation. *Journal of Experimental Research in Personality*, 1967, **2**, 154–159.

Bem, D. J. An experimental analysis of self-persuasion. *Journal of Experimental Social Psychology*, 1965, **1**, 199–218.

Benedict, Ruth. *The chrysanthemum and the sword*. Boston: Houghton-Mifflin, 1946.

Berg, I. A., and Bass, B. M. (Eds.) *Conformity and deviation*. New York: Harper, 1961.

Berger, S. M. Conditioning through vicarious instigation. *Psychological Review*, 1962, **69**, 450–466.

Berger, S. M. Observer practice and learning during exposure to a model. *Journal of Personality and Social Psychology*, 1966, **3**, 696–701.

Berges, J., and Lezine, I. *Test d'imitation de gestes: Techniques d'exploration du schema corporel et des praxies chez l'enfant de 3 à 6 ans* (Test of imitation of gestures: Methods for plotting body image and movements from 3 to 6 years). Paris: Masson et Cie, 1963.

Beritov, J. S. *Neural mechanisms of higher vertebrate behavior*. Boston: Little, Brown, and Company, 1964.

Berkowitz, L. *Aggression: A social psychological analysis*. New York: McGraw-Hill, 1962.

Berkowitz, L. Some aspects of observed aggression. *Journal of Personality and Social Psychology*, 1965, **2**, 359–369.

Berkowitz, L., and Daniels, Louise R. Affecting the salience of the social responsibility norm: Effects of past help on the response to dependency relationships. *Journal of Abnormal and Social Psychology*, 1964, **68**, 275–281.

Berkowitz, L., and Friedman, P. Some social class differences in helping behavior. *Journal of Personality and Social Psychology*, 1967, **5**, 217–225.

Berkowitz, L., and Geen, R. G. Film violence and the cue properties of available targets. *Journal of Personality and Social Psychology*, 1966, **3**, 525–530.

Berkowitz, L., and Geen, R. G. Stimulus qualities of the target of aggression: A further study. *Journal of Personality and Social Psychology*, 1967, **5**, 364–368.

Berlyne, D. E. *Conflict, arousal, and curiosity*. New York: McGraw-Hill, 1960.

Berlyne, D. E. *Structure and direction in thinking*. New York: Wiley, 1965.

Berscheid, Ellen, and Walster, Elaine. When does a harm-doer compensate a victim? *Journal of Personality and Social Psychology*, 1967, **6**, 435–441.

Bettelheim, B. Individual and mass behavior in extreme situations. *Journal of Abnormal and Social Psychology*, 1943, **38**, 417–452.

Bijou, S. W. Experimental studies of child behavior: Normal and deviant. In L. Krasner and L. P. Ullman (Eds.), *Research in behavior modification: New developments and implications*. New York: Holt, Rinehart, and Winston, 1965. Pp. 36–81.

Bijou, S. W., and Baer, D. M. Operant methods in child behavior and development. In W. K. Honig (Ed.), *Operant behavior: Areas of research and application*. New York: Appleton-Century-Crofts, 1966. Pp. 718–789.

Birch, D. Verbal control of nonverbal behavior. *Journal of Experimental Child Psychology*, 1966, **4**, 266–275.

Bixenstine, V. E. Secondary drive as a neutralizer of time in integrative problem-solving. *Journal of Comparative and Physiological Psychology*, 1956, **49**, 161–166.

Black, A. H. The extinction of avoidance responses under curare. *Journal of Comparative and Physiological Psychology*, 1958, **51**, 519–524.

serial responses to color cues. *Journal of Social Psychology,* 1941, **13,** 259–280.

Crespi, L. P. Quantitative variations of incentive and performance in the white rat. *American Journal of Psychology,* 1942, **55,** 467–517.

Crowley, P. M. Effect of training upon objectivity of moral judgment in grade-school children. *Journal of Personality and Social Psychology,* 1968, **8,** 228–232.

Curlin, Elizabeth R., and Donahue, J. W. Effects of shock intensity and placement on the learning of a food-reinforced brightness discrimination. *Journal of Experimental Psychology,* 1965, **69,** 349–356.

D'Amato, M. R., and Fazzaro, J. Discriminated lever-press avoidance learning as a function of type and intensity of punishment. *Journal of Comparative and Physiological Psychology.* 1966, **61,** 313–315.

D'Amato, M. R., Fazzaro, J., and Etkin, M. Discriminated bar-press avoidance maintenance and extinction in rats as a function of shock intensity. *Journal of Comparative and Physiological Psychology,* 1967, **63,** 351–354.

D'Amato, M. R., and Gumenik, W. E. Some effects of immediate versus randomly delayed shock on an instrumental response and cognitive processes. *Journal of Abnormal and Social Psychology,* 1960, **60,** 64–67.

D'Andrade, R. G. Sex differences and cultural institutions. In Eleanor E. Maccoby (Ed.), *The development of sex differences.* Stanford, California: Stanford University Press, 1966. Pp. 174–204.

Daniels, V. Communication, incentive, and structural variables in interpersonal exchange and negotiation. *Journal of Experimental Social Psychology,* 1967, **3,** 47–74.

Darby, C. L., and Riopelle, A. J. Observational learning in the rhesus monkey. *Journal of Comparative and Physiological Psychology,* 1959, **52,** 94–98.

Darlington, R. B., and Macker, C. E. Displacement of guilt-produced altruistic behavior. *Journal of Personality and Social Psychology.* 1966, **4,** 442–443.

Darwin, C. *The descent of man and selection in relation to sex.* London: J. Murray, 1871.

Dashiell, J. F. Experimental studies of the influence of social situations on the behavior of individual human adults. In C. C. Murchison (Ed.), *Handbook of social psychology.* Worcester, Massachusetts: Clark University Press, 1935. Pp. 1097–1158.

Davis, A. H., and Havighurst, R. J. Social class and color differences in child-rearing. *American Sociological Review,* 1946, **11,** 698–710.

Davitz, J. R., and Mason, D. J. Socially facilitated reduction of a fear response in rats. *Journal of Comparative and Physiological Psychology,* 1955, **48,** 149–151.

deCharms, R., and Rosenbaum, M. E. Status variables and matching behavior. *Journal of Personality,* 1960, **28,** 492–502.

deLorge, J. Fixed-interval behavior maintained by conditioned reinforcement. *Journal of the Experimental Analysis of Behavior,* 1967, **10,** 271–276.

Denenberg, V. H., and Bell, R. Critical periods for the effects of infantile experience on adult learning. *Science,* 1960, **131,** 227–228.

Denenberg, V. H., Hudgens, G. A., and Zarrow, M. X. Mice reared with rats: Modification of behavior by early experience with another species. *Science,* 1964, **143,** 380–381.

DeNike, L. D. The temporal relationship between awareness and performance in verbal conditioning. *Journal of Experimental Psychology,* 1964, **68,** 521–529.

Dennis, W. Animism and related tendencies in Hopi children. *Journal of Abnormal and Social Psychology,* 1943, **38,** 21–36.

Desiderato, O. Generalization of conditioned suppression. *Journal of Comparative and Physiological Psychology,* 1964, **57,** 434–437.

Deutsch, J. A., and Howarth, C. J. Some tests of a theory of intracranial self-stimulation. *Psychological Review,* 1963, **70,** 444–460.

Deutsch, M., and Gerard, H. B. A study of normative and informational social influences upon individual judgment. *Journal of Abnormal and Social Psychology,* 1955, **51,** 629–636.

Deutsch, M., and Krauss, R. M. The effect of threat upon interpersonal bargaining. *Journal of Abnormal and Social Psychology,* 1960, **61,** 181–189.

DeVore, I. (Ed.) *Primate behavior: Field studies of monkeys and apes.* New York: Holt, Rinehart, and Winston, 1965.

De Vos, G. The relation of guilt toward parents to achievement and arranged marriage among the Japanese. *Psychiatry,* 1960, **23,** 287–301.

DiLollo, V., and Berger, S. M. Effects of apparent pain in others on observer's reaction time. *Journal of Personality and Social Psychology,* 1965, **2,** 573–575.

Dinsmoor, J. A., and Clayton, Marilyn H. A conditioned reinforcer maintained by temporal association with the termination of shock. *Journal of the Experimental Analysis of Behavior,* 1966, **9,** 547–552.

Ditrichs, R., Simon, S., and Greene, B. Effect of vicarious scheduling on the verbal conditioning of hostility in children. *Journal of Personality and Social Psychology,* 1967, **6,** 71–78.

Doland, D. J., and Adelberg, Kathryn. The learning of sharing behavior. *Child Development,* 1967, **38,** 695–700.

Dollard, J., Doob, L. W., Miller, N. E., Mowrer, O. H., and Sears, R. R. *Frustration and aggression.* New Haven: Yale University Press, 1939.

Dollard, J., and Miller, N. E. *Personality and psychotherapy: An analysis in terms of learning, thinking, and culture.* New York: McGraw-Hill, 1950.

Donin, Janet A., Surridge, C. T., and Amsel, A. Extinction following partial delay of reward with immediate continuous reward interpolated, at 24-hour intertrial intervals. *Journal of Experimental Psychology,* 1967, **74,** 50-53.

Dornbush, Rhea L., and Winnick, Wilma A. Short-term intentional and incidental learning. *Journal of Experimental Psychology,* 1967, **73,** 608–611.

Douvan, Elizabeth. Social status and success strivings. *Journal of Abnormal and Social Psychology,* 1956, **52,** 219–223.

Douvan, Elizabeth, and Adelson, J. *The adolescent experience.* New York: Wiley, 1966.

Dulany, D. E. The place of hypotheses and intentions: An analysis of verbal control in verbal conditioning. In C. W. Eriksen (Ed.), *Behavior and awareness.* Durham, North Carolina: Duke University Press, 1962. Pp. 102–129.

Duncker, K. Experimental modification of children's food preferences through social suggestion. *Journal of Abnormal and Social Psychology,* 1938, **33,** 489–507.

Durkheim, E. *Suicide.* Glencoe, Illinois: Free Press, 1951.

Durkin, Dolores. Children's concepts of justice: A comparison with the Piaget data. *Child Development,* 1959, **30,** 59–67. (a)

Durkin, Dolores. Children's acceptance of reciprocity as a justice principle. *Child Development,* 1959, **30,** 289–297. (b)

Durkin, Dolores. Children's concepts of justice: A further comparison with the Piaget data. *Journal of Educational Research,* 1959, **52,** 252–257. (c)

Durkin, Dolores. The specificity of children's moral judgments. *Journal of Genetic Psychology,* 1961, **98,** 3–13.

Easterbrook, J. A. The effect of emotion on cue utilization and the organization of behavior. *Psychological Review,* 1959, **66,** 183–201.

Egger, M. D., and Miller, N. E. Secondary reinforcement in rats as a function of information value and reliability of the stimulus. *Journal of Experimental Psychology*, 1962, **64**, 97–104.

Elkin, D. G. On conditioned reflexes to complex verbal stimuli in school children. In B. G. Anan'yev, A. N. Leontiev, A. R. Luria, N. A. Menuinshkaia, C. L. Rubinstein, A. A. Smirnov, M. V. Sokolov, and B. M. Teplov (Eds.), *Materials of the conference on psychology.* Moscow: Akad. Pedag. Nauk RSFSR, 1957. Pp. 370–379.

Elkonin, D. B. The physiology of higher nervous activity and child psychology. In B. Simon (Ed.), *Psychology in the Soviet Union.* London: Routledge and Kegan Paul, 1957. Pp. 47–68.

Endler, N. S. Conformity as a function of different reinforcement schedules. *Journal of Personality and Social Psychology*, 1966, **4**, 175–180.

Endsley, R. C. Effortfulness and blocking at different distances from the goal as determinants of response speed and amplitude. *Journal of Experimental Child Psychology*, 1966, **3**, 18–30.

Epstein, R. Aggression toward outgroups as a function of authoritarianism and imitation of aggressive models. *Journal of Personality and Social Psychology*, 1966, **3**, 574–579.

Eriksen, C. W. Discrimination and learning without awareness: A methodological survey and evaluation. *Psychological Review*, 1960, **67**, 279–300.

Erikson, E. H. *Childhood and society.* New York: Norton, 1950.

Eron, L. D., Walder, L. O., Toigo, R., and Lefkowitz, M. M. Social class, parental punishment for aggression, and child aggression. *Child Development*, 1963, **34**, 849–867.

Escalona, Sibylle K. Feeding disturbances in children. *American Journal of Orthopsychiatry*, 1945, **15**, 76–80.

Estes, W. K. An experimental study of punishment. *Psychological Monographs*, 1944, **57**, No. 3 (Whole No. 263).

Estes, W. K. Discriminative conditioning. II. Effects of a Pavlovian conditioned stimulus upon a subsequently established operant response. *Journal of Experimental Psychology*, 1948, **38**, 173–177.

Estes, W. K., and Skinner, B. F. Some quantitative properties of anxiety. *Journal of Experimental Psychology*, 1941, **29**, 390–400.

Etzel, Barbara C., and Gewirtz, J. L. Experimental modification of caretaker-maintained high-rate operant crying in a 6- and a 20-week-old infant (infans tyrannotearus): Extinction of crying with reinforcement of eye contact and smiling. *Journal of Experimental Child Psychology*, 1967, **5**, 303–317.

Fagan, J. F., III, and Witryol, S. L. The effects of instructional set and delay of reward on children's learning in a simultaneous discrimination task. *Child Development*, 1966, **37**, 433–438.

Fantino, E. Immediate reward followed by extinction vs. later reward without extinction. *Psychonomic Science*, 1966, **6**, 233–234.

Farber, I. E. Response fixation under anxiety and non-anxiety conditions. *Journal of Experimental Psychology*, 1948, **38**, 111–131.

Ferraro, D. P. Persistence to continuous punishment as a function of amount of reinforcement. *Psychonomic Science*, 1966, **6**, 109–110.

Ferster, C. B. Sustained behavior under delayed reinforcement. *Journal of Experimental Psychology*, 1953, **45**, 218–224.

Ferster, C. B. Withdrawal of positive reinforcement as punishment. *Science*, 1957, **126**, 509.

Ferster, C. B. Control of behavior in chimpanzees and pigeons by time-out from positive reinforcement. *Psychological Monographs,* 1958, **72**, No. 8 (Whole No. 461).

Ferster, C. B., and Appel, J. B. Punishment of S^Δ responding in matching-to-sample by time-out from positive reinforcement. *Journal of the Experimental Analysis of Behavior,* 1961, **4**, 45–56.

Ferster, C. B., and Hammer, C. Variables determining the effects of delay in reinforcement. *Journal of the Experimental Analysis of Behavior,* 1965, **8**, 243–254.

Ferster, C. B., and Skinner, B. F. *Schedules of reinforcement.* New York: Appleton-Century-Crofts, 1957.

Feshbach, S. The stimulating versus cathartic effects of a vicarious aggressive activity. *Journal of Abnormal and Social Psychology,* 1961, **63**, 381–385.

Festinger, L. *A theory of cognitive dissonance.* Stanford, California: Stanford University Press, 1957.

Festinger, L. *et al. Conflict, decision, and dissonance.* Stanford, California: Stanford University Press, 1964.

Festinger, L., and Carlsmith, J. M. Cognitive consequences of forced compliance. *Journal of Abnormal and Social Psychology,* 1959, **58**, 203–210.

Festinger, L., and Freedman, J. L. Dissonance reduction and moral values. In P. Worchel and D. Byrne (Eds.), *Personality change.* New York: Wiley, 1964. Pp. 220–247.

Festinger, L., Pepitone, A., and Newcomb, T. M. Some consequences of deindividuation in a group. *Journal of Abnormal and Social Psychology,* 1952, **47**, 382–389.

Fischer, W. F. Sharing in preschool children as a function of amount and type of reinforcement. *Genetic Psychology Monographs,* 1963, **68**, 215–245.

Fort, Jane G. Discrimination based on secondary reinforcement. *Child Development,* 1965, **36**, 481–490.

Foss, B. M. (Ed.) *Determinants of infant behaviour.* Volume II. London: Methuen, 1963.

Fowler, H., and Wischner, G. J. Discrimination performance as affected by problem difficulty and shock for either the correct or incorrect response. *Journal of Experimental Psychology,* 1965, **69**, 413–418.

Fox, R. E., and King, R. A. The effects of reinforcement scheduling on the strength of a secondary reinforcer. *Journal of Comparative and Physiological Psychology,* 1961, **54**, 266–269.

Freedman, D. G. Constitutional and environmental interactions in rearing of four breeds of dogs. *Science,* 1958, **127**, 585–586.

Freedman, J. L. Long term behavioral effects of cognitive dissonance. *Journal of Experimental Social Psychology,* 1965, **1**, 145–155.

Freedman, J. L., Wallington, Sue A., and Bless, E. Compliance and pressure: The effect of guilt. *Journal of Personality and Social Psychology,* 1967, **7**, 117–124.

French, J. R. P., Morrison, H. W., and Levinger, G. Coercive power and forces affecting conformity. *Journal of Abnormal and Social Psychology,* 1960, **61**, 93–101.

Freud, Anna, and Dann, Sophie. An experiment in group upbringing. In *The psychoanalytic study of the child.* Volume VI. New York: International Universities Press, 1951. Pp. 127–168.

Freud, S. *The ego and the id.* London: Hogarth, 1927.

Freud, S. *New introductory lectures in psychoanalysis.* New York: Norton, 1933.

Freud, S. *The problem of anxiety.* New York: Norton, 1936.

Friedrichs, R. W. Alter versus ego: An exploratory assessment of altruism. *American Sociological Review,* 1960, **25**, 496–508.

Gerard, H. B. Conformity and commitment to the group. *Journal of Abnormal and Social Psychology*, 1964, **68**, 209–211.

Gerard, H. B. Compliance, expectation of reward, and opinion change. *Journal of Personality and Social Psychology*, 1967, **6**, 360–364.

Gesell, A. *et al*. *The first five years of life*. New York: Harper, 1940.

Gewirtz, J. L. A learning analysis of the effects of normal stimulation, privation, and deprivation on the acquisition of social motivation and reinforcement. In B. M. Foss (Ed.), *Determinants of infant behaviour*. Volume I. London: Methuen, 1961. Pp. 213–290.

Gewirtz, J. L. The course of infant smiling in four child-rearing environments in Israel. In B. M. Foss (Ed.), *Determinants of infant behaviour*. Volume III. London: Methuen, 1965. Pp. 205–248.

Gewirtz, J. L., and Baer, D. M. The effect of brief social deprivation on behaviors for a social reinforcer. *Journal of Abnormal and Social Psychology*, 1958, **56**, 49–56. (a)

Gewirtz, J. L., and Baer, D. M. Deprivation and satiation of social reinforcers as drive conditions. *Journal of Abnormal and Social Psychology*, 1958, **57**, 165–172. (b)

Gibbon, J. Discriminated punishment: Avoidable and unavoidable shock. *Journal of the Experimental Analysis of Behavior*, 1967, **10**, 451–460.

Glass, D. C. Changes in liking as a means of reducing cognitive discrepancies between self-esteem and aggression. *Journal of Personality*, 1964, **32**, 531–549.

Gleitman, H., and Steinman, Fredda. Depression effect as a function of retention interval before and after shift in reward magnitude. *Journal of Comparative and Physiological Psychology*, 1964, **57**, 158–160.

Glickman, S. E., and Schiff, B. B. A biological theory of reinforcement. *Psychological Review*, 1967, **74**, 81–109.

Glueck, S., and Glueck, Eleanor. *Unravelling juvenile delinquency*. New York: Commonwealth Fund, 1950.

Gold, M. Suicide, homicide, and the socialization of aggression. *American Journal of Sociology*, 1958, **63**, 651–661.

Goldfarb, W. Psychological privation in infancy and subsequent adjustment. *American Journal of Orthopsychiatry*, 1945, **15**, 247–255.

Goodall, Jane. Chimpanzees of the Gomba Stream Reserve. In I. DeVore (Ed.), *Primate behavior: Field studies of monkeys and apes*. New York: Holt, Rinehart, and Winston, 1965. Pp. 425–473.

Goodson, F., and Brownstein, A. Secondary reinforcing and motivating properties of stimuli contiguous with shock onset and termination. *Journal of Comparative and Physiological Psychology*, 1955, **48**, 381–386.

Goranson, R. E., and Berkowitz, L. Reciprocity and responsibility reactions to prior help. *Journal of Personality and Social Psychology*, 1966, **3**, 227–232.

Gottschaldt, K., and Frühauf-Ziegler, Christiane. Über die Entwicklung der Zusammenarbeit im Kleinkindalter (On the development of cooperative behavior in young children). *Zeitschrift für Psychologie*, 1958, **162**, 254–278.

Gouldner, A. W. The norm of reciprocity: A preliminary statement. *American Sociological Review*, 1960, **25**, 161–178.

Greene, W. A. Operant conditioning of the GSR using partial reinforcement. *Psychological Reports*, 1966, **19**, 571–578.

Greenspoon, J. The reinforcing effect of two spoken sounds on the frequency of two responses. *American Journal of Psychology*, 1955, **68**, 409–416.

Grim, P. F., Kohlberg, L., and White, S. H. Some relationships between conscience and attentional processes. *Journal of Personality and Social Psychology,* 1968, **68,** 239–252.

Grinder, R. E. Parental child rearing practices, conscience, and resistance to temptation of sixth-grade children. *Child Development,* 1962, **33,** 803–820.

Grinder, R. E. Relations between behavioral and cognitive dimensions of conscience in middle childhood. *Child Development,* 1964, **35,** 881–891.

Grinder, R. E., and McMichael, R. E. Cultural influence on conscience development: Resistance to temptation and guilt among Samoans and American Caucasians. *Journal of Abnormal and Social Psychology,* 1963, **66,** 503–507.

Grings, W. W. Verbal-perceptual factors in the conditioning of autonomic responses. In W. F. Prokasy (Ed.), *Classical conditioning: A symposium.* New York: Appleton-Century-Crofts, 1965. Pp. 71–89.

Grossman, S. P., and Grossman, Lore. Effects of chemical stimulation of the midbrain reticular formation on appetitive behavior. *Journal of Comparative and Physiological Psychology,* 1966, **61,** 333–338.

Grusec, Joan. Some antecedents of self-criticism. *Journal of Personality and Social Psychology,* 1966, **4,** 244–252.

Grusec, Joan, and Mischel, W. Model's characteristics as determinants of social learning. *Journal of Personality and Social Psychology,* 1966, **4,** 211–215.

Gwinn, G. T. The effects of punishment on acts motivated by fear. *Journal of Experimental Psychology,* 1949, **39,** 260–269.

Hagen, J. W., and Sabo, Ruth A. A developmental study of selective attention. *Merrill-Palmer Quarterly,* 1967, **13,** 159–172.

Hake, D. F., and Azrin, N. H. Conditioned punishment. *Journal of the Experimental Analysis of Behavior,* 1965, **8,** 279–293.

Hake, D. F., Azrin, N. H., and Oxford, Rebecca. The effects of punishment intensity on squirrel monkeys. *Journal of the Experimental Analysis of Behavior,* 1967, **10,** 95–107.

Hake, D. F., and Laws, D. R. Social facilitation of responses during a stimulus paired with electric shock. *Journal of the Experimental Analysis of Behavior,* 1967, **10,** 387–392.

Hall, G. F. Association of neutral objects with rewards: Persistence of effect upon verbal evaluation. *Journal of Verbal Learning and Verbal Behavior,* 1967, **6,** 291–294.

Hall, Julia C. Some conditions of anxiety extinction. *Journal of Abnormal and Social Psychology,* 1955, **51,** 126–132.

Hall, K. R. L. Observational learning in monkeys and apes. *British Journal of Psychology,* 1963, **54,** 201–226.

Hallowell, A. I. The social function of anxiety in a primitive society. In D. G. Haring (Ed.), *Personal character and cultural milieu.* (Second Edition) Syracuse, New York: Syracuse University Press, 1949. Pp. 375–388.

Hamilton, W. D. The genetical evolution of social behavior. I and II. *Journal of Theoretical Biology,* 1964, **7,** 1–16, 17–52.

Handlon, Britomar J., and Gross, Patricia. The development of sharing behavior. *Journal of Abnormal and Social Psychology,* 1959, **59,** 425–428.

Haner, C. F. and Whitney, E. R. Empathic conditioning and its relation to anxiety level. *American Psychologist,* 1960, **15,** 493. (Abstract)

Hanlon, Camille. The effects of social isolation and characteristics of the model on accent imitation in fourth-grade children. Unpublished doctoral dissertation, Stanford University, 1964.

Hare, R. D. Temporal gradient of fear arousal in psychopaths. *Journal of Abnormal Psychology,* 1965, **70,** 442–445.

Hare, R. M. *The language of morals*. London: Oxford University Press, 1952.

Harlow, H. F. Motivation as a factor in the acquisition of new responses. In *Current theory and research in motivation: A symposium*. Lincoln, Nebraska: University of Nebraska Press, 1953. Pp. 24–49.

Harlow, H. F. Learning set and error factor theory. In S. Koch (Ed.), *Psychology: A study of a science*. Volume II. *General systematic formulations, learning, and special processes*. New York: McGraw-Hill, 1959. Pp. 492–537. (a)

Harlow, H. F. Basic social capacity of primates. In J. N. Spuhler (Ed.), *The evolution of man's capacity for culture*. Detroit: Wayne State University Press, 1959. Pp. 40–53. (b)

Harlow, H. F., and Harlow, Margaret K. The affectional systems. In A. M. Schrier, H. F. Harlow, and F. Stollnitz (Eds.), *Behavior of nonhuman primates: Modern research trends*. Volume II. New York: Academic Press, 1965. Pp. 287–334.

Harlow, H. F., and Yudin, H. C. Social behavior of primates. I. Social facilitation of feeding in the monkey and its relation to attitudes of ascendance and submission. *Journal of Comparative Psychology*, 1933, **16**, 171–188.

Harlow, H. F., and Zimmerman, R. R. Affectional responses in the infant monkey. *Science*, 1959, **130**, 421–432.

Harper, F. B. W., Hoving, K., Holm, Gretchen, Sasso, Joanna, and Dubanoski, R. Young children's yielding to false adult judgments. *Child Development*, 1965, **36**, 175–183.

Harrower, Molly R. Social status and the moral development of the child. *British Journal of Educational Psychology*, 1934, **4**, 75–95.

Hartshorne, H., and May M. A. *Studies in the nature of character*. Volume I. *Studies in deceit*. New York: Macmillan, 1928.

Hartshorne, H., May, M. A., and Maller, J. B. *Studies in the nature of character*. Volume II. *Studies in service and self-control*. New York: Macmillan, 1929.

Hartup, W. W. Patterns of imitative behavior in young children. *Child Development*, 1964, **35**, 183–191.

Hartup, W. W., and Coates, B. Imitation of peers as a function of reinforcement from the peer group and rewardingness of the model. *Child Development*, 1967, **38**, 1003–1016.

Hartup, W. W., and Himeno, Y. Social isolation vs. interaction with adults in relation to aggression in preschool children. *Journal of Abnormal and Social Psychology*, 1959, **59**, 17–22.

Hatfield, J. S., Ferguson, Lucy R., and Alpert, R. Mother-child interaction and the socialization process. *Child Development*, 1967, **38**, 365–414.

Havenga, C. F. B. *Die sederlike oordeel van die agt- tot twallfjarige kind* (The moral judgment of children between the ages of eight and twelve years). Pretoria, South Africa: University of Pretoria, 1958.

Havighurst, R. J., and Neugarten, Bernice L. *American Indian and white children*. Chicago: University of Chicago Press, 1955.

Hayes, K. J., and Hayes, Catherine. Imitation in a home-reared chimpanzee. *Journal of Comparative and Physiological Psychology*, 1952, **45**, 450–459.

Hearst, E. Concurrent generalization gradients for food-controlled and shock-controlled behavior. *Journal of the Experimental Analysis of Behavior*, 1962, **5**, 19–31.

Hearst, E. Stress- induced breakdown of an appetitive discrimination. *Journal of the Experimental Analysis of Behavior*, 1965, **8**, 135–146.

Hearst, E. Oscillatory behavior during approach-avoidance conflict. *Journal of the Experimental Analysis of Behavior*, 1967, **10**, 75–84.

Hebb, D. O. *The organization of behavior*. Philadelphia: Saunders, 1949.

Hebb, D. O. The motivating effects of exteroceptive stimulation. *American Psychologist,* 1958, **13,** 109–113.

Hebb, D. O., and Thompson, W. R. The social significance of animal studies. In G. Lindzey (Ed.), *Handbook of social psychology.* Volume I. *Theory and method.* Cambridge, Massachusetts: Addison-Wesley, 1954. Pp. 532–561.

Hefferline, R. F., Keenan, B., and Harford, R. A. Escape and avoidance conditioning in human subjects without their observation of the response. *Science,* 1962, **135,** 1338–1339.

Heider, F. *The psychology of interpersonal relations.* New York: Wiley, 1958.

Heinecke, C. M. Some antecedents and correlates of guilt and fear in young boys. Unpublished doctoral dissertation, Harvard University, 1953.

Henry, A. F., and Short, J. F., Jr. *Suicide and homicide: Some economic, sociological, and psychological aspects of aggression.* Glencoe, Illinois: Free Press, 1954.

Herbert, J. J., and Harsh, C. M. Observational learning by cats. *Journal of Comparative Psychology,* 1944, **37,** 81–95.

Herrnstein, R. J. Superstition: A corollary of the principles of operant conditioning. In W. K. Honig (Ed.), *Operant behavior: Areas of research and application.* New York: Appleton-Century-Crofts, 1966. Pp. 33–51.

Hess, E. H. The relationship between imprinting and motivation. In M. R. Jones (Ed.), *Nebraska symposium on motivation.* Volume VII. Lincoln, Nebraska: University of Nebraska Press, 1959. Pp. 44–77.

Hetherington, E. Mavis. A developmental study of the effects of sex of the dominant parent on sex-role preference, identification, and imitation in children. *Journal of Personality and Social Psychology,* 1965, **2,** 188–194.

Hetherington, E. Mavis, and Frankie, G. Effects of parental dominance, warmth, and conflict on imitation in children. *Journal of Personality and Social Psychology,* 1967, **6,** 119–125.

Hicks, D. J. Imitation and retention of film-mediated aggressive peer and adult models. *Journal of Personality and Social Psychology,* 1965, **2,** 97–100.

Hill, Frances A. Effects of instructions and subject's need for approval on the conditioned galvanic skin response. *Journal of Experimental Psychology,* 1967, **73,** 461–467.

Hill, W. F. Learning theory and the acquisition of values. *Psychological Review,* 1960, **67,** 317–331.

Hockman, C. H., and Lipsitt, L. P. Delay-of-reward gradients in discrimination learning with children for two levels of difficulty. *Journal of Comparative and Physiological Psychology,* 1961, **54,** 24–27.

Hoffman, H. S., and Fleshler, M. Stimulus factors in aversive controls: The generalization of conditioned suppression. *Journal of the Experimental Analysis of Behavior,* 1961, **4,** 371–378.

Hoffman, H. S., and Fleshler, M. Stimulus aspects of aversive controls: The effects of response-contingent shock. *Journal of the Experimental Analysis of Behavior,* 1965, **8,** 89–96.

Hoffman, H. S., Fleshler, M., and Jensen, P. Stimulus aspects of aversive controls: The retention of conditioned suppression. *Journal of the Experimental Analysis of Behavior,* 1963, **6,** 575–583.

Hoffman, H. S., Selekman, W. S., and Fleshler, M. Stimulus aspects of aversive controls: Long term effects of suppression procedures. *Journal of the Experimental Analysis of Behavior,* 1966, **9,** 659–662.

Hoffman, M. L. Power assertion by the parent and its impact on the child. *Child Development,* 1960, **31,** 129–143.

Hoffman, M. L. Child-rearing practices and moral development: Generalizations from empirical research. *Child Development,* 1963, **34,** 295–318.

Hoffman, M. L. *Early processes in moral development.* Chicago: Aldine, 1968, in press.

Hoffman, M. L., and Saltzstein, H. D. Parent discipline and the child's moral development. *Journal of Personality and Social Psychology,* 1967, **5,** 45–57.

Holder, Elaine E. Learning factors in social facilitation and social inhibition in rats. *Journal of Comparative and Physiological Psychology,* 1958, **51,** 60–64.

Holder, W. B., Marx, M. H., Holder, Elaine E., and Collier, G. Response strength as a function of delay of reward in a runway. *Journal of Experimental Psychology,* 1957, **53,** 316–323.

Hollenberg, Eleanor, and Sperry, Margaret. Some antecedents of aggression and effects of frustration in doll play. *Personality: Topical Symposia,* 1951, **1,** 32–43.

Holmes, S. J. The reproductive beginnings of altruism. *Psychological Review,* 1945, **52,** 109–112.

Holt, E. B. *Animal drive and the learning process.* Volume I. New York: Holt, 1931.

Holz, W. C., and Azrin, N. H. Interactions between the discriminative and aversive properties of punishment. *Journal of the Experimental Analysis of Behavior,* 1962, **5,** 229–236.

Holz, W. C., and Azrin, N. H. A comparison of several procedures for eliminating behavior. *Journal of the Experimental Analysis of Behavior,* 1963, **6,** 399–406.

Holz, W. C., Azrin, N. H., and Ayllon, T. Elimination of behavior of mental patients by response-produced extinction. *Journal of the Experimental Analysis of Behavior,* 1963, **6,** 407–412.

Homans, G. C. *Social behavior: Its elementary forms.* New York: Harcourt, Brace, and World, 1961.

Honig, W. K. (Ed.) *Operant behavior: Areas of research and application.* New York: Appleton-Century-Crofts, 1966.

Horel, J. A., Treichler, F. R., and Meyer, D. R. Coercive behavior in the rhesus monkey. *Journal of Comparative and Physiological Psychology,* 1963, **56,** 208–210.

Humphrey, G. Imitation and the conditioned reflex. *Pedagogical Seminary,* 1921, **28,** 1–21.

Humphrey, G. The conditioned reflex and the elementary social reaction. *Journal of Abnormal and Social Psychology,* 1922, **17,** 113–119.

Hunt, J. McV. Intrinsic motivation and its role in psychological development. In D. Levine (Ed.), *Nebraska symposium on motivation.* Volume XIII. Lincoln, Nebraska: University of Nebraska Press, 1965. Pp. 189–282.

Hyman, H. H. The value systems of different classes: A social psychological contribution to the analysis of stratification. In R. Bendix and S. M. Lipset (Ed.), *Class, status, and power: A reader in social stratification.* Glencoe, Illinois: Free Press, 1953. Pp. 426–442.

Imanishi, K. Social behavior in Japanese monkeys, *Macaca fuscata. Psychologia,* 1957, **1,** 47–54.

Inhelder, Bärbel, and Piaget, J. *The growth of logical thinking from childhood to adolescence.* New York: Basic Books, 1958.

Irwin, F. W. On desire, aversion, and the affective zero. *Psychological Review,* 1961, **68,** 293–300.

Isaacs, Susan. *Social development in young children.* London: Routledge and Kegan Paul, 1933.

Iscoe, I., and Williams, Martha S. Experimental variables affecting the conformity behavior of children. *Journal of Personality,* 1963, **31,** 234–246.

Itani, J. On the acquisition and propagation of a new food habit in the natural group of the Japanese monkey at Takasakiyama. *Journal of Primatology,* 1958, **1,** 84–98.

Ivanov-Smolenski, A. G. *Works of the Institute of Higher Nervous Activity: Pathophysiological series.* Volume II. Moscow: Academy of Sciences of the USSR, 1956.

Ivanov-Smolenski, A. G. Ways and perspectives of the development of the physiology and pathophysiology of the higher nervous activity of the child. In *The central nervous system and behavior.* Washington, D.C.: United States Public Health Service Russian Scientific Translation Program, 1959.

Jacobs, R. C., and Campbell, D. T. The perpetuation of an arbitrary tradition through several generations of a laboratory micro-culture. *Journal of Abnormal and Social Psychology,* 1961, **62,** 649–658.

Jahoda, G. Immanent justice among West African children. *Journal of Social Psychology,* 1958, **47,** 241–248.

Jakubczak, L. F., and Walters, R. H. Suggestibility as dependency behavior. *Journal of Abnormal and Social Psychology,* 1959, **59,** 102–107.

James, W. T. The development of social facilitation of eating in puppies. *Journal of Genetic Psychology,* 1960, **96,** 123–127.

Janis, I. L. Psychological effects of warnings. In G. W. Baker and D. W. Chapman (Eds.), *Man and society in disaster.* New York: Basic Books, 1962. Pp. 55–92.

Janis, I. L., and King, B. T. The influence of role playing on opinion change. *Journal of Abnormal and Social Psychology,* 1954, **49,** Pp. 211–218.

Janis, I. L., and Mann, L. Effectiveness of emotional role-playing in modifying smoking habits and attitudes. *Journal of Experimental Research in Personality,* 1965, **1,** 84–90.

Jeffrey, W. E. The effects of verbal and nonverbal responses in mediating an instrumental act. *Journal of Experimental Psychology,* 1953, **45,** 327–333.

Johnson, R. C. A study of children's moral judgments. *Child Development,* 1962, **33,** 327–354.

Jones, Mary C. Elimination of fears in children. *Journal of Experimental Psychology,* 1924, **7,** 382–390.

Kagan, J. The concept of identification. *Psychological Review,* 1958, **65,** 296–305.

Kahn, M. W. The effect of severe defeat at various age levels on the aggressive behavior of mice. *Journal of Genetic Psychology,* 1951, **79,** 117–130.

Kamin, L. J. The delay of secondary reward gradient in avoidance learning tested on avoidance trials only. *Journal of Comparative and Physiological Psychology,* 1957, **50,** 450–456.

Kamin, L. J. The delay-of-punishment gradient. *Journal of Comparative and Physiological Psychology,* 1959, **52,** 434–436.

Kamin, L. J. Temporal and intensity characteristics of the conditioned stimulus. In W. F. Prokasy (Ed.), *Classical conditioning: A symposium.* New York: Appleton-Century-Crofts, 1965. Pp. 118–147.

Kanareff, Vera T., and Lanzetta, J. T. Effects of task definition and probability of reinforcement upon the acquisition and extinction of imitative responses. *Journal of Experimental Psychology,* 1960, **60,** 340–348.

Kanfer, F. H. Vicarious human reinforcements: A glimpse into the black box. In

L. Krasner and L. P. Ullman (Eds.), *Research in behavior modification: New developments and implications.* New York: Holt, Rinehart, and Winston, 1965. Pp. 244–267.

Kanfer, F. H., Bradley, Marcia M., and Marston, A. R. Self-reinforcement as a function of degree of learning. *Psychological Reports,* 1962, **10**, 885–886.

Kanfer, F. H., and Duerfeldt, Pryse H. Effects of pretraining on self-evaluation and self-reinforcement. *Journal of Personality and Social Psychology,* 1967, **7**, 164–168.

Kanfer, F. H., and Goldfoot, D. A. Self-control and tolerance of noxious stimulation. *Psychological Reports,* 1966, **18**, 79–85.

Kanfer, F. H., and Marston, A. R. Human reinforcement: Vicarious and direct. *Journal of Experimental Psychology,* 1963, **65**, 292–296. (a)

Kanfer, F. H., and Marston, A. R. Determinants of self-reinforcement in human learning. *Journal of Experimental Psychology,* 1963, **66**, 245–254. (b)

Karsh, Eileen B., and Williams, Joanna P. Punishment and reward in children's instrumental learning. *Psychonomic Science,* 1964, **1**, 359–360.

Kasatkin, N. I. Early ontogenesis of reflex activity in the child. *Zhurnal vysshey nervnoy deyatel'nosti,* 1957, **7**, 805–818 (Washington, D.C.: United States Public Health Service Russian Scientific Translation Program, 1960).

Katahn, M., Blanton, R. L., and Gipson, M. T. Speed and amplitude of response as a function of anxiety and degree of conflict. *Journal of Experimental Research in Personality,* 1967, **2**, 169–172.

Kaufman, A. Effects of punishment intensity on human operant behavior. *Psychological Reports,* 1964, **15**, 287–294.

Kaufman, A., and Baron, A. Use of withdrawal of reinforcement within the escape-avoidance paradigm. *Psychological Reports,* 1966, **19**, 959–965.

Kaufman, A., Baron, A., and Kopp, Rosemarie E. Some effects of instructions on human operant behavior. *Psychonomic Monograph Supplements,* 1966, **1**, 243–250.

Kaufmann, M. E., and Peterson, W. M. Acquisition of a learning set by normal and retarded children. *Journal of Comparative and Physiological Psychology,* 1958, **51**, 619–621.

Kausler, D. H., and Trapp, E. P. Motivation and cue utilization in intentional and incidental learning. *Psychological Review,* 1960, **67**, 373–379.

Kawamura, S. The process of sub-culture propagation among Japanese macaques. In C. H. Southwick (Ed.), *Primate social behavior.* Princeton, New Jersey: Van Nostrand, 1963. Pp. 82–90.

Kelleher, R. T. Chaining and conditioned reinforcement. In W. K. Honig (Ed.), *Operant behavior: Areas of research and application.* New York: Appleton-Century-Crofts, 1966. Pp. 160–212.

Kelleher, R. T., and Gollub, L. R. A review of positive conditioned reinforcement. *Journal of the Experimental Analysis of Behavior,* 1962, **5**, 543–597.

Kelleher, R. T., Riddle, W. C., and Cook, L. Persistent behavior maintained by unavoidable shocks. *Journal of the Experimental Analysis of Behavior,* 1963, **6**, 507–517.

Kelley, H. H., Condry, John C., Jr., Dahlke, A. E., and Hill, A. H. Collective behavior in a simulated panic situation. *Journal of Experimental Social Psychology,* 1965, **1**, 20–54.

Kelley, H. H., and Ring, K. Some effects of "suspicious" versus "trusting" training schedules. *Journal of Abnormal and Social Psychology,* 1961, **63**, 294–301.

Kelley, H. H., Thibaut, J. W., Radloff, R., and Mundy, D. The development of cooperation in the "minimal social situation." *Psychological Monographs*, 1962, **76**, No. 19 (Whole No. 538).

Kellmer Pringle, M. L., and Edwards, J. B. Some moral concepts and judgments of junior school children. *British Journal of Social and Clinical Psychology*, 1964, **3**, 196–215.

Kelman, H. C. Compliance, identification, and internalization. In H. Proshansky and B. Seidenberg (Eds.), *Basic studies in social psychology*. New York: Holt, Rinehart, and Winston, 1965. Pp. 140–148.

Kendler, H. H., and Kendler, Tracy S. Vertical and horizontal processes in problem-solving. *Psychological Review*, 1962, **69**, 1–16.

Kendler, Tracy S. Development of mediating responses in children. In J. C. Wright and J. Kagan (Eds.), Basic cognitive processes in children. *Monographs of the Society for Research in Child Development*, 1963, **28**, No. 2 (Serial No. 86). Pp. 33–48.

Kendler, Tracy S., Kendler, H. H., and Carrick, Martha A. Verbal labels and inferential problem solution of children. *Child Development*, 1966, **37**, 749–763.

Kessen, W., and Kuhlman, Clementina (Eds.) Thought in the young child. *Monographs of the Society for Research in Child Development*, 1962, **27**, No. 2 (Serial No. 83).

Kessen, W., and Mandler, G. Anxiety, pain, and inhibition of distress. *Psychological Review*, 1961, **68**, 396–404.

Kimble, G. A. *Hilgard and Marquis' conditioning and learning.* (Second Edition) New York: Appleton-Century-Crofts, 1961.

Kimble, G. A. Classical conditioning and the problem of awareness. In C. W. Eriksen (Ed.), *Behavior and awareness*. Durham, North Carolina: Duke University Press, 1962. Pp. 27–45.

Kimbrell, D. L., and Blake, R. R. Motivational factors in the violation of a prohibition. *Journal of Abnormal and Social Psychology*, 1958, **56**, 132–133.

Kimmel, H. D. Instrumental inhibitory factors in classical conditioning. In W. F. Prokasy (Ed.), *Classical conditioning: A symposium*. Appleton-Century-Crofts, 1965. Pp. 148–171.

Kimmel, H. D. Instrumental conditioning of autonomically mediated behavior. *Psychological Bulletin*, 1967, **67**, 337–345.

Kimmel, H. D., and Baxter, R. Avoidance conditioning of the GSR. *Journal of Experimental Psychology*, 1964, **68**, 482–485.

King, B. T. Relationships between susceptibility to opinion change and child-rearing practices. In C. I. Hovland and I. L. Janis (Eds.), *Personality and persuasibility*. New Haven: Yale University Press, 1959. Pp. 207–221.

Kinsman, R. A., and Bixenstine, V. E. Secondary reinforcement and shock termination. *Journal of Experimental Psychology*, 1968, **76**, 62–68.

Kintz, B. L., and Bruning, J. L. Punishment and compulsive avoidance behavior. *Journal of Comparative and Physiological Psychology*, 1967, **63**, 323–326.

Klopfer, P. H. Observational learning in birds: The establishment of behavioral modes. *Behaviour*, 1961, **17**, 71–79.

Kluckhohn, Florence R., and Strodtbeck, F. L. *Variations in value orientations.* Evanston, Illinois: Row, Peterson, 1961.

Knapp, R. K., Kause, R. H., and Perkins, C. C., Jr. Immediate vs. delayed shock in T-maze performance. *Journal of Experimental Psychology*, 1959, **58**, 557–562.

Knott, P. D., and Clayton, K. N. Durable secondary reinforcement using brain stimulation as the primary reinforcer. *Journal of Comparative and Physiological Psychology,* 1966, **61,** 151–153.

Knott, P. D., Nunnally, J. C., and Duchnowski, A. J. Effects of frustration on primary and conditioned incentive value. *Journal of Experimental Research in Personality,* 1967, **2,** 140–149.

Kobasigawa, A. Observation of failure in another person as a determinant of amplitude and speed of a simple motor response. *Journal of Personality and Social Psychology,* 1965, **1,** 626–630.

Kohlberg, L. The development of children's orientations toward a moral order. I. Sequence in the development of moral thought. *Vita Humana,* 1963, **6,** 11–33. (a)

Kohlberg, L. Moral development and identification. In H. W. Stevenson (Ed.), *Yearbook of the National Society for the Study of Education.* Part I. *Child psychology.* Chicago: University of Chicago Press, 1963. Pp. 277–332. (b)

Kohlberg, L. Development of moral character and moral ideology. In M. L. Hoffman and Lois W. Hoffman (Eds.), *Review of child development research.* Volume I. New York: Russell Sage Foundation, 1964. Pp. 383–431.

Kohlberg, L. *Stage and sequence: The developmental approach to moralization* (tentative title). New York: Holt, Rinehart, and Winston, 1969, in preparation.

Kohn, M. L. Social class and the exercise of parental authority. *American Sociological Review,* 1959, **24,** 352–366.

Kohn, M. L. Social class and parent-child relationships: An interpretation. *American Journal of Sociology,* 1963, **68,** 471–480.

Konorski, J. *Conditioned reflexes and neuron organization.* New York: Cambridge University Press, 1948.

Konorski, J. On the mechanism of instrumental conditioning. *Proceedings of the Seventeenth International Congress of Psychology, Washington, D.C., 1963.* Amsterdam: North-Holland Publishing Company, 1964. Pp. 45–59.

Krasner, L., and Ullman, L. P. (Eds.) *Research in behavior modification: New developments and implications.* New York: Holt, Rinehart, and Winston, 1965.

Krus, D., Werner, H., and Wapner, S. Studies in vicariousness: Motor activity and perceived movement. *American Journal of Psychology,* 1953, **66,** 603–608.

Kuenne, Margaret R. Experimental investigation of the relation of language to transposition behavior in young children. *Journal of Experimental Psychology,* 1946, **36,** 471–490.

Kuhn, Deanna Z., Madsen, C. H., Jr., and Becker, W. C. Effects of exposure to an aggressive model and "frustration" on children's aggressive behavior. *Child Development,* 1967, **38,** 739–745.

Kuo, Z. Y. Studies on the basic factors in animal fighting: VII. Inter-species coexistence in mammals. *Journal of Genetic Psychology,* 1960, **97,** 211–225.

Kurtz, K. H., and Walters, G. C. The effects of prior fear experiences on an approach-avoidance conflict. *Journal of Comparative and Physiological Psychology,* 1962, **55,** 1075–1078.

Kwint, L. Ontogeny of motility of the face. *Child Development,* 1934, **5,** 1–12.

LaBarre, W. Some observations on character structure in the Orient: The Japanese. *Psychiatry,* 1948, **8,** 319–342.

Lacey, J. I., and Smith, R. L. Conditioning and generalization of unconscious anxiety. *Science,* 1954, **120,** 1045–1052.

Lambert, W. W., Triandis, Leigh M., and Wolf, Margery. Some correlates of beliefs in the malevolence and benevolence of supernatural beings: A cross-societal study. *Journal of Abnormal and Social Psychology*, 1959, **58**, 162–169.

Landau, Rivka, and Gewirtz, J. L. Differential satiation for a social reinforcing stimulus as a determinant of its efficacy in conditioning. *Journal of Experimental Child Psychology*, 1967, **5**, 391–405.

Lanzetta, J. T., and Driscoll, J. M. Preference for information about an uncertain but unavoidable outcome. *Journal of Personality and Social Psychology*, 1966, **3**, 96–102.

Lavery, J. J., and Foley, P. J. Altruism or arousal in the rat? *Science*, 1963, **140**, 172–173.

Lawrence, D. H., and Festinger, L. *Deterrents and reinforcements: The psychology of insufficient reward.* Stanford, California: Stanford University Press, 1962.

Lazarus, R. S., Speisman, J. C., Mordkoff, A. M., and Davidson, L. A. A laboratory study of psychological stress produced by a motion picture film. *Psychological Monographs*, 1962, **76**, No. 34 (Whole No. 553).

Lefcourt, H. M. Internal vs. external control of reinforcement. *Psychological Bulletin*, 1966, **65**, 206–220.

Lefcourt, H. M., Barnes, K., Parke, R. D., and Schwartz, F. Anticipated social censure and aggression-conflict as mediators of response to aggression induction. *Journal of Social Psychology*, 1966, **70**, 251–263.

Leff, R. The effects of punishment intensity and consistency on the internalization of behavioral suppression in children. Unpublished doctoral dissertation, University of Pennsylvania, 1967.

Lefkowitz, M. M., Blake, R. R., and Mouton, Jane S. Status factors in pedestrian violation of traffic signals. *Journal of Abnormal and Social Psychology*, 1955, **51**, 704–705.

Lefkowitz, M. M., Walder, L. O., and Eron, L. D. Punishment, identification, and aggression. *Merrill-Palmer Quarterly*, 1963, **9**, 159–174.

Leighton, Dorothea, and Kluckhohn, C. *Children of the people: The Navaho individual and his development.* Cambridge, Massachusetts: Harvard University Press, 1947.

Leitenberg, H. Punishment training with and without an escape contingency. *Journal of Experimental Psychology*, 1967, **74**, 393–399.

Lenrow, P. B. Studies of sympathy. In S. S. Tomkins and C. E. Izard (Eds.), *Affect, cognition, and personality: Empirical studies.* New York: Springer, 1965. Pp. 264–294.

Lerner, E. *Constraint areas and the moral judgment of children.* Menasha, Wisconsin: George Banta Publishing Company, 1937.

Lerner, M. J., and Matthews, Gale. Reactions to the suffering of others under conditions of indirect responsibility. *Journal of Personality and Social Psychology*, 1967, **5**, 319–325.

Lesser, G. S., and Abelson, R. P. Personality correlates of persuasibility in children. In C. I. Hovland and I. L. Janis (Eds.), *Personality and persuasibility.* New Haven: Yale University Press, 1959. Pp. 187–206.

Levin, H., and Baldwin, A. L. Pride and shame in children. In M. R. Jones (Ed.), *Nebraska symposium on motivation.* Volume VII. Lincoln, Nebraska: University of Nebraska Press, 1959. Pp. 138–173.

Levin, H., and Sears, R. R. Identification with parents as a determinant of doll play aggression. *Child Development*, 1956, **27**, 136–153.

Levin, H., and Turgeon, Valerie F. The influence of the mother's presence on children's doll play aggression. *Journal of Abnormal and Social Psychology*, 1957, **55**, 304–308.

Lewis, D. J., and Duncan, C. P. Vicarious experience and partial reinforcement. *Journal of Abnormal and Social Psychology,* 1958, **57,** 321–326.

Lewis, M., Wall, A. M., and Aronfreed, J. Developmental change in the relative values of social and nonsocial reinforcement. *Journal of Experimental Psychology,* 1963, **66,** 133–137.

Liddell, H. S. Conditioned reflex method and experimental neurosis. In J. McV. Hunt (Ed.), *Personality and the behavior disorders.* Volume I. New York: Ronald Press, 1944. Pp. 389–412.

Liebert, R. M., and Ora, J. P., Jr. Children's adoption of self-reward patterns: Incentive level and method of transmission. *Child Development,* 1968, **39,** in press.

Lifton, R. J. *Thought reform and the psychology of totalism.* New York: Norton, 1961.

Linder, D. E., Cooper, J., and Jones, E. E. Decision freedom as a determinant of the role of incentive magnitude in attitude change. *Journal of Personality and Social Psychology,* 1967, **6,** 245–254.

Lipsitt, L. P. Learning in the first year of life. In L. P. Lipsitt and C. C. Spiker (Eds.), *Advances in child development and behavior.* Volume I. New York: Academic Press, 1963. Pp. 147–195.

Lipsitt, L. P., and Castaneda, A. Effects of delayed reward on choice behavior and response speeds in children. *Journal of Comparative and Physiological Psychology,* 1958, **51,** 65–67.

Livson, N., and Mussen, P. The relation of ego control to overt aggression and dependency. *Journal of Abnormal and Social Psychology,* 1957, **55,** 66–71.

Lockard, Joan S. Choice of a warning signal or no warning signal in an unavoidable shock situation. *Journal of Comparative and Physiological Psychology,* 1963, **56,** 526–530.

Logan, F. A. A comparison of avoidance and nonavoidance eyelid conditioning. *Journal of Experimental Psychology,* 1951, **42,** 390–393.

Logan, F. A. *Incentive: How the conditions of reinforcement affect the performance of rats.* New Haven: Yale University Press, 1960.

Logan, F. A., Olmsted, D. L., Rosner, B. S., Schwartz, R. D., and Stevens, C. M. *Behavior theory and social science.* New Haven: Yale University Press, 1955.

Logan, F. A., and Wagner, A. R. *Reward and punishment.* Boston: Allyn and Bacon, 1965.

Long, E. R., Hammack, J. T., May, F., and Campbell, B. J. Intermittent reinforcement of operant behavior in children. *Journal of the Experimental Analysis of Behavior,* 1958, **1,** 315–339.

Longstreth, L. E. The relationship between expectations and frustration in children. *Child Development,* 1960, **31,** 667–671.

Longstreth, L. E. Incentive stimuli as determinants of instrumental response strength in children. *Journal of Comparative and Physiological Psychology,* 1962, **55,** 398–401.

Lorenz, K. Contribution to the comparative sociology of colonial-nesting birds. *Proceedings of the Eighth International Ornithology Congress, Amsterdam, 1934.* Pp. 207–218.

Lorenz, K. *On aggression.* New York: Harcourt, Brace, and World, 1966.

Lövaas, O. I. Effect of exposure to symbolic aggression on aggressive behavior. *Child Development,* 1961, **32,** 37–44. (a)

Lövaas, O. I. Interaction between verbal and nonverbal behavior. *Child Development,* 1961, **32,** 329–336. (b)

Lövaas, O. I. Control of food intake in children by reinforcement of relevant verbal behavior. *Journal of Abnormal and Social Psychology,* 1964, **68,** 672–678.

Lövaas, O. I., Berberich, J. P., Perloff, B. F., and Schaeffer, B. Acquisition of imitative speech by schizophrenic children. *Science,* 1966, **151,** 705–707. (a)

Lövaas, O. I., Freitag, G., Kinder, M. I., Rubenstein, D. B., Schaeffer, B., and Simmons, J. Q. Establishment of social reinforcers in two schizophrenic children on the basis of food. *Journal of Experimental Child Psychology,* 1966, **4,** 109–125. (b)

Lövaas, O. I., Schaeffer, B., and Simmons, J. Q. Building social behavior in autistic children by use of electric shock. *Journal of Experimental Research in Personality,* 1965, **1,** 99–109.

Luria, A. R. *The role of speech in the regulation of normal and abnormal behavior.* New York: Liveright, 1961.

Luria, Zella, Goldwasser, Miriam, and Goldwasser, Adena. Response to transgression in stories by Israeli children. *Child Development,* 1963, **34,** 271–280.

Lykken, D. T. A study of anxiety in the sociopathic personality. *Journal of Abnormal and Social Psychology,* 1957, **55,** 6–10.

Lynn, D. B. A note on sex differences in the development of masculine and feminine identification. *Psychological Review,* 1959, **66,** 126–135.

Maccoby, Eleanor E. Role-taking in childhood and its consequences for social learning. *Child Development,* 1959, **30,** 239–252.

Maccoby, Eleanor E. The taking of adult roles in middle childhood. *Journal of Abnormal and Social Psychology,* 1961, **63,** 493–503.

Maccoby, Eleanor E. Class differences in boys' choices of authoritative roles. *Sociometry,* 1962, **25,** 117–119.

Maccoby, Eleanor E. Dependency behavior. In P. Mussen (Ed.), *Carmichael's manual of child psychology.* (Third Edition) New York: Wiley, 1969, in press.

Maccoby, Eleanor E., and Bee, Helen L. Some speculations concerning the lag between perceiving and performing. *Child Development,* 1965, **36,** 367–377.

Maccoby, Eleanor E., and Gibbs, Patricia K. *et al.* Methods of child-rearing in two social classes. In W. Martin and Celia B. Stendler (Eds.), *Readings in child development.* New York: Harcourt, Brace, 1954. Pp. 380–396.

Maccoby, Eleanor E., and Hagen, J. W. Effects of distraction upon central versus incidental recall: Developmental trends. *Journal of Experimental Child Psychology,* 1965, **2,** 280–289.

Maccoby, Eleanor E., and Whiting, J. W. M. Some child-rearing correlates of young children's responses to deviation stories. Unpublished manuscript, Stanford University, 1960.

MacKinnon, D. W. Violation of prohibitions. In H. A. Murray *et al., Explorations in personality.* New York: Oxford University Press, 1938. Pp. 491–501.

MacRae, D., Jr. A test of Piaget's theories of moral development. *Journal of Abnormal and Social Psychology,* 1954, **49,** 14–18.

Maier, N. R. F. *Frustration: The study of behavior without a goal.* New York: McGraw-Hill, 1949.

Maier, S. F., Seligman, M. E. P., and Solomon, R. L. Pavlovian fear conditioning and learned helplessness: Effects on escape and avoidance behavior of (a) the CS-US contingency and (b) the independence of the US and voluntary responding. In B. A. Campbell and R. M. Church (Eds.), *Punishment.* New York: Appleton-Century-Crofts, 1968, in press.

Maller, J. B. General and specific factors in character. *Journal of Social Psychology,* 1934, **5,** 97–102.

Malmo, R. B. Anxiety and behavioral arousal. *Psychological Review,* 1957, **64,** 276–287.

Mandel, I. J., and Bridger, W. H. Interaction between instructions and ISI in conditioning and extinction of the GSR. *Journal of Experimental Psychology,* 1967, **74,** 36–43.

Mandler, G., and Watson, D. L. Anxiety and the interruption of behavior. In C. D. Spielberger (Ed.), *Anxiety and behavior.* New York: Academic Press, 1966. Pp. 263–288.

Marler, P. Optical systems. In T. A. Sebeok (Ed.), *Animal communication: Techniques of study and results of research.* Bloomington, Indiana: Indiana University Press, 1968, in press.

Marston, A. R. Imitation, self-reinforcement, and reinforcement of another person. *Journal of Personality and Social Psychology,* 1965, **2,** 255–261.

Marston, A. R. Determinants of the effects of vicarious reinforcement. *Journal of Experimental Psychology,* 1966, **71,** 550–558.

Marston, A. R., and Kanfer, F. H. Human reinforcement: Experimenter and subject controlled. *Journal of Experimental Psychology,* 1963, **66,** 91–94.

Martin, B. Reward and punishment associated with the same goal response: A factor in the learning of motives. *Psychological Bulletin,* 1963, **60,** 441–451.

Martin, B., and Ross, L. E. Effects of consummatory response punishment on consummatory and runway behavior. *Journal of Comparative and Physiological Psychology,* 1964, **58,** 243–247.

Mason, W. A. Development of communication between young rhesus monkeys. *Science,* 1959, **130,** 712–713.

Mason, W. A. The effects of social restriction on the behavior of rhesus monkeys. II. Tests of gregariousness. *Journal of Comparative and Physiological Psychology,* 1961, **54,** 287–290.

Mason, W. A., and Hollis, J. H. Communication between young Rhesus monkeys. *Animal Behaviour,* 1962, **10,** 211–221.

Masserman, J. H. *Behavior and neurosis.* Chicago: University of Chicago Press, 1943.

Masserman, J. H. *Principles of dynamic psychiatry.* Philadelphia: Saunders, 1946.

Masserman, J. H., Wechkin, S., and Terris, W. "Altruistic" behavior in rhesus monkeys. *American Journal of Psychiatry,* 1964, **121,** 584–585.

Maynard Smith, J. The evolution of alarm calls. *American Naturalist,* 1965, **99,** 59–63.

McAllister, W. R., and McAllister, Dorothy E. Variables influencing the conditioning and measurement of acquired fear. In W. F. Prokasy (Ed.), *Classical conditioning: A symposium.* New York: Appleton-Century-Crofts, 1965. Pp. 172–191.

McBride, A. F., and Hebb, D. O. Behavior of the captive bottle-nose dolphin, *Tursiops truncatus. Journal of Comparative and Physiological Psychology,* 1948, **41,** 111–123.

McClelland, D. C. Some social consequences of achievement motivation. In M. R. Jones (Ed.), *Nebraska symposium on motivation.* Volume III. Lincoln, Nebraska: University of Nebraska Press, 1955. Pp. 41–65.

McClelland, D. C. *The achieving society.* Princeton, New Jersey: Van Nostrand, 1961.

McConnell, O. L. Perceptual versus verbal mediation in the concept learning of children. *Child Development,* 1964, **35,** 1373–1383.

McCord, Joan, and Clemes, S. Conscience orientation and dimensions of personality. *Behavioral Science,* 1964, **9,** 19–29.

McCord, Joan, and McCord, W. The effects of parental role models on criminality. *Journal of Social Issues,* 1958, **14,** 66–75.

McCord, Joan, McCord, W., and Howard, A. Family interaction as antecedent to the direction of male aggressiveness. *Journal of Abnormal and Social Psychology*, 1963, **66**, 239–242.

McCord, W., and McCord, Joan. A tentative theory of the structure of conscience. In Dorothy Willner (Ed.), *Decisions, values, and groups*. Oxford: Pergamon Press, 1960. Pp. 108–134.

McCord, W., McCord, Joan, and Howard, A. Familial correlates of aggression in nondelinquent male children. *Journal of Abnormal and Social Psychology*, 1961, **62**, 79–83.

McCullers, J. C., and Stevenson, H. W. Effects of verbal reinforcement in a probability learning situation. *Psychological Reports*, 1960, **7**, 439–445.

McDavid, J. W. Imitative behavior in preschool children. *Psychological Monographs*, 1959, **73**, No. 16 (Whole No. 486).

McDavid, J. W. Effects of ambiguity of environmental cues upon learning to imitate. *Journal of Abnormal and Social Psychology*, 1962, **65**, 381–386.

McDougall, W. *An introduction to social psychology*. London: Methuen, 1908.

McMains, M. J., and Liebert, R. M. The influence of discrepancies between successively modeled self-reward criteria on the adoption of a self-imposed standard. *Journal of Personality and Social Psychology*, 1968, **8**, 166–171.

McMichael, R. E., and Grinder, R. E. Children's guilt after transgression: Combined effect of exposure to American culture and ethnic background. *Child Development*, 1966, **37**, 425–431.

McMillan, D. E. A comparison of the punishing effects of response-produced shock and response-produced time out. *Journal of the Experimental Analysis of Behavior*, 1967, **10**, 439–449.

Mead, G. H. *Mind, self, and society*. Chicago: University of Chicago Press, 1934.

Mead, Margaret. *Cooperation and competition among primitive peoples*. New York: McGraw-Hill, 1937.

Mead, Margaret. Some anthropological considerations concerning guilt. In M. L. Reymert (Ed.), *Feelings and emotions*. New York: McGraw-Hill, 1950. Pp. 362–373.

Mead, Margaret. *Cultural patterns and technical change*. New York: Columbia University Press, 1953.

Mead, Margaret. Social change and cultural surrogates. In C. Kluckhohn, H. A. Murray, and D. M. Schneider (Eds.), *Personality in nature, society, and culture*. (Second Edition) New York: Knopf, 1961. Pp. 651–662.

Medinnus, G. R. Objective responsibility in children: A comparison with the Piaget data. *Journal of Genetic Psychology*, 1962, **101**, 127–133.

Medinnus, G. R. Behavioral and cognitive measures of conscience development. *Journal of Genetic Psychology*, 1966, **109**, 147–150.

Melvin, K. B., and Martin, R. C. Facilitative effects of two modes of punishment on resistance to extinction. *Journal of Comparative and Physiological Psychology*, 1967, **62**, 491–494.

Melvin, K. B., and Smith, F. H. Self-punitive avoidance behavior in the rat. *Journal of Comparative and Physiological Psychology*, 1967, **63**, 533–535.

Metz, J. R. Conditioning generalized imitation in autistic children. *Journal of Experimental Child Psychology*, 1965, **2**, 389–399.

Metzner, R. Effects of work requirements in two types of delay of gratification situations. *Child Development*, 1963, **34**, 809–816.

Meyer, W. J., and Offenbach, S. I. Effectiveness of reward and punishment as a function of task complexity. *Journal of Comparative and Physiological Psychology*, 1962, **55**, 532–534.

Meyer, W. J., and Seidman, S. B. Relative effectiveness of different reinforcement combinations on concept learning of children at two developmental levels. *Child Development,* 1961, **32,** 117–128.

Midlarsky, Elizabeth, and Bryan, J. H. Training charity in children. *Journal of Personality and Social Psychology,* 1967, **5,** 408–415.

Migler, B. Experimental self-punishment and superstitious escape behavior. *Journal of the Experimental Analysis of Behavior,* 1963, **6,** 371–385.

Milgram, S. Behavioral study of obedience. *Journal of Abnormal and Social Psychology,* 1963, **67,** 371–378.

Milgram, S. Group pressure and action against a person. *Journal of Abnormal and Social Psychology,* 1964, **69,** 137–143.

Miller, D. R., and Swanson, G. E. *The changing American parent: A study in the Detroit area.* New York: Wiley, 1958.

Miller, D. R., and Swanson, G. E. *et al. Inner conflict and defense.* New York: Holt, 1960.

Miller, G. A., Galanter, E., and Pribram, K. H. *Plans and the structure of behavior.* New York: Holt, 1960.

Miller, N. Acquisition of avoidance dispositions by social learning. *Journal of Abnormal and Social Psychology,* 1961, **63,** 12–19.

Miller, N. E. Studies of fear as an acquirable drive: I. Fear as motivation and fear-reduction as reinforcement in the learning of new responses. *Journal of Experimental Psychology,* 1948, **38,** 89–101.

Miller, N. E. Learnable drives and rewards. In S. S. Stevens (Ed.), *Handbook of Experimental Psychology.* New York: Wiley, 1951. Pp. 435–572.

Miller, N. E. Liberalization of basic S-R concepts: Extensions to conflict behavior, motivation, and social learning. In S. Koch (Ed.), *Psychology: A study of a science.* Volume II. *General systematic formulations, learning, and special processes.* New York: McGraw-Hill, 1959. Pp. 196–292.

Miller, N. E. Some reflections on the law of effect produce a new alternative to drive reduction. In M. R. Jones (Ed.), *Nebraska symposium on motivation.* Volume XI. Lincoln, Nebraska: University of Nebraska Press, 1963. Pp. 65–112.

Miller, N. E., and Carmona, A. Modification of a visceral response, salivation in thirsty dogs, by instrumental training with water reward. *Journal of Comparative and Physiological Psychology,* 1967, **63,** 1–6.

Miller, N. E., and DiCara, L. Instrumental learning of heart rate changes in curarized rats: Shaping, and specificity to discriminative stimulus. *Journal of Comparative and Physiological Psychology,* 1967, **63,** 12–19.

Miller, N. E., and Dollard, J. *Social learning and imitation.* New Haven: Yale University Press, 1941.

Miller, R. E., Banks, J. H., and Ogawa, N. Role of facial expression in "cooperative-avoidance conditioning" in monkeys. *Journal of Abnormal and Social Psychology,* 1963, **67,** 24–30.

Miller, R. E., Caul, W. F., and Mirsky, I. F. Communication of affects between feral and socially isolated monkeys. *Journal of Personality and Social Psychology,* 1967, **7,** 231–239.

Miller, R. E., and Murphy, J. V. Social interactions of rhesus monkeys. II. Effects of social interaction on the learning of discrimination tasks. *Journal of Comparative and Physiological Psychology,* 1956, **49,** 207–211.

Mills, J. Changes in moral attitudes following temptation. *Journal of Personality,* 1958, **26,** 517–531.

Mischel, W. Preference for delayed reinforcement: An experimental study of a cultural observation. *Journal of Abnormal and Social Psychology,* 1958, **56,** 57–61.

Mischel, W. Preference for delayed reinforcement and social responsibility. *Journal of Abnormal and Social Psychology,* 1961, **62,** 1–7. (a)

Mischel, W. Delay of gratification, need for achievement, and acquiescence in another culture. *Journal of Abnormal and Social Psychology,* 1961, **62,** 543–552. (b)

Mischel, W. Father-absence and delay of gratification: Cross-cultural comparisons. *Journal of Abnormal and Social Psychology,* 1961, **63,** 116–124. (c)

Mischel, W. Theory and research on the antecedents of self-imposed delay of reward. In B. A. Maher (Ed.), *Progress in experimental personality research.* Volume III. New York: Academic Press, 1966. Pp. 85–132.

Mischel, W., and Gilligan, Carol. Delay of gratification, motivation for the prohibited gratification, and responses to temptation. *Journal of Abnormal and Social Psychology,* 1964, **69,** 411–417.

Mischel, W., and Grusec, Joan. Determinants of the rehearsal and transmission of neutral and aversive behaviors. *Journal of Personality and Social Psychology,* 1966, **3,** 197–205.

Mischel, W., and Grusec, Joan. Waiting for rewards and punishments: Effects of time and probability on choice. *Journal of Personality and Social Psychology,* 1967, **5,** 24–31.

Mischel, W., and Liebert, R. M. Effects of discrepancies between observed and imposed reward criteria on their acquisition and transmission. *Journal of Personality and Social Psychology,* 1966, **3,** 45–53.

Mischel, W., and Masters, J. C. Effects of probability of reward attainment on responses to frustration. *Journal of Personality and Social Psychology,* 1966, **3,** 390–397.

Mischel, W., and Staub, E. The effects of expectancy on working and waiting for larger rewards. *Journal of Personality and Social Psychology,* 1965, **2,** 625–633.

Montague, M. F. A. The origin and nature of social life and the biological basis of cooperation. In P. Sorokin (Ed.), *Explorations in altruistic love and behavior: A symposium.* Boston: Beacon Press, 1950. Pp. 74–92.

Moore, G. E. *Principia ethica.* Cambridge, England: Cambridge University Press, 1903.

Morris, J. F. Symposium on the development of moral values in children. II. The development of adolescent value-judgements. *British Journal of Educational Psychology,* 1958, **28,** 1–14.

Morse, W. H. Intermittent reinforcement. In W. K. Honig (Ed.), *Operant behavior: Areas of research and application.* New York: Appleton-Century-Crofts, 1966. Pp. 52–108.

Mowrer, O. H. A stimulus-response analysis of anxiety and its role as a reinforcing agent. *Psychological Review,* 1939, **46,** 553–565.

Mowrer, O. H. *Learning theory and personality dynamics.* New York: Ronald Press, 1950.

Mowrer, O. H. *Learning theory and behavior.* New York: Wiley, 1960. (a)

Mowrer, O. H. *Learning theory and the symbolic processes.* New York: Wiley, 1960. (b)

Mowrer, O. H., and Lamoreaux, R. R. Avoidance conditioning and signal duration—a study of secondary motivation and reward. *Psychological Monographs,* 1942, **54,** No. 5 (Whole No. 247).

Mowrer, O. H., and Ullman, A. D. Time as a determinant in integrative learning. *Psychological Review,* 1945, **52,** 61–90.

Mowrer, O. H., and Viek, P. An experimental analogue of fear from a sense of helplessness. *Journal of Abnormal and Social Psychology,* 1948, **43,** 193–200.

Muenzinger, K. F., Brown, W. O., Crow, W. J., and Powloski, R. F. Motivation in learning. XI. An analysis of electric shock for correct responses into its avoidance and accelerating components. *Journal of Experimental Psychology,* 1952, **43,** 115–119.

Munsinger, H., and Kessen, W. Uncertainty, structure, and preference. *Psychological Monographs,* 1964, **78,** No. 9 (Whole No. 586).

Murdock, G. P. Correlations of matrilineal and patrilineal institutions. In G. P. Murdock (Ed.), *Studies in the science of society.* New Haven: Yale University Press, 1937. Pp. 445–470.

Murphy, Lois B. *Social behavior and child personality: An exploratory study of some roots of sympathy.* New York: Columbia University Press, 1937.

Murray, A. K., and Strandberg, J. M. Development of a conditioned positive reinforcer through removal of an aversive stimulus. *Journal of Comparative and Physiological Psychology,* 1965, **60,** 281–283.

Murray, Marcia, and Nevin, J. A. Some effects of correlation between response-contingent shock and reinforcement. *Journal of the Experimental Analysis of Behavior,* 1967, **10,** 301–309.

Mussen, P. Some antecedents and consequents of masculine sex-typing in adolescent boys. *Psychological Monographs,* 1961, **75,** No. 2 (Whole No. 506).

Mussen, P., and Distler, L. M. Masculinity, identification, and father-son relationships. *Journal of Abnormal and Social Psychology,* 1959, **59,** 350–356.

Mussen, P., and Parker, Ann L. Mother nurturance and girls' incidental imitative learning. *Journal of Personality and Social Psychology,* 1965, **2,** 94–97.

Mussen, P., and Rutherford, E. Effects of aggressive cartoons on children's aggressive play. *Journal of Abnormal and Social Psychology,* 1961, **62,** 461–464.

Mussen, P., and Rutherford, E. Parent-child relations and parental personality in relation to young children's sex role preferences. *Child Development,* 1963, **34,** 589–608.

Myer, J. S., and Baenninger, R. Some effects of punishment and stress on mouse killing by rats. *Journal of Comparative and Physiological Psychology,* 1966, **62,** 292–297.

Myers, J. L. Secondary reinforcement: A review of recent experimentation. *Psychological Bulletin,* 1958, **55,** 284–301.

Myers, J. L., and Myers, Nancy A. Effects of schedules of primary and secondary reinforcement on extinction behavior. *Child Development,* 1963, **34,** 1057–1063.

Myers, Nancy A. Extinction following partial and continuous primary and secondary reinforcement. *Journal of Experimental Psychology,* 1960, **60,** 172–179.

Myers, Nancy A., and Myers, J. L. Secondary reinforcement as a function of training and testing schedules. *Child Development,* 1966, **37,** 645–652.

Najarian-Svajian, P. H. The idea of immanent justice among Lebanese children and adults. *Journal of Genetic Psychology,* 1966, **109,** 57–66.

Nelson, F. Effects of two counterconditioning procedures on the extinction of fear. *Journal of Comparative and Physiological Psychology,* 1966, **62,** 208–213.

Nelson, F. B., Reid, I. E., and Travers, R. M. W. Effect of electric shock as a reinforcer of the behavior of children. *Psychological Reports,* 1965, **16,** 123–126.

Newcomb, T. M. *Social psychology.* New York: Dryden, 1950.

Nissen, H. W., and Crawford, M. P. A preliminary study of food-sharing behavior in young chimpanzees. *Journal of Comparative Psychology,* 1936, **22,** 383–419.

Oakes, W. F. Verbal operant conditioning, intertrial activity, awareness, and the extended interview. *Journal of Personality and Social Psychology,* 1967, **6,** 198–202.

O'Connell, E. J., Jr. The effect of cooperative and competitive set on the learning of imitation and nonimitation. *Journal of Experimental Social Psychology,* 1965, **1,** 172–183.

Offenbach, S. I. Reinforcer acquisition in discrimination learning. *Psychological Reports,* 1966, **19,** 843–849.

Olds, J. The influence of practice on the strength of secondary approach drives. *Journal of Experimental Psychology,* 1953, **46,** 232–236.

Olds, J. Physiological mechanisms of reward. In M. R. Jones (Ed.), *Nebraska symposium on motivation.* Volume III. Lincoln, Nebraska: University of Nebraska Press, 1955. Pp. 73–139.

Olds, J., and Olds, Marianne. Drives, rewards, and the brain. In *New directions in psychology.* Volume II. New York: Holt, Rinehart, and Winston, 1965. Pp. 329–410.

Osgood, C. E. Motivational dynamics of language behavior. In M. R. Jones (Ed.), *Nebraska symposium on motivation.* Volume V. Lincoln, Nebraska: University of Nebraska Press, 1957. Pp. 348–424.

Overmier, J. B., and Seligman, M. E. P. Effects of inescapable shock upon subsequent escape and avoidance responding. *Journal of Comparative and Physiological Psychology,* 1967, **63,** 28–33.

Painting, D. H. The performance of psychopathic individuals under conditions of positive and negative partial reinforcement. *Journal of Abnormal and Social Psychology,* 1961, **62,** 352–355.

Papoušek, H. Experimental studies of appetitional behavior in human newborns and infants. In H. W. Stevenson, E. H. Hess, and Harriet L. Rheingold (Eds.), *Early behaviour: Comparative and developmental approaches.* New York: Wiley, 1967. Pp. 249–277.

Parke, R. D., and Walters, R. H. Some factors influencing the efficacy of punishment training for inducing response inhibition. *Monographs of the Society for Research in Child Development,* 1967, **32,** No. 1 (Serial No. 109).

Parker, R. K., and Nunnally, J. C. Association of neutral objects with rewards: Effects of reward schedules on reward expectancy, verbal evaluation, and selective attention. *Journal of Experimental Child Psychology,* 1966, **3,** 324–332.

Parsons, T. A revised analytical approach to the theory of social stratification. In R. Bendix and S. M. Lipset (Eds.), *Class, status, and power: A reader in social stratification.* Glencoe, Illinois: Free Press, 1953. Pp. 92–128.

Parsons, T., and Bales, R. F. *et al. Family, socialization and interaction process.* Glencoe, Illinois: Free Press, 1955.

Parton, D. A., and DeNike, L. D. Performance hypotheses of children and response to social reinforcement. *Journal of Personality and Social Psychology,* 1966, **4,** 444–447.

Pavlov, I. P. *Conditioned reflexes.* London: Oxford University Press, 1927.

Pavlov, I. P. *Lectures on conditioned reflexes.* New York: International Publishers, 1928.

Pearl, J., Walters, G., and Anderson, R. C. Suppressing effects of aversive stimulation on subsequently punished behavior. *Canadian Journal of Psychology,* 1964, **18,** 343–348.

Pearlin, L. I., Yarrow, Marian R., and Scarr, H. A. Unintended effects of parental aspirations: The case of children's cheating. *American Journal of Sociology,* 1967, **73,** 73–83.

Peck, R. F., and Havighurst, R. J. *et al. The psychology of character development.* New York: Wiley, 1960.

Penney, R. K. Effect of reward and punishment on children's orientation and discrimination learning. *Journal of Experimental Psychology,* 1967, **75,** 140–142.

Penney, R. K., and Lupton, A. A. Children's discrimination learning as a function of reward and punishment. *Journal of Comparative and Physiological Psychology,* 1961, **54,** 449–451.

Pepitone, A., McCauley, C., and Hammond, P. Change in attractiveness of forbidden toys as a function of severity of threat. *Journal of Experimental Social Psychology,* 1967, **3,** 221–229.

Pepper, S. C. *The sources of value.* Berkeley, California: University of California Press, 1958.

Perkins, C. C., Jr., Seymann, R. G., Levis, D. J., and Spencer, H. R., Jr. Factors affecting preference for signal-shock over shock-signal. *Journal of Experimental Psychology,* 1966, **72,** 190–196.

Perry, R. B. *The general theory of value.* New York: Longmans, Green, 1926.

Piaget, J. *The child's conception of the world.* New York: Harcourt, Brace, 1929.

Piaget, J. *The moral judgment of the child.* Glencoe, Illinois: Free Press, 1948. (First English edition: London: Kegan Paul, 1932)

Piaget, J. *Play, dreams, and imitation in childhood.* New York: Norton, 1951.

Piaget, J. *The origins of intelligence in children.* New York: International Universities Press, 1952.

Pick, H. Some Soviet research on learning and perception in children. In J. C. Wright and J. Kagan (Eds.), Basic cognitive processes in children. *Monographs of the Society for Research in Child Development,* 1963, **28,** No. 2 (Serial No. 86). Pp. 185–190.

Piers, G. Shame and guilt. In G. Piers and M. B. Singer, *Shame and Guilt: A psychoanalytic and a cultural study.* Springfield, Illinois: Charles C. Thomas, 1953. Pp. 5–41.

Poliakova, A. G. Analiz protsessa usvaeniia navykov putem podrazhaniia u detei doshkol'nogo vozrasta (Analysis of the process of acquiring habits by means of imitation in children of preschool age). *Voprosy Psikhologii,* 1958, **4,** 88–97.

Postman, L. Short-term memory and incidental learning. In A. W. Melton (Ed.), *Categories of human learning.* New York: Academic Press, 1964. Pp. 145–201.

Premack, D. Reinforcement theory. In D. Levine (Ed.), *Nebraska Symposium on motivation.* Volume XIII. Lincoln, Nebraska: University of Nebraska Press, 1965. Pp. 123–180.

Prince, A. I., Jr. Effect of punishment on visual discrimination learning. *Journal of Experimental Psychology,* 1956, **52,** 381–385.

Prokasy, W. F. The acquisition of observing responses in the absence of differential external reinforcement. *Journal of Comparative and Physiological Psychology,* 1956, **49,** 131–134.

Prokasy, W. F. (Ed.) *Classical conditioning: A symposium.* New York: Appleton-Century-Crofts, 1965.

Rachlin, H. The effect of shock intensity on concurrent and single-key responding in concurrent-chain schedules. *Journal of the Experimental Analysis of Behavior,* 1967, **10,** 87–95.

Raven, B. H., and Fishbein, M. Acceptance of punishment and change in belief. *Journal of Abnormal and Social Psychology,* 1961, **63,** 411–416.

Razran, G. Stimulus generalization of conditioned responses. *Psychological Bulletin,* 1949, **46,** 337–365.

Razran, G. Backward conditioning. *Psychological Bulletin,* 1956, **53,** 55–69.

Razran, G. The observable unconscious and inferable conscious in current Soviet psychophysiology: Interoceptive conditioning, semantic conditioning, and the orienting reflex. *Psychological Review,* 1961, **68,** 81–147.

Rebelsky, Freda G., Allinsmith, W., and Grinder, R. E. Sex differences in children's use of fantasy confession and their relation to temptation. *Child Development,* 1963, **34,** 955–962.

Reese, H. W. Discrimination learning set in children. In L. P. Lipsitt and C. C. Spiker (Eds.), *Advances in child development and behavior.* Volume I. New York: Academic Press, 1963. Pp. 115–145.

Reese, H. W. Verbal effects in the intermediate-size transposition problem. *Journal of experimental Child Psychology,* 1966, **3,** 123–130.

Renner, K. E. Delay of reinforcement: A historical review. *Psychological Bulletin,* 1964, **61,** 341–361.

Renner, K. E. Temporal integration: The effect of early experience. *Journal of Experimental Research in Personality,* 1966, **1,** 201–210. (a)

Renner, K. E. Temporal integration: The relative utility of immediate vs. delayed reward and punishment. *Journal of Experimental Psychology,* 1966, **72,** 901–903. (b)

Rescorla, R. A., and LoLordo, V. M. Inhibition of avoidance behavior. *Journal of Comparative and Physiological Psychology,* 1965, **59,** 406–412.

Rescorla, R. A., and Solomon, R. L. Two-process learning theory: Relationships between Pavlovian conditioning and instrumental learning. *Psychological Review,* 1967, **74,** 151–182.

Rettig, S. Ethical risk taking in group and individual conditions. *Journal of Personality and Social Psychology,* 1966, **4,** 648–654.

Rettig, S., and Rawson, H. E. The risk hypothesis in predictive judgment of unethical behavior. *Journal of Abnormal and Social Psychology,* 1963, **66,** 243–248.

Rettig, S., and Sinha, J. B. Bad faith and ethical risk sensitivity. *Journal of Personality,* 1966, **34,** 275–286.

Rheingold, Harriet L. The effect of environmental stimulation upon social and exploratory behavior in the human infant. In B. M. Foss (Ed.), *Determinants of infant behaviour.* Volume I. London: Methuen, 1961. Pp. 143–171.

Rice, G. E., Jr. Aiding behavior vs. fear in the albino rat. *Psychological Record,* 1964, **14,** 165–170.

Rice, G.E., Jr., and Gainer, Priscilla. "Altruism" in the albino rat. *Journal of Comparative and Physiological Psychology,* 1962, **55,** 123–125.

Riesman, D., Denney, R., and Glazer, N. *The lonely crowd: A study of the changing American character.* New Haven: Yale University Press, 1950.

Riopelle, A. J. Observational learning of a position habit by monkeys. *Journal of Comparative and Physiological Psychology,* 1960, **53,** 426–428.

Rosekrans, Mary A. Imitation in children as a function of perceived similarity to a social model and vicarious reinforcement. *Journal of Personality and Social Psychology,* 1967, **7,** 307–315.

Rosekrans, Mary A., and Hartup, W. W. Imitative influence of consistent and inconsistent response consequences to a model on aggressive behavior in children. *Journal of Personality and Social Psychology,* 1967, **7,** 429–434.

Rosen, B., and D'Andrade, R. G. The psychosocial origins of achievement motivation. *Sociometry,* 1959, **22,** 185–218.

Rosenbaum, M. E., and deCharms, R. Direct and vicarious reduction of hostility. *Journal of Abnormal and Social Psychology,* 1960, **60,** 105–111.

Rosenbaum, M. E., and Tucker, I. F. The competence of the model and the learning of imitation and nonimitation. *Journal of Experimental Psychology,* 1962, **63,** 183–190.

Rosenblith, Judy F. Imitative color choices in kindergarten children. *Child Development,* 1961, **32,** 211–223.

Rosenhan, D., and White, G. M. Observation and rehearsal as determinants of prosocial behavior. *Journal of Personality and Social Psychology,* 1967, **5,** 424–431.

Ross, Dorothea. Relationship between dependency, intentional learning, and incidental learning in preschool children. *Journal of Personality and Social Psychology,* 1966, **4,** 374–381.

Rotter, J. B. Generalized expectancies for internal vs. external control of reinforcement. *Psychological Monographs,* 1966, **80,** No. 1 (Whole No. 609).

Sandler, J. Some aspects of self-aversive stimulation in the hooded rat. *Journal of the Experimental Analysis of Behavior,* 1964, **7,** 409–414.

Sandler, J., and Davidson, R. S. Punished avoidance behavior in the presence of a nonpunished alternative. *Psychonomic Science,* 1967, **8,** 297–298.

Sandler, J., Davidson, R. S., Greene, W. E., and Holzschuh, R. D. Effects of punishment intensity on instrumental avoidance behavior. *Journal of Comparative and Physiological Psychology,* 1966, **61,** 212–216.

Schachter, S. The interaction of cognitive and physiological determinants of emotional state. In L. Berkowitz (Ed.), *Advances in experimental social psychology.* Volume I. New York: Academic Press, 1964. Pp. 49–80.

Schachter, S., and Latané, B. Crime, cognition, and the autonomic nervous system. In D. Levine (Ed.), *Nebraska symposium on motivation.* Volume XII. Lincoln, Nebraska: University of Nebraska Press, 1964. Pp. 221–273.

Schachter, S., and Singer, J. E. Cognitive, social, and physiological determinants of emotional state. *Psychological Review,* 1962, **69,** 379–399.

Schaffer, H. R., and Emerson, Peggy E. The development of social attachments in infancy. *Monographs of the Society for Research in Child Development,* 1964, **29,** No. 3 (Serial No. 94).

Schein, E. H. The effect of reward on adult imitative behavior. *Journal of Abnormal and Social Psychology,* 1954, **49,** 389–395.

Schein, E. H. Patterns of reaction to severe chronic stress in American Army prisoners of war of the Chinese. In *Methods of forceful indoctrination: Observations and interviews.* New York: Group for the Advancement of Psychiatry, 1957.

Schnierla, T. C. An evolutionary and developmental theory of biphasic processes underlying approach and withdrawal. In M. R. Jones (Ed.), *Nebraska symposium on motivation.* Volume VII. Lincoln, Nebraska: University of Nebraska Press, 1959. Pp. 1–42.

Schopler, J., and Bateson, N. The power of dependence. *Journal of Personality and Social Psychology,* 1965, **2,** 247–254.

Schopler, J., and Matthews, Marjorie W. The influence of the perceived causal locus of partner's dependence on the use of interpersonal power. *Journal of Personality and Social Psychology,* 1965, **2,** 609–612.

Scott, J. P. *Aggression.* Chicago: University of Chicago Press, 1958.

Scott, J. P. The process of primary socialization in canine and human infants. *Monographs of the Society for Research in Child Development,* 1963, **28,** No. 1 (Serial No. 85).

Scott, J. P., and Fuller, J. L. *Genetics and the social behavior of the dog.* Chicago: University of Chicago Press, 1965.

Scott, J. P., and McCray, C. Allelomimetic behavior in dogs: Negative effects of competition on social facilitation. *Journal of Comparative and Physiological Psychology,* 1967, **63,** 316–319.

Scott, J. P., Shepard, J. H., and Werboff, J. Inhibitory training of dogs: Effects of age at training in basenjis and Shetland sheepdogs. *Journal of Psychology,* 1967, **66,** 237–252.

Sears, Pauline S. Doll play aggression in normal young children: Influence of sex, age, sibling status, father's absence. *Psychological Monographs,* 1951, **65,** No. 6 (Whole No. 323).

Sears, Pauline S. Child-rearing factors related to playing of sex-typed roles. *American Psychologist,* 1953, **8,** 431. (Abstract)

Sears, R. R. Relation of early socialization experiences to aggression in middle childhood. *Journal of Abnormal and Social Psychology,* 1961, **63,** 466–492.

Sears, R. R., and Hovland, C. I. Experiments on motor conflict. II. Determination of mode of resolution by comparative strength of conflicting responses. *Journal of Experimental Psychology,* 1941, **28,** 280–286.

Sears, R. R., Maccoby, Eleanor E., and Levin, H. *Patterns of child rearing.* Evanston, Illinois: Row, Peterson, 1957.

Sears, R. R., Rau, Lucy, and Alpert, R. *Identification and child training.* Stanford, California: Stanford University Press, 1965.

Sears, R. R., Whiting, J. W. M., Nowlis, V., and Sears, Pauline S. Some child-rearing antecedents of aggression and dependency in young children. *Genetic Psychology Monographs,* 1953, **47,** 135–234.

Seligman, M. E. P. CS redundancy and secondary punishment. *Journal of Experimental Psychology,* 1966, **72,** 546–550.

Seligman, M. E. P., and Campbell, B. A. Effect of intensity and duration of punishment on extinction of an avoidance response. *Journal of Comparative and Physiological Psychology,* 1965, **59,** 295–297.

Seligman, M. E. P., and Maier, S. F. Failure to escape traumatic shock. *Journal of Experimental Psychology,* 1967, **74,** 1–9.

Setterington, R. G., and Walters, R. H. Effects of concurrent delays of material rewards and punishments on problem-solving in children. *Child Development,* 1964, **35,** 275–280.

Seward, J. P. The structure of functional autonomy. *American Psychologist,* 1963, **18,** 703–710.

Seward, J. P., King, R. M., Chow, T., and Shiflett, S. C. Persistence of punished escape responses. *Journal of Comparative and Physiological Psychology,* 1965, **60,** 265–268.

Sgan, Mabel L. Social reinforcement, socioeconomic status, and susceptibility to experimenter influence. *Journal of Personality and Social Psychology,* 1967, **5,** 202–210.

Shearn, D. W. Operant conditioning of heart rate. *Science,* 1962, **137,** 530–531.

Sheffield, F. D. Theoretical considerations in the learning of complex sequential tasks from demonstration and practice. In A. A. Lumsdaine (Ed.), *Student response in programmed instruction: A symposium.* Washington, D.C.: National Academy of Sciences—National Research Council, 1961. Pp. 13–32.

Sheffield, F. D. Relation between classical conditioning and instrumental learning. In W. F. Prokasy (Ed.), *Classical conditioning: A symposium.* New York:

Appleton-Century-Crofts, 1965. Pp. 302–322.

Shirley, Mary M. *The first two years*. Volume II. *Intellectual development*. Minneapolis: University of Minnesota Press, 1933.

Sidman, M. Two temporal parameters of the maintenance of avoidance behavior by the white rat. *Journal of Comparative and Physiological Psychology*, 1953, **46**, 253–261.

Sidman M. Delayed punishment effects mediated by competing behavior. *Journal of Comparative and Physiological Psychology*, 1954, **47**, 145–147.

Sidman, M. On the persistence of avoidance behavior. *Journal of Abnormal and Social Psychology*, 1955, **50**, 217–220.

Sidman, M. Conditioned reinforcing and aversive stimuli in an avoidance situation. *Transactions of the New York Academy of Sciences*, 1957, **19**, Series II, 534–544.

Sidman, M., and Boren, J. J. The relative aversiveness of warning signal and shock in an avoidance situation. *Journal of Abnormal and Social Psychology*, 1957, **55**, 339–344.

Sidman, M., Herrnstein, R. J., and Conrad, D. G. Maintenance of avoidance behavior by unavoidable shocks. *Journal of Comparative and Physiological Psychology*, 1957, **50**, 553–557.

Sidowski, J. B., Kass, N., and Wilson, Helen. Cue and secondary reinforcement effects with children. *Journal of Experimental Psychology*, 1965, **69**, 340–342.

Sidowski, J. B., Wyckoff, L. B., and Tabory, L. The influence of reinforcement and punishment in a minimal social situation. *Journal of Abnormal and Social Psychology*, 1956, **52**, 115–119.

Siegel, Alberta E. Aggressive behavior of young children in the absence of an adult. *Child Development*, 1957, **28**, 371–378.

Siegel, Alberta E., and Kohn, Lynette G. Permissiveness, permission, and aggression: The effect of adult presence or absence on aggression in children's play. *Child Development*, 1959, **30**, 131–141.

Siegel, A. W., and Stevenson, H. W. Incidental learning: A developmental study. *Child Development*, 1966, **37**, 811–817.

Silverman, I. W. The incidence of guilt reactions in children. *Journal of Personality and Social Psychology*, 1967, **7**, 338–340.

Simmel, E. C. Social facilitation of exploratory behavior in rats. *Journal of Comparative and Physiological Psychology*, 1962, **55**, 831–833.

Singer, J. E., Brush, Claudia A., and Lublin, Shirley C. Some aspects of deindividuation: Identification and conformity. *Journal of Experimental Social Psychology*, 1965, **1**, 356–378.

Singer, M. B. Shame cultures and guilt cultures. In G. Piers and M. B. Singer, *Shame and guilt: A psychoanalytic and a cultural study*. Springfield, Illinois: Charles C. Thomas, 1953. Pp. 45–86.

Skinner, B. F. *The behavior of organisms: An experimental analysis*. New York: Appleton-Century-Crofts, 1938.

Skinner, B. F. Superstition in the pigeon. *Journal of Experimental Psychology*, 1948, **38**, 168–172.

Skinner, B. F. *Science and human behavior*. New York: Macmillan, 1953.

Skinner, B. F. Two "synthetic social relations." *Journal of the Experimental Analysis of Behavior*, 1962, **5**, 531–533.

Smith, B., and Epstein, S. Influence of incentive on adequacy and mode of conflict resolution. *Journal of Experimental Psychology*, 1967, **75**, 175–179.

Solomon, R. L. Punishment. *American Psychologist,* 1964, **19,** 239–253.

Solomon, R. L., and Brush, Elinor S. Experimentally derived conceptions of anxiety and aversion. In M. R. Jones (Ed.), *Nebraska symposium on motivation.* Volume IV. Lincoln, Nebraska: University of Nebraska Press, 1956. Pp. 212–305.

Solomon, R. L., and Coles, M. R. A case of failure of generalization of imitation across drives and across situations. *Journal of Abnormal and Social Psychology,* 1954, **49,** 7–13.

Solomon, R. L., Kamin, L. J., and Wynne, L. C. Traumatic avoidance learning: The outcomes of several extinction procedures with dogs. *Journal of Abnormal and Social Psychology,* 1953, **48,** 291–302.

Solomon, R. L., and Turner, Lucille H. Discriminative classical conditioning in dogs can later control discriminative avoidance responses in the normal state. *Psychological Review,* 1962, **69,** 202–219.

Solomon, R. L., Turner, Lucille H., and Lessac, M. S. Some effects of delay of punishment on resistance to temptation in dogs. *Journal of Personality and Social Psychology,* 1968, **8,** 233–238.

Solomon, R. L., and Wynne, L. C. Traumatic avoidance learning: Acquisition in normal dogs. *Psychological Monographs,* 1953, **67,** No. 4 (Whole No. 354).

Solomon, R. L., and Wynne, L. C. Traumatic avoidance learning: The principles of anxiety conservation and partial irreversibility. *Psychological Review,* 1954, **61,** 353–385.

Spear, N. E. Retention of reinforcer magnitude. *Psychological Review,* 1967, **74,** 216–234.

Spence, Janet T. Verbal discrimination performance as a function of instructions and verbal reinforcement combination in normal and retarded children. *Child Development,* 1966, **37,** 269–281.

Spence, Janet T., and Segner, Leslie L. Verbal versus noverbal reinforcement combinations in the discrimination learning of middle- and lower-class children. *Child Development,* 1967, **38,** 29–38.

Spence, K. W. *Behavior theory and conditioning.* New Haven: Yale University Press, 1956.

Spence, K. W., and Platt, J. R. Effects of partial reinforcement on acquisition and extinction of the conditioned eyeblink in a masking situation. *Journal of Experimental Psychology,* 1967, **74,** 259–263.

Spielberger, C. D., and DeNike, L. D. Descriptive behaviorism vs. cognitive theory in verbal operant conditioning. *Psychological Review,* 1966, **73,** 306–326.

Spielberger, C. D., Southard, L. D., and Hodges, W. F. Effects of awareness and threat of shock of verbal conditioning. *Journal of Experimental Psychology,* 1966, **72,** 434–438.

Spiker, C. C. Performance on a difficult discrimination following pretraining with distinctive stimuli. *Child Development,* 1959, **30,** 513–521.

Spiker, C. C. Verbal factors in the discrimination learning of children. In J. C. Wright and J. Kagan (Eds.), Basic cognitive processes in children. *Monographs of the Society for Research in Child Development,* 1963, **28,** No. 2 (Serial No. 86). Pp. 53–69.

Spiro, M. E., and D'Andrade, R. G. A cross-cultural study of some supernatural beliefs. *American Anthropologist,* 1958, **60,** 456–466.

Spitz, R. A., and Wolf, Katherine M. The smiling response: A contribution to the ontogenesis of social relations. *Genetic Psychology Monographs,* 1946, **34,** 57–125.

Steigman, M. J., and Stevenson, H. W. The effect of pretraining reinforcement schedules on children's learning. *Child Development,* 1960, **31,** 53–58.

Stein, Aletha H. Imitation of resistance to temptation. *Child Development,* 1967, **38,** 157–169.

Stein, Aletha H., and Wright, J. C. Imitative learning under conditions of nurturance and nurturance withdrawal. *Child Development,* 1964, **35,** 927–938.

Stein, L. Secondary reinforcement established with subcortical stimulation. *Science,* 1958, **127,** 466–467.

Stevenson, C. L. *Ethics and language.* New Haven: Yale University Press, 1944.

Stevenson, H. W. Social reinforcement of children's behavior. In L. P. Lipsitt and C. C. Spiker (Eds.), *Advances in child development and behavior.* Volume II. New York: Academic Press, 1965. Pp. 97–126.

Stevenson, H. W., Weir, M. W., and Zigler, E. F. Discrimination learning in children as a function of motive-incentive conditions. *Psychological Reports,* 1959, **5,** 95–98.

Stone, W. F. Autokinetic norms: An experimental analysis. *Journal of Personality and Social Psychology,* 1967, **5,** 76–81.

Strickland, L. H., and Grote, F. W. Temporal presentation of winning symbols and slot-machine playing. *Journal of Experimental Psychology,* 1967, **74,** 10–13.

Suedfeld, P., and Vernon, J. Attitude manipulation in restricted environments. II. Conceptual structure and the internalization of propaganda received as a reward for compliance. *Journal of Personality and Social Psychology,* 1966, **3,** 586–589.

Taffel, C. Anxiety and the conditioning of verbal behavior. *Journal of Abnormal and Social Psychology,* 1955, **51,** 496–501.

Terman, L. M. *et al. Genetic studies of genius.* Volume I. *Mental and physical traits of a thousand gifted children.* Stanford, California: Stanford University Press, 1925.

Terman, L. M., and Merrill, Maud A. *Measuring intelligence.* Boston: Houghton-Mifflin, 1937.

Terman, L. M., and Miles, Catherine C. *Sex and personality: Studies in masculinity and femininity.* New York: McGraw-Hill, 1936.

Terrell, G. Reinforcement in discrimination learning with special attention to the effects of delayed reinforcement. *Journal of Genetic Psychology,* 1964, **104,** 225–233.

Thibaut, J. W., and Kelley, H. H. *The social psychology of groups.* New York: Wiley, 1959.

Thorndike, E. L. *Animal intelligence.* New York: Macmillan, 1911.

Thorndike, E. L. Reward and punishment in animal learning. *Comparative Psychology Monographs,* 1932, **8,** No. 39.

Thorpe, W. H. *Learning and instinct in animals.* (Second Edition) London: Methuen, 1963.

Tighe, T. J., and Leaton, R. N. Escape from conflict. I. The effects of increasing difficulty of discrimination. *Psychonomic Science,* 1966, **6,** 129–130.

Trowill, J. A. Instrumental conditioning of the heart rate in the curarized rat. *Journal of Comparative and Physiological Psychology,* 1967, **63,** 7–11.

Tuma, E., and Livson, N. Family socioeconomic status and adolescent attitudes to authority. *Child Development,* 1960, **31,** 387–399.

Turiel, E. An experimental test of the sequentiality of developmental stages in the child's moral judgments. *Journal of Personality and Social Psychology,* 1966, **3,** 611–618.

Turner, Elizabeth A., and Wright, J. C. Effects of severity of threat and perceived availability on the attractiveness of objects. *Journal of Personality and Social Psychology*, 1965, **2**, 128–132.

Turner, Lucille H., and Solomon, R. L. Human traumatic avoidance learning: Theory and experiments on the operant-respondent distinction and failures to learn. *Psychological Monographs*, 1962, **76**, No. 40 (Whole No. 559).

Turner, W. D. Altruism and its measurement in children. *Journal of Abnormal and Social Psychology*, 1948, **43**, 502–516.

Ugurel-Semin, R. Moral behavior and moral judgment of children. *Journal of Abnormal and Social Psychology*, 1952, **47**, 463–474.

Uhl, C. N., and Young, A. G. Resistance to extinction as a function of incentive, percentage of reinforcement, and number of nonreinforced trials. *Journal of Experimental Psychology*, 1967, **73**, 556–564.

Ulrich, R. Interaction between reflexive fighting and cooperative escape. *Journal of the Experimental Analysis of Behavior*, 1967, **10**, 311–317.

Verplanck, W. S. The operant conditioning of human motor behavior. *Psychological Bulletin*, 1956, **53**, 70–83.

Vygotsky, L. S. *Thought and language.* Cambridge, Massachusetts: M.I.T. Press, 1962.

Wagman, W., and Allen, J. D. The development of a conditioned positive reinforcer based upon the termination of shock. *Psychonomic Science*, 1964, **1**, 363–364.

Wagner, A. R., Siegel, Linda, and Fein, Greta G. Extinction of conditioned fear as a function of percentage of reinforcement. *Journal of Comparative and Physiological Psychology*, 1967, **63**, 160–164.

Wallace, J., and Sadalla, E. Behavioral consequences of transgression. I. The effects of social recognition. *Journal of Experimental Research in Personality*, 1966, **1**, 187–194.

Walster, Elaine. Assignment of responsibility for an accident. *Journal of Personality and Social Psychology*, 1966, **3**, 73–79.

Walster, Elaine, and Prestholdt, P. The effect of misjudging another: Over-compensation or dissonance reduction. *Journal of Experimental Social Psychology*, 1966, **2**, 85–97.

Walters, R. H. Delay of reinforcement gradients in children's learning. *Psychonomic Science*, 1964, **1**, 307–308.

Walters, R. H., Bowen, Norma V., and Parke, R. D. Influence of looking behavior of a social model on subsequent looking behavior of observers of the model. *Perceptual and Motor Skills*, 1964, **18**, 469–483.

Walters, R. H., and Brown, M. A test of the high-magnitude theory of aggression. *Journal of Experimental Child Psychology*, 1964, **1**, 376–387.

Walters, R. H., and Demkow, Lillian. The timing of punishment as a determinant of response inhibition. *Child Development*, 1963, **34**, 207–214.

Walters, R. H., Leat, M., and Mezei, L. Inhibition and disinhibition of responses through empathetic learning. *Canadian Journal of Psychology*, 1963, **17**, 235–243.

Walters, R. H., and Llewellyn Thomas, E. Enhancement of punitiveness by visual and audiovisual displays. *Canadian Journal of Psychology*, 1963, **16**, 244–255.

Walters, R. H., Llewellyn Thomas, E., and Acker, C. W. Enhancement of punitive behavior by audiovisual displays. *Science*, 1962, **136**, 872–873.

Walters, R. H., and Parke, R. D. Influence of response consequences to a social model on resistance to deviation. *Journal of Experimental Child Psychology*, 1964, **1**, 269–280. (a)

Walters, R. H., and Parke, R. D. Social motivation, dependency, and susceptibility to social influence. In L. Berkowitz (Ed.), *Advances in experimental social psychology.* Volume I. New York: Academic Press, 1964. Pp. 231–276. (b)

Walters, R. H., and Parke, R. D. The role of the distance receptors in the development of social responsiveness. In L. P. Lipsitt and C. C. Spiker (Eds.), *Advances in child development and behavior.* Volume II. New York: Academic Press, 1965. Pp. 59–96.

Walters, R. H., and Parke, R. D. The influence of punishment and related disciplinary techniques on the social behavior of children: Theory and empirical findings. In B. A. Maher (Ed.), *Progress in experimental personality research.* Volume IV. New York: Academic Press, 1967. Pp. 179–228.

Walters, R. H., Parke, R. D., and Cane, Valerie. Timing of punishment and the observation of consequences to others as determinants of response inhibition. *Journal of Experimental Child Psychology,* 1965, **2**, 10–30.

Warden, C. J., Fjeld, H. A., and Koch, A. M. Imitative behavior in the Cebus and Rhesus monkeys. *Journal of Genetic Psychology,* 1940, **56**, 311–322.

Ware, R., and Terrell, G. Effects of delayed reinforcement on associative and incentive factors. *Child Development,* 1961, **32**, 789–793.

Washburn, S. L., Jay, Phyllis C., and Lancaster, Jane B. Field studies of Old World monkeys and apes. *Science,* 1965, **150**, 1541–1547.

Watson, D., and Baumal, Evelyn. Effects of locus of control and expectation of future control upon present performance. *Journal of Personality and Social Psychology,* 1967, **6**, 212–215.

Watts, W. A. Commitment under conditions of risk. *Journal of Personality and Social Psychology,* 1966, **3**, 507–515.

Weber, M. *The Protestant ethic and the spirit of capitalism.* New York: Charles Scribner's Sons, 1930.

Weinberger, N. M. Effect of detainment on extinction of avoidance responses. *Journal of Comparative and Physiological Psychology,* 1965, **60**, 135–138.

Weingold, H. P., and Webster, R. L. Effects of punishment on a cooperative behavior in children. *Child Development,* 1964, **35**, 1211–1216.

Weir, M. W., and Stevenson, H. W. The effect of verbalization in children's learning as a function of chronological age. *Child Development,* 1959, **30**, 143–149.

Weiskrantz, L., and Cowey, A. The aetiology of food reward in monkeys. *Animal Behaviour,* 1963, **11**, 225–234.

Weisman, R. G., Denny, M. R., Platt, S. A., and Zerbolio, F. J., Jr. Facilitation of extinction by a stimulus associated with long nonshock confinement periods. *Journal of Comparative and Physiological Psychology,* 1966, **62**, 26–30.

Wheeler, L. Toward a theory of behavioral contagion. *Psychological Review,* 1966, **73**, 179–192.

Wheeler, L., and Caggiula, A. R. The contagion of aggression. *Journal of Experimental Social Psychology,* 1966, **2**, 1–10.

Wheeler, L., and Smith, S. Censure of the model in the contagion of aggression. *Journal of Personality and Social Psychology,* 1967, **6**, 93–98.

White, R. W. Motivation reconsidered: The concept of competence. *Psychological Review,* 1959, **66**, 297–333.

White, S. H. Evidence for a hierarchical arrangement of learning processes. In L. P. Lipsitt and C. C. Spiker (Eds.), *Advances in child development and behavior.* Volume II. New York: Academic Press, 1965. Pp. 187–220.

Whiteman, P. H., and Kosier, K. P. Development of children's moralistic judgments: Age, sex, IQ, and certain personal-experiential variables. *Child Development,* 1964, **35**, 843–850.

Whiting, J. W. M. Sorcery, sin, and the superego: Some cross-cultural mechanisms of social control. In M. R. Jones (Ed.), *Nebraska symposium on motivation.* Volume VII. Lincoln, Nebraska: University of Nebraska Press, 1959. Pp. 174–195.

Whiting, J. W. M. Resource mediation and learning by identification. In I. Iscoe and H. W. Stevenson (Eds.), *Personality development in children.* Austin, Texas: University of Texas Press, 1960. Pp. 112–126.

Whiting, J. W. M., and Child, I. L. *Child training and personality.* New Haven: Yale University Press, 1953.

Whiting, J. W. M., and Mowrer, O. H. Habit progression and regression: A laboratory study of some factors relevant to human socialization. *Journal of Comparative Psychology,* 1943, **36,** 229–253.

Wike, E. L. (Ed.). *Secondary reinforcement: Selected experiments.* New York: Harper and Row, 1966.

Williams, D. R. Classical conditioning and incentive motivation. In W. F. Prokasy (Ed.), *Classical conditioning: A symposium.* New York: Appleton-Century-Crofts, 1965, Pp. 340–357.

Williams, D. R., and Barry, H., III. Counter-conditioning in an operant conflict situation. *Journal of Comparative and Physiological Psychology,* 1966, **61,** 154–156.

Wilson, W. C. Imitation and the learning of incidental cues by preschool children. *Child Development,* 1958, **29,** 393–397.

Winterbottom, Marian R. The relation of need for achievement to learning experiences in independence and mastery. In J. W. Atkinson (Ed.), *Motives in fantasy, action, and society.* Princeton, New Jersey: Van Nostrand, 1958. Pp. 453–478.

Withey, S. B. Reaction to uncertain threats. In G. W. Baker and D. W. Chapman (Eds.), *Man and society in disaster.* New York: Basic Books, 1962. Pp. 93–123.

Wolfe, J. B. Effectiveness of token rewards for chimpanzees. *Comparative Psychology Monographs,* 1936, **12,** 1–72.

Wolfle, D. L., and Wolfle, Helen M. The development of cooperative behavior in monkeys and young children. *Journal of Genetic Psychology,* 1939, **55,** 137–175.

Wright, Beatrice A. Altruism in children and the perceived conduct of others. *Journal of Abnormal and Social Psychology,* 1942, **37,** 218–233.

Wright, J. C., and Smothergill, D. Observing behavior and children's discrimination learning under delayed reinforcement. *Journal of Experimental Child Psychology,* 1967, **5,** 430–440.

Wyckoff, L. B. The role of observing responses in discrimination learning. Part I. *Psychological Review,* 1952, **59,** 431–442.

Wyckoff, L. B. Toward a quantitative theory of secondary reinforcement. *Psychological Review,* 1959, **66,** 68–78.

Wynne-Edwards, V. C. *Animal dispersion in relation to social behavior.* New York: Hafner, 1962.

Yerkes, R. M., and Dodson, J. D. The relation of strength of stimulus to rapidity of habit-formation. *Journal of Comparative Neurology and Psychology,* 1908, **18,** 458–482.

Yerkes, R. M., and Learned, B. W. *Chimpanzee intelligence and its vocal expressions.* Baltimore: Williams and Wilkins, 1925.

Young, P. T. *Motivation and emotion: A survey of the determinants of human and animal activity.* New York: Wiley, 1961.

Zajonc, R. B. Social facilitation. *Science,* 1965, **149,** 269–274.

Zamble, E. Classical conditioning of excitement anticipatory to food reward. *Journal of Comparative and Physiological Psychology,* 1967, **63,** 526–529.

Zigler, E. F., and Williams, Joanna. Institutionalization and the effectiveness of social reinforcement: A three-year follow-up study. *Journal of Abnormal and Social Psychology,* 1963, **66,** 197–206.

Zimbardo, P. G. Involvement and communication discrepancy as determinants of opinion conformity. *Journal of Abnormal and Social Psychology,* 1960, **60,** 86–93.

Zimmerman, D. W. Durable secondary reinforcement: Method and theory. *Psychological Review,* 1957, **64,** 373–383.

Zimmerman, D. W. Sustained performance in rats based on secondary reinforcement. *Journal of Comparative and Physiological Psychology,* 1959, **52,** 353–358.

Zimmerman, Elaine H., and Zimmerman, J. The alteration of behavior in a special classroom situation. *Journal of the Experimental Analysis of Behavior,* 1962, **5,** 59–60.

Zimmerman, J. Technique for sustaining behavior with conditioned reinforcement. *Science,* 1963, **149,** 682–684.

Zimmerman, J., and Baydan, N. T. Punishment of S^Δ responding of humans in conditional matching-to-sample by time-out. *Journal of the Experimental Analysis of Behavior,* 1963, **6,** 589–597.

Zimmerman, J., and Hanford, P. V. Sustaining behavior with conditioned reinforcement as the only response-produced consequence. *Psychological Reports,* 1966, **19,** 391–401.

INDEX OF AUTHORS

Numbers in italic type indicate the pages on which complete references are listed.

A

Abel, Theodora M., 266, *334*
Abelson, R. P., 38, 40, 101, *334, 356*
Acker, C. W., 95, *372*
Adelberg, Kathryn, 135, 141, *344*
Adelson, J., 330, *344*
Ader, R., 96, *334*
Adler, H. E., 99, 100, *334*
Adorno, T. W., 41, 239, *334*
Akhtar, M., 168, *334*
Alekin, R. O., 85, *342*
Allen, J. D., 213, 225, *372*
Allen, V. L., 38, *334*
Allinsmith, Beverly B., 317, 328, *334*
Allinsmith, W., 38, 126, 128, 167, 181, 206, 226, 235, 239, 275, 304, 317, 318, 321, *334, 341, 366*
Alpert, R., 10, 38, 126, 128, 167, 274, 275, 304, 305, 308, 318, 321, 330, *349, 368*
Allport, F. H., 86, 96, 117, *334*
Allport, G. W., 149, *334*
Angermeier, W. R., 120, *334*
Amsel, A., 23, 58, 59, 198, *334, 344*
Anderson, D. C., 167, *340*
Anderson, R. C., 199, 200, *364*
Angermeier, W. R., 120, *334*
Antonova, T. G., 48, *340*
Appel, J. B., 59, *346*
Argyle, M., 38, *334*
Aronfreed, J., 4, 8, 9, 27, 29, 31, 34, 40, 50, 62, 63, 70, 89, 109, 113, 143, 152, 173, 174, 184, 191, 213, 215, 218, 223, 226, 231, 239, 240, 274, 293, 295, 313, 316, 317, 318, 319, 322, 328, 329, 330, *334, 335, 357*
Aronson, E., 39, 281, 282, 286, 288, 292, 293, *335*
Asch, S. E., 38, 149, *335*
Ausubel, D. P., 250, 305, *335*
Ayer, A. J., 2, *335*
Ayllon, T., 59, *351*
Azrin, N. H., 27, 50, 59, 62, 127, 163, 164, 165, 168, 172, 196, *335, 348, 351*

B

Bach, G. R., 279, *335*
Bacon, Margaret K., 304, 330, *335, 337*
Badia, P., 64, 201, 226, *336*
Baenninger, R., 202, *363*
Baer, D. M., 23, 49, 50, 59, 94, 98, 114, *336, 338, 347*
Baldwin, A. L., 252, *356*
Baldwin, J. M., 3, 87, *336*
Bales, R. F., 3, *364*
Bandura, A., 9, 29, 31, 83, 84, 87, 89, 91, 92, 102, 103, 104, 105, 106, 107, 108, 110, 111, 112, 113, 115, 119, 120, 122, 126, 127, 129, 132, 133, 134, 135, 187, 189, 190, 225, 264, 307, 310, 318, 320, 321, *336, 337*
Banks, J. H., 141, 142, 150, *361*
Banks, R. K., 23, 30, 172, 209, *337*
Barbu, Z., 330, *337*
Barnes, K., 95, 189, *356*
Baron, A., 59, 71, 172, *337, 353*
Barry, H., III, 168, 304, 330, *335, 337, 374*
Bass, B. M., 39, *338*
Bateson, N., 150, *367*
Baumal, Evelyn, 64, *373*
Baxter, R., 52, *354*
Baydan, N. T., 59, *375*
Bayer, E., 96, *337*
Bayroff, A. G., 97, *337*
Beauchamp, R. D., 196, *342*
Becker, W. C., 107, 319, *337, 355*
Bee, Helen L., 83, 105, 133, *337, 358*
Belanger, R. M., 36, 64, 201, 226, *338*
Bell, R., 200, *343*
Bem, D. J., 51, 214, *338*
Benedict, Ruth, 249, *338*
Berberich, J. P., 94, 98, 114, *358*
Berg, I. A., 39, *338*
Berger, S. M., 89, 119, *338, 344*
Berges, J., 85, *338*
Beritov, J. S., 68, *338*
Berkowitz, L., 58, 95, 122, 141, *338, 347*
Berlyne, D. E., 22, 68, *338*
Berscheid, Ellen, 227, *338*

INDEX OF SUBJECTS

A

Achievement motivation, parental rewards as antecedents of, 128

Acquired aversive value
  without behavioral contingencies, 27–28, 151–156, 165–166, 190, 287–289
  of conditioned suppressors, 26–28, 58, 165–166, 179
  of distress signals, 151–159
  extinction of, 30
  as a function of informational signals, 27–28, 36–37, 65, 73, 117, 165–166
  generalization of, 27–28, 182–183
  under intermittent contingencies, 27–28, 165
  intrinsic, 55, 58, 169–172, 176–187, 190–196, 208–209, 212–216, 287–289
  resistance to extinction of, 27–28, 165
  of warning signals, 19, 26–27, 55–56, 117, 165–166, 179, 188–189, 219–221

Acquired positive value
  without behavioral contingencies, 26, 81–82, 118, 144–149, 306–308
  of conditioned reinforcers, 21–22, 24–26, 81, 144–149
  as a function of informational signals, 25, 36–37, 65, 73, 164–165
  generalization of, 74, 88, 90, 308
  under intermittent contingencies, 21, 24
  intrinsic, 54, 56, 73, 81–82, 88, 125, 132, 236, 306–308
  of motivational incentives, 56, 58, 90, 118, 131
  of punishment as a signal of positive outcomes, 164–165
  resistance to extinction of, 21–22, 24–25, 145–146
  of sequential components of reinforced behavior, 73, 80
  and unlearned predispositions toward social stimulation, 21–22, 25, 45–46, 82, 90, 162

Affection
  in conditioning of empathic and vicarious experience, 144–148
  in observational learning and imitation, 221–223, 306–308
  physical, 144–148, 221–223
  reinstatement of, 229, 321–322
  withdrawal of, *see* Withdrawal of affection
  see also Child-rearing *and* Nurturance

Affective states, *see* Affectivity

Affectivity
  autonomic determinants of, 208–209
  in behavior-contingent learning, 49, 51–56, 58, 72, 74, 124–125, 132, 144, 149, 151, 166, 168–172, 176–187, 193–203, 205–209, 229, 233, 236–240
  classification of, 45–46, 243–245, 249–250
  cognitive specification of, 45, 54, 115–116, 209, 215, 242–254
  as a component of values, 5–6, 12–13, 278, 285–292, 296–297
  conditioned excitation and inhibition of, 21, 44, 47–49, 51–56, 58, 71–72, 76–77, 81–82, 88, 90, 94, 109, 117–119, 125, 132, 144, 151–155, 157, 165–166, 169–172, 176–189, 193–196, 208–209, 213, 217–219, 221–223, 225, 233, 306–308, 310–314
  control of outcomes over, 52
  as a determinant of self-evaluation, 217–218, 221–223, 225–226, 245, 247–248, 254
  empathic and vicarious extinction of, 119
  empathic and vicarious mediation of, 115–119, 139, 144, 149–153, 157–159, 188, 190
  generalization of, 77, 117, 182–183
  internalized transmission of, 44–47, 49, 53–56, 58, 70, 74, 76–78, 81–82, 84, 86, 88, 94, 106–107, 109, 111, 113–114, 117–118, 125, 127, 132, 139, 149, 151–152, 157–159, 169–172, 176–190, 193–196,

see also Altruistic behavior, Co-operative behavior, *and* Sharing

T

Templates, *see* Cognitive templates
Transgression
concept of, 169
guilt versus shame and type of, 251–254
judgements of severity of, 258, 270
perception of, 216, 258, 270
see also Conscience, Reactions to transgression, *and* Suppression of behavior

U

Unlearned dispositions
toward aggression, 162–163
toward altruistic behavior, 140–141
toward observational learning and imitation, 82
toward "psychopathic" behavior, 208–209
toward sensitivity to punishment, 208
toward the value of social stimuli, 21–22, 25, 45–46, 90, 162, 166

V

Values
acquisition of, 12–13, 259-261, 265–272, 276–277, 293, 296-297, 306
affective components of, 5–6, 12–13, 278, 285–292, 296–297
anxiety and the engagement of, 285–292, 296
aversive control of behavior and engagement of, 280, 282–299
behavioral engagement of, 105, 133, 278–300
cognitive complexity and change in, 263–268
cognitive structure of, 278, 287, 293

cultural variations in, 3, 261–262, 267
dimensions of, 2–5, 11, 35, 102–103, 246, 258, 264, 267, 270–272
discrepancies between conduct and, 9–11, 30
and experienced versus anticipated outcomes of behavior, 295–297, 299–300
internal versus external control of, 279–300
moral, *see* Moral judgement
observational elicitation of, 104–106, 133
positive control of engagement of, 283–284
situational specificity of, 11, 104–105, 133
social experience in development of, 260–261, 268–272, 276–277
social influence on, 263–265
structure versus substance of, 263–264, 266–268
verbal elicitation of, 105, 133
see also Conscience *and* Moral judgement
Verbal mediation, *see* Cognitive and verbal representation
Vicarious experience, *see* Empathic and vicarious experience
Violation, *see* Punishment *and* Transgression

W

Withdrawal of affection
as a component of punishment, 57, 221, 229, 311–313, 321–322
as a determinant of observational learning and imitation, 88–90, 221, 306
as a type of discipline, 315, 321–322